New Gill History of Ireland 3

# Seventeenth-Century Ireland

## Making Ireland Modern

**New Gill History of Ireland**

The Gill History of Ireland originally appeared in eleven volumes between 1972 and 1975. It was succeeded by a proposed six-volume series entitled New Gill History of Ireland in 1990, although in the event only five volumes were published. Now the revised and rewritten series is published in its entirety.

New Gill History of Ireland 3

# Seventeenth-Century Ireland

Making Ireland Modern

**Raymond Gillespie**

*Gill Books*

Gill Books
Hume Avenue
Park West
Dublin 12
www.gillbooks.ie

Gill Books is an imprint of M.H. Gill & Co.

© Raymond Gillespie 2006
Paperback ISBN-13: 978 07171 3946 0
Paperback ISBN-10: 0 7171 3946 8

Index compiled by Helen Litton
Typography design by Make Communication
Print origination by O'K Graphic Design, Dublin
Printed by Replika Press Pvt. Ltd.

This book is typeset in 10.5/13 pt Minion.

The paper used in this book comes from the wood pulp of
managed forests. For every tree felled, at least one tree is
planted, thereby renewing natural resources.

A CIP catalogue record for this book is available from the British
Library.

10 9 8

# Contents

# Preface and Acknowledgments

This is a book which, in its own way, attempts to tell a story the outlines of which are well known. Indeed some episodes of the evolution of a relatively primitive society, still dominated in the 1590s by the structures and systems of late medieval lordship, to a recognisably modern world, characterised by the triumph of central government and county society, have been documented in great detail. However, it is not the task of this book, like that of a biblical commentary, to expand on all the aspects of that transformation. There are, for instance, large areas of the seventeenth-century experience, particularly in the social and cultural spheres, of which so little has been recovered that attempts to write about it at a general level would be premature. Rather, I have chosen to view the processes of change through the lens of what might be called the social history of governance in seventeenth-century Ireland. What this means is not a dissection of the minutiae of politics, political thought or administration, or even the broad sweep of economic shifts, although all these subjects will appear, sometimes fleetingly, in the pages that follow. Rather, this book tries to chart the processes by which the diverse ethnic and religious groups which made up the social networks of Ireland constructed and reconstructed the ideas of social order and government that held their world together during the first forty and most of the last thirty years of the century. Equally it is an attempt to explain how those brittle arrangements broke down under the particular stresses and specific problems of the 1640s and 1680s. The result is a rather schematised view of the seventeenth century. Early modern societies did not develop in straight lines; rather, they evolved, often in an inherently unpredictable way, and their elements are never exactly in the same relationship over time. In a narrative history such as this something of the messiness of that evolution, often seen only in the detail of local life, is tidied up and rendered more comprehensible.

Inevitably there are areas in such a work which lie outside my own area of expertise, and so I have relied on the advice and research of others. Three groups of people have influenced this book. I have been fortunate to belong to a generation of early modern historians who have transformed their field of research. That the approach of this volume is rather different to what might have been written twenty years ago is due to their efforts. I have had to be selective in what I can discuss, especially in the 1640s, but I hope that I have not misrepresented the present state of our understanding. Secondly, I have tried to teach this period of history in N.U.I. Maynooth for over ten years. On many occasions I have learned more from students than I have taught them, and they have proved the value of an encounter with those who can challenge assumptions, often those dearly held. Thirdly, I have been shaped by those who taught me, both formally and informally. I hope that Lewis Warren would find something of his approach to medieval political history in this volume. Aidan Clarke and Toby Barnard have contributed more than they suspect; and Bill Crawford may have wished to see more about regional economies and societies than is presented here, but without his enthusiasm there would be nothing at all.

Finally there are specific debts. Jimmy Kelly persuaded a Doubting Thomas that writing such a book as this was worthwhile and has also read and commented on the entire text. In this thankless task he was joined by Toby Barnard and Marian Lyons. All three have saved me from at least some of my own follies, and if there are errors remaining, they are the result of my own obstinacy despite their best efforts. As always, Bernadette Cunningham has had a powerful influence in moulding the final product in many scholarly and other ways.

I have opted for a chronological rather than a thematic approach in this book. Chapter 1 is, however, intended to set out some of the broader problems that will be dealt with. This presumes some knowledge of the period, and some readers may wish to begin with Chapter 2 and return to the first chapter later when some of its implications may be clearer. I have reckoned the year as beginning on 1 January, rather than 25 March as contemporaries did, although I have left other dates in 'old style'. Irish currency has been identified as such but in most cases sterling is used, without being explicitly specified as such. Space constraints mean that footnotes have been used only to identify the sources of quotations. A guide to background reading and more general references will be found in the bibliographical essay.

Map 1  Provinces, counties and principal places mentioned in the text

Map 2  Dioceses in the seventeenth century

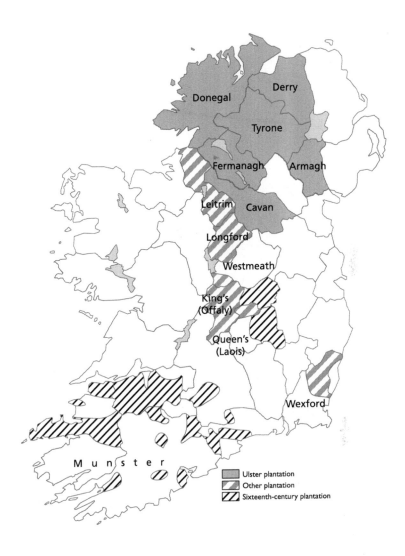

Map 3 Seventeenth-century plantations

# Introduction: Seventeenth-Century Ireland and its Questions

Seventeenth-century Ireland was an enigma to many contemporaries. Some attempted to sort out the apparently labyrinthine political, religious and economic problems characteristic of the country by committing to paper ideas on how they thought that system worked and, more often, how it should be reformed. These anatomisers of Ireland, from Edmund Spenser's *View of the present state of Ireland* written in the 1590s to William Petty's *Political anatomy of Ireland* (published in the 1690s, though it had been written in the 1670s), were, in the main, theorists with particular political or ideological agendas and their impact on the shaping of Irish society was limited. They dealt in ideas rather than realities. Others abandoned the intellectual and political challenges that Ireland presented. As one M.P. in the English 'Addled Parliament' of 1614 declared, 'Ireland is not a thorn in our foot but a lance in our side. If [there is] a revolt there what shame and disgrace would it be either to leave [it] or misery to recover it.'[1] Such ambivalent attitudes towards seventeenth-century Ireland are not the sole prerogative of contemporaries. As one modern historian has characterised the situation, 'Whether we attempt to view the British problem [in the early modern period] as an example of the development of "composite monarchies" or as an aspect of the colonial expansion of the Atlantic seaboard powers, Ireland is a special case. It just will not fit into any of the established patterns.'2

This perplexity as to how to describe seventeenth-century Ireland is, to some extent, of our own making. We attempt to use models which, ultimately, fail to take cognisance of all the evidence. Some have attempted to characterise the period as 'an age of disruption' or the age of 'wars of religion'. However, such attempts conceal as much as they reveal. They emphasise division in society, which certainly existed, at the expense of shared assumptions of God, hierarchy, deference and honour that made social arrangements work. Large numbers of the Old English gentry, for example, shared a common educational formation with settlers through their training at the Inns of Court in London which provided both groups with a shared common-law context for their understanding of the world. Again, those educated in colleges on continental Europe and Trinity College Dublin shared assumptions about the importance of hierarchy and order. Though ethnic and economic fault-lines ran through Irish society, the elite shared many common social assumptions, and from their position of strength they dictated taste, manners and morals, convinced of the importance of their leadership both culturally and politically. Much of the conflict in Ireland was, paradoxically, between people who shared similar values and assumptions about how society worked.

One example of this problem of trying to describe seventeenth-century Irish society in slogans is the understanding of that society as the product of a revolution. Evidence for this sense of a revolutionary age is not wanting. In some respects it shared in processes that can be traced in outline across contemporary Europe. The centralisation of authority in Dublin after the end of the Nine Years' War in 1603 and the undermining of powerful local magnates such as Hugh O'Neill, Earl of Tyrone, for example, reflect trends at work elsewhere in Europe. The state increasingly monopolised violence and the machinery of war at the expense of local nobilities. Similarly, the economic transformation of Ireland, with the rise of a market economy and the greater commercialisation of economic life, echoed a broader European process. In religious terms too, the progress of the Reformation and Counter-Reformation in Ireland needs to be seen in a European context, if only to emphasise some of the aberrant features of the Irish experience.

In other areas the development of Irish society in the sixteenth and seventeenth centuries was unique. The composition of the Irish social and political elite underwent a dramatic shift in the years between 1580 and 1700 in a way that did not happen in most other countries. Only in parts of the Holy Roman Empire, for instance Bohemia after 1620, was there a similar change in the social elite as Catholics replaced Protestants as part of a process of changing political configurations. The Irish peerage summoned to the parliament of 1585 was drawn from five Gaelic or gaelicised families and twenty Old English landed families who thought of themselves as the descendants of the medieval Anglo-Norman settlers. By the end of the seventeenth century, of the fifty-nine elite families who were summoned to the House of Lords, thirty-nine (or about two-thirds) were drawn from New English settler families, most of whom had arrived in the country in the half-century before 1641. A further five were from settler families of post-1641 origin. Old English families had thirteen representatives, while just two were of native Irish extraction. Confessionally, in 1613 the Irish House of Commons was fairly evenly divided between Protestants and Catholics, yet after 1690 it was entirely composed of members of the Church of Ireland. The changing composition of parliament reflects a major transfer of power from one social group to another. Underpinning this transfer of political influence was a dramatic shift in the pattern of Irish landownership as land passed from Catholic to Protestant landowners through both formal plantation and informal colonisation, reflecting shifts not simply in economic power but in social relationships also. However, the traditional estimates of the fall in the proportion of Irish land held by Catholics from 61 per cent in 1641 to 22 per cent in 1688 and by 1703, after the Williamite land settlement, to 15 per cent, may be too sweeping. The simple equations of Protestant with settler and Catholic with native are far from perfect. At least some new settlers, such as the Hamilton family, Earls of Abercorn in Ulster, or the Browne family, Lords Altamont in Mayo, were Catholic. Some former Catholic families, such as the Butlers, Earls of Ormond, converted to Protestantism. Yet the shift in landholding patterns is striking enough to delineate, at least in outline, the decline of one elite and its replacement by another.

Such patterns of change are the stuff of history, but they are rarely as simple as they appear at first glance. Only occasionally is it possible to see anything which might even resemble a single, coherent revolution. Irish Catholics may have lost land, but in many cases they retained considerable social prestige. As Archbishop Oliver Plunkett of Armagh noted in Ulster during the 1670s, many of the 'ancient vassals' who were now reduced to the rank of tenants living on land owned by new settlers 'are more or less so well disposed to their former overlords that they always give them some contribution'.[3] It may have been easy to effect a change in landownership, but social attitudes proved more difficult to alter. In the sphere of religion, too, it is possible to map out the institutional revolution that took place in early modern Ireland. However, the effects of these developments on religious belief are much more problematic because the laity shaped their own ideas about God for day-to-day use in the world. Changes in the various spheres of human existence happened at differential rates. Some areas of experience, such as belief or social attitudes, shifted only slowly, while other aspects, such as economic status or institutional change, responded more quickly to external stimuli. To this already complex situation it is necessary to add a consideration of regional variation in the distribution of power and wealth. Such variations in power and wealth help to explain why the province of Ulster, where the social and political vacuum which followed the flight to Europe of the northern earls in 1607 allowed a major social engineering project to be carried out, was so different from County Longford, in north Leinster, where local native families devised survival strategies to minimise the impact of plantation. All of this suggests that early modern Ireland did not undergo a single revolution but rather a series of interlinked revolutions moving at varying speeds. Their differential progress in various parts of the country may go some way to explaining not only the highly localised nature of early modern Irish society but also why large-scale movements, such as the Reformation, comprising a series of linked revolutions in institutions and beliefs had the character that they did.

If the idea of revolution proves a more complex interpretative tool than seems at first glance, equally problematical are the two politico-geographical contexts in which Ireland is usually viewed: on the one hand a colony like the world of North America, which was settled by colonists in the same manner as Munster in the 1580s and Ulster at the beginning of the seventeenth century, or, on the other, a European-style kingdom, with the associated political structures. Clear as these paradigms may appear, in reality they present enormous interpretative difficulties. The new worlds of North America slowly came to influence English and Scottish sensibilities during the seventeenth century as information about them became available. Ireland, and especially the east coast, was well known by people in England and Scotland through trading contacts and Irish migration to London, Glasgow and Wales in the sixteenth century. In 1604 10.8 per cent of those arrested for vagrancy in England were of Irish origin, with much higher proportions on the west coast, while the occurrence of Irish names among the apprentice population in London suggests a more settled community there. Moreover, those arriving in Ireland during the seventeenth century discovered that the country had a well-established social structure and a system of governance not unlike that found in most of Western Europe, both features which were lacking in North America.

However, economic and demographic experiences, at least initially, showed some similarities between the world of the North American colonies and Ireland. In the early part of the seventeenth century, at least, the driving force in population growth in both regions was immigration, encouraged by the availability of land as a result of confiscations. In consequence, Ireland's population growth was more rapid than that of Europe, but it was somewhat slower than that of North America. By 1700, however, while migration continued to be significant in some regions of Ireland, the dynamic of population growth was moving away from immigration to natural increase. The limits on Irish resources meant that Ireland's capacity to absorb large numbers of immigrants was much reduced, whereas in the colonial world large-scale settlement was still possible. In economic terms also, Irish and colonial trade showed similar characteristics in the seventeenth century. Both were concerned with the export of raw materials. This situation arose from similar economic problems: shortage of capital and skilled labour. However, in the later seventeenth century economic trends diverged as the Irish economy developed, producing more processed goods for export to a European market. Thus, in demographic and economic terms, Ireland lay somewhere between the colonial model of North America and the experiences of the kingdoms of mainland Europe.

The paradox of Ireland's position is clear: an Old World kingdom underpinned by social arrangements which seem entirely colonial in their nature. The position of a Protestant governing elite, who claimed their place on the basis of social and moral authority to rule, was in effect guaranteed by a series of apparently colonial land settlements and economic structures. The full vigour of colonial exploitation was, in effect, constrained by the political ideas of hierarchy, deference and honour associated with a kingdom. Such contradictions were commonplace in seventeenth-century Ireland, and understanding what some of these were will help to elucidate the difficulties with which those who lived in seventeenth-century Ireland had to grapple.

## CONTRADICTIONS OF KINGSHIP
The most basic statement on the organisation of the government of seventeenth-century Ireland was an unambiguous one. Henry VIII's 1541 act which framed Ireland's constitutional position declared that 'the king's highness, his heirs and successors, kings of England, be always kings of this land of Ireland' and that they were 'to have, hold and enjoy the said style, title, majesty and honours of king of Ireland . . . as united and knit to the imperial crown of the realm of England'. When King James I succeeded to the crown in 1603, he was greeted with expressions of loyalty not only from his settler subjects but also from their Old English and Gaelic Irish counterparts. The poets Eoghan Ruadh Mac an Bhaird and Eochaidh Ó hEodhasa hailed the new king with verse that celebrated a monarch who would bring peace, banish strife and under whom Ireland would prosper. Mac an Bhaird provided the king with a suitable Irish genealogy, through his Scottish ancestors to Fergus mac Eirc, the first Irish King of Scotland, and in doing so provided the basis for the powerful royalism which the Irish repeatedly demonstrated throughout the seventeenth century. Few disagreed with this proposition. In the 1620s an unrealistic proposal was floated among some of the Irish in Spain that the country might be declared a republic in order to prevent bickering between the O'Neill and O'Donnell factions over who should be king in a reconquered Ireland. Again in the early 1640s a small group in

Limerick, possibly influenced by Dutch settlers there, called for a 'free state of themselves as they had in Holland'.[4] Such views were firmly in a minority. Throughout the seventeenth century the dominant political idea in Ireland was that of monarchy. Support of monarchy underpinned both seventeenth-century Irish Catholicism and the Church of Ireland. As the Franciscan author Bonaventure Ó hEodhasa put it starkly in his commentary on the fourth commandment (on honouring parents), 'Not only are we bound to honour our fathers and mothers but we are likewise bound to give the same honour to every superior either of church of state.'[5] Protestants too felt uneasy without the stability a king could offer, and in 1656, during the Protectorate, seventeen of Ireland's thirty M.P.s at Westminster voted to offer the crown to Oliver Cromwell. Equally, Irish Protestants were prominent in bringing Charles II back to the throne in 1660.

The problem with monarchy in seventeenth-century Ireland was not the idea itself but rather its implications. First, kingship created a particular set of governmental structures which were similar to those found in kingdoms across contemporary Europe. The principal division in society was between the ruler and the ruled, the ruler having no superior but God. All power rested in the hands of the king and from thence it proceeded, creating a long chain of dependence which bound king and people together. Authority and liberty flowed not from political organisations but through the structure of personal relationships. As a result, the ruled were regarded as an organic, coherent body, a hierarchical order rather than a society with internal divisions. This made discord within the order of the ruled particularly difficult to deal with. Social hierarchy could be accommodated within the traditional language of deference and subversion, well set out and satirised in the Irish tract *Pairlement Chloinne Tomáis* of the 1630s. However, the religious fractures which criss-crossed those governed by the King of Ireland were more difficult to contain. Divisions such as this opened gaps in the ideal world of hierarchy. In such interstices of power, difficulties in practical government emerged. Whereas in most other European countries the principle of Augsburg (1555) that the religion of the ruler was also the religion of the ruled applied, in Ireland that was not the case. This presented a dilemma for personal relations within the world of the ruled and often required resort to the language of rebellion and disloyalty or allegations of unworthiness regarding one's place in the social order so as to stigmatise an opposition. It also created a powerful incentive to emphasise loyalty, hierarchy, authority and social deference over division, a trend some of the Old English used to good effect when playing politics in the early seventeenth century.

Such relationships with the king and one's peers not only defined an individual's place in society, but also determined what functions a person could play in that society. The status of the gentry was determined by a combination of economic power and cultural capital. Both of these were under the control of the king, who made grants of land and conferred honour through titles and offices. There was a bewildering range of such offices linked in a long chain from the king through to local sheriffs, justices of the peace, churchwardens and parish constables. In the 1670s it was estimated there were some 40 sheriffs, 400 sub-sheriffs and 900 justices of the peace in Ireland. Assuming that parishes appointed churchwardens, this would have swelled the administrative ranks by over 4,500 part-time officials. This figure does not include the clergy, who were also government agents, or the salaried office-holders in the customs or revenue service. Some of these offices were for life, but others, such as parochial office, were annual appointments involving the middling sort of people, whose behaviour and suitability for office were therefore under continual scrutiny. Thus government business was carried out not by impersonal bureaucracies but by people who were known to each other. Government authority was intimate, none of its activities too insignificant to be dealt with by a prominent local official. Local administrative and judicial offices were held by neighbourhood gentry whose lack of knowledge of the law was more than offset by the respect they commanded in the local community. The power of local sheriffs and magistrates, the main link between central and local government, lay in their local superiority. Law could often be what they said it was, and as a result legal proceedings were as much about social judgments as they were about findings upon the facts of a case. This was a society that thrived on the public exploitation of private power. The greater one's private position, the greater one's public office. As a result, government service, such as office-holding or advising the king in parliament, was part of a duty which was held to be commensurate with social rank. Important offices were, in theory, to be held by those whose talents, wealth and, above all, social authority allowed it. Government effectiveness depended on local interest, while local gentry depended on government office to validate their social position. Thus attacks on local magistrates were not simple episodes of mugging, but were viewed as 'tending to overthrow and supplant the root, and to dry up the fountain and spring-head of justice without which no commonwealth can exist'.[6]

There were varying reactions to these types of social constructs across Ireland. Those who were most familiar with them, those who thought of themselves as the descendants of the Anglo-Norman settlers of the country and who by the early seventeenth century referred to themselves as Old English, saw the King of Ireland as a central focus of loyalty and patronage. As David Rothe, later Catholic Bishop of Ossory, arguing for toleration of religious diversity, expressed it in 1614,

> That as a body natural, compounded of many dissimilar parts—
> flesh, bone gristles, muscles and sinews—yet, in one and the self-
> same integrity of a total form, is moved, fashioned, ruled and
> quickened by one natural form of the animating soul, which
> overswayeth and governeth all those parts and members—even so
> the politic body of this republic, plotted and compacted of divers
> nations not agreeing in one idea and form of religion (though but
> one true) may stand upon one frame of civil allegiance and be
> swayed under one sceptre, under one Imperial diadem.[7]

The leader of the convinced Catholic recusants in the 1613–15 Dublin parliament reflected a similar view when declaring that James I was the King of Ireland, 'whereof we no more doubted than the day is day and the night is night'.[8] From a Gaelic Irish perspective, many agreed. Throughout the seventeenth century the vast majority of the Old English and native Irish were deeply and profoundly royalist. In practical terms, the King of Ireland, like his predecessors, could not reside in the country (except briefly in 1689–90) since he was also King of England and Scotland, and hence appointed a provincial administrator to act as his agent, the Lord Deputy or later in the century the Lord Lieutenant. These office-holders were exactly that: provincial administrators. For the Old English, the locus of power really resided at the royal court in London. Consequently, throughout the century they were not afraid to appeal directly to the monarch to overturn decisions they thought unfavourable. They had used this technique with devastating effect in the late sixteenth century, undermining successive Lords Deputy by appealing directly to the King of Ireland in London.

This view, while entirely legitimate in its own terms, was underpinned by a system of values, traditional concepts and principles that had failed to keep pace with political reality as the New English settlers saw it. For this group (a few of whom had arrived in Ireland in the late sixteenth century, though most had come in the early seventeenth century), contemporary political realities were set out in the apparently colonial nature of Irish society, reflected most clearly in the various land settlements. Ireland was not a distinct kingdom but a conquered country, and the institutions of government could not work in the same way as the English model which they emulated without endangering the basis of the social order. This was a dangerous argument, for it implied that Ireland, as a conquered country, could be treated in any way the king wished, including ignoring the rights of settlers as Englishmen abroad. The administration of Thomas Wentworth (subsequently Earl of Strafford) in the 1630s proved the point. To resolve this dilemma in 1612, the Irish Attorney General, Sir John Davies, argued that after 1603

> there had been a perfect union between the nations and consequently a perfect conquest of Ireland. For the conquest is never perfect till the war be at an end, and the war is not at an end until there be peace and unity and there can never be unity and concord in any one kingdom but where there is but one king, one allegiance and one law.[9]

Seen in this way the social changes that characterised seventeenth-century Ireland were proof of its colonial status, although Ireland maintained its common-law rights despite colonisation, a position that the Old English rejected. In the 1660s the Old English priest John Lynch, in his work *Cambrensis eversus*, tried to refute the conquest argument, citing the survival of Irish language and customs as evidence of the fact that a full conquest, which should have eliminated all traces of a former society, did not take place. Such a view of conquest was not a simple one. Postulating colonial relationships inevitably raised problems for that actual constitutional reality—the crown of Ireland. The 1541 act may have established such an entity, but it had failed to say anything about the relationships between the crowns of England and Ireland (and after 1603 Scotland). Even more complex was the relationship of those crowns to the parliament in Westminster. In the course of the seventeenth century the Westminster parliament was to interest itself increasingly in Irish affairs. The first significant incursion could be seen as a matter of convenience, the impeachment of an Irish official, the Earl of Strafford, in 1640. The second, the trial of Conor Maguire, second Baron of Enniskillen, for his part in the 1641 rising before a jury in Middlesex in February 1645, was much more dubious. Again, the passage of the Adventurers' Act in 1642, which raised funds for the suppression of the Irish rising to be repaid from Irish land after the war, might seem to be a wartime measure, but the Cattle Acts of 1663 and 1667, which prohibited the import of Irish cattle into England, or the Woollen Act of 1699, which did the same for woollen goods, could not be so regarded. The Navigation Acts of 1663 and 1671, restricting Irish trading networks, were also viewed by contemporaries as clear examples of interference in Irish matters by the Westminster parliament.

These complexities resulted not in one set of ideas about kingship but in a number of constructions of what kingship meant in different circumstances. Consequently, what seemed to be a uniting factor actually became a divisive one, as the wars of the 1640s proved. As the secretary of the Confederated Catholics, Richard Bellings, ruefully observed, the war was 'of many parts, carried on under the notion of so many interests, perplexed with such diversity of rents and divisions among those who seem to be of a side'.[10] Monarchy, supposedly the unifying focus for all the combatants, was in reality a profoundly divisive factor.

The second implication of kingship and its structures of government was that it called for the creation of a commonwealth. One New English commentator on the role of plantations in the early seventeenth century declared: 'By this means [the land settlement] shall that people [the Irish] now grow into a body commoned and into a commonwealth; before they wholly consisted of poor, proud gentry.'[11] That process of creating a commonwealth was complicated. It involved a reciprocal process of negotiation and renegotiation between ruler and subjects in an attempt to balance public and private interests. The implication of this was, first, that a large number of people should be involved in the political process, and, secondly, that they should have the moral authority to do so. In this world the king did not rule, in the sense of handing down laws; rather he was a guarantor of the system of government. As such, the king had an obligation to consult with those in society who had the moral and social authority to give him advice, and through this process his power and authority would be enhanced. As Richard Bellings wrote in the 1620s, 'Thus he whom God ordained a king to be / Obeys his subjects and is never free.'[12] In the eyes of the Old English community, it was they who were the group with the appropriate authority to rule. Bellings explained this in the context of the Grand Council of 1640, dominated by Old English peers and usually meeting before parliament, in which the right to give counsel was 'a privilege which they [the members of the Grand Council] may claim as their birth right by the fundamental laws of the government'.[13] The failure to accord this elite their due was a frequent complaint made by commentators on seventeenth-century Irish society. The Old English priest and historian Geoffrey Keating, for example, stressed the 'virtues or good qualities of nobles among the *sean ghallaibh* [Old English]' and complained bitterly that their patronage, piety and hospitality were ignored by New English historians who 'take notice of the ways of inferiors and wretched little hags, ignoring the worthy actions of the gentry'.[14]

In the minds of the New English settlers, however, it was to them that the providence of God and military circumstances had delivered the reins of power. In reality, the New English settlers had much less claim to the moral authority to govern Ireland. It is true that they had almost exclusive claim on what might be described as transactional power, since they controlled the army and particularly the system of provost-marshals that formed a quasi-military local government structure in the early part of the seventeenth century. However, this was a contested view. The Old English argued that in the early part of the seventeenth century the New English simply did not understand Ireland. They did not have the social contacts necessary to make society work, and, as new arrivals were often from poor social backgrounds as younger sons or impoverished gentlemen trying to make their fortune, they did not have the moral authority to hold a social hierarchy together. The Old English lawyer Richard Hadsor, argued in 1604 that so long as the Old English 'were employed as principal officers and counsellors of estate in time of war and peace in the realm, being such men who were thoroughly informed of all matters therein, and acquainted with the disposition of the people, the realm was well governed and daily increased in civility'. The New English, on the other hand, whether in the army or 'employed as inferior magistrates', were held responsible for 'the enormities of that commonwealth [which] hath brought forth many rebellions, and especially the last general and dangerous combination of the mere Irish throughout the whole realm'.[15]

In the early part of the seventeenth century New English settlers made attempts to lay claim on some justification for rule. For instance, the accumulation of titles of honour was seen as a strong basis for the moral authority to govern, and settlers accumulated such honours with enthusiasm. The Irish peerage expanded over the seventeenth century and perhaps most dramatically in the period from 1615 to 1628 when honours were freely available for sale. Seventy-five individuals availed of their opportunity to purchase an Irish title, compared with forty-six in the wealthier, and much larger, world of England. Moreover, those in Ireland who possessed titles also strove to acquire an English title, usually junior to their Irish one, and to intermarry with the English peerage as a way of further underpinning their position. Below the level of the peerage between 1603 and 1629 there were 258 new Irish knighthoods of which just over two-thirds went to settlers. Acquiring a title was an attempt to repair the social problems created by rapid upward mobility. One may have had an Irish landed estate, but that counted for little; such estates were easily come by. Titles of honour were not the only ones in use. Long after they had ceased to mean anything on the field of command, settlers continued to use military ranks as a means of indicating status. In the course of time the New English settlers began to accumulate the sort of prestige which, in their own eyes, allowed them to describe themselves as the governors of Ireland. Since New English society was, in the main, the result of a migration process, individuals lacked the sort of familial and factional contacts that smoothed the operation of government in England or Scotland. Social bonds, fractured in the migration process, had to be slowly rebuilt to create a new structure. There were advantages to this. The absence of a dense network of genealogical bonds meant that feuding, which characterised parts of Scotland, did not resurrect itself in Ulster. On the negative side, it made the acquisition of social authority, as demonstrated by familial connections and accumulated cultural capital, difficult. This may partly explain the conspicuous consumption associated with these families in matters such as hospitality and funerary monuments which can be traced back into the sixteenth century. New English settler society had to be created in the seventeenth century. Settlers built social capital through the formation of networks of association, obligation and support. This was a gradual process but an inevitable one. Some individuals followed the practice of Richard Boyle, Earl of Cork, who arranged a series of prestigious marriages for his children with the offspring of influential men, including the Earl of Kildare, that linked him into the older network of the Old English authority. However, origins were not easily forgotten. When one peer, the Earl of Drogheda, complained in 1662 that the members of the Irish House of Commons all wanted to be peers, he elicited the retort that 'Another rebellion may make us so, as a former made your ancestors.'[16] Settlers also built cultural capital by acquiring an understanding of Ireland and the rules by which the social world might work. Thus at the onset of the wars of the 1640s some abandoned their estates in England and began to see Ireland as their home. By the 1660s many were second-generation settlers who thought of themselves as Anglo-Irish rather than as settlers and began to build a 'Protestant interest'. They interested themselves in new fashions and adopted new ways of thinking about their world, evidenced by the founding of the Dublin Philosophical Society and Royal College of Physicians in the late seventeenth century. By the end of the century the language of conquest was flatly rejected by their political theorist William Molyneux in his *Case of Ireland's being bound by acts of parliament in England . . . stated* (1698). In short, the settlers had adopted the political language of the Old English of the early seventeenth century.

Such changing ideas highlight the dangers of associating one political philosophy with a particular ethnic or social group. Ideas about how Ireland was to be governed were continually in flux. They were determined by many different circumstances. Immediate difficulties might well set in train a set of political meditations by an individual which resulted in convictions rather different to those of friends or neighbours. Thus in 1625 an Old Englishman of impeccable credentials, John Cusack, can be found in London arguing that

Ireland was a colony to be governed by royal will. That may be related to the fact that he wished the English courts to overrule their Irish counterparts in a land suit in which he was involved. Again, unpredictable political alliances were often formed against the later historian's expectations. Thus in 1646 the Protestant parliamentarian Earl of Essex can be found moving to protect the estates and position of the Catholic royalist Earl of Clanricard. Similarly, in the scramble for land at the Restoration in the 1660s the Protestant William Montgomery secured land for a Catholic family known to him, while objecting to the restoration of others. All this is a reminder that political positions were almost always taken up in social contexts. In most cases that was the context of kinship, friendship and community, and hence the social reproduction of political ideas and positions tended to perpetuate particular types of view within particular communities, though with considerable complexity at the edges of those communities.

## CONTRADICTIONS OF BELIEF

Belief, as opposed to religion, is a difficult area for the historian to deal with, yet it lies at the heart of reconstructing how contemporaries perceived their world. Indeed, religion in the early modern world can only be effective as an explanatory force for change when underpinned by an understanding of it as a set of beliefs. Few, if any, in seventeenth-century Ireland saw their world as the outcome of impersonal social, economic and political forces. They tended to explain the changes in their lives as being the result of interpersonal relationships or the effect of divine will. Thus Fear Flatha Ó Gnímh in early seventeenth-century Ulster interpreted the political crisis which followed the 'flight of the earls' in 1607 as God's judgment on the Irish, and Dáibhí Ó Bruadair used the same explanation to account for the Williamite victory in 1690. Protestants also accounted for disasters, such as the rising of 1641 or personal misfortunes, in terms of God's judgment for sin. God was therefore a present reality in the lives of people in seventeenth-century Ireland.

Measuring the impact of the intangible spiritual lives of contemporaries on their actions is fraught with difficulty, which is why historians have preferred to deal with belief in the organised, corporate form of religion. However, this is to ignore the untidy reality which belief represents. People were part of a religious grouping for many overlapping reasons. For some it was custom;

many reformers in the early seventeenth century argued that Catholics could be easily converted if taken away from the influence of great lords. For others it was primarily a badge of belonging. As one Corkman told insurgents in the 1640s, 'I am of the religion that both the king and the Lord Lieutenant General of Ireland profess which is the true Protestant religion.'[17] For others, religion was the result of emotionally charged experiences that convinced them of their need for supernatural assistance in their lives.

Historians have tended to view religion in a rather simplistic way, treating it as a marker of identity or badge of belonging, with newcomers being equated with Protestantism and natives with Catholicism. However, the problem of belief muddies the waters here. Not all newcomers were Protestant. English Catholics had migrated to Munster in the sixteenth century, creating a Catholic settler group there. In Ulster too there were Catholic settlers. The Hamilton family in the barony of Strabane were to prove particularly obstreperous. As the Earl of Cork recorded in 1629, 'The Master of Abercorn, Sir George Hamilton, Sir Claud Hamilton and Sir William Hamilton [four of the main undertakers in the barony of Strabane] drew priests and Jesuits to Strabane and had a meeting there of them with some papists whom the laws had ejected from Scotland.' Consequently, Cork complained that 'Far from encouraging Protestantism they have countenanced and drawn thither Scottish papists.' Indeed, the Bishop of Derry alleged that they 'countenanced papists so much that there will be a revolt in Strabane if any more of the Scotch papists come there'. Worse was to come when Sir William Hamilton 'perverted' his wife, a daughter of Hugh Montgomery, Viscount Ards, and a Jesuit also converted one of her maids.[18] Cases such as this warn us that religion in early modern Ireland is a complicated matter and that religious rifts are often less clear-cut than they seem.

Any attempt to chart confessional relations forged in seventeenth-century Ireland needs to be done in two contexts. The first is that of geography. For many Catholics who lived in seventeenth-century Ireland, relations with the Protestant Established Church were not a difficulty, since there were no Protestants to have relations with. On the very crude assumption that most of those described as 'English' in the poll money return of 1660 were Protestant and that most of those described as 'Irish' were Catholic, it may be possible to hazard some guesses as to the religious geography of Ireland. On this basis, it is clear that there were large parts of Ireland, especially in the west and south-west of the country, where Protestants formed less than 5 per cent of the population. There were equally large areas in the province of Munster where Protestants comprised less than 10 per cent. This reality was reflected in the dilapidated state of Church of Ireland churches in these areas, with less than a third of all churches in the ecclesiastical province of Cashel in a fit state to be used in 1615. In many of these regions a Protestant was a rarity. It was in Ulster and the eastern seaboard of the country, as well as in the hinterland of the major towns such as Cork and Dublin, that the Protestant population clustered. In those areas the issue of their relationship with their Catholic neighbours could, under certain circumstances, become significant. Conversions, following Jesuit or Franciscan missions or Church of Ireland preaching or mixed marriages, might raise local tensions in such areas where the confessional balance may have been a sensitive issue. In the 1640s as military success in rebellion shifted power into the hands of local Catholics in some localities they also attempted to impose local confessional unity. In Longford, for example, they declared that 'none should live in Ireland but such as would go to Mass', and in one Monaghan instance it was claimed that some Protestants 'could not be Christians unless they were so christened anew'. Threats were made to force Protestants to conform to Catholicism, and more practically in a state of warfare it was claimed in Longford that soldiers 'could give quarter to them that were Catholics but not to the heretics'. Others converted to save their goods or lives.[19] In this way shifts in local power resulted in confessional change, but this was rarely more than local in its effect. As a result, attitudes to confessional division displayed considerable regional variation, even over short distances, which reflected local priorities and perceptions. Thus a late seventeenth-century landlord such as Arthur Brownlow at Lurgan was happy to have as his tenants Catholics, Quakers, Presbyterians and even members of the Church of Ireland, while only a few miles away on the Conway estates the agent, George Rawdon, was utterly opposed to any group as tenants except those who attended the Church of Ireland parish church.

The second important context is the realisation that negotiating social and religious relations was not simply about Protestants and Catholics, either within a confessional model or within one driven by belief, because within those two traditions there were sub-traditions contending among themselves. Most obviously, those Protestants who regarded themselves as 'godly' saw around them a host of the 'ungodly' or reprobate. From the perspective of the godly preachers, these nominal Protestants were a dangerous threat to social order. Their polarised view of the godly and the ungodly led to condemnation of the profanity, hypocrisy and individualism of the ungodly. This was tempered by calls for repentance. The language used by some godly preachers against the ungodly was every bit as violent as that directed against Catholics. In the eyes of Steven Jerome, chaplain to the Earl of Cork, they appeared as 'hypocrite, idolater, blasphemer, drunkard, atheist, profane person, murderer [and] the devil incarnate'.[20] Within Catholicism too there were divergent devotional traditions which created tensions. For many who had been exposed to the ideas of the Council of Trent, some elements of traditional Irish Catholic practices seemed no better than heathenism. The synodal legislation of the early seventeenth century attempted to dismantle as superstition traditional communal rites of inclusion such as pilgrimages to holy wells. Religious change in early modern Ireland was not one simple binary opposition, but a set of social relationships traversed by a lattice of potential fracture lines.

Given this potential for social division over religious issues in early seventeenth-century Ireland, it is interesting to consider what did not happen. Before the late 1630s it is hard to detect anything within Irish Protestantism that could be described as widespread tendencies to form separate confessions despite the potential for such separatism. Church of Ireland preachers continually emphasised the principle of *adiaphora*, that certain rites and ceremonies which might have split Protestantism were matters of indifference. Again, the Eucharist was an important manifestation of community cohesiveness providing a way of defusing tensions within Protestant communities. The Church of Ireland canons of 1634, for instance, laid great stress on the importance of reconciliation both with God and their neighbours before communion. That at least some Protestants took this seriously is suggested by the low numbers who came to communion despite large attendances at services. In 1638 one minister in County Cavan refused to administer communion because he was not in charity with some of his congregation. Developments of the late 1630s, particularly the introduction of the 'black oath' against Presbyterianism, caused splits to emerge. Reactions to the war of the 1640s resulted in the separation from the Church of Ireland fold of those who thought of themselves as the godly, and this trend was dramatically accentuated in the 1650s with the arrival of Cromwellian soldiers who had backgrounds in radical religion. Similarly within Catholicism, the two key strands, one traditional and one following the reforms enjoined by the Council of Trent, generated at least some tension. There were disputes between secular or diocesan clergy and regular clergy who were members of religious orders over rights of pastoral care and the income that this generated. Commonalities such as the mass held differing Catholic groups together, and while in theory clergy were seen as having a limited social role, in practice they acted as creators and regulators of social peace and order. Again, in the case of relations between Catholics and Protestants, it is often difficult to detect the sort of confessional rifts that might be expected. It is clear, for example, that Protestants, both locally and in Dublin Castle, knew the whereabouts of Catholic churches. They compiled lists of them, but apparently made little effort to close them down. Moreover, Catholics did not hide their churches. One Dublin priest, Edmund Doyle, in 1637 described his church, vestments and ornaments in some detail in his will which was duly proved in the testamentary court of the Protestant Archbishop of Dublin. For some this was a confusing situation. As one commentator wrote to the Earl of Arran, later Lord Deputy, in 1681, Catholics in Dublin went to mass 'without any shyness or indeed prudence'. Moreover, it seemed strange that 'the Lord Primate [Church of Ireland Archbishop of Dublin] should see these meetings [going] publicly to mass every Sunday morning on his way to Church and not endeavour to remove them'.[21] When circumstances dictated that government should close Catholic churches, as in Dublin in 1629, it is clear that they knew exactly where the churches were located. At least one Jesuit house, closed in that raid, was located within a few hundred yards of Christ Church Cathedral and had been visited by an interested Protestant tourist.

This absence of overt religious conflict on the scale that might be expected, together perhaps with the lack of witchcraft trials (which were prevalent across Europe) in early seventeenth-century Ireland, all point to some measure of social cohesion, or drive for peace and order, which existed in tension with the desire to enforce confessional division and helped to mitigate its disruptive tendencies. Thus the literature of formal religious controversy failed to penetrate seventeenth-century Ireland until the late 1680s. Social and economic factors were important here. While administrators in Dublin Castle, Church of Ireland bishops and Catholic missionary clergy used the rhetoric of confessional division and reformation—urging recusancy rather than the accommodation with the Established Church (or church-papistry) on Catholics—as part of large-scale and ultimately unsuccessful policy objectives, the language and institutions of everyday life were rather different. The structures of everyday life were focused on the manor or civil parish and, frequently, on the law as expressed at community level. Such sites provided ways of diffusing the more destabilising influences from outside local communities.

Despite these qualifications, religious divisions were a reality of Irish life in the seventeenth century. Such divisions were clearly visible in times of social and economic tension from the Mandates controversy of 1605–6, through the proclamations expelling Catholic clergy from Ireland in 1624 and 1629, to the riot which accompanied the closing of the Dublin religious houses in the latter year. At a more popular level, the outbreak of religious violence during the rising of 1641–2 provides ample evidence that government did not have a monopoly on the production of religious tension. Yet the trauma of the 1640s should not obscure the fact that there were long periods when tensions were subdued, and even during the 1640s many Protestants lived unmolested in Catholic-controlled areas. Ideas of religious division might well be encapsulated in government proclamation or statute, yet how these ideas were activated, or remained quiescent, depended a great deal on contemporary social contexts.

## CONTRADICTIONS OF CULTURE

If culture is to be understood not simply as the arts and learning but in a broader sense as a way of organising meaning in everyday life, then it is appropriate to focus on a number of important cultural ideas that contemporaries used to master and interpret their worlds. Some of these, such as kingship and God, have been discussed above, but two others are of importance here since they were frequently resorted to in order to explain changes in the world: history and language. For most people living in seventeenth-century Ireland, it was axiomatic that the good was to be equated with the old. In particular, custom provided an important legal validator for and arbitrator of actions, since, in the view of the Attorney General, Sir John Davies, customary law was 'better than all the written laws in the world to make men honest and happy in this life' and from this all other law flowed.[22] Or as the traditionalist Duke of Ormond characterised the 1640s, 'the breach of ancient custom brought disorder'.[23] Despite this belief, people lived in a world that was rapidly changing. The result was a range of historical works generated both within and outside Ireland which attempted to explain to contemporaries the significance of the past for the present and to justify the present in the light of past events.

Sir John Davies's *Discovery of the true causes why Ireland was never entirely subdued* (1612), using the archives in Dublin Castle, provided an explanation of how the people of Ireland had become the subjects of the king and how the errors of the past had been corrected under King James. This was a significant new development for those who hitherto had relied on the frequently reprinted twelfth-century works of Giraldus Cambrensis or the censored sixteenth-century history of Ireland written by Richard Stanihurst. It explained how and why the present situation had developed and used the past to prove the inevitability of the present.

Davies's *Discovery* became an important text, read by many including Lord Deputy Wentworth in the 1630s, but it was not the only one of its kind to appear. In the 1630s the work of Sir James Ware, a Dublin government official, also contributed to understanding the contemporary situation by resorting to the past. Rather than writing a new history, in 1633 Ware published editions of what he regarded as key texts from Ireland's past. In subtle ways these were made relevant to the present. Ware removed the names of Anglo-Irish magnates, such as the Earls of Ormond, who had been involved in dubious activities in the past but who were now significant figures in the new order, from his edition of Spenser's *View of the present state of Ireland*. Such works thus helped to integrate an older tradition into the world of the New English, then only in the process of formation.

The native Irish too used history to contextualise and explain the society which they saw forming around them. However, these questions were being addressed not so much by those who remained within Ireland but rather among the Irish living and working in continental Europe. Hence the position of Ireland in a wider world became an important element of that study. The Franciscans of the

Irish College at Louvain reshaped the history of Ireland to meet new circumstances by using the lives of its saints, the succession of its kings and the political struggles of its lords as their interpretative framework. The most comprehensive presentation of Irish history emerging from this context was the work of the Four Masters. Their Annals of the Kingdom of Ireland, compiled in County Donegal between 1632 and 1636, was the culmination of a decade of research into the sources for Irish history, both ecclesiastical and secular, by a team of scholars led by the Franciscan lay brother, Mícheál Ó Cléirigh. Drawing on authoritative primary sources, and using a traditional annalistic format, the history of Ireland compiled by the Four Masters emphasised the antiquity of the Irish kingdom and the achievements of its local leaders, both ecclesiastical and secular. Some of the same scholars also compiled a martyrology, or calendar of saints' feast-days, the Martyrology of Donegal, and a document detailing the genealogies of saints and kings which used chronology to link hagiography and history. While the research and compilation was done in Ireland, the inspiration came principally from Mícheál Ó Cléirigh's superiors in the Franciscan convent of St Anthony at Louvain, not least Hugh Ward and Patrick Fleming. After the premature deaths of Fleming in 1631 and Ward in 1635 the Louvain project was continued by another Irish Franciscan, John Colgan, who made extensive use of Ó Cléirigh's annals and transcripts of the saints' lives in his own publications.

In so far as this Louvain project had an underlying theory of history, it was articulated by John Colgan in the preface to his *Acta Sanctorum Hiberniae* (1645). Colgan argued that Ireland, the land of saints and scholars, had developed through a series of golden ages and times of crisis which were resolved from outside. The coming of Patrick, the British holy man, had produced the first golden age of the Irish church, revealed clearly in the lives of the saints which had been collected by Ó Cléirigh. This era had been shattered by the coming of the Vikings. That church was again revitalised by the twelfth-century reform under the guidance of the holy man St Malachy (who had close links with the European reformer St Bernard), which again produced a golden age of the medieval Irish church. This was in turn brought to an end by Henry VIII and the coming of the Reformation in the early sixteenth century. While Colgan did not explicitly say so, he probably believed the church would again require renewal by holy men from abroad in the seventeenth century, and there is little doubt that it was himself and his colleagues, the Louvain Franciscans, who had been cast in this role. The cultural source of this model of external influences on Ireland is not difficult to find. The twelfth-century *Leabhar Gabhála* had postulated the pre-Christian settlement of Ireland through waves of settlers, and this key interpretative framework influenced the way in which Colgan and others conceptualised later Irish history. Others abroad, such as the Catholic Archbishop of Armagh, Peter Lombard, shaped similar interpretations of the Irish past in the light of contemporary circumstances.

Colgan's success in explaining Europe to the Irish and Ireland to the Europeans dominated the shaping of Irish perceptions of Europe. By contrast, Colgan's contemporary, the secular priest Geoffrey Keating, saw history moving in a straight line rather than in a series of cycles. For him, the continuities of ecclesiastical structures, dioceses and parishes, rather than waves of disruption and renewal, were the organising principles of Irish history. Such telling differences in these works reflect contrasting views of how Catholic religious reform was to be implemented in Ireland. Colgan's model emphasised the role of religious orders, while Keating's saw the secular priest within his parish, responsible to a bishop, as the central element of Catholic organisation. Again, for Keating the papacy's issuing of the bull *Laudabiliter*, in which Adrian iv was supposed to have allowed Henry ii to reform the Irish church, was crucial in the historical interpretation of the evolution of the Irish church (as it was for Protestant commentators), but it did not feature in Colgan's analysis.

Colgan's view of the history of Ireland explained to the Irish what their links with Europe were. First, Colgan was intent on explaining to Europeans the significance of the Irish. Colgan's works were issued in Latin from the press in Louvain. They were large folio volumes which were not easily portable. They were intended for scholarly rather than devotional reading. The most important context for such scholarly works is the establishment by the pope in 1588 of the Sacred Congregation of Rites and Ceremonies, the responsibilities of which included canonisation and the recognition of saints. Procedures for the recognition of saints became increasingly rigorous with new regulations in 1629 and 1634. Neither Patrick, Brigit, Columcille nor almost any other Irish saint had ever had papal approval, being saints 'by acclamation' according to an older medieval custom. Colgan's work was therefore, in part, designed to explain to European scholars and Vatican reformers the world of Irish sanctity and the validity of its national saints at a time of reform. Secondly, as Colgan pointed out to Irish readers, spiritual regeneration of Ireland had come from outside the country, whether through St Patrick or St Bernard's disciple Malachy, and hence Ireland belonged to a wider tradition of Christianity. That was not an alien tradition. The early Irish church had provided missionaries who had evangelised Britain and Europe in the early Middle Ages in a way that the Roman church had not. One of Colgan's heroes, St Columcille, was the quintessential missionary monk, and the stories of his life, together with those of Patrick and Brigit, were collected by Colgan in a large Latin volume entitled *Trias thaumaturga* in 1647. In this way Irish and European ideas were firmly intertwined. The rewriting of early Irish history in its European context thus had the effect of imbuing at least some Irish Catholics with a European underpinning for their sense of Irishness, a process enhanced by the education of many Old English clergy in the European Irish colleges in the seventeenth century.

The tensions between what happened in the past and its relevance to the present reveal a good deal about the concerns of those who lived in seventeenth-century Ireland, but there are yet further examples of these tensions in the history of language in that period. The 1534 act for the 'English order, habit and language' had laid down clearly that in creating a commonwealth '[there is] nothing which doth more contain and keep many of the [king's] subjects of this his said land in a savage and wild kind and manner of living than the diversity that is betwixt them in tongue, language, order and habit'. Despite this, the Irish language was not destroyed in the seventeenth century. In naming the features of the landscape, there was little systematic attempt to change Irish-language placenames, apart from an abortive requirement in the 1665 Act of Explanation that 'new and proper names more suitable to the English tongue than the barbarous and uncouth names' be used for townlands. Rather, English, as a language, made considerable progress in seventeenth-century Ireland. In the 1620s Conell Mageoghegan in Westmeath and in the 1660s Dáibhí Ó Bruadair in Limerick lamented the decline of the Irish language. By 1700 Ireland was, in large measure, a bilingual society. While many were not fluent, or perhaps literate, in English, they could at least recognise the basic significance of different types of document and understood what their effect was. This expansion of the English language alongside Irish was not random. In the Irish satire entitled *Pairlement Chloinne Tomáis*, composed in the early 1630s, the context in which English is used by one of the native Irish peasants is to buy tobacco from an English merchant. If commercial activity was one point of contact for language change, another was the law, a fact appreciated by Sir John Davies as early as 1612. With the spread of the common law, writing became a more widespread activity because it was used to conduct commercial transactions and determine land title. Thus reading became more common, and the language in which this skill was acquired was English. People learned both something of English and Irish legal terminology. Irish-language texts of the seventeenth century contain a large number of legal terms all borrowed directly from English. By the 1620s the legal vocabulary included such phrases as *síothcháin an ríogh* (the king's peace) and *proiseas* (a legal process). By the 1630s *suigheacháin* seems to have been the quarter-sessions while *sioson mór* is probably the assizes. More commonly the borrowing of words into Irish took place by incorporating the terms heard at legal proceedings. Thus, by the 1650s, terms such as writ, assize, commission, replevin, *nisi prius* and *capias* were all familiar enough to appear in Irish-language poetry. All this is testimony to how deeply the legal system penetrated the lives of those who lived in seventeenth-century Ireland. English was a language that did not merely exist; it became important to be able to speak it, at least in certain social contexts. Thus when in the early seventeenth century the east Ulster poet Fear Flatha Ó Gnímh praised his patron Henry O'Neill, the virtues he highlighted were nobility and knowledge of English law and learning in preference to the older warlike motifs of the sixteenth century. Thus law provided a common language through which social order could be negotiated and, in some cases, a venue such as the assize or quarter-sessions, where such social bargains could be struck. Consequently, more and more people with native Irish backgrounds can be traced using the common-law processes in the seventeenth century. At the lowest level, the manorial courts attracted Irish suitors, and at Finavarra in County Clare in the 1670s some of the most important figures at the manor courts were the local Gaelic legal family, the O'Davorens, who seem to have adapted easily from brehon to common law. The paucity of evidence means that it is not possible to say whether this trend was widespread.

In addition to these borrowings from English, the Irish language also devised new terms to express new realities. Outside Ireland those with a different perspective on developments in the country borrowed new words, such as *perseacuision* (persecution), to express what they felt were changing situations. Within Ireland the traditional term for lord, *tigherna*, changed its meaning from lordship over men to ownership of land, or landlord. In the sixteenth century lords had not owned land in Gaelic Ireland; rather, property was vested in families who owed lordship to greater lords but owed it only in so far as it could be enforced. In return for renders of goods, such as cattle or butter, greater lords provided services such as military protection and the administration of justice, distributing the surplus goods they received through guesting and feasting. Society was thus held together by the ties of obligation of lordship rather than formal contracts such as land grants or leases, and there were few formal market structures or towns. Those who analysed that world thought that this left too many freeholders at the mercy of great lords, and in the course of the sixteenth century the crown had attempted to transform lords into landlords through policies such as composition, and surrender and regrant. In short, there was an attempt to transform land into a means of wealth rather than a source of personal power. Many native lords saw the benefit of a steady rental income as a landlord and co-operated by trying to reduce the status of freeholders to that of tenants. By the end of the sixteenth century even the most powerful Ulster lord, the O'Neill, was moving in this direction. The spread of the common law and the market economy made the landlord a universal feature in seventeenth-century Ireland, and a cash rent was an increasingly common way of determining social bonds.

### A WORLD OF AMBIGUITIES

The contradictions inherent in a wide range of aspects of early modern Irish life undoubtedly presented challenges. For those Protestants who lived in a world dominated by Catholicism there was a tension between an abhorrence of Catholic practices and a fascination with them. A case in point is Samuel Waring, the son of William Waring, who acquired a modest but significant estate in County Down, with a rental of about £600 on his death in 1703. Towards the end of his life William betrayed his religious position by writing a memorandum for his son 'of God's providences which hath attended me'. The Warings were of the solidly Protestant county gentry which then controlled provincial Ireland. Samuel was educated in Trinity College Dublin, and in 1687 he was dispatched on his European tour to round off his education. The tour was intended to introduce him to the cultured world of Europe. He prepared himself in the manner of any good tourist by reading guidebooks on Holland, Venice, Geneva, Naples and Rome. Perhaps not surprisingly, given his background, Samuel Waring had a sensitivity to the religious geography of the areas through which he travelled. Passing through Germany, he noted that villages of forty or fifty houses were either Lutheran or Catholic and 'one may soon know which by the many crosses we see about ye popish towns'. Yet he was fascinated by Catholic religious ceremonial. In Rome he visited convents and recorded their practices and went to hear a Jesuit preach, 'addressing and caressing the cross and crucifix after an old manner'. He went to the exposition of relics in another convent. He witnessed the Easter ceremonies in Rome, with the washing of the feet on Holy Thursday, and noted the procession of penitents with thousands of wax candles 'making a most glorious show'. He also visited five churches on Good Friday, witnessed the display of relics, and recorded the traditions associated with the Roman churches and the crucifixion. In a Dominican cemetery on the Hill of Julian he saw two coats of arms, one representing the guardians of England trampled by Cromwell, and the other Britannia throwing her sceptre at the pope's feet and the Church of Rome's feet. A Jesuit college in Rome also had pictures representing England, Scotland and Ireland 'with a harp and this motto "Gaudet Hiberniae"'. Despite the obvious political meaning of this iconography, Waring did not comment further in his travel journals. Displaying yet more curiosity about Catholicism, Waring, the paragon of the Protestant establishment, was assisted in gaining access to Catholic sites by a number of Catholic clergy. At one point he noted his contacts on the tour who had helped him. These included a Dominican priest in Naples, a 'Fr Maguire, a priest in Venice', Fr Sheldon, a Jesuit, 'very civil to us at Loretto giving us papers of the place in English'. In Rome Cardinal Howard, an English cardinal, received him and showed him around Rome on Good Friday, and he was helped by 'Fr Plunkett, ye agent for the popish clergy of Ireland'. He also happily visited the Irish Franciscan friars at

St Isidore's, where he listened to their theological disputations.[24] It is difficult to detect any immediate intellectual consequences of Waring's European tour, but in other instances such contacts between Protestant and Catholic certainly led to leakages across the confessional divides. Irish Protestants certainly visited Catholic holy wells, and, as one author observed in a treatise on cattle in 1673, some Protestants did not look for help in managing sick cattle until many were dead, 'and then to save those that are kept alive they make use of those that have charms, enchanted water, enchanted rings and bells', all of which would have been rejected by formal Protestant doctrine.[25]

Such tensions between how people were supposed to behave in areas of everyday life, apart from the religious, and what they actually did gave rise to agonising among some. Robert Boyle, the younger son of the first Earl of Cork, displayed considerable moral scruples throughout his life about the way in which the land and ecclesiastical livings which provided his income had been acquired. Behind this lay the quest for something more intangible, namely virtue which 'is the cement of humane society, without which they would confound themselves into a chaos'. To remove it would be to 'take away the foundations and cornerstones of the commonwealth'.[26] His brother Roger showed a similar interest in one branch of virtue—heroics—in his plays. While others had similar interests, the fabric of the commonwealth had an importance for those trying to construct it. It was, for instance, no coincidence that the idea of virtue had been most closely associated with sixteenth-century republics in which social authority had been continually in motion. More practically, tensions between image and reality gave rise to a search for solutions to immediate political, social and economic problems. Archbishop Ussher's writings on the early history of the British and Irish churches, for instance, were a response to the wider problem of explaining whether or not there had been a breach with the early Christian church at the Reformation. The creativity that such problems inspired can be identified in many aspects of Irish life. In science the challenge of learning about and devising ways of settling Ireland produced work of significance. In England in 1650 Samuel Hartlib inquired about the natural history of Ireland, noting: 'I suppose this may be one means whereby Ireland may be peopled again, and get good tenants; especially if the other parts which are wanting to that [natural] history, were more particularly discovered and described.'[27] Part of that work of description fell to Sir William Petty in his mapped survey of Ireland, the Down Survey, in the 1650s and the continual outpouring of descriptions of and proposals for Ireland in the late seventeenth century, all dedicated to solving the problems of Ireland. Indeed, it may be significant that Dublin managed to form a sustainable scientific society, the Dublin Philosophical Society, in the 1680s when Edinburgh failed to do so.

Early science was not the only intellectual area in which the educated elite in Ireland were engaged. Some of its inhabitants showed an interest in the literary world. Roger Boyle and his brother Robert were both sufficiently curious about the world of French romance literature to try to emulate the genre, the first volume of Roger Boyle's *Parthenissa* being published at Waterford in 1654. Not all literary developments were imitative. The first modern novel may well be the anonymous *Virtue rewarded, or The Irish princess* (London 1693) set in the area around Clonmel, County Tipperary, possibly written by a settler resident there during the Williamite wars. That the search for literary innovation was conscious is clear from the comment of William Congreve in his novel *Incognita* (1692), written shortly after he left Ireland the previous year, saying of what he was attempting: 'I have not observed it before in a novel.'[28] Authorship had limited outlet in Ireland, and while the numbers of printed books grew rapidly in the late seventeenth century, this was largely the result of imports from England. Thus Irish authors had to live in two worlds, that of Ireland and the literary world of England where their work was published and where most of their readership lay. The tensions which this created may well be one of the sources of creative energy which gave rise to this literary output.

Innovation was not confined to learning and literature. In the realm of land law, economic conditions created a form of tenure in Ireland unparalleled in other countries. It combined elements of both leasehold and freehold. This became known as the three-life lease renewable for ever which first appeared in Ulster in the late seventeenth century. The freehold element derived from the fact that new lives could be continuously inserted into the lease on payment of a fine as each of the originally named individuals died. Thus the tenure was effectively a perpetuity. However, it also contained the normal stipulations of a lease relating, for instance, to distraint and re-entry for non-payment of rent. In this way the interests of landlords were protected by retaining the elements of a lease while permitting long leases that encouraged substantial tenants to settle on an estate at a point when such tenants were in short supply.

## PROBLEMS AND POSSIBILITIES

The creativity Irish society manifested in many spheres in the seventeenth century can best be seen not as the result of the work of a central authority but as the participatory creativity of many who attempted to solve the problems generated by their own worlds. Those problems were unique and complex. They resulted from the attempts to blend two worlds: the world of old Europe, with its emphasis on monarchy, hierarchy and an integrated society, with a colonial world associated with migration, social fragmentation and the failure of the conditions set out in the Treaty of Augsburg that the religion of the ruler should be the religion of the people. The solutions to those problems were what made Ireland different to the medieval world that had gone before, a more modern construct, and different to many other societies in the seventeenth century. Ultimately those solutions produced the web of interactions, mutualities, reciprocities and antagonisms that comprised that hybrid world.

# Part I
An Old World Made New

## 2
# Distributing Power, 1603–20

On 30 March 1603, six days after the death of Elizabeth I, Hugh O'Neill, Earl of Tyrone signed the Treaty of Mellifont which brought the Nine Years' War to a formal close. The war had begun as a guerrilla campaign in the middle of the 1590s, but after the attempted Spanish invasion at Kinsale in 1601 it had become a bloody conflict. In Ulster, in particular, the scorched-earth campaign that brought hostilities to an end had been particularly severe, forcing O'Neill into submission. The consequences of that submission triggered responses which, as they evolved over the next few years, were complex and contingent. On the one hand, the Irish poet Eochaidh Ó hEodhasa celebrated the changes that James I's accession had brought in terms of the brilliant sun of the king which dispersed the mist and the 'mutual mourning' and changed it to glory. In the same year, however, he wrote an 'answer' poem in the love-poetry tradition which was a biting satire on the literary changes then becoming fashionable. He complained of the changes in the social order and the consequent decline of literary patronage and abandonment of the traditional difficult bardic verse, with its complex rules for composition, for the 'common sort of easy art' that dunces and others practised.[1] Among the New English community too there were contradictory responses to the end of the war. O'Neill had, after all, been defeated, but had apparently emerged unscathed. As one officer, Sir John Harrington, expostulated in 1603, 'I have lived to see that damnable rebel Tirowen brought to England, courteously received and well liked. O my Lord, what is there doth not prove the inconstancy of worldly matters.' Nine years of war and deprivation for soldiers, which had achieved everything, had apparently achieved nothing, so that 'now doth Tyrone dare us old commanders with his presence [in London] and protection'.[2] More importantly, there was no sign of the expected land confiscation and allocation of the spoils of war among the victors.

On 25 April, almost a month after O'Neill's surrender, the victorious Lord Deputy Mountjoy wrote to the king that 'This kingdom is now capable of what form it shall please the king to give it, and in time it may be made no small ornament and addition of honour and commodity to the crown of England.'[3] Mountjoy was, of course, wrong. Instead of expanding the political possibilities after the Nine Years' War, the Treaty of Mellifont constrained them by opting for the maintenance of the existing social order, with some adjustments to meet new realities, rather than creating a new departure through plantation, as in Munster after the Desmond rebellion in the 1580s. Such room for manoeuvre as did exist was closed off by a proclamation in the spring of 1603 of pardon for those involved in the insurrection.

Ireland in 1603 had existing political and governmental structures which gave the kingdom cohesion and established it as more than just a cultural construct. It had a central authority, the King of Ireland, a governmental administrative structure and judicial institutions. The effectiveness of these systems was, admittedly, patchy, and the sense of belonging to an Irish kingdom varied a great deal across the country. Regionalism remained strong. As late as the 1670s Oliver Plunkett, the Catholic Archbishop of Armagh, could observe: 'Ulster men and Leinster men have never agreed and will not in the future either and the same is true of the Munster men and Connacht men. Connacht men and Ulster men will easily agree as will Munster men and Leinster men.'[4] Cultural regions were accentuated as commercialisation created a series of distinctive economic regions. However, the sense of belonging to a kingdom grew after 1603. Between the 1570s and the 1630s the number of decrees handed down by the Irish Court of Chancery more than tripled; part of the reason for this was the integration of the provinces of Ulster and Connacht into the ambit of the Dublin administration. Thus in the first decade of the seventeenth century the number of decrees issued by the Court of Chancery relating to Ulster and Connacht expanded from 50 a year to 715, while the fines in the Court of Common Pleas multiplied almost fivefold. It was within these pre-existing administrative structures and judicial institutions that a new settlement of the kingdom was created in the seventeenth century. Yet the enthusiasm implicit in Mountjoy's comment suggests that minds had turned to the question of the governance of Ireland within days of the ending of the war in the spring of 1603.

## GOVERNING IRELAND

A number of developments over the years 1603 to 1606 indicate how the minds of those charged with governing Ireland were working. In April 1605 a proclamation was issued that all inhabitants in Ireland were free, natural and immediate subjects of the king and not subjects of any local lord or chief. It also pardoned all offences committed before 1603 on condition of an oath of fealty to the king and required that royal grants of land were to be set to tenants at fixed rents. This was an innovative move, and in some parts of the country, at least, this proclamation was translated into Irish. What the government had in mind here was the establishment of a fundamental set of relationships which were to govern the new Irish polity. Their importance lay in the fact that every individual was connected to everyone else through their common link with the king: a long train of dependence arranged in hierarchy, with authority percolating from top to bottom. As one member of the 1613–15 parliament put it, 'All honour is derived from the king.'[5] This was more than simply about government. This meant the creation of a new set of social and political relationships.

How these relationships would actually work depended on the main point of contact between government and subject: the gentry and major landowners of Ireland. The crown clearly believed that as a result of establishing men of substance in the Irish localities they would act as its agents in governing the country in the way that the Earl of Argyll had done in western Scotland for the Edinburgh government. It was such thinking that encouraged the king in 1605 to make a grant of almost 340,000 acres in County Antrim to Randal

MacDonnell, whose family had already established itself there in the late sixteenth century. James did so in an endeavour to secure the coastline of eastern Ulster against the Scottish mercenaries who had been such a destabilising force there in the late sixteenth century. Similar ideas may lie behind another grant in the same year of substantial property in north County Down to Scottish settlers. Other mechanisms were also available to stabilise the tenure of large estates and, hopefully, to provide a solid basis for local governance. In June 1606 a royal commission was issued to allow commissioners to grant letters patent to any subject holding a grant from the crown since 1541 and who wished to obtain a more secure title in law to their land. It was also agreed that no further grants of concealed lands would be made, again in an attempt to calm a land market noted for dubious dealings. The commission was certainly open to abuse by those who had acquired their property by underhand means. The most spectacular example of this was the case of Richard Boyle, first Earl of Cork, who used the commission to secure the title to lands acquired in doubtful ways in the 1590s so that it would not be open to further inquiry either by the crown or by rival adventurers, and in doing so also improved the tenure by which it was held from the crown.

The security conferred upon such great magnates brought stability to seventeenth-century Irish society, but it did not always give stability to the state. A danger of this system was that it could promote political fragmentation in which a number of great landlords would use the system to replace the generally shared values envisaged by the 1605 proclamation with a multiplicity of individual ones. Some larger landlords did take such advantage. Royal officers were to find men like Boyle, Earl of Cork, and MacDonnell, later Earl of Antrim, notoriously difficult to deal with during the early seventeenth century. As if to demonstrate his power as a feudal magnate, MacDonnell constructed castles across his estate which adhered to medieval forms but functionally had no defensive purpose. These were not the only two culprits. In the west the Earls of Clanricard and Thomond both moved quickly after 1603 to exempt themselves and their estates from the authority of the provincial presidencies which had been established in Connacht and Munster in 1569–70 with the objective of increasing the effectiveness of the Dublin administration outside the Pale. Richard Burke, fourth Earl of Clanricard, having proved his loyalty to the crown during the Nine Years' War, succeeded in being nominated as President of Connacht in late 1603 and in effect became both landowner and royal governor of his property. He resigned the post in 1616, by which time he was permanently resident in England, but only after ensuring that the entire county of Galway, in which his estates lay, was exempt from the jurisdiction of any future provincial president. Further south Donogh O'Brien, fourth Earl of Thomond, became Vice-President of Munster in 1607 and President in 1615, a post he retained until his death in 1624. In 1616 he transferred the governorship of Thomond to his son and heir, Henry, Baron of Ibrackan, thus ensuring that the Thomond lordship remained exempt from the authority of the Munster presidency. In 1605 it was not clear how effective these moves would be. There were signs that landlord power could be challenged. Judicial decisions abolishing gavelkind (or inheritance of property among all sons), which clearly consolidated the powers of freeholders, might allow them to challenge the expanding powers of Clanricard and Thomond. Some did so, using the Court of Chancery to sue their landlord for breaching customary rights.

The danger of fragmented power was not one of which the government was unaware. In some respects Clanricard and Thomond, as well as MacDonnell, were permitted to behave as they did because of their anglicising credentials. The fourth Earl of Clanricard, Richard Burke, although a Catholic, had been educated in England and was married to the daughter of Francis Walsingham, one of the Elizabethan secretaries of state. Those who became owners of large estates in the early seventeenth century were to be given suitable credentials. Significant Catholic families were targeted for this treatment. The son of Randal MacDonnell, first Earl of Antrim, spent an extended period at court in the hope of making him as acceptable as Clanricard. The most successful of these experiments was James Butler, grandson of the Catholic eleventh Earl of Ormond, who succeeded to the Ormond title in 1633. James Butler was educated in the household of George Abbot, Archbishop of Canterbury, which provided him not only with the sort of contacts a future Irish Lord Lieutenant needed, but, as he told his first biographer Sir Robert Southwell, 'My father and mother lived and died papists and bred all their children so. Only I, by God's merciful providence, was educated in the true Protestant religion from which I never swerved towards either extreme.'[6] In other cases the treatment was less successful.

Arthur Magennis, son of Sir Arthur, of County Down was sent by the English Privy Council first to the University of Oxford and then to the Middle Temple Inn of Court in London, often seen as a 'finishing school' for educated gentlemen. However, all this, according to the Privy Council, 'has in no way bettered him in those things which we specially desired nor had sorted to that effect as was expected'.[7] A few others went to the newly founded Trinity College Dublin, encouraged by government grants. Others arrived there as a result of the terms under which land grants had been made to their parents under the 1606 commission on defective titles. In the main these grants were made with the tenure of knight service attached, which required that should the landowner die before his heir had reached his majority, the property would be administered in the Court of Wards, which in turn required that heirs of university age were sent to Trinity College Dublin. On achieving their majority, heirs were required to take the Oath of Supremacy before they could claim their inheritance. Long-term this strategy might have been, but reform was a slow and unpredictable business.

The second danger for this fledgling government system was the problem of the apparent fragility of the loyalty of the king's Irish subjects to their new master. There were certainly complaints about the king. One man in Tyrone in 1613 was alleged to have said that 'the King of England was a very poor fellow . . . and that he did wonder that he should be King of England, for if it should be tried by histories or chronicles, himself had as much right to be king as he'.[8] However, such comments were infrequently reported and came well within the range of sedition that might be expected even in England. More worrying was the problem of religion. This was an issue that weighed heavily on the minds of contemporaries early in the new king's reign. In April and early May of 1603, following the accession of James I, the corporations and inhabitants of the Munster towns virtually declared their independence from the provincial and national government. Emboldened by the rumour that the new king was a Catholic, there were public demonstrations of Catholicism throughout the Munster towns. In Cork, Waterford and Kilkenny there were a number of Catholic processions, and in Cashel, according to the Lord Deputy's secretary, a Protestant goldsmith was tied to a tree and threatened with burning, with copies of the Bible and the Book of Common Prayer being used as fuel. Mass-houses were opened in a number of towns. In late April Lord Deputy Mountjoy mustered all the forces he could and marched on the towns, extinguishing the revolt bloodlessly by the sheer size of his force. By early May, when Cork submitted, the so-called recusancy revolt was over and, perhaps unusually, no retaliatory action was taken, it being considered on both sides that it was best that the entire business should be forgotten. Undoubtedly motives here were complex. One line of fracture was economic. The problems generated for the towns by the Nine Years' War and the debasement of the coinage in the latter years of that war had a powerful destabilising effect. Again, the mercantile elites of the towns feared that their privileges were being eroded by the Dublin administration. The charters of Limerick and Kinsale had recently been called in, and in other places the provincial president had overridden chartered rights. For all this, religion was undoubtedly the most significant motivating factor. While economics and governance may have been underlying motivations, these were subsumed in a demand for religious diversity which became a way of articulating other grievances as well. The same pattern of events would appear some years later in Dublin, where the challenging of civic privilege alienated many of the Old English merchant community from the government and made them ready recruits to outright recusancy as the Counter-Reformation movement began to flourish in the city.

The revolt of the towns had little immediate impact in London. King James himself appreciated that the Catholic Old English were the key to governing Ireland, and it seemed that a solution to the problem might be at hand. James was, by inclination, a reconciler and in England sought to devise a religious settlement that would accommodate Catholics and Protestants. In January 1604 he issued a proclamation expelling Jesuits and other priests whose submission to foreign, papal jurisdiction made them less than fully subject to the king's authority. A similar proclamation was issued in Ireland in July 1605. In the same month a royal commission designed to undertake inquisitions into church property with a view to establishing learned Protestant clergy in the Irish countryside was established. At the same time, however, James was making overtures to the pope for the calling of an ecumenical council to resolve religious differences. Bishop Bancroft of London was negotiating with a group of Catholic clergy about the form of an oath of allegiance to the king. The object was to create a political middle ground to the exclusion of doctrinal and political extremists. Ultimately the plan proved too divisive within Catholicism because of its position on the source of political power. However, at least it offered a view with which the Old English would have been sympathetic. James himself attempted to conciliate the Puritan faction within the Church of England at the Hampton Court Conference of 1604. In these circumstances, it seemed that the Irish problem might just be as solvable as those which had been successfully dealt with by means of politico-religious accommodations in the United Provinces and with Protestants in France.

If the purpose of such initiatives was to identify a solution to the underlying problem of divergence between the religion of the majority of the Irish population and that of their king, it proved short-lived. The discovery of the Catholic Gunpowder Plot to assassinate James in November 1605 brought a new urgency to the problem, and the Dublin administration took matters into its own hands on 13 November by issuing 'Mandates' or instructions requiring sixteen prominent Dublin Catholics to attend worship in the Established Church. The Mandates were disregarded. Fines of up to £100 were imposed on the recusants, or committed Catholics, by the Court of Castle Chamber, and they were imprisoned until they at least nominally conformed. The gentry of the Pale were outraged and petitioned Lord Deputy Chichester, who took particular offence at the large-scale protest and imprisoned several instigators of the petition, including Viscount Gormanston and Sir Patrick Barnewall. Further Mandates were issued and duly ignored before the London administration intervened in late January 1606. The London Privy Council, appalled that Chichester had acted without its consent and afraid that there would be dangerous repercussions from Pale Catholics who effectively controlled power in the localities, ordered Dublin to proceed more circumspectly. The petitioners, and those imprisoned for failure to obey the Mandates, were to be released. The exception was Patrick Barnewall, who was summoned to England. There, after imprisonment, he was forced to apologise for his actions. Meanwhile Chichester and his administration continued to apply pressure on prominent Catholics in the hope that by making examples of them they would promote allegiance to the Established Church. Other New English officials did likewise. Towards the end of 1605 and into 1606 the practice of issuing Mandates was taken up by Sir Henry Brouncker, Lord President of Munster, and Mandates were also issued in Galway. Brouncker carried out his task with enthusiasm, seeking the Oath of Supremacy from municipal officials in Munster and deposing from office those who refused it, including five successive mayors of Waterford, and raising almost £7,000 in fines in the process. Such successes inspired the Dublin administration to reactivate the policy in the capital towards the end of 1606, and a number of Catholics were fined in the Court of Castle Chamber for not attending the Church of Ireland. There are indications that it was proposed to extend the scheme to Drogheda in 1607. As word of the escalation of these actions reached London, with a petition of Munster Catholics against Brouncker and his actions, it elicited a sharp response from the Privy Council, which was furious that its attempts to moderate Chichester's actions had been ignored. This situation was not helped by rumours in the summer of 1607 that Hugh O'Neill, Earl of Tyrone, was conspiring with the Spanish, contrary to the Treaty of Mellifont. The London administration feared a fusion of a politicised Old English group, aggrieved by the Mandates, with O'Neill. Chichester was ordered in no uncertain terms to halt his actions.

The Mandates controversy needs to be interpreted not in isolation but as part of a wider attempt by the Dublin administration to test the limits of its authority. On the one hand it pressed on the Old English of the Pale in an attempt to assess the limits of loyalty, and on the other it compelled the London government to see how far a royal policy of religious conciliation would stretch. There would be other such forays to test loyalties, such as the execution of the Catholic Bishop of Down and Connor, Conor O'Devany, in 1612, which would help the Dublin administration to gauge the limits to which it could go in dealing with Irish Catholics in shaping the post-1603 political configuration.

What is significant about the aftermath of the Mandates controversy is what did not happen. In England legislation passed in early 1606 required that Catholics who attended the Church of England on an occasional basis to evade penal legislation had to receive the sacrament at least once a year or be subject to heavy fines. Those who refused to come to the services of the Established Church had to pay £20 a month or lose two-thirds of their property. An oath was also required from those suspected of recusancy. In Ireland none of these penalties was introduced. Some time later, in 1616, it seemed that the oath might be applied since a work associated with it was ordered to be reprinted in Dublin, but there is no evidence that it ever was. The Irish administration was obliged to rely on the Elizabethan Act of Uniformity, which levied a hopelessly inadequate fine of 12d for absence from church. The failure to tighten Irish law to conform to English norms can be seen as an attempt to conciliate Irish Catholics; yet despite such conciliatory gestures, there can be no doubt that the Mandates experiment resulted in a considerable souring of relations between the Dublin administration and its Catholic subjects.

## THE POSITION OF THE ULSTER EARLS

Religion was not, however, the only thing that separated the governors of Ireland from the governed. The most important test case for the creation of a new order occurred in the province of Ulster. The political settlement agreed at the end of the Nine Years' War was extremely generous to O'Neill. If he had raised a rebellion in England, he would almost certainly have lost his head. In Ulster, however, his position was such that the government had to rely on his authority in the region to make any political settlement work. In the view of the Dublin administration, such authority would need to be woven into the new reality of Irish governance in which O'Neill could no longer behave like an independent lord. In west Ulster Rory O'Donnell received less favourable treatment, and his scope for manoeuvre locally was limited by the problem of a rival for power within his area of influence: Niall Garbh O'Donnell. Hugh O'Neill, by contrast, tightened his grip on his zone of influence in mid-Ulster after the war, by claiming all the land of the earldom of Tyrone in freehold against the claims of other Ulster lords, such as the O'Cahans. In effect, he sought to transform himself from an Irish lord, who held the allegiance of followers but not title to their lands, into a powerful English-style landlord with palatinate jurisdiction which exempted him from Dublin's control.

In order to minimise the danger of O'Neill becoming too powerful, Sir John Davies, the Solicitor General, obtained instructions from James I that Tyrone's and O'Donnell's lands should be divided into freeholds held directly from the crown by their inhabitants to prevent either of the great lords having too much power over their followers. In effect, Davies was following the model established in the late sixteenth-century settlement of Monaghan that would be repeated in

Cavan, Monaghan and Fermanagh in 1606. Initially Tyrone and O'Donnell seemed prepared to co-operate with the commissioners appointed to effect these new arrangements, thinking changes would be superficial; but when in 1606 it became clear that a thoroughgoing reform was intended, Tyrone and the other Ulster lords became seriously concerned. Other restrictions on Tyrone's power became apparent as ecclesiastical reform spread into his lordship with the appointment of George Montgomery as Church of Ireland Bishop of Derry, Raphoe and Clogher in 1605. Moreover, rumours about the appointment of a President of Ulster, along the lines of the provincial presidencies of Munster and Connacht, began to circulate. This would have placed Tyrone under the power of a local official who could constantly pry into the earl's affairs if he wished. All this was compounded by the accumulation of considerable financial debts as a result of the war which also weakened O'Neill's position, although this was not as severe a problem for him as it was for O'Donnell. Many of these fears were groundless, but the eruption of a dispute within Tyrone's own lordship fatally weakened his ability to resist central government encroachment. Donal O'Cahan, the chieftain of 'O'Cahan's country' in what would become north-east County Londonderry, objected to having to pay rent for his land to O'Neill, since he claimed his lordship had always been independent from that of O'Neill. Davies, seeing an opportunity to force O'Neill to create freeholds, and thus weaken his power, took up the case, hoping that others would follow. Later Hugh O'Neill claimed that he fled Ireland fearing that Chichester was about to accuse him falsely of treason. That may not have been true, but by the middle of 1607 O'Neill may have thought it was the final element in Dublin's strategy to constrain his authority. In fact Tyrone still stood high in the king's estimation in the summer of 1607 despite his problems with the Dublin administration, and the earl well appreciated the importance of royal favour in dealing with provincial administrations.

Tyrone's problems were far from unusual. Conflicts between local rights and central authority were often enmeshed with issues of loyalty and religion. The revolt of the Munster towns in 1603 had been a good example of that. What made the outcome in O'Neill's case different was another context. It is clear, at least as early as 1604, that O'Donnell had made contact with the Spanish authorities and was receiving payments from them. He may well have been building contacts within Ireland with the aim of fomenting some sort of insurrection in alliance with a few of the more radical Old English gentry, including Christopher St Lawrence of Howth, radicalised by the Mandates campaign. How deeply O'Neill was involved in this is a matter of conjecture, since most of the surviving evidence is in the form of rumour and innuendo by contemporaries. When some of the alleged conspirators were arrested in early 1607, Tyrone was certainly afraid that suspicion would fall on him, whether justified or not. Suspicion certainly did fall on Tyrconnell and Maguire, who were involved in the plot, they having been warned from Flanders in August of the impending arrest. Tyrconnell and Maguire arranged an escape route in a ship hired to take them to the Spanish Netherlands. Tyrone on a spur of the moment made the serious misjudgment of deciding to go with them. The ship sailed from Rathmullan in County Donegal on 4 September 1607. Hugh O'Neill, Earl of Tyrone, was not to see Ireland again.

## THE ULSTER EXPERIMENT

The flight of the Ulster earls on 4 September 1607 was regarded by the native Irish poets as a disaster. Yet they saw it not as the result of political manoeuvring but as a judgment of God for the sins of the earls. For the Dublin administration, it created a state of confusion. Their first reaction was to issue a proclamation declaring that the natives of Counties Donegal and Tyrone, the areas most affected, would be left on their lands as long as they behaved as dutiful subjects of the king. Towards the end of the year the legal processes to confiscate the lands of the earls for treason, having left the realm without the king's permission, were set in train to provide a legal basis for the settlement of Ulster. The only impediment to this technical process came in April 1608 when Sir Cahir O'Doherty rose in rebellion and seized Culmore and Derry. O'Doherty had been a beneficiary of the initial settlement after the flight of O'Donnell and had been granted the large property of Inishowen. However, relations between O'Doherty and some of the local and former military men were difficult. A personal insult by Sir George Paulet, governor of Derry, in April 1608 seems to have provoked O'Doherty into a rising. It was suppressed within two months, but it enabled the government to confiscate the property of a second level of Gaelic lords, below those of the earls, who had been involved. Thus the property of the

O'Cahans, O'Doherty and Niall Garbh O'Donnell fell to the crown, allowing an expansion of the area intended for plantation. The principal beneficiary was the Lord Deputy, Sir Arthur Chichester, who received O'Doherty's Inishowen property. Throughout 1608 the technicalities of establishing an Ulster settlement were put in place. The six escheated counties were surveyed by inquisition. This material was sent to London in the middle of 1608 to help with the detailed planning of the plantation scheme then being devised there. A second commission in 1609 was authorised to resurvey the escheated lands and divide them into precincts, and as part of this process a set of maps of the escheated counties was produced.

Parallel with this process there was a second train of events which was intended to establish structures for the creation of a new society in Ulster. This was conducted by the King of Ireland and his Privy Council in London. As such, it followed normal practice whereby the king determined policy for Ireland and the Dublin administration was responsible for its implementation. This was a matter for the royal prerogative in which parliament played no part. Indeed, in 1623 the English parliament incurred the royal rage when members tried to raise Irish matters, since they were encroaching on the royal prerogative of the King of Ireland. For all this, the king and his council did not lack advice, which came from many sources. John Bell, the vicar of Christ Church in London, for instance, urged the king to develop a plantation to absorb the poor of England and Wales. Another suggestion offered by the former Munster planter Richard Spert emphasised profit as the main function of plantation, and a third advocated that it would prevent rebellion. However, the main sources which the Privy Council drew on for advice were the English administrators based in Ireland.

A number of different approaches to the problem of how to create a new society in Ulster can be identified among this group of men. The first approach can be associated with Lord Deputy Chichester. He was a soldier who had a pragmatic view of how societies worked. As he wrote to George Abbot, Archbishop of Canterbury, in 1612, 'I observed that a commonwealth is nothing more than a commencement or continual suppeditacion [exchange] of benefits mutually received and done between men.'[9] This practical view was based on daily experience. A second line of thought might be associated with the Irish Attorney General, Sir John Davies. As a lawyer, Davies had a different view of how people related to each other, and for him law was at the centre of that process. The failure to normalise social relationships in medieval Ireland, he argued, was the result of not extending the common law to the native Irish, since that should have created a coherent society. Unlike English common lawyers, Davies could not argue for the supremacy of Irish common law on historical grounds and thus had to resort to the civil-law idea of conquest to justify the importance of law as the basis of the common good. Davies thus framed his view of social relations as a conquest which 'doth reduce all the people thereof to the condition of subjects: and those I call subjects which are governed by the ordinary laws and magistrates of the sovereign'.[10] In Davies's view, law provided the basic framework for social interaction which regulated behaviour.

These two views, grounded in practicalities and law, were reflected in the approaches taken to planning the plantation scheme. Chichester's understanding of how Ulster society should develop was set out in a letter to the king on 17 September 1607. In keeping with his practical approach, he advocated the division of the escheated lands of Ulster among the native Irish inhabitants, former soldiers (or 'servitors') and some 'colonies of civil people of England and Scotland at His Majesty's pleasure'.[11] However, servitors were to be given priority, with most Irish being left on the land they already occupied. This was an extension of what had previously been happening in Ulster, with settlements of soldiers around Chichester's own property at Carrickfergus and Sir Thomas Phillips's settlement at Limavady. A second scheme propounded by Chichester favoured the removal of all inhabitants from the escheated counties together with their goods and cattle, but this was clearly unworkable and was probably included for effect. These ideas were developed in Chichester's 'Notes of remembrance' of March 1608 in which he used the sixteenth-century freeholding of Monaghan as his precedent for a proposed settlement which, by the creation of freeholds, would remove the Irish landowners from the control of greater lords. In Tyrone he argued strenuously that those 'who are in my opinion most fit to undertake this plantation are the captains and officers who have served in these parts'. They were to receive the best land, with the remainder going to the new settlers.[12] Chichester was, in effect, arguing for a continuation of the sort of methods by which Ireland had been governed in the past: small military colonies with native settlement around them.

The second strand of the argument, which seems to have come into play after O'Doherty's rising in 1608, and might be associated with Sir John Davies, contained a more sophisticated element. Much of this may have been Davies's own plan, but it is clear that he was also reflecting the views of the king and the Privy Council in the planning process. Davies introduced into the scheme a stronger element of social engineering based on the supremacy of law. As he later described the process, it was an advance on the sixteenth-century idea of surrender and regrant (under which native lords had surrendered their lands to the crown and received a new grant of them, thus making them royal subjects) in so far as it introduced enough new colonists to outnumber the Irish and at the same time restricted the powers of undertakers, since 'His Majesty gave not an entire country or county to any particular person, much less did he grant *jura regalia* or any extraordinary liberties'. Secondly, the mixing of settler and native was to promote social change so that 'they might grow up together in one nation', although some natives had to be transplanted 'that they might grow milder'.[13] What the king had to do, in Davies's view, was to create a balanced world under crown and law in a new initiative that would avoid repeating the mistakes of the past. This involved creating a new world driven by immigration as an alternative to the continuation of older social thought and practices.

The details of how the final scheme emerged for the plantation of the six escheated Ulster counties are unclear owing to the destruction of the records of the English Privy Council, where most of the planning was done, for these years. It is known that in December 1608 a scheme did emerge, and this was slightly revised in the 'Orders and conditions' of 1610. The original 1608 'Project' for the plantation represents a compromise of the views of Chichester and Davies. There were to be three classes of beneficiaries under the scheme: English and Scottish undertakers who were to plant their proportions with English and Scottish tenants; servitors who could take either settler or native Irish tenants; while the third group comprised native freeholders. The confiscated property was divided into precincts which were allocated to groups of English or Scottish undertakers, with a chief undertaker in each precinct. Forty per cent of the total land was set aside for the undertakers, split equally between Scots and English, and divided into three classes: 2,000 acres, 1,500 acres, and 1,000 acres. These were smaller than the proposed estates in the sixteenth-century plantation of Munster, thereby reflecting government concerns about how large landowners had succeeded in monopolising Munster. Undertakers were to build a castle on their property by 1613 and were obliged 'within two years to plant a competent number of English and Scottish tenants upon their proportion'. They were to remove any native Irish living there. The revised conditions of 1610 were more specific, requiring larger undertakers to plant 'twenty-four able men of the age of eighteen years or upwards being English or inland Scottish' within three years of receiving their grants. Smaller undertakers were only required to introduce ten families onto their lands.

The revised arrangements also stipulated how the property was to be divided between fee-farmers, leaseholders and tenants at will, thus attempting to plan the social structure and social relationships of the new settlement. The use of the lease as a way of shaping society is of particular importance here. Within Gaelic Ireland, families had thought of their social and economic relationships primarily in terms of the extended family and regarded them as a set of mutual rights and obligations between lords and followers regulated by tradition and, when necessary, violence. The lease departed from this tradition by spelling out relationships in writing and by being subject to legal interpretation, although within a clear context of hierarchy and inequality. However unequal the parties to the contract were, the existence of the written lease recognised that each had rights and obligations. Moreover, the lease represented an asset that could be sold, in a way that a social relationship could not, and hence a market could develop in land. In time many of the rights created by leases would be absorbed into local custom, such as the practice of tenant right which gave tenants the right to renewal of their leases or the right to sell the renewal. Such contracts were as important in defining relationships between people as they were in making specific promises of action by landlords and tenants.

In addition to undertakers, servitors were allocated fifty-seven precincts, amounting to 13 per cent of the escheated lands, but their estates were mixed with the native Irish for security reasons and they were not required to take settlers as tenants. Finally, some 208 of the native Irish were to receive 14 per cent of the escheated property (more than the servitors, suggesting that Chichester's influence in drafting the scheme was less than might be thought), although only twenty-six were assigned estates in excess of 1,000 acres. Two other groups were allocated land in the plantation scheme. Some 18 per cent was given over to support the church, and under 1 per cent to maintain schools.

One significant exception to the whole scheme was the county then known as Coleraine, which, it was agreed in 1610, was to be managed by the City of London through a new body later known as the Irish Society. This, like the Virginia Company established to settle part of North America, was a joint-stock company set up as a way of attracting mercantile capital into the plantation scheme. In 1613 the county, renamed Londonderry, was parcelled up into estates of about 3,000 acres which were then granted to twelve groups of the London guilds. The governing body, the Irish Society, was also to hold the ports and customs of Coleraine and Derry, the main outlets for the economic products of the plantation, and presumably London's trading connections were felt to be beneficial here. Derry and Coleraine were to be the urban success stories of the plantation, with populations of about 1,000 by 1630, making them the same size as an English market town, and with a wide range of trades and a more complex occupational structure.

This overall scheme was a highly innovative one, concentrating as it did as much on social engineering as on the redistribution of land. Just how innovative it was is clear by comparing it with other contemporary schemes. In the Scottish context, attempts in 1597, 1605 and 1607 by a group of Fife merchants to settle the Isle of Lewis bore no parallel with the social reorganisation envisaged in the Ulster scheme. Indeed, the closest Scottish example to the blueprint for Ulster, and one which may have been affected by developments there, was the scheme for the Western Isles of Scotland detailed in the Statutes of Iona (1609). The Statutes of Iona attempted to reorder the society of the Scottish Isles along the standards of Lowland Scotland. Within Ireland too the Ulster initiative had few imitators. A number of other plantation plans were certainly undertaken in early seventeenth-century Ireland. In Munster the late sixteenth-century plantation continued to expand, with perhaps 22,000 settlers in 1641, but this proceeded in a rather unregulated way. In Counties Wexford and Longford and west Queen's County plantations were more about the transfer of land from native inhabitants to settlers—and particularly into the hands of officials of the Dublin administration and royal favourites—than about social change. The terms of the Longford settlement of 1619, for instance, required undertakers to build a castle on their estates and to establish market towns. Land was also set aside for the Established Church and schools, and undertakers were required to sow hemp. There was nothing in the conditions of plantation about introducing new settlers or regulating society by stipulating the tenures for holding their land. The closest that any of the these later settlements came to that of Ulster was the 1620 scheme for Leitrim in which undertakers were to build castles and introduce between one and five British freeholders onto their estates, and there was some attempt to regulate tenures. In comparison to the Ulster scheme, such numbers were small and insignificant.

The distinctiveness of the Ulster scheme arose from the desire on the part of the king and his counsellors not simply to plant Ulster but to use the unique opportunity it presented to establish social norms there that could be imitated throughout the rest of the island. The underlying aim was probably best summed up by the terminology used in the first document setting out the scheme in 1608, which referred to the 'project' of the Ulster plantation. In seventeenth-century terms, a 'project' was a practical initiative which could be used for exploiting material things. The forms in which such 'projects' developed varied a great deal. In some Irish cases royal support was provided to farmers to introduce new crops, such as woad or jute, onto their estates in response to rising consumer demand. More ambitious projects were surrounded by legal protections in the form of grants of monopoly from the crown, for which payments were made, thus allowing their originators to make a profit. The latter provides the best model for what the planners in Ulster were trying to do. Individual landlords were given, in effect, monopolies over their lands in the form of land grants. The payment to the crown for these monopolies was intended to be the investment which settlers would make in their estates.

Such a model for development could only work within certain parameters. Most importantly, the legal structures that reinforced these arrangements needed to be clear and required institutional underpinning. These arrangements impacted on many aspects of the immigrant experience. Apart from general issues of law and order, manorial and market courts were required to resolve disputes between landlord and tenant and to ensure that commercial transactions could be carried on securely. The sort of arrangements that were required are exemplified in the provision that estates granted under the plantation scheme were to be erected into manors. Thus what was granted under the scheme was not simply land but a range of legal rights which made that land work. Crucially important were the manorial courts. Such courts were clearly vital for both landlords and tenants, and the one surviving manor court roll for the Archbishop of Armagh's property for 1625–7 suggests that both Irish and settlers used the court extensively. Little evidence has survived to allow the reconstruction of the detail of how manor courts worked in practice, but one of their functions was to define the manor, or estate, as a particular entity. The evolution of manorial customs and the language of the law that tenants encountered at the manorial courts were clearly intended to facilitate the formation of local collectivities that would transcend other ethnic or social divisions such as those between newcomer and native.

Since the Ulster settlement comprised two settler ethnic groups (Scots and English), those thinking about plantations had also to consider relations between them. What is striking about the Ulster settlement is how few immediate social and cultural problems the large influx of Scots and English into the area created. There were a few technical difficulties. In 1624 some Scottish undertakers complained that the clerk of the Irish council could not read Scottish handwriting and hence had difficulty in understanding petitions sent to him. They asked for a second clerk to be appointed to deal with Scottish business. Patrick Hannay, a minor poet and Chancery official, was appointed as second clerk a few weeks later. In the more general area of law, the Scottish settlers adapted remarkably quickly to the ideas and institutions of common law. On most Scottish estates in the escheated counties of Ulster by 1622 the written lease, then relatively rare in Scotland, was the normal means of landholding. Moreover, there seems to have been very little tension between Scottish and English settlers. A few isolated cases of friction can be identified, as in 1614 when some of the Scottish tenants of the Earl of Abercorn at Strabane made an assassination attempt on Lord Audley, a nearby English settler. The reason offered was that he had uttered some words 'against the Scottish nation'. The attempt was unsuccessful, and Audley denied that he had spoken any such words. He pointed out he had planted the required number of English settlers on his lands, 'and I have so many more of Scotchmen besides which sheweth no malice but my love and good opinion towards that nation and we all agree very well'.[14] Such cases of antagonism between English and Scottish settlers were unusual.

In general, what appears to have developed in the first thirty years of the Ulster plantation was some kind of accommodation between the various groups of settlers. This is what the government seems to have intended, and a number of strategies were devised to promote it. Settlers were enjoined to live together and not to disperse, so that cohabitation would 'breed unity and civility' and 'some course would be taken that the English and Scottish may be placed both near and woven one with another'.[15] In particular, planners emphasised the idea of a 'British' identity for the settlers, stressing that the plantation was the work of the King of Great Britain rather than the government of England. This message was conveyed by the designation of settlers in Ulster as 'British' after 1611 in the surveys of the plantation scheme.

How the common building blocks of this social order were constructed is difficult to trace, but there are at least two sites where such new relationships could be negotiated. In a 1610 list of the division of the precincts between the English and Scots in the plantation scheme the author added a note that the anticipated 'places of intercourse and meeting of the English and Scotch in the several counties' would be at markets and the quarter-sessions and assizes. In County Armagh these were to be the markets of Armagh, Mountnorris and Charlemont and 'the quarter-sessions and assizes held at Armagh'. In County Tyrone, apart from the markets of Omagh, Mountjoy, Dungannon and Clogher, such meetings could occur 'at the quarter-sessions held at Dungannon where they shall be joined in juries and other public services and the like in other counties'.[16] The assize, of course, was only the pinnacle of a network of courts incorporating the quarter-sessions and manorial courts. These local institutions were also intended to promote co-operation; ethnic and social groups were not distinguished in the daily grind of local government. The summonister rolls for County Tyrone, for instance, record the presentment of inhabitants of Donaghmore parish in 1632 for not mending the highways on the mountain and those of Cappagh parish for not mending 'cashes' on the king's highway. In 1628 the inhabitants of Clonfeakle parish were presented at the assizes for failing to maintain a bridge at Castlemoyle, and a number of parishes were fined in 1633 for not building a bridge on the highway between Newtownstewart and Strabane. Such corporate responsibility suggests that in civil matters Catholics as well as Protestants were expected to participate in resolving local problems. In short, Ulster was being thought of not as a set of lineages, as other places were, or even as a collection of estates, but as a set of communities with local responsibilities. The thinking which underpinned the Ulster plantation scheme was not simply about land redistribution, although a great deal of energy was put into drafting and redrafting the plans for that. Rather, it was aimed at creating a social framework using the law, markets, schools and the church, which were endowed with land under the scheme, to provide the infrastructure for what can only be described as a significant piece of social engineering.

## THE LIMITS TO SOCIAL CHANGE

While government was prepared to provide the framework for the Ulster plantation scheme, it did not become directly involved in promoting the project. That was left to landlords who were presumed to have a vested interest in settling their estates. However, the process by which the final pattern of landholding emerged was socially selective. Those most concerned to acquire plantation land were those most interested in increasing their social and economic status quickly. Thus they tended to be people in pursuit of profit to reverse declining income at home or as a way to enhance social mobility restricted by lack of opportunities at home. Either way, they had limited capital to spend on their Irish estates. As Chichester explained in 1610, the settlers in the plantation were disappointing, since 'those from England are, for the most part, plain country gentlemen. . . . If they have any money they keep it close; for hitherto they have disburst but little. . . . The Scottish come with greater part and better accompanied, but it may be with less money in their purses.' Chichester's impressions were confirmed by a survey of undertaker wealth. None had an income of more than £2,000 per annum, and less than a fifth of those who provided income figures had over £1,000.[17] Even Chichester himself fell victim to the problem of estate capitalisation and was forced to make long leases to tenants for cash payments, thus mortgaging away future income, a strategy that would have long-term consequences.

As a result of their financial difficulties, many undertakers failed to fulfil the terms of their grants. When the plantation scheme was surveyed in 1619, of 164 estates, thirty-eight (24 per cent) had no principal dwelling, the largest estates being the greatest offenders. Others yielded to the temptation of taking Irish tenants on their estates because of a lack of British settlers. The migration to Ulster fell far short of the level intended. By the 1630s, when settlement was at its peak, there were some 6,550 British adult males in the escheated counties and probably 6,000 adults in Counties Down and Antrim. If allowance is made for children, but remembering that many of those who migrated were young and single, a figure of 16,000 Scottish settlers in Ulster by 1630 may be close to reality. Colonial North America by mid-century received some 210,000 people, mainly from England (4.2 per cent of the English population). The Scottish migration to Ulster, by contrast, was less than that from Scotland to Poland and Scandinavia. Settler tenants, particularly tenants of sufficient quality, were often in short supply in Ulster and tended to cluster near ports, so that landlords often succumbed to the temptation of taking Irish as tenants on their estates, especially since they frequently offered higher rents than many settler tenants. By 1628 this process was formalised when settlers were allowed to take Irish as tenants on a quarter of their estates, but this proved impossible to police. By 1660 the number of townlands in Ulster with no Irish inhabitants ranged between 5 and 10 per cent at the margins of the settlement in west and south Ulster, while in core of the plantation regions (north Armagh, parts of Tyrone and Londonderry) the number rose to 20 per cent.

The social background of settlers meant they were driven more towards the pursuit of profit than towards creation of a commonwealth. Undercapitalisation of their estates encouraged them to seek a quick profit. By the 1620s they were complaining that the allocations of land they had received were not large enough, despite the fact that most had failed to introduce the required number of settlers onto their estates. The lack of landlord capital for intensive development meant that in order to continue generating income, landholding had to expand continually. Initially this had been done through the purchase of land from those who had little interest in becoming Irish landlords, but by the 1620s this avenue was exhausted. The failure of the settlers to obey the rules of the scheme became painfully obvious through the formal surveys of the plantation scheme made in 1611, 1615, 1619 and 1622. The 1622 commissioners were bombarded by complaints from tenants about the failure of their landlords to fulfil promises to make leases and their failure to remove native Irish tenants from the property. As one settler put it, they 'have so little encouragement as they wish themselves again in their own country'.[18] Attempts to regulate the social structure of the new settlement had fallen victim to the undertakers' drive to optimise profit returns from their new property.

## THE PARLIAMENT OF 1613–15

If the plantation of Ulster provides a unique opportunity to examine how the king and his counsellors were thinking about the governance of Ireland, then the Dublin parliament of 1613–15 provides an insight into alternative ways of considering the same problem. By the beginning of the second decade of the seventeenth century it had become clear to most of the political elite in Ireland that it would be necessary to summon a parliament. There had been no parliament since 1585, and since 1603 Ireland had been governed by a series of *ad hoc* expedients which had not allowed for the venting of Old English grievances. Decisions had been implemented through proclamation and administrative action. Perhaps most radical was the use of judicial decisions to govern Ireland in the form of Sir John Davies's published collection of Irish law reports (1615), which dealt with the difficulties of land inheritance in the cases of gavelkind and tanistry, and in other kinds of property rights in cases on the customs and on base money. A parliament, suggested by Davies himself in 1604, had not been summoned, and by 1610 the Dublin Castle administration was beginning to compile lists of statutes that were necessary for the effective governing of Ireland. Proposed legislation was to cover ecclesiastical matters, the royal revenue, 'the king's person and government' and 'civil policy and justice'. In addition, a number of English acts were thought necessary to be passed in Ireland to regularise matters. Almost ninety acts were proposed, a completely impractable number given the rate at which legislation passed in the sixteenth-century Irish parliaments. There were even more pressing financial reasons for calling a parliament. While the military establishment had been reduced significantly at the end of the Nine Years' War, it still remained at a very high level, almost three times that of the civil establishment. Moreover, Ireland was not generating sufficient income to service this large force. In 1611 total income was £20,000 and expenditure was £74,903. The shortfall was met by subventions from England, as had been the case in the sixteenth century, but these were usually inadequate and late. The grant of a subsidy from the Irish parliament was urgently needed.

While the Dublin administration was convinced of the need for a parliament, it was not convinced that summoning such a body would deliver the desired result, namely the passage of the required legislation. The Attorney General, Sir John Davies, in 1611 carefully worked out what the balance of power in the parliament should be, declaring: 'It is to be doubted that the Irish and such as are descended of English race, of whom both the houses of parliament consist, being for the most part popish recusants, will distaste and reject such bills as shall be transmitted out of England to be propounded here in Ireland although they be for the benefit of the crown and kingdom.'[19] Davies was only partly right. Religion would emerge as a divisive issue in the parliament and reveal the strength and tactics of various groups involved in the Irish polity, but the parliament would play other roles also.

The parliament which met in May 1613 comprised 232 members of the Commons and forty-three members of the Lords. At the opening of the session 100 of the Commons were recusant and 132 Protestant, a narrow but working majority. Revision after an inquiry in 1613 into the election reduced the number of seats to 210, which number comprised 101 recusants and 109 Protestants. At elections there had been some violence, especially in Dublin, which did not bode well for what was to follow. The initial flashpoint between the various groups emerged over the election of a Speaker of the House of Commons. The Catholic faction urged the claim of Sir John Everard, placing him in the Speaker's chair, while the Protestant camp claimed greater numerical support for Sir John Davies and enforced their claim by physically ejecting Everard. While Everard's party did not deny that Davies could command a majority for the Speakership, they refused to admit that this vote had legitimacy, since some of the elections of M.P.s, it was claimed, were illegal: false returns had been made by sheriffs, and boroughs had been created to pack the parliament and their M.P.s were not resident in them. Parliament, which hitherto had been the main bulwark of the Old English interest and an important element in their conception of the governance of Ireland, was being removed from their control. The Catholic members and Catholic peers in the Lords withdrew, a tactic which it has been suggested was prearranged and possibly even influenced by Catholic clergy. The parliament was effectively prorogued in May 1613. Twelve Old English Catholics acted as their sixteenth-century predecessors had done in similar circumstances and appealed above the head of Lord Deputy Chichester, whom they regarded as a provincial official, to the King of Ireland in London, and two delegations went to the seat of royal authority itself. Once at the royal court they broadened the scope of their attack, hoping for the recall of the Lord Deputy. What eventually resulted in May 1613 was a commission of inquiry into the elections to the parliament, which the king hoped would allow the recusants to let off steam. In the event, the commissioners reported against the Catholic interest on all but two points, those concerning the M.P.s for Clogher and those for Kildare and Cavan. Perhaps more significantly, the anti-Catholic legislation which was intended to be introduced in parliament was quietly dropped. However, the recusants had overplayed their strong hand and interpreted this conciliatory move as weakness. They succeeded only in annoying James, who summoned them to London in April 1614 and deemed them 'half-subjects' since they were not prepared to recognise his position as governor of the Established Church as well as head of state. Fortunately for the recusants, within a few months the king was in a conciliatory mood again, overturning more of the results of the 1613 elections in Ireland and thereby changing, though not decisively, the configuration of the Commons.

In October 1614 the parliament reassembled and business moved fairly smoothly, with four bills passing in the Commons. Some legislation was rejected by the Catholic faction, who occasionally held a majority in the Commons because of poor attendance by Protestants. The parliament was prorogued on 29 November, since the bills for the royal subsidy had not reached Dublin. It was April 1615 before the parliament reassembled for a third session, intended mainly to deal with the subsidy. The Catholic minority used the passage of the subsidy as a bargaining counter for concessions on such measures as recusancy fines and recognition of the right of Catholic lawyers to practise in Ireland. As one Catholic M.P. from Kildare put it, 'Least said soon amended / Subsidy granted, parliament ended'. The accuracy of his prognostication was clear when the parliament passed the subsidy on 28 April. Undoubtedly Chichester's revelation on 18 April of the discovery of a largely imaginary plot in Ulster concentrated minds to ensure an easy passage of the subsidy. Given the ramshackle nature of this conspiracy—a fact that Chichester was well aware of—its stage-managed revelation can only be seen as a tactic to speed up deliberations. Parliament was prorogued on 16 May 1615 but never met again, and it was dissolved in October.

It would be wrong to understand the events of the 1613–15 parliament purely in terms of religious conflict. Parliament did a great deal of other business which was not reflected in the statute roll, the contents of which were constrained by Poynings' Law and its requirement that all draft Irish legislation had to be approved by the English Privy Council before it could be introduced into the Irish parliament. It received petitions from a range of individuals dealing with sometimes very local matters. During its lifetime the parliament discussed watercourses on the River Dodder in Dublin, thatched houses in Dublin, the vicarage of Carlingford in County Louth, the assize of bread and bere in the capital city, and Sir Thomas Phillips's castle at Limavady in County Londonderry. It received petitions from Mulmore O'Reilly and Walter Brady, both of County Cavan, from the Church of Ireland Bishop of Dromore, and from John Codd concerning lands in County Wexford, as well as petitions for individuals' debts. It adjudicated on Thomas Luttrell's marriage settlement, Paul Sherlock's attempts to bribe local officials, the lands of Christopher Eustace, and the reversal of the attainder on the late Earl of Desmond's daughters. Little is known about the handling of these local matters, since they were usually delegated to committees constituted to deal with petitions and the details do not appear in the official sources that survive. Again, the proposals for legislation from parliament itself dealt mainly with social and economic regulation, the interest of landowners, and administrative and legal abuses. All this reflects the fact that parliament was important as a point of contact between the regions of Ireland and the royal governor at which disputes, unresolvable locally, were settled. It was also the occasion on which the Lord Deputy had the opportunity to consult, take advice and hear grievances from the representatives of local communities. As David Rothe, future Catholic Bishop of Ossory, expressed it in the Irish parliament, 'There be a suitable correspondence between both—the head with influence of royal clemency and pity to ease and relieve the distressed body of the subjects—and they, with the real vapours of their best digested substance, to refresh the head in due proportion.' The parliament was a forum for 'our recognition of duty, affection and allegiance' to the king, but members of parliament were 'employed by our commonwealth to represent her sighs to the ears of our common father, as we are one day to yield account to the high judge of our inward minds, so we are at our return from hence to be accountants to the counties and corporations whose voice and suffrage we were entrusted withal'.[20] Legislation was part, but only part, of this process.

The consultative process can be seen in 1610 and 1611 when Chichester held discussions with the nobility and gentry, dominated by the Old English, as to what new legislation should be promoted. In 1611 those whose counsel he sought declared themselves to be the Grand Council traditionally summoned before parliament and therefore entitled to see the bills which the administration intended to transmit to London for approval before the parliament. Chichester refused them this right, prompting complaints from the Old English gentry that their entitlement to be consulted had been ignored. It may have been that they simply wanted to know the nature of any anti-recusant legislation which, it was rumoured, was to be introduced into the parliament, but it may well be that they felt that their duty and right to give advice to the king, which was a reflection of their social standing and part of the function of the parliament, was being ignored. It might have been in an attempt to repair this insult that in September Chichester asked for Poynings' Law to be suspended for private bills; however, the king and council in London firmly refused.

Social strategies can be detected not only in the workings of parliament but also the way in which the electoral campaigns for that body were organised. The recusants' argument about the deficiencies in the electoral process, which they made both in parliament in 1613 and before the king in 1614, was essentially a moral one. They argued that the New English M.P.s who had been chosen for certain boroughs were not suitable or qualified to be summoned to give advice to the king and resolve the problems of the community of the kingdom. A profile of the recusant M.P.s suggests they were all influential in their own constituencies and had held significant local offices as sheriff, mayor, bailiff, or justice of the peace. Collective action in parliament came naturally to men of such backgrounds. By contrast, the Dublin administration had little interest in moral authority and was principally concerned with ensuring that it had a working majority to pass legislation which, in the opinion of Sir John Davies, was 'for the benefit of the crown and kingdom'. The government electoral strategy rested on minimising the number of recusants in the Commons, and to that end it attempted to control the selection of sheriffs and mayors who acted as returning officers, arranged for the return of government supporters, and manipulated the number of new boroughs that would return Protestant M.P.S. Forty-one new boroughs had been created since 1604, partly reflecting the expansion of English authority since the previous meeting of parliament in 1585. These were castigated by the Old English as little more than groups of hovels. The result was the return of what Old English critics described as 'mere clerks, and other, who have little or no interest' in the county they represented. This was rather unjust, since almost 90 per cent of the Protestant members returned in 1613 were resident in their constituencies. A much smaller number had wider family connections with their constituencies. This was an inevitable consequence of the fact that most were recent arrivals in Ireland; only a quarter of Protestant M.P.S were second-generation settlers. It was the apparently unsuitable social backgrounds of these men rather than their residency that upset the older, well-established families of the Old English. The 'upstart' composition of the Protestant M.P.S is confirmed by the fact that a third of Protestant M.P.S had been knighted, whereas under 10 per cent of the recusants held knighthoods, since knighthoods tended to be acquired by those only currently moving up the social hierarchy, mainly through military achievement.[21] During the Nine Years' War 157 knights bachelor had been created in Ireland, almost four times as many as in the previous decade, and many of them from the ranks of junior officers. The message seemed clear: Protestant members had to rely on titles for their social authority rather than the older, more acceptable forms of social recognition by their peers possessed by the Catholic Old English group. Thus, the parliament of 1613–15 can be seen not simply as a clash of religious groups over the role of Catholics in Irish governance—although it certainly was that—but also as a clash of different ideas about what the institution was, how it was to function, and what its social basis was intended to reflect. As such, it reflected deeper conflicts about the governance of Ireland rather than simply arguments about affiliation to a particular religious institution.

## THE IRISH KINGDOM

Despite the fractious nature of proceedings in the Irish parliament of 1613–15, those involved in the reshaping of Irish society in the first two decades of the seventeenth century had good cause to be pleased with themselves. As the English Lord Keeper observed in an address to the Irish Lord Chancellor in 1617, the 'civilisation' of Ireland 'is not yet conducted to perfection but is far advanced . . . it is likely to become a garden and a younger sister to Great Britain'. From an Old English perspective, David Rothe agreed, claiming in 1614 that 'This green tendril of [the] Irish commonwealth [is] taking of late some vigour of life.'[22] In particular, contemporaries might have congratulated themselves that the plantations and religious changes had been effected with almost no serious repercussions from the native population. The reasons why this should have been so are complicated. Part of the explanation may lie in the way in which the native population explained the changed circumstances in which they found themselves. In the political poetry written after the 'flight of the earls', the Ulster poets Fear Flatha Ó Gnímh and Eochaidh Ó hEodhasa directed the blame for recent developments not on the settlers but on the Irish themselves. The flight and its consequences were a punishment by God for the sins of the Irish and their failure to be 'submissive to God'.

For those who were not prepared to accept their fate with resignation there was a safety-valve in emigration. In the early decades of the seventeenth century, building on a late sixteenth-century base, there emerged a substantial Irish community in continental Europe. The foundation of Irish colleges at a number of locations including Paris (1578), Salamanca (1592), Louvain (1607), Bordeaux (1615) and Rome (1625) created focal points for Irish overseas networks and generated discussion on Irish affairs within a different social context from that found in Ireland itself. Moreover, the amalgamation of a number of independent Irish companies in Spanish Flanders into one military regiment commanded by Henry O'Neill, son of the Earl of Tyrone, gave cohesion to the Irish serving in the armies of Spanish Flanders. Between 1605 and 1659 at least fourteen Irish regiments were formed in the Netherlands. In the years between 1586 and 1620 probably up to 10,000 people migrated from Ireland to the Low Countries. Others, such as Philip O'Sullivan Beare, went to Spain, where they, by their writings, created new perspectives on Ireland.

Many of these might otherwise have stayed in Ireland venting their discontent with the new social arrangements there.

In the latter half of the second decade of the seventeenth century many of those who had been involved in shaping events in Ireland began to move off stage. In 1615 the Lord Deputy, Sir Arthur Chichester, was removed from office. This had probably been prearranged. His main contacts in the London court, Robert Cecil, Earl of Salisbury, and Henry Howard, Earl of Northampton, were now dead, and it would have been difficult to establish a new patronage network to ensure his voice was heard in London. He was also ill and his interest in Irish politics waning. It does not seem that he retired in disgrace, since he reappeared in 1622 as a senior Privy Councillor in England, dealing particularly with foreign affairs. His *alter ego*, Sir John Davies, returned to England in 1619 with his insane wife, and later prophetess, Eleanor. There is little doubt that Davies had always seen his sojourn in Ireland as temporary, and he was relieved of office at his own request. He passed his final years, until his death in 1626, as an author of poetry and legal treatises as well as practising law, being appointed Chief Justice of the Court of King's Bench in 1626, although he died the night before he was to take office. In 1621 he also represented Newcastle-under-Lyme in parliament. The third major actor in the shaping of Ireland in the first decade of the seventeenth century, Hugh O'Neill, Earl of Tyrone, died in Rome in 1616. That this was a decisive event was clear to Mícheál Ó Cléirigh and the other compilers of the Annals of the Kingdom of Ireland, commonly known as the Annals of the Four Masters, in the 1630s, for it was with his obituary that they brought their history of Ireland to a close. In diplomatic terms, O'Neill's death certainly marked the end of any real threat of an Irish invasion from Europe. For the major powers of continental Europe, O'Neill had become something of an embarrassment as they tried to place themselves on good terms with King James 1 of England. O'Neill spent his later years planning to return to Ireland, having lived to regret his impetuous decision of 1607. His plaintive letters to James seeking permission to return home went unheeded. Moreover, relations with former friends became progressively less cordial. Peter Lombard, Archbishop of Armagh, who had been O'Neill's agent in Rome during the Nine Years' War, read the signs of the time in European politics and threw his support behind the king in the hope of gaining toleration for Irish Catholics.

Hugh O'Neill, Earl of Tyrone, was a man who had indeed been destroyed by the peace that had fallen on Ireland before 1620.

# 3
# Money, Land and Status, 1620–32

On the death of James I in March 1625, his son Charles succeeded to the crowns of the three kingdoms. What was already obvious was that the near euphoria which characterised discussions on Ireland of the second half of the 1610s had dissipated. The early 1620s revealed a host of problems that had been building up for nearly a decade and which were caused by the failure to formulate any real programme for the government of Ireland in the second decade of the seventeenth century. Ireland may have been moving towards being a unified kingdom, but it was far from being a unified state, and that problem was compounded by the fact that the government of Ireland was being allowed to drift.

## THE PROBLEMS OF THE EARLY 1620S

The problems of the early 1620s were brought vividly to light from three quarters. The first was a commission established in 1622 to survey the state of Ireland. The immediate impetus for the creation of this body was concern in England at the financial drain that subsidising the government of Ireland was causing the English exchequer. The polemical literature of the years after 1603 had promised the London administration profit from Irish plantations and trade, but this was slow in materialising. Between 1603 and 1619 two-thirds of Irish expenditure was funded from the treasury in London and one-third from Irish revenue, although the English subventions did fall over time, especially after 1613. By 1618 an additional problem was identified, since it was believed the sheer volume of coin which was being shipped to Ireland to balance the books was depleting money supply in England. The rising financial genius in England, Lionel Cranfield, Earl of Middlesex, who became Lord Treasurer in 1621, maintained that the quantity of specie exported to Ireland was a significant contributory factor to English financial difficulties in the early 1620s. He immediately stopped the subventions, leaving Ireland with a deficit in 1622 of £24,376 (Irish) and an accumulated debt of £99,805 (Irish). With Cranfield's ascent to power, the changing configurations of English court politics singled out a victim to factional interests: the Irish Lord Deputy, Sir Oliver St John, who had held the office since 1616. In 1622 he was recalled and replaced by Viscount Falkland.

In the light of these changes, cost-cutting reforms were necessary to balance the books in Ireland. In particular, measures were required to control the size of the Irish army, which had not been reduced as much as was necessary after 1603. The army had, in effect, become a branch of government. Its reduction left the government with the problem of finding people to exercise the local administrative functions which officers had carried out previously. After 1604 colonels were transformed into governors of the areas in which they lived and provost-marshals supplemented the normal workings of local government. As a result, many officers stayed on the military list for close on twenty-five years. It was against this backdrop that Cranfield was the prime mover in establishing a commission in March 1622 to consider almost every aspect of Irish society and its financing. What the commissioners found was not simply a financial deficit but 'manifold disorders and confusion in the exchequer', negligent collection of revenue, and doubtful rents left in arrears and with no attempts made to collect them. The judicial system, it was agreed, needed a thorough overhaul, and directions for reordering the courts were issued in 1622. The commission made recommendations, but in practice little was done, although the customs farm was revised. Cranfield was powerless to stem the mounting Irish deficit or to make the kingdom self-supporting when faced with well-established vested interests in England and Ireland. However, his attempts made him enough enemies to ensure that by 1623 Cranfield had been effectively sidelined, and in 1624 he was impeached. As Lord Deputy Falkland gleefully wrote to the Duke of Buckingham in May 1624, 'We say here that Michael and his angels hath overthrown the Dragon and his angels, and mightily we rejoice that Lucifer is fallen.'[1]

While the 1622 commission concentrated, in the main, on finance and administrative matters, it did not do so exclusively. The final report included a section on the Established Church which did not paint a rosy picture. It noted the failure of the official government policy of conversion stretching back to before the Mandates controversy in 1605, observing that in some corporate towns few or none of the principal citizens attended the Church of Ireland. This it attributed to the failure of the Church of Ireland to put in place the sort of infrastructure to support the sort of campaign of religious convincement that some in London had in mind. Even those in 1620 who took a positive view of Ireland saw the problems of the church all too clearly. In 1620 the civil lawyer Thomas Ryves observed:

> The prosperous and happy peace which this poor kingdom of Ireland hath of late years enjoyed, is such as neither our fathers ever saw, nor can be sampled out of the records or histories of former ages. . . . Only the church in this common joy mourneth, looking pale and wan, as if she had been either newly taken out of a burning fever, or came lately out of a bloody battle. The churches in most places lie waste, and where churches are, there want rather able ministers able to instruct the people than people capable of instruction.[2]

A dramatic instance of the problems with the church was the revelation by the 1622 commission that there were only 380 licensed preaching ministers among the 2,492 parishes of the Church of Ireland. These revelations were fleshed out in greater detail by the returns of the regal visitation taken in the same year in conjunction with the inquiry. The visitation revealed that of the 380 preachers some 136 (or nearly 36 per cent) were in Ulster. This admittedly represented some growth in the numbers of clergy since 1615, but it also indicated that provision for reform was somewhat unbalanced. Part of the explanation for this situation was revealed when impropriate livings, of which laymen owned the tithes, were investigated. Of the 2,492 parishes, some 1,289 were impropriated to laymen, and hence the officiating clergy had no source of income other than what the impropriator might pay them. In cases where the tithes were held by a Catholic, such payment may not have been forthcoming. Few of these impropriations were in Ulster because the plantation had reorganised the ecclesiastical structure there. This meant that most of these livings were located disproportionately in other parts of Ireland (and especially in Connacht, where 85 per cent of the livings in the ecclesiastical province of Tuam were impropriate); hence finding incumbents for these unprofitable livings was a problem. Regional variations in the prevalence and intensity of this problem are important. The Pale had a higher level of impropriations and church buildings in poor repair than south Leinster. In Munster the dioceses of Killaloe, Cork, Cloyne and Ross were all much more attractive than livings in a corridor stretching from Clonmel to Limerick which had levels of impropriation and church dereliction comparable with those in the Pale.

Outside Ulster many parishes were small and incapable of supporting a rector; pluralist clergy holding two or more parishes were appointed in an effort to obtain a respectable income. This was a situation the commissioners found unacceptable. A further difficulty arose from the fact that most of the graduate clergy—those who were preachers as opposed to those who simply read the liturgy—who were summoned to appear before the 1622 visitation had received their education in England. The fledging Trinity College Dublin had not yet begun to produce local clergy in any numbers. There were some clergy with Irish names, usually Catholic priests who had conformed, but these were few, widely scattered, and usually served only as reading ministers who did not preach. This meant that, notwithstanding the fact that the Book of Common Prayer had been translated into Irish and was available in print from 1608, and that the New Testament had appeared in an Irish translation six years earlier, few Protestant clergy had the linguistic skills to use these aids to reach the Irish-speakers who made up the bulk of the population. These factors combined to create circumstances for which someone else was perceived to be to blame. The commissioners, not unreasonably, thought it was a problem for the church and issued thirty-eight orders for its reform, beginning with the basic requirement that church buildings be repaired. The bishops, on the other hand, blamed the state, claiming that there was no point in preaching the reformed faith unless people were compelled to come to church in order to hear sermons. This situation seemed to be getting worse with the suspension in 1621 of the recusancy fine of 12d for failure to attend parish churches on Sunday. The Dublin government in turn blamed London for curbing its enthusiasm in enforcing reform, as evidenced in the events surrounding the Mandates in 1605. Indecision simply made worse what already seemed to be a serious problem.

Another view into the world of the early 1620s is provided by the tracts written by private individuals, probably spurred on by the events surrounding the commission and visitation. In contrast to the unrelieved gloom of the official inquiries, those who wrote private treatises sometimes took a rather more positive view of the state of Ireland and raised different questions. Their views provided an alternative perspective to that of the 1622 commission, which recounted a sorry story of the failure of plantation policy. In Longford, the commissioners reported, the settlers had done 'little or nothing' and were 'likely to leave the country more waste and unpeopled than they found it'. In Leitrim only four out of forty-eight undertakers were resident, no building had been started and no leases made. In Munster the English population was 'greater in show than substance', and in Ulster settler immigration had slowed and settlers were failing to meet the conditions of their grants.[3] One author, Sir Arthur Blundell, who was a member of the 1622 commission, echoed the views of the commission when he produced a rather dark overview of plantations. He admitted some progress in Ulster, although it was 'a poor ragged quarter plantation', but overall he tended to be pessimistic about the prospects of removing the Irish, and the plantation was, in his estimation, generally weak. Longford, for instance, he thought was 'a show of something where nothing is done'. Blundell urged better planning, exhorted that men of greater substance might be involved, argued for smaller land grants, and pressed for greater policing of conditions and less rushing for profit by stumbling from one plantation to another.[4]

Another analysis of plantations written in 1622 provides a more positive analysis of the social effects of the process. The writer, possibly Sir William Parsons, though identified only as Sir W.P. in the manuscript, pointed to what had been achieved. Plantations, he argued, had brought peace by effectively breaking the power of the great Gaelic lords. The sort of power blocks associated with traditional Irish lordships, which had been underpinned by social customs such as fosterage, were on the wane. Newly created freeholders were now able to oppose great lords, and the king's law was generally obeyed, so that through 'the common use of law being brought in by these plantations the people's minds will be thereby busied in legal passages which before generally indicated how to break peace and law'.[5] As a result, there was a convergence of interests, and those Irish who were now part of the new order were benefiting from it. There is no doubt that both of these 1620s authors were correct in their assessments, though from very different perspectives. By the 1630s the native Irish gentry of King's County were petitioning the Lord Deputy to 'take away all manner of distinction between the natives of the Irish blood and birth and other His Majesty's subjects of this kingdom'.[6] The Ulster jail delivery rolls of 1613–15 bear out the accuracy of Parsons's comments about the increasing use of the common law by the native Irish. They were present not only as parties in legal actions but as participants in the common-law process, acting as jurors, sub-sheriffs or sheriff's bailiffs. They also appeared at more localised courts, such as manor courts, but here the evidence is thinner. According to one tract of 1615, there was a great demand among native Irish at the top of the social scale to become involved with the world of the common law as justices of the peace, for 'if any gentleman of the Irishry be of ten pounds revenues or of any manner of fashion or can speak English . . . he will use one means or another to be put in the commission of the peace'.[7] How many succeeded is not known, although one list of justices for County Clare in 1633 suggests that about half the J.P.s were of local origin. Moreover, the literature from within Gaelic Ireland suggests that the older order was being undermined by unprecedented social mobility spurred on by economic growth. The poet Brian Mac Giolla Phádraig, for instance, spoke of beggar-women's sons being dressed as princes, and the Tipperary priest and preacher Geoffrey Keating attacked the 'new sort' who were 'base by right' and who had now become a feature of Irish society. The most sustained attack on this process came in the prose tract *Pairlement Chloinne Tomáis*, probably written in the early 1630s, which satirised those who had moved beyond their place in the social order by acquiring land in the new settlements and becoming *ceannuibh bailte*, or village headmen. They now had money, bought themselves the sort of clothes worn by their social superiors, and had begun to educate their children in a manner which the author thought decidedly inappropriate for social climbers.

This sort of social fluidity gave rise to other reflections. Writing as early as 1614, one commentator, probably Sir George Carew, former President of Munster, thought he detected a significant change in the nature of Irish society. He observed that formerly the Old English of the Pale had 'despised the mere Irish race', but now he believed 'these latter times have produced a change' with the two groups growing together. There was intermarriage, the Irish 'by their travel abroad . . . are civilised', and the plantations had forced them together. Carew concluded from this that another rebellion was inevitable and urged that action be taken to prevent this.[8] Carew was correct in his observation that the two groups were becoming less distinguishable, but wrong in his short-term deduction that this would mean trouble. It is true that some of the native Irish looked back enviously to the high point of their world in the late sixteenth century and its crumbling after the battle of Kinsale in 1601. Probably in the early 1620s Lughaidh Ó Cléirigh from Donegal composed a life of Red Hugh O'Donnell which recorded stirring stories of the Nine Years' War, linking faith with fatherland, and which ended with the Irish giving up 'bravery for cowardice, courage for weakness, pride for servility', as a result of which they were 'dispersed and scattered' throughout Europe.[9] While this was an important strain of thought among the native Irish after 1603, and was to reappear in the 1640s, it was not the only one. Most of those who remained in Ireland after 1603 had a rather different agenda.

The Old English and some native Irish were indeed becoming more alike. Part of the explanation was economic. The social solvent of the market that developed as part of the economic expansion of the early seventeenth century had a significant effect on the social order. Gaelic poets, for instance, complained that their privileged position as members of an older social elite was declining as society became more commercialised and the status conveyed by praise poetry had been much reduced. Poets urged more profitable trades on their children such as fullers, needle-makers or comb-makers. Moreover, the sort of dress and fashion accessories being acquired by those Irish satirised in *Pairlement Chloinne Tomáis* made them look indistinguishable from the Old English. In the smarter parts of Gaelic Ireland the traditional dress of mantle and glib were a thing of the past.

However, economics will not explain all. As Carew observed, the Irish were also becoming more 'civil'. This sort of civility was what the Dublin government desired, but its origin was not what they had hoped for. At least some social change was the result of the spread of Counter-Reformation ideas and practices in Ireland. By the early 1630s it is clear from episcopal reports to Rome that in the areas identified in the 1622 visitation as having few Church of Ireland clergy and high levels of impropriations the Counter-Reformation revival was strongly under way. The Catholic reform movement required clergy, and the numbers of Catholic clergy were growing by the 1630s. This expansion in the clerical body provided another mechanism for social mobility without economic agrandisement. In 1633 the Dublin priest Paul Harris, for example, noted that the Franciscans recruited from the younger sons of the gentry, apprentices, farmers' sons, 'serving men, soldiers, tailors and horse boys who are now become R[everend] Fathers though neither learned nor civil men'.[10] Not surprisingly, according to Harris, scandals followed, but such men nonetheless moved rapidly up the social ladder.

The pattern of Catholic reform lay in the enforcement of a code of religious observance within a frame of parochial uniformity which required a range of social reforms before it could be effective. For example, the code of religious observance relating to marriage, baptism and mass attendance frequently conflicted with Gaelic Irish practices associated with kinship solidarity and particularly with its counterpart, feud. Thus one of the most effective of the Counter-Reformation bishops, David Rothe of Ossory, was clear that the role of Tridentine Catholicism in Ireland was to 'eliminate barbarous customs . . . and convert the detestable intercourse of savages into polite manners and a care for maintaining the commonwealth' and also to promote 'civil prudence, urbanity, industry' and other social virtues.[11] This was to be done in a way that would not offend the king or the temporal authorities. In the early 1620s Catholics were increasingly testing the bounds of recent moves to toleration to discover what might or might not offend the government. In Navan, County Meath, in 1622 it was complained that Catholics carried a cross openly at funerals, and in Drogheda Franciscan activity became more public. The Catholic episcopal hierarchy was largely reconstructed by the 1620s, and a series of reforming synods were held, ranging from one at Drogheda for the province of Armagh in

1614 to another at Tuam in 1640. This ecclesiastical legislation reshaped social practices in a wide range of Irish life. Clandestine marriage, for instance, was outlawed. All marriages were now to take place before a priest; if possible, banns were to be read beforehand; and marriages within prescribed degrees of kinship were not permitted. An attempt was made to regulate the number of godparents at baptism in order to limit the formation of artificial lineages that contributed to feud. Controls were also applied to social behaviour at wakes and funerals. Clearly, given the shortage of properly trained clergy, there were problems in enforcing such reform practices, but they seem to have penetrated the world of the Old English with considerable speed and provided a sense of identification with the wider religious cultures of Western Europe. In the case of Gaelic Irish society, it took considerably longer for the Tridentine reforms to be adopted. The ways of articulating belief, and the ecclesiastical structures which underpinned that belief, differed in various parts of Ireland, and this produced tensions, most notably between the secular (or diocesan) clergy associated with the Pale and the regular clergy (especially the Franciscans) in Gaelic Ireland. This does not mean that there were no points of contact between those two groups. Those of the Gaelic Irish world who had survived, and possibly benefited from, the reorganisation of landownership at the beginning of the century began to move in much the same social and religious circles as their Old English counterparts and came to absorb the same economic, political and religious ideas.

A rather different perspective on Ireland in the early 1620s is provided by the tract now known as the 'Advertisements for Ireland' written by the Old English lawyer from County Louth and one of the 1622 commissioners, Richard Hadsor. Many of the themes associated with the commission are present in his account of Ireland, in particular stories of official corruption, difficulties with the workings of courts, reform of the army, and the problems of trade and the customs. Strikingly, one of the most important themes running through Hadsor's writing is that which also concerned Parsons, though from a rather different perspective—the position of the native Irish in the new order. Whereas in Parsons's tract the integration of the native Irish into the new order is seen as a positive development, in Hadsor's work it is regarded as an insidious innovation. Hadsor was clear that there existed between the 'mere Irish' and the inhabitants of the Pale 'so large a distance between them really as there be betwixt two several nations of sundry regions'. The Palesmen, he stressed, were always loyal and prepared to serve the king, and he prayed: 'Would to God His Majesty and the state there would be pleased to make trial of our English Pale gentlemen . . . and would vouchsafe to employ them in some acceptable service that would give testimony of their duty and make expression of their hearts and willingness to discharge the parts of good subjects and commonwealth men.' Such honesty he contrasted with the behaviour of New English 'sharks there that be of obscure fortunes, birth and quality, which having not much to take unto before their arrival there, do more to look more to their own ends than either to advance His Majesty's revenue or profit'. The aim of the discourse, as Hadsor set it out, was to demonstrate that such unworthy men were the 'chiefest causes of the slow progress of the now growing commonwealth to perfection'.[12] In many ways this was a deeply conservative tract, arguing against the changes that were occurring in the planted areas, and instead advocating the shoring up of the social order characteristic of late sixteenth-century Ireland within which the Old English were natural governors of the country. An argument in favour of sumptuary legislation was advanced as a way of containing the sort of rapid change depicted in *Pairlement Chloinne Tomáis*, and a thoroughgoing reform of the Heralds' Office was required so that men would know their own arms, descents and pedigree as a bulwark against the *nouveau riche*.

If the 1622 commission set out the problems of Ireland from the centralised view of the London administration and the work of Sir William Parsons reflected what was occurring within the newly emerging societies of provincial Ireland from a planter's perspective, the work of Richard Hadsor presented a third way of looking at Ireland in the 1620s. It was a world in which the Old English still had a clear view of their own role as an elite within society. At local level they still had considerable power. In the early 1620s, for instance, Lord Deputy Falkland decided to enforce the anti-recusant legislation in Ireland, instructing sheriffs to present recusants at the assizes. No sooner had he done so than he received a letter from the Catholic Countess of Kildare complaining of his actions which immediately resulted in the withdrawal of all the writs against her tenants. The sheriff was informed that this was 'for reasons best known to ourself'.[13] Thereafter relations between the powerful elite and Lord Deputy Falkland became more circumspect. Complaining to the Protestant Earl of Thomond that one Catholic bishop was becoming bold in exercising his episcopal functions, Falkland was careful not to prohibit such functions explicitly but stipulated that Catholics 'may be contained within the bounds of moderation as formerly they were'.[14] The realities of the early 1620s were that, in the light of the Mandates controversy and subsequent events, their Catholicism was a considerable liability in exercising what they regarded as their moral authority to rule. Events were to open a new set of possibilities.

## THE GRACES

The economic and political problems of the early 1620s were not resolved by the 1622 commission. Rather, if anything, they were intensified by factors outside the control of the Dublin administration. The failure of the attempted match between Prince Charles (King Charles I after 1625) and the Infanta of Spain resulted in the outbreak of war between England and Spain in early 1625 which presented particular security problems for Ireland. Preparations for war were expensive, and the 1625 parliament at Westminster, unhappy about the new king's marriage to the French Catholic Henrietta Maria, refused to pay the bill, voting only a sum which was one-sixth of the administration's requirements. The weakest point in the English defence was Ireland. The Irish army was augmented from 1,350 to 3,850 foot and the cavalry increased from 170 to 400 horse. This force needed to be equipped, fed and trained; in short, it needed even more money spent on it. The simple solution to this problem was to follow the example of England and raise 'trained bands' of unpaid ordinary citizens who could be trained into a militia by a professional muster-master. The difficulty lay in the question of whether the membership of these bodies should be confined to Protestants or extended to embrace loyal Catholics who would see involvement in such a scheme as part of their duty. The case for the latter was put by the Dublin Catholic Sir John Bathe, who had influential friends at the court of Charles I. Bathe pointed to the loyalty of the Old English in the past and to the fact that they had been entrusted by London with governing Ireland. Recent events may have undermined that trust, but all that was required was a show of goodwill by London for that relationship to be renewed. From the Old

English point of view, it would have allowed them to perform public service which was both a marker of their status and something they regarded as part of their natural obligations. This was a timely and attractive offer because when the Privy Council agreed to the scheme, Bathe promised a gift of £3,000 as a contribution towards the cost of the regular army. At Bathe's suggestion, others emulated this generosity, which had the opposite effect to that intended. The government, now with its financial difficulties temporarily eased, thought twice about putting arms in the hands of Catholics, and in the spring of 1626 the scheme was abandoned.

As the military situation with Spain deteriorated rapidly in 1626, so the financial position worsened. Ireland's defence was now a matter of urgency. The problem was compounded by the chaotic retreat of English forces from Spain, which meant that a large number of English soldiers were dumped in Ireland, raising the Irish force to almost 5,000, being maintained on a budget intended for only 1,350. In this context, the Lord Deputy, Falkland, turned to Sir John Bathe again. The intention was that in return for concessions the Old English of the Pale might once again make a substantial financial contribution to the army. The king helpfully supplied a list of twenty-six matters, mainly administrative reforms of a minor nature, which he was prepared to grant as matters of 'grace and bounty' in return for a contribution towards the cost of the army to be approved by a meeting of the Catholic lords. The most significant matter was undoubtedly the offer to stop collecting recusancy fines and an undertaking to do away with religious tests for inheritance, office-holding and legal practice.

Reactions to these promises were somewhat muted. The Old English, understandably rather suspicious of government's motives after the failure of the trained bands scheme, were unconvinced. Falkland was equally ambivalent towards the proposal. On the one hand, money solved some of his problems, but the source of that money could be potentially unreliable. The meeting of the Old English lords in November was fractious and quickly degenerated into a litany of grievances against the administration and its ways of raising money. Significantly for an understanding of the Old English position, they alleged that the increase in the army was only necessary because the trained bands proposal had been shelved, and they demanded that it be reintroduced. One important outcome was an agreement to hold a full-scale meeting of local delegates in Dublin to deal with the matter 'after a parliamentary way'. In the event, this meeting of the 'Great Assembly', as it came to be called, did not take place until April 1627, and the government expected little of it. Nor did the 'Great Assembly' deliver much. Among a welter of addresses professing loyalty there were complaints of poverty, many of which were examples of special pleading, and a desire that the Old English should be trusted with what was, after all, their duty owed to the king: the defence of Ireland. Indeed, this exercise of duty could be nowhere better expressed than through the summoning of a parliament in which the king could consult his subjects in the traditional manner. In all of this, Irish Protestants were deeply uneasy. The religious implications of political developments were easy to see, and in late 1626 the Church of Ireland bishops, led by James Ussher, Archbishop of Armagh, drew up a protest about recent worrying developments and followed it with a series of sermons in Christ Church Cathedral, Dublin, about the dangers of toleration and Catholic conversions. Ironically, Ussher himself was an agent for royal policy, since he had been commissioned to oversee the raising of the army for which the revenue raised by the Graces was to pay.

The failure of the 'Great Assembly' to yield funds left Falkland with no alternative but to use force to feed the Irish army. In May 1627 the lords of the Pale were summoned before the Privy Council and informed that money had to be raised. This resulted in stalemate, with the government agreeing that arrangements to raise money would have to be forced through. Four Old English lords were summoned to a meeting, only to find themselves swamped by a Protestant majority who agreed to a levy of £43,000. However, the Old English had not been idle. Following the failure of the 'Great Assembly', Richard Nugent, Earl of Westmeath, had gone to Charles and persuaded him to receive a delegation from the Old English in Ireland. In June elections were held for a convention to nominate the delegation to the king. This was a slow process, and it was not until early 1628 that eleven agents were chosen and departed for England. The delegation included three Protestant settlers and eight Catholic Old Englishmen, all of whom were substantial landowners, some well known in government circles. The deputation had its first formal audience with the king on 20 March 1628, at which they presented him with a petition promising substantial contributions to the army in return for the granting of sixty requests. Following an examination of these, some fifty-three were allowed to stand, and after further negotiations their price was fixed at £40,000 sterling each year for three years in addition to what had been paid already. The list was redrafted into fifty-one 'Instructions and Graces' which were dispatched to the Irish government.

The Graces, as they became known, covered a wide range of issues, some minor and others major. The opportunity was taken to impose controls on the army, including stopping the billeting of soldiers on private individuals, and on the collection of crown rents. This problem was not unique to Ireland; indeed, the English Petition of Right of 1628 included clauses dealing with the same problem of military control. Limits were also placed on the actions of the Court of Wards and Liveries. The court managed feudal obligations, including the administration of the estates of minors. Previously heirs were not allowed to enter their estates without taking the Oath of Supremacy, but the Graces replaced this with a straightforward oath of allegiance. Thirteen of the Graces dealt with reforms in the courts of law in an attempt to limit discretionary powers. At the centre of the agreement were three Graces dealing with land title (Articles 24, 25 and 26). The last of these confirmed Ulster planters in their estates, on certain financial conditions, notwithstanding the breaches of the conditions on which they held them as revealed by the 1622 commission. In practice this meant that the condition that no Irish should be taken as tenants on undertakers' lands was being abandoned. Article 24 promised security of tenure to the Old English by directing that an act would pass in the next Irish parliament to uphold the existing distribution of land and therefore remove the threat of confiscation. For this purpose, as with the English Concealment Act of 1624, sixty years' possession would constitute good title against royal claims. Article 25 provided security of titles for those in the province of Connacht, made necessary because of a misunderstanding concerning the 1585 Composition which some thought constituted title to land whereas it only dealt with taxation. It was intended that all these promises should be finalised by a parliament that was to meet at Dublin in November 1628. For the Old English, such promises represented a dramatic advance on what had been on offer, or even sought, in 1626.

In Dublin Lord Deputy Falkland set about summoning the

required parliament, but he made the serious mistake of assuming that Charles's agreement with the delegation constituted authority to summon a parliament without going through the procedures set down in Poynings' Law. In September he was informed by the English Privy Council that his failure to do so meant the parliament could not be convened by the required date. Falkland had already begun to collect the first part of the subsidy, and the Irish army had been increased to 5,000 men (although this was not meant to happen until the autumn). Falkland attempted to find a solution without success, and while elections were being held in October 1628 he issued a proclamation postponing parliament's meeting.

The early increase in the size of the army and the proclamation were both viewed by the Old English as signs of betrayal. A protest meeting in Dublin denounced the fact that parliament had been postponed and alleged that others of the Graces which were of an administrative nature had not been implemented. A petition from the meeting threatened that if what had been promised was not delivered, there would be no further payments. In fact enough had been achieved, including the reforms in the Court of Wards and Liveries, to ensure that further payments were made. The government seized on this situation and in the middle of 1630 declared that no parliament would meet until the contribution for the army, which was, after all, to defend the Old English from invasion, had been paid in full. By then the context had changed. Peace had been made with Spain in 1629, and the size of the Irish army had been reduced. Charles already regarded parliaments in England as inconvenient nuisances which could be dispensed with and saw no need to call one in Ireland. Lord Deputy Falkland was recalled in 1629. The Old English attempts to prove their loyalty had been stymied.

However, all had not been lost. After 1628 there was a surge of fines for liveries of land in the Court of Wards. This can only be taken to mean that those suing out liveries did not have to take the Oath of Supremacy. For landholders it meant that property remained under the jurisdiction of the Court of Wards for a shorter period of time, and consequently the profit which the crown could make at the expense of others was reduced. At least something had been achieved by the Old English group.

## THE DYNAMICS OF CRISIS

The immediate circumstances of 1624–7 certainly explain why the crisis over the Graces occurred at this point of the early seventeenth century, but it does not explain why it happened at all. To understand that problem, we need to examine something of the character of the Old English community in the early seventeenth century and its reaction to the changes which were taking place. Perhaps one of the most characteristic features of the Old English community was its sense of moral authority to behave as the rulers of Ireland. It was this concern to demonstrate their position as the natural rulers of Ireland, with obligations to serve the crown and be consulted by it, that had motivated most of the Old English activity through the episode of the Graces. This sense of moral authority associated with the Old English community was both underpinned and disrupted by the changes taking place in the Irish economy.

The most characteristic feature of the Irish economy in the years before 1638 was its expansionary nature. The yield of the customs, for instance, though not strictly comparable because of revisions to the tax rates, shows near continuous growth over the early seventeenth century. The extent of the expansion is indicated by the scale of Irish trade passing through Chester, one of the main destinations of Irish exports. In the late 1580s somewhere between twenty-five and sixty dickers of hides (a dicker being a pack of ten hides) were landed at Chester from Ireland each year, whereas by 1639 this had increased to 1,289 dickers a year. Similarly, in the 1580s between eleven and seventy packs of yarn were sent annually to Chester; by 1639 the number had grown to 113 packs. Tallow exports also increased from fifty hundredweight in 1592–3 to 619 hundredweight in 1639. More dramatic was the growth in wool exports from between 100 and 200 stone in the late 1580s to 6,666 stone in 1639. The spectacular success of the live cattle trade, which rose from nothing in the late sixteenth century to 15,000 beasts a year in the late 1630s, provides yet further evidence of the expansion of Irish trade. Similar patterns appear in other ports, with the result that the Irish balance of trade was usually in a healthy state in the early seventeenth century. In the main this involved an expansion of the existing structure of the economy rather than the introduction of new products or activities, although some new sectors such as ironworking, fishing and timber did become important.

The reasons for these changes are fairly clear. The Irish population expanded in the early seventeenth century from probably 1.4 million in 1600 to about 2.1 million in 1641 as a result of immigration and, to a lesser extent, natural increase. In fact the growth was greater than it appears, since there was also emigration to continental Europe for education and military service which reduced the potential population growth. This population rise resulted in a significantly expanded labour force, growing from a low level, and this resulted in increased output. Coupled with this was the evolution of a more commercialised economy associated with the spread of a common-law framework for trade and the emergence of a land market. These developments meant that increasingly surpluses, previously circulated through gifts or tribute to overlords, were now brought to markets for sale. As one commentator put it in 1611, 'It is confessed necessary that all merchandise shall be sold only in markets [since] markets increase commerce and procure one produce to be brought for sale for the buying of another which tends that [he] that has access to the market shall be more readily furnished with commodities wherein to employ his money and so the seller is furnished with money to buy.'[15] As a result, local markets boomed, with some 500 grants of market rights being issued between 1600 and 1649. Not all of these proved viable as markets in the longer term. Larger port towns, such as Cork and Youghal, probably doubled their populations between 1600 and 1641. In particular, the dominance of Dublin in Irish trade became clear, with some 21 per cent of the island's customs revenue generated there in 1616–17, rising to almost a third by 1630 and 47 per cent by 1662–3. In such an environment, the market was an important social solvent, allowing the sort of mobility within Gaelic Ireland that some English commentators hoped for, since it gave the native Irish a stake in the new order, but which the Old English feared, perceiving it to be socially disruptive.

There was a wide range of beneficiaries from this pattern of economic growth, and prominent among them were the Old English. Since a high proportion of Irish trade was in the hands of Old English merchants trading in foreign ships, the accumulation of wealth in the hands of this group was considerable. One rather crude measure is the growth of the quantity of land owned by the Old English outside the counties of the Pale. By 1641 the Old English, whose landholding before 1603 had been largely concentrated in the east and south of the country, held 48.4 per cent of the profitable land in County Mayo, and 20 per cent and 63.6 percent of the profitable land in Counties Roscommon and Galway respectively. In County Sligo they held 21.3 per cent of the profitable land, and in County Kerry 17.9 per cent. Some of this was inherited property; and in the case of the 15.6 per cent of the profitable land they held in County Cavan, the Ulster plantation was responsible for some land grants. The bulk of this property, however, had been purchased recently by the Old English. As the 1622 commissioners complained, 'The merchants here in all the cities of the kingdom do as they grow unto wealth withdraw themselves into the country and settle upon farms and neglect their trade of merchandise in which they were bred.'[16] Most of these merchants were Old English who had benefited from the spread of peace and the single land market created by the implementation of English law across Ireland. The process by which they acquired this property is clearly demonstrated in the case of the mercantile elite in Galway city. By 1641 some 150 Old English merchants from Galway held about 18 per cent of the profitable land in County Galway, 11 per cent in County Mayo, and 14 per cent in County Sligo. Most of these merchants probably owned less than 150 profitable acres each, but others had large landholdings: Sir Richard Blake had over 10,000 profitable acres, two others had over 7,000, and a further eleven had over 1,000.[17] The burden of taxation and a number of harvest crises in the early 1620s had an adverse effect on the smaller Gaelic Irish landholders in Mayo and Galway. As a result, they arranged mortgages with those who had cash on hand, mainly Galway city merchants who, under the terms of the mortgage, occupied the land; this pattern can be traced, for example, in the Wentworth survey of County Mayo in 1635. The Dublin staple books also suggest an increased amount of borrowing and lending in these years. Most of the small freeholders of land were never in a position to redeem their mortgages, and so in time title passed absolutely to the merchants. In the province of Connacht especially the greater lords welcomed this, since it strengthened the position of the larger landowners who were consolidating their own local power bases, a process which had sixteenth-century roots but which became more noticeable after 1605. In addition, the availability of crown lands in Connacht, mainly as a result of the dissolution of religious houses, enhanced the landownership possibilities for Galway residents. Perhaps half of the land they acquired came from this source, most of which was in place by 1617. Galway merchants were not alone in growing rich. Around the cities of Cork and Kilkenny local merchants acted in similar ways to their Connacht counterparts, buying up land owned by the native Irish in the hinterlands of their towns.

Translating this personal, social and economic power of the Old English into political authority through a system of patronage was one of the central tasks of the system of governance. In theory it should have been self-intensifying: social and economic power should have created political authority, which in turn should have created more social influence. In practice this failed to happen. Land titles, for instance, were less secure than they should have been. The fact that economic success was not reflected in the acquisition of political power, and the resulting divergence of economic and political influence, constituted one of Ireland's post-1603 problems that the Graces were meant to address, though with limited effect.

## THINKING ABOUT THE GRACES

The events surrounding the Graces episode are revealing of the tensions inherent in Irish society. However, the responses to those events are at least as important. The politics of the late 1620s seem to have prompted many to ponder the nature of authority within the Irish polity and how that was exercised. One form in which that thinking took shape was an exploration of the Irish past, since the past could be used to validate present positions. Writing history in the early seventeenth century was not so much the articulation of a common understanding of the Irish past as an important power struggle. Stories of the past needed to be made usable so that they could serve the needs of the present. Those who could use historical evidence to make a case that their vision of how things should be done was, in fact, identical with the way in which they had always been done wielded a potentially powerful instrument for shaping social and political culture. It is not coincidental that three significant antiquarians began producing their reflections on the Irish past in the wake of the Graces. The implications of the questions raised in the late 1620s lie at the core of some of these works as such men tried to make their pasts usable in the present.

The first of those antiquarians was the Old English priest Geoffrey Keating, who completed his *Foras feasa ar Éirinn* no later than 1635, with a preliminary draft probably in circulation by 1629, just as the Graces débâcle was drawing to a close. A Catholic priest from County Tipperary who trained in Bordeaux and Douai, Keating was proud of his Old English background and told the story of Ireland's past from the earliest times to the coming of the Anglo-Normans in the late twelfth century in a way that incorporated the Old English into the Irish origin myth based on the *Leabhar Gabhála*. Whereas the traditional story had ended with the coming of the sons of Míl, ancestors of the *Gaeil*, Keating's version added the Anglo-Normans as a final stage of that origin legend—presenting them as a people who had long ago chosen Ireland as their homeland. This ensured that his representation of the early Irish past could be read as the history of the Old English as well as the Gaelic Irish. Keating's work was conceived as the history of those he termed *Éireannaigh*, or Irish people, whom he defined as of Gaelic or Anglo-Norman descent, who had been born in Ireland and were confessionally Catholic. The definition thus created an older cohesive block in opposition to the New English which helped deny the latter any constitutional legitimacy as defined by Irish history.

This allowed the Old English to appropriate to themselves the historical legitimation of the political arrangements which Keating thought he saw in the early Irish sources. His view of the nature of kingship was not based on kingship by divine right. Irish kingship, Keating argued, was elective rather than hereditary, and he asserted that

> We do not read in the *seanchus* that there was ever any king of Ireland from the time of Sláinghe to the Norman invasion but a king who obtained the sovereignty of Ireland by the choice of the people, by the excellence of his exploits and by the strength of his hand.[18]

The ceremony of inauguration affirmed the contract between the king and people which underpinned sovereignty:

> [A] chronicler came forward bearing the book called the Instructions for Kings, in which there was a brief summary of the customs and laws of the country, and where it was explained how God and the people would reward the doing of good and the punishment that awaited the king and his descendants if he did

not carry out the principles of justice and equity which the Book of Kings and the Instructions for Kings direct to put in practice.[19]

This was clearly meant to be interpreted by contemporary readers in the light of the experience of kingship in early seventeenth-century Ireland, and in particular the role of King Charles I in the failure of the Graces episode. Good kingship, portrayed as being essential to prosperity and sovereignty, was in the gift of the political nation. Since it was necessary to explain the legitimacy of the Stuart kings within this context, Keating was careful to present the first Anglo-Norman monarch to rule Ireland, Henry II, as one who had earned the trust of the nobility and clergy of Ireland. He had been assigned the sovereignty of Ireland by Pope Adrian IV in the twelfth-century bull *Laudabiliter* so that he could offer his protection. While admitting that there had initially been an element of conflict associated with the coming of the Anglo-Normans, Keating explained this as the actions of a small minority who had been punished by God for their misdeeds and who had no descendants in contemporary Ireland. Those Irish who resisted Anglo-Norman rule were excused on the grounds that they had been unjustly treated and that, given good government, they were a law-abiding people—again a message for those involved in the Graces. In this way Keating, as historian, could present both Gaels and Anglo-Normans in a favourable light, a point that was essential to underpin the moral authority of Old English Catholics in the seventeenth century as the legitimate holders of power in Ireland.

In a further elaboration of the historical origins of the Irish polity, Keating's description of the *feis* of Tara created an origin myth for the parliament and social hierarchy which lay at the cornerstone of Old English political thought. Emphasising the close relationship between the high king and the nobility in establishing and revising the laws to be used in governing Ireland, he explained:

Now the *feis* of Tara was a great general assembly like a parliament [*parlaimeint*], in which the nobles and the ollamhs of Ireland used to meet at Tara every third year at Samhain, where they were wont to lay down and to renew rules and laws, and to approve the annals and records of Ireland. There, too, it was arranged that each of the nobles of Ireland should have a seat according to his rank and title.

There, also, a seat for every leader that commanded the soldiery who were in the service of the lords of Ireland.[20]

Keating's version of the 'ancient constitution' of Ireland was a product of the ongoing historiographical process whereby the ideas of the high kingship and supporting institutions such as the assembly of Tara were created retrospectively. Moreover, it demonstrated that the Irish parliament had certain inherent rights to make law that did not derive from a royal grant of those prerogatives as a result of conquest. It also provided a model of how kingship and decision-making should operate in contrast to the world of the Graces.

History was used also to affirm the status of the contemporary Catholic Church as the true successor of the church of the early Christians. Simply by emphasising the continuity of the Irish polity over time it was possible to cultivate the idea of a Catholic kingdom with its roots in the ancient past. Echoing the division of the Bible into Old and New Testaments, Keating's history was written in two books, the second beginning with the coming of Christianity to Ireland with the holy man, St Patrick, bearing the truth. Patrick was presented as the founding father of the Irish church, and the loyalty of the Irish to that church over time was deemed sufficient explanation of the legitimacy of the Catholic Church in Keating's day as the successor, in an unbroken tradition, of the church founded by Patrick. Unlike the Protestant ecclesiastical historian James Ussher, who discussed the same questions of continuity, Keating felt no need to elaborate on this argument concerning the continuity of Catholicism. Keating, as a secular priest, was more concerned to emphasise the origins of ecclesiastical structures, such as dioceses, thereby reducing the significance of the religious orders. Thus the Synod of Kells in 1152, which resulted in the creation of the four archbishoprics of Armagh, Cashel, Dublin and Tuam, was integrated into the closing section of the *Foras feasa* so that it too became part of the origin myth of Catholic Ireland. As such it stressed the message of the Council of Trent that regular clergy were subject to bishops and served as an historical commentary on an ongoing dispute in Keating's own day about the respective and hotly contested rights of secular and regular clergy and parochial dues.

Keating's placing of the discussion of the twelfth-century church at the end of a long discourse on the origins of the Old English and

Gaelic Irish provided a shared Catholic version of their history. His revision of Irish history was designed to remind his Catholic readers of the need to live up to the standards of their illustrious ancestors and, in particular, to affirm the moral authority of the Old English to be entrusted with supporting the legitimately appointed king. Such reaffirmation of support for just rule as the means of maintaining an ordered society was central to reinforcing the moral authority of the Old English that had been damaged by the Graces episode.

The second sort of usable past that emerged from the problems of the Graces was the work of the Protestant Archbishop of Armagh, James Ussher. Ussher had more in common with Keating than might appear at first glance. Both were ethnically Old English in background, and the language difference between them is more attributable to the fact that Ussher grew up in Dublin, where the English language was the norm, while Keating's Tipperary background and education predisposed him to Irish. Both scholars were well read, particularly in Irish and British material, both printed and manuscript, and they were in touch with wider developments in continental Europe. The yawning gap between them lay in the matter of religion. While Keating was a secular Catholic priest, Ussher was Church of Ireland Archbishop of Armagh and a convinced Calvinist who held that the pope was Antichrist. The handling of the Graces were deeply worrying to Ussher, for it suggested that the godly prince, who should have been the champion of reformed religion, was instead temporising with the enemy. Ussher assumed the leadership of the Irish bishops in their opposition to the Graces. The Graces initiative was coupled with another development, the withdrawal of Charles's support from the sort of Calvinist consensus that had developed in Ireland in favour of a different soteriology. As this occurred in the late 1620s Ussher's letters became more apocalyptic. Writing to Samuel Ward in Cambridge, Ussher advised that 'All men's hearts [are] failing them for fear, and for looking after those things which are coming on the land. The Lord prepare us for the day of visitation, and let His blessed will be done.'[21] The trauma of the Graces and the failure of the godly prince seemed to Ussher to foreshadow the final tribulation of the elect. And so he turned to history for explanation. This was not an illogical move, since, for Ussher, history was not an academic subject but rather the unfolding of God's providential will. Moreover, in 1613 he had produced a work of church history using as its model the Book of Revelation and contemporary European ideas about the evolution of the church. Ussher argued that the primitive church had become progressively corrupt through the Middle Ages and that the Reformation process had not created anything new but simply returned the contemporary church to its ancient state of purity.

One way in which Ussher's historical drive manifested itself in the years after the Graces was the republication in 1631 of his *A discourse of the religion anciently professed by the Irish and British*. This had first appeared as an appendix to a work of controversy by Christopher Sibthorpe in 1622, but its significance only became clear in the aftermath of the trauma of the Graces when the weaknesses of the Church of Ireland had been laid bare in the face of the need to compromise with Catholicism. Like Keating's *Foras feasa*, the *Discourse* was an attempt to create a usable past, but in this case for the Church of Ireland. It adapted Ussher's earlier work on the history of the church to Irish circumstances. As such it tried to demonstrate, using the evidence from the early Irish church, and a Calvinist framework, that the Church of Ireland of which Ussher was primate was the direct successor of the church of St Patrick. This he did by using evidence from early medieval texts to argue that the church of St Patrick was firmly centred on the Bible and that the central Protestant tenet of justification by faith alone was present in Patrick's church. Equally, belief in purgatory could not be found in the early evidence relating to that church. However, Ussher's historical work is strongest on reconstructing the sacramental tradition of the early Irish church. As Ussher read the evidence, the liturgy of the early Irish church was a pure form not like 'the new Mass of the Romanists': communion was given in both kinds, and transubstantiation was a corruption introduced in the twelfth century. Confession was not a mechanical device for absolution, and penance was done to reflect inward repentance, unlike the Roman tradition of casuistry. Marriage was not a sacrament, and clerical celibacy was not mandatory. In short, the Patrician church provided the model for the seventeenth-century Church of Ireland, although the problem of monasticism remained unresolved in Ussher's scheme, despite some discussion of it. Crucial for Ussher's argument was the status of Rome in the early church. Here he argued that Ireland acknowledged no dependence on the see of Rome, no appeals were sent to Rome, and no papal legates came to Ireland until the twelfth century. It was at this point, argued Ussher, that corruption first appeared in the Irish church, and one manifestation of this was the papal bull *Laudabiliter*, which had authorised the intervention of Henry II in Ireland. This inevitably created a clash of political loyalties resolved by dismissing the bull and relying on the submission of the Irish bishops and lords to Henry in 1171, thereby creating the Irish polity with which Ussher in the seventeenth century was familiar.

This was an impressive argument, bolstered by Ussher's wide reading in Latin and English sources and his massive learning. He displayed much less engagement with the Irish-language sources, which was the result of the problem of access as well as cultural sympathy. Ussher did have contacts in the Gaelic world, notably Conell Mageoghegan of Westmeath, and he employed translators who provided him with texts. Despite this scholarly network, some key works seemed to elude him, and he usually relied on the evidence of Latin rather than Irish texts. The interpretation of the history of the early Irish and British churches was a problem that he would pursue in the late 1630s, culminating in the publication of his substantial Latin work of historical interpretation *Britannicarum ecclesiarum antiquitates* in 1639. However, the English *Discourse* had a much greater effect in creating a usable past for Protestants in the wake of the instability created by the Graces and was, potentially, a controversial work against those who had precipitated the crisis: the Catholics.

In a rather different form, the early work of Sir James Ware can also be related to that of Ussher and the need to create a Protestant past for a new generation after the Graces. Ware, a second-generation settler in Ireland, seems to have become interested in history in the early 1620s, possibly as a result of his investigations into land titles as Auditor General of Ireland. He quickly fell under the influence of Ussher, and his earliest published work from 1626 is a succession list of the Archbishops of Cashel and Tuam and on the Cistercian houses in Ireland. This was followed in 1628 by further a succession list of the Archbishops of Dublin. It is not difficult to see the influence of Ussher here in the preoccupation with episcopal succession, reflecting Ussher's case for the Church of Ireland being the lineal descendant of the church of St Patrick. In the 1630s Ware's interests changed as he turned his historical expertise to providing justifications for other political positions.

## AN HONOURABLE SOCIETY

The experience of the Graces was, in many ways, a defining moment in the pattern and direction of Irish governance. It demonstrated to the Old English that it was possible for the Dublin and London administrations to differentiate between Catholics and Catholicism. The same differentiation seems to have applied in the area of printed religious controversy in Ireland. First, there was very little of it. While the English presses produced hundreds of tracts of a controversial nature, their Irish counterparts produced almost nothing. Some of the reasons for this may lie in the technicalities of printing in Dublin, but a major feature seems to have been a lack of interest in spending money on this type of literature, since there is little evidence of its importation into the country. That does not mean there was no controversy. Manuscript tracts did circulate, and there were public confrontations, as in 1630 when an exorcism was performed in Dublin by the Discalced Carmelite Stephen Brown before a large crowd who had previously witnessed a Church of Ireland minister fail to have any impact on the demoniac. At least part of the explanation may be the concern that printed controversy could have disturbing effects on society because of its potential for widespread circulation. Certainly writers such as Richard Bellings, the secretary of the Kilkenny Confederates, refused to let their works be printed for this reason. If one was going to attack Catholicism, one had to do it without offending too many Catholics who, after all, were the majority of the population. When printed works of controversy did appear from the pen of Archbishop Ussher and others, directed to the Catholic laity, they often stopped short of the full logic of their arguments against Catholicism, possibly so as not to offend excessively the Catholic reader.

There was no doubt that Catholicism was potentially a deeply divisive issue between natives and newcomers. Yet it was possible to deal with Catholics in making arrangements for the day-to-day workings of government and defence. The idea of Catholicism was one that could be mobilised or suppressed in varying circumstances to create, if not integration, at least a *modus vivendi*. However, what the Graces demonstrated was that such an arrangement was difficult to achieve, not because of religious differences, but because of something more fundamental: a lack of trust between the parties. The idea of trust led to one of the core organising principles of all aspects of seventeenth-century society: the concept of honour. Honour was the value that gentry society placed on its members and a value which a gentleman placed on himself. It subsumed a wide range of other ideas, including loyalty, duty, lineage, pride, reputation and, increasingly, religion. Lineage, for instance, was as much a blessing of God as a human construct, and duty involved not only relations between people but duties to God also, a fact emphasised by George Downham, Bishop of Derry, in his sermons published as *The Covenant of Grace* (1631). Honour presumed a stratified world in which a few could claim moral superiority over the rest, defending it in a potentially fatal duel if necessary. The language of honour and loyalty was central to both the Old English and the New English understanding of themselves, since elites were defined more by shared sets of cultural values within each elite than by wealth or landownership.

The New English demonstrated their sense of honour in their funeral monuments with heraldic devices, intended to create a sense of lineage and manipulated to enhance the status of one's ancestors if necessary, and the use of titles and description of noble service (especially military service) in inscriptions. From an Old English perspective, the diminution of position of honour and trust had obvious implications. Geoffrey Keating in his *Foras feasa ar Éirinn* asked rhetorically what course of action was 'more honourable, more noble or more loyal to the crown of England', and the answer may well have been given by the chronicler, Mícheál Ó Cléirigh, when he described his compilation of the Annals of the Kingdom of Ireland as being 'for the glory of God and the honour of Ireland'.[22] In this context, it is not difficult to see how the language of honour, with ideas of duty, reputation and betrayal, which was shared by both sides in the events surrounding the Graces came to be highly divisive. The defence of Ireland, which for the Old English was regarded as an honourable duty that enhanced their reputation, was something they were not being allowed to carry out because they were regarded as untrustworthy. Hence divisions ran deeper than confessional positions and were not easily resolved despite the possibility of creating a series of temporary accommodations. One possible solution was the emergence of a common enemy who would be regarded by both Old and New English as acting in a dishonourable way. On this common ground battles which joined both parties in the reconstruction of an honourable position might be fought. That situation, which emerged in the 1630s, was more imminent than many might have thought.

# 4
# The Challenge to the Old World, 1632–9

The events surrounding the attempts to have the Graces confirmed in the late 1620s highlighted the tensions inherent in Irish society. The recall of Lord Deputy Falkland in 1629 and the swearing in of Adam Loftus, the Lord Chancellor, and Richard Boyle, Earl of Cork, as Lords Justices to act until a new Lord Deputy could be appointed gave no hint that progress might be made on the political agenda laid out in the Graces. The Treaty of Madrid of November 1630, which ended the war between England and Spain, seemed to alter the political circumstances that had favoured the Old English in the late 1620s. Indeed, there appeared to be signs that a more conservative regime, associated with the New English political elite, was emerging. In December 1629 sixteen Catholic religious houses in Dublin that had been opened in the course of the 1620s were closed, including the Jesuit house in Back Lane and the Franciscan chapel in Cook Street. That rare event in early seventeenth-century Ireland, a religious riot, ensued. Clearly the authorities knew where such houses were but had taken no action against them until after the recall of Falkland, which suggests a high level of toleration in the late 1620s. Moreover, those who visited the Jesuit house in Back Lane realised that within sight of the Protestant cathedral of Christ Church there was a Catholic religious complex of some sophistication, under the patronage of the Countess of Kildare. The Jesuit chapel was as large as a Dublin parish church, the altar was raised up and railed in and was richly adorned with pictures. There were also four European-style confession boxes, relative novelties in the world of Irish Catholicism. The closure of a number of Dublin Catholic churches was not a unique occurrence, since in 1632 the government ordered the closure of the traditional pilgrimage site of St Patrick's Purgatory in Donegal. However, before too many sweeping generalisations are made about these isolated episodes it needs to be remembered that a number of Catholic mass-houses in Dublin, not run by those in religious orders but recorded by Archbishop Bulkeley in his 1630 visitation, remained open.

In July 1633, however, the conventions by which early modern Irish society operated changed fundamentally with the appointment of Thomas Wentworth, later Earl of Strafford, as Irish Lord Deputy. Wentworth's analysis of the problems in Ireland, and his solutions to those problems, were radically different to what had gone before. While in the 1620s Wentworth in England had been one of the champions of the rights of the English parliament, by the 1630s he was closely associated with the king in a way that no previous Irish Lord Deputy had been. Consequently, the manner in which the Irish polity was managed in the 1630s was to be determined by priorities that were not entirely Irish. The context in which the problem of governing Ireland came to be seen was a common one in contemporary Europe —the dilemma of multiple monarchies.

In 1603 the crowns of England and Scotland had been united by the accession of James VI of Scotland to the throne of England. Rather more than fifty years earlier the crown of Ireland had been united to that of England. By the 1630s one monarch ruled over three distinct entities, each with its own governmental, legal, religious and cultural structures. In this sense the new British monarchy was not unlike that of Spain or indeed that of the Holy Roman Empire, whose emperor presided over a *mélange* of lesser political entities. While the monarch was prepared to allow local cultures, in which shared assumptions of religion, government and law were predominantly local, to survive, this need not have given rise to concern. In the main that is what James VI & I had done. Innovations in, for example, religious practice in Scotland had been limited and were introduced slowly. King James, for all his foibles, was still treated as an effective monarch, and his changes were backed up by personal authority. He managed to strike a balance between royal authority and the expectation that he would act as arbiter between the various institutions of the state and provide good government. That could not be said of his son Charles, who succeeded him in 1625. Moreover, what had become clear in the débâcle surrounding the failure of the planned parliament of 1629 was that there was considerable confusion concerning procedural arrangements for the governance of Ireland, as Falkland's misreading of Poynings' Law suggests. It was possible to think that the crown of Ireland was equal to but nonetheless part of the imperial crown, as the Old English had argued, and that within that arrangement balances needed to be struck between the power of the executive and the subject in Ireland, using parliament and appeal to the king as counterbalances to executive authority. Alternatively it could be argued that somehow Ireland was a dependency of England to be ruled by royal will, as many New English colonists suggested, or that it was some sort of combination of these positions not yet explored.

## ANATOMISING IRELAND

In January 1632, before his formal appointment to the Irish Lord Deputyship, Thomas Wentworth wrote a treatise entitled 'A survey of the government of Ireland'.[1] Wentworth was the first viceroy in the seventeenth century to have no Irish connections before his appointment, and hence he needed to inform himself on the country and its customs. There was little that was new in the treatise, indeed much of it seems to have been derived from reading John Davies's *A discovery of the true causes why Ireland was never entirely subdued* (1612). Like Davies, Wentworth identified two crucial reasons why Ireland had been an unstable entity in the past. The first was that large estates had been given to Strongbow and his fellow Anglo-Norman settlers in the twelfth century, and this had resulted in the establishment of palatinates that were difficult to control. This was a situation he would easily recognise, when he came to Ireland, as being far from simply a problem in the past. Three weeks after his swearing-in Wentworth wrote to the Earl of Arundel:

I find myself in the society of a strange people, their own privates altogether their study without any regard at all to the public. . . . I find this kingdom abandoned for these late years to every man that could please himself to purchase what he best liked for his money.[2]

What Wentworth wanted to create in Ireland was a rather different world, familiar to other powerful European royal servants such as Richelieu and Olivares in France and Spain respectively, in which the priority for those in positions of power was not their own profit but his understanding of royal service, although those two things were not necessarily incompatible. As he counselled the young Earl of Ormond in 1634, 'That power your birth and quality give you in this kingdom [use] the right way, that is to the service of the crown.'[3] Wentworth had come face to face with one of the key problems in the governance of Ireland: how to delegate royal authority without either losing control of it or putting too much discretionary power in the hands of subordinates.

The second reason why Ireland had been so problematic in the past, in Wentworth's reading of Davies, was that it was a mistake to try to segregate the settlers from the natives. A better policy was to try to bring them together under the umbrella of the common law. This was a more challenging idea. Given the exceptional circumstances to be found in Ireland whereby the crown had alienated, or been cheated out of, all its assets so that, as Wentworth put it, 'all the crown revenue [is] reduced into fee farms . . . so as . . . there is little left either to benefit the king's servants or to improve his own revenues by', the question arose whether the common law could achieve its aims of delivering royal justice.[4] In short, had the procedures of the common law and the royal administration not been perverted by those who were supposed to uphold them? Wentworth could not deny that Magna Carta and the common law operated in Ireland and provided the touchstone of royal authority, and throughout his Irish career he always worked through established structures rather than creating new ones. However, he could argue that the exceptional circumstances of Ireland called for exceptional solutions to its problems.

Indeed, the recent introduction of common law as a result of Elizabethan conquest might even require such exceptional measures, since, unlike England, Ireland outside the Pale had no tradition of common law. The argument here rested on a legal case of 1607, Calvin's case, which had dealt with the rights of those born in Scotland after the union of the crowns. Among other things this case established the principle that conquered countries could be governed by the will of the king alone, although that right was, presumably, limited by natural equity. It was, for Wentworth, an effective argument, since it swept aside both Old English and New English ideas of rights, and hence it proved a dangerous precedent. The principal area of concern was the administration of justice, and especially the law-giving and enforcing functions of the Lord Deputy and council. In particular, the expansion of the equitable jurisdiction of the Irish Privy Council under Wentworth at the expense of the common-law courts and parliament gave cause for serious concern among many contemporaries. The key issue of Wentworth's administration was therefore to be the relationship of the executive government to the law. Wentworth, with some justification, might have argued that his executive powers were simply roles vested in his office of Irish Lord Deputy whereby he had extraordinarily wide powers when compared with other royal officials, including the king's ministers, within the British Isles. The viceroy, from the sixteenth century, as the personal representative of the king, could make leases and land grants, issue proclamations and pardons, deliver judgments, make treaties, proclaim rebels and introduce martial law. What constrained him was his instructions from the king, usually a rather vague and imprecise document. This was a subject that Wentworth studied in some detail, and among his papers are copies of royal instructions to Lords Deputy from 1611 and a variety of Irish state papers. As Wentworth saw it, both the character of landed society and the nature of the viceroyalty made an eloquent case for Irish exceptionalism.

In short, Wentworth's reading of Davies's analysis of the Irish problem had brought him to a position directly opposite that of his instructor. What Davies had tried to do was to integrate the world of England and Ireland through the common law, and in doing so separate them from the civil-law tradition in Scotland. The logic of Wentworth's argument was that, notwithstanding the workings of the common law, in both areas what was needed was a decoupling of the English and Irish systems of justice and administration. This was not a view much liked by the Old English lawyers, who looked on the king and common law as their bulwark against exactly the sort of argument for increasing executive power that Wentworth made. In the sixteenth century they had happily appealed to the king in London over the heads of viceroys who put forward similar arguments. To contemporaries, Wentworth's arguments looked suspiciously like what they would describe at his trial in 1641 as tyranny.

In Wentworth's analysis, the only way to grapple with the basic exceptionalism of Irish society was a multi-pronged approach which mobilised the rights and powers of the holder of the anomalous post of Irish Lord Deputy. First, land, the basis of political power and wealth, had to be more effectively managed to the king's advantage than hitherto. This involved a range of strategies, but the most prominent was the rearrangement of land tenure known as plantation, though without the sort of social restructuring associated with the Ulster scheme. Secondly, the institutions of state needed to be overhauled to ensure that they too operated in the crown's interests. Thirdly, religious policy needed tightening to reflect royal will. Finally, it needed to be demonstrated to the inhabitants of Ireland that their country really was a kingdom in which royal rights should prevail and that it was not a centre of colonial exploitation for the benefit of settlers. In short, Wentworth's strategy was an experiment in the social rules of governance.

## LAND AND ITS OWNERS

Since the ownership of land was the principal source of wealth and social prestige in seventeenth-century Ireland, the matter required urgent attention. Wentworth's genius in dealing with land lay not in instituting new procedures or devising new strategies to deal with what he thought were abuses, but in identifying weaknesses in the existing system. This he achieved with devastating effect through the Commission for Defective Titles. This was not a new idea. In 1606 there had been a similar commission which had offered new grants, and hence tenurial security, of property where the title was doubtful because of the way in which the land had been acquired. Wentworth reinvigorated the idea in 1634 as a revenue-raising measure for the crown. His move could even be defended as a response to Article 24 of the Graces, which demanded that a sixty-one-year title should be enough in law to guarantee security of tenure. New land grants would solve this problem at a price. At the simplest, crown rents on property regranted under the scheme were increased. According to one list of 1636, in the case of about a hundred proprietors the old rents were increased by over 50 per cent, while new rents in excess of £138 were imposed. Moreover, the terms on which new grants were made were often tenurially less favourable than those already existing. Those in the plantation of Ulster had their tenures changed from common soccage to the more burdensome feudal tenure of knight service, which carried a range of obligations that would further enrich the crown through the Court of Wards (discussed below). The precise number of new grants taken out is not known, but it was alleged that on one occasion 150 letters patent were declared void, and certainly pressure was brought to bear on some landowners to take out new grants for their property.

If the Commission for Defective Titles was a generalised way of dealing with the problem of land, Wentworth also adopted more focused approaches. Some of the specific problems which related to land were inherited by Wentworth from earlier initiatives. In the case of the settlement of Londonderry by the London Companies, the problem of the failure to comply with the terms of the grant went back more than twenty years. One settler who had been there before the Londoners, Sir Thomas Phillips, regarded them as having restricted his expansion and continually pointed out to London their failures. An inquiry of 1628, finding negligence on the part of the Londoners, had been reinforced by a collection of material put together by Phillips in the following year and this resulted in the pursuit of a Court of Star Chamber suit against the city of London between 1630 and 1635. Wentworth almost inevitably interfered with proceedings, claiming that the customs of the ports of Derry and Coleraine, which the city of London held without payment, was 'a liberty unfit to be in grant to any subject' and demanded they be resumed.[5] The judgment in 1635 fined the city £70,000 and resumed their patent. In 1636 Wentworth decided to make a personal bid for the lease of the property with an annual rent of £8,000 and £32,000 for the customs. Others in England and Scotland had their eye on the property, including James Hamilton, third Marquis of Hamilton in Scotland, and his partner the Earl of Antrim. Sir John Clotworthy from Antrim headed a settler consortium also hopeful of success. No bid succeeded since the king decided to keep the property for himself, but the episode is revealing of the complex and porous world of

Scotland, England and Ireland within which Wentworth moved and drew his ideas. In addition, the failure of some of those English and Scottish bidders for the Londonderry property and other Irish land or offices under Wentworth would have repercussions for the Lord Deputy in the longer term.

A landed problem with a less venerable lineage was that of the O'Byrnes' country, which ran along the coast of County Wicklow from Delgany to Arklow and inland into south County Wicklow. In the late 1620s there had been threats of confiscation and plantation of this property. The Earl of Carlisle had obtained a grant of part of the property, which by the early 1630s he was proposing to sell to two New English property speculators, Sir William Parsons and Lord Ranelagh. Wentworth, however, wished to exploit what seemed to be a weakness in the title to royal advantage, but had no desire to annoy Carlisle, whose support he needed at court in London. In 1634 the Lord Deputy began inquiring into the royal title to the O'Byrnes' country, but with a promise of favourable treatment for those holding property. The proceedings were characterised by a good deal of duplicity, particularly in the buying out of Carlisle's interest, and it was not until 1639 that real progress was made towards some sort of settlement. The result of the reorganisation by 1641, as it appears in the Books of Survey and Distribution, was that the O'Byrnes secured legal possession of some 19,900 acres, and settlers, mainly along the coast, acquired 23,300 acres, largely split between Parsons and Wentworth. A number of Old English speculators, such as Richard Bellings, also acquired land as part of this settlement. The real economic potential of this area lay in timber exports and in the closely allied activity of iron-making. While Wentworth encouraged both activities on his estates, establishing an ironworks there in 1638, the coming of war in 1641, in which Wicklow was one of the earliest counties affected, meant that little profit was realised. That exploitation was to be more effective after 1660.

The final land problem that Wentworth inherited was the plantation of the barony of Ormond in Tipperary. In 1630 Charles I had instructed the Lords Justices that he intended to plant Ormond. This was, in many ways, a logical development from the nearby midland plantations in the 1620s. The plan seems to have been that a quarter of the land should go to settlers and that this would be divided into lots of 1,500 and 2,000 acres; the settlers would then be introduced and three towns built. The remainder of the property was to be given to native freeholders, who were to hold it directly from the king. How far this plan progressed is not known, and it was not until 1637 that crown title was to be found in the area. In the interim Wentworth reached an agreement with one of the landlords in the area, James Butler, twelfth Earl of Ormond, by which the latter would have a fourth part of the planted lands for himself. This arrangement would undoubtedly have increased the earl's local power at the expense of the native freeholders, but it was not implemented. Royal title was found and surveys were made in 1639, but then the process was cut short by the crisis of 1640 and Wentworth's impeachment. In addition to these schemes, Wentworth also involved himself in lesser expropriations including the establishment of royal title to the barony of Ida (Idough) in County Kilkenny and its subsequent sale to his cousin Christopher Wandesford, the Irish Master of the Rolls.

Of course, Wentworth did press ahead with more extensive settlements himself. The most significant of these lay in Connacht. The weakness in arrangements for Connacht landholding had been signalled almost five years before Wentworth's arrival in Ireland. Article 25 of the Graces had sought to regularise the landholding position of the Connacht gentry. Questions had been repeatedly raised about their land title. By 1610 some Connacht landowners believed that the 1585 Composition agreements, if only they had been enrolled in Chancery, would have secured their land title under common law. This misconception was to have been resolved by the 1613–15 parliament, but it failed to do so. In 1615 James I, possibly as a result of lobbying by the largest of the Connacht landowners, Richard Burke, fourth Earl of Clanricard, authorised the acceptance of new surrenders of land in Connacht and Thomond with a view to regranting the lands by patent. Inquisitions were held in 1617, but opposition emerged to the scheme from those ambitious to profit from wardships, alienations, fines and other potentially lucrative sources of income from defects in Connacht land titles. In consequence, the planned patents were never enrolled in Chancery. Attempts by the 1622 commissioners to regularise the position, and ensure a greater flow of income to the crown, failed because the Earl of Clanricard thought it might impinge upon his rights. Tenurial instability attracted discussion of the possibility of plantation in the 1620s, but this was neutralised by the power of Clanricard. By the beginning of the 1630s the Earl of Cork among others was talking about a Connacht plantation, excluding County Galway so as to avoid confrontation with the Earl of Clanricard, the bulk of whose land lay in that county. Viscount Ranelagh, one of the Vice-Presidents of Connacht, was openly preparing the way for a plantation in Counties Mayo, Roscommon and Sligo despite opposition from the Old English families who had acquired land there, not least the Dillons who had extensive property interests in Mayo and Roscommon. Indeed, the Dillons had entered into the spirit of local Connacht society and had even sponsored a traditional bardic *duanaire* compiled in their honour which provided them with impeccable cultural credentials as though they were native Irish. The arrival of Wentworth saw a significant broadening of the base of the proposed Connacht plantation scheme so that it would include County Galway. This placed the Lord Deputy in direct conflict with that other powerful courtier, the Earl of Clanricard. The involvement of Clanricard, who had a long history of effectively excluding royal authority from his property, together with the awareness that if Wentworth's strategy succeeded in County Galway then all Old English land titles were in doubt, entrenched Old English opposition further. The defence of the Connacht land titles was entrusted to the earl's agent and lawyer, John Donellan, and the earl's brother John Burke, Viscount Clanmorris, in consultation with the Galway lawyer Patrick Darcy. In the face of this, in 1635 Wentworth began the process of establishing crown title to the lands as a prelude to resuming them into royal hands for the plantation. Juries were carefully selected, and in some cases bribed, and they found royal title in Mayo, Sligo and Roscommon. Wentworth himself arrived at Clanricard's house at Portumna, where the County Galway inquisition was to be taken. The Galway jurors, however, were not prepared to find royal title for the entire county. As a result of their defiance, they were bound to appear at the Court of Castle Chamber in Dublin to account for their actions.

In these circumstances, the Old English behaved as they usually did when there was trouble with a provincial official such as a Lord Deputy: they appealed directly to the king in London. This strategy was facilitated by the presence of Clanricard at court, where he had been active for over twenty years, and a petition was sent to the king asking him to receive a delegation. In August 1635 two Galway lawyers, Patrick Darcy and Richard Martin, and one prominent landowner,

Roger O'Shaughnessy, were appointed to present the case to the king. This was undoubtedly the most dangerous crisis of Wentworth's administration. If Clanricard and the Galway gentry were to triumph, it would mean the end of Wentworth's political career in Ireland and the destruction of his most important advantage, his link with the king. On the other hand, should he defeat Clanricard, it would be a considerable triumph for the power of the Dublin administration over provincial magnates. Wentworth asked the king that the delegation be allowed a formal hearing, be required to present their proposals in writing, be arrested for leaving Ireland without licence, and then sent home for legal action to be taken against them. To all this the king agreed. With the death of the Earl of Clanricard in November 1635, Wentworth's triumph seemed complete.

However, matters were not to end quite so neatly. Martin, Darcy and O'Shaughnessy remained at liberty until well into 1636, and Old English resentment toward the Lord Deputy was clear to all. Beginning in May 1636 the Galway jury was tried in Castle Chamber. The trial lasted until February 1637, during which time the jurors retreated slowly from their previous recalcitrant position until they finally accepted the reality of finding royal title to the County Galway land. Ulick Burke, the new Earl of Clanricard, however, knew how to play the politics of the court and, unlike Wentworth, was near the king. In February 1639 he managed to extract from the king a regrant of all his lands, thus effectively removing much of County Galway from the proposed Connacht settlement. By 1640 the idea of a Connacht plantation was dead. Some land may have been allocated, but settlers could not be induced to come to the province, and by then political developments elsewhere were demanding attention.

The sort of reorganisation of land tenure that was proposed in the province of Connacht was not simply intended to bring short-term financial gain to the crown. Wentworth also saw it as part of a longer-term strategy for the improvement of Ireland's finances by increasing trade and hence generating customs revenue for the crown. In the process, of course, Wentworth himself became rich. In the late 1630s he controlled the customs farm, dominated the tobacco monopoly, and held property in Counties Wicklow, Wexford, Kildare and Sligo. His annual income from Ireland was more than twice that from his Yorkshire property. His critics would accuse him of lining his own pockets, but that is to misunderstand the role of the Irish Lord

Deputy. The Lord Deputyship could only work on the basis of public exploitation of private power. Thus a powerful Lord Deputy, such as Wentworth, saw no contradiction in enhancing his private wealth, because it formed the basis of his public authority.

## INSTITUTIONAL EFFICIENCY

As in the case of landholding, Wentworth's approach to administrative reform was not to innovate but rather to use to the full the powers inherent in the office of Lord Deputy. In the main he used institutions which already existed in Ireland or for which there was precedent to pursue his aims. Established institutions could also be used in new and innovative ways, as was the case with parliament. In the parliament that met in 1634 the House of Commons had 254 members, of whom 112 were Catholic and 142 Protestant. In the Lords there were fourteen New English peers, thanks to the creations of the 1620s, twenty-four of Old English backgrounds, and six from the native Irish grouping. However, this house was dominated by Wentworth's party, led by the Earl of Ormond and Lord Esmond, through the use of proxies from absentee peers and the votes of the bishops.

This parliament had a number of tasks. The most urgent was financial, since Ireland was currently running a deficit of some £20,000 a year (with cumulative arrears of £80,000). That had been plugged in the early 1630s by the payments from the Graces, which had been extended in the hope of having the concessions confirmed. Money in the form of a subsidy was needed, but the price to be paid would be political concessions, most importantly confirmation of the Graces. Wentworth, however, was determined not to be dependent on local influences for financial resources. Much of his economic policy for Ireland was driven by the need for financial solvency. His introduction of a monopoly on tobacco imports and sales and his reform of the customs was intended to generate increased royal revenue. More indirectly, his attempt to increase manufactures in Ireland by controlling the export of unprocessed goods, such as linen yarn and wool, in the expectation that they would be worked up into cloth, was driven by the greater customs yield for manufactured goods. The export of raw wool was controlled through a licensing system, and Wentworth himself set up a weaving operation at Chapelizod, near Dublin, to encourage the manufacture of linen cloth. Neither plan had much effect on Irish economic life.

The second task for the parliament was to modernise the legislative framework, particularly in relation to land law. The Lord Deputy's plan to ensure that the parliament passed this legislation was not to rely on traditional Protestant–Catholic divisions, but rather to create his own 'deputy's party' which could hold the balance of power. What lay at the root of this tactic was the realisation that inherited legal controls, and particularly Poynings' Law, could be used to obstruct parliamentary actions rather than to control government initiative, as had originally been intended. The first session of the parliament was largely given over to a discussion of the necessity that the Graces should be passed into law, drafting the bills and passing the subsidies. Once the financial business of the parliament was completed, Wentworth had little interest in the Graces and refused to transmit the bills to London. The message was clear: by re-examining Poynings' Law, Wentworth had ensured that parliament could do nothing without royal authority and could communicate officially with the crown only through the Irish council. Parliament, as in contemporary France, had been reduced to the subordinate status of a legislative agency which could give or withhold statutory effect to executive policy but could do no more. What the Old English were given was not confirmation of the Graces as they had been promised, but a proposal that only ten should be enacted. These excluded the most important ones relating to land title, while a number of others were to be left to the king's pleasure. Perhaps understandably the second session of the parliament was fractious, but in April 1635 the parliament was dissolved having achieved Wentworth's principal objective.

Wentworth's chief reliance was not on institutions such as parliament, but rather on those that strengthened the executive arm of government. In particular, his use of the two executive tribunals, the Court of Castle Chamber and the Court of Wards, reveals his strategy for using institutions in the government of Ireland. The Court of Castle Chamber was the Irish equivalent of Star Chamber in London and dealt with the same sort of business: riots, conspiracy, perjury, forgery and extortion. It was not a Wentworthian innovation and had operated in Ireland sporadically through the sixteenth century. It was firmly under the control of the executive, the main members of the court being the Lord Deputy, the Lord Chancellor, the Treasurer and the Vice-Treasurer. Wentworth quickly moved to gain control of the court. In 1635 the Vice-Treasurer, Lord Mountnorris, was court-martialled and removed from his government posts, including his position in Castle Chamber. In the process, Wentworth ensured that the other posts in the court went to his own supporters, leaving him in control of the institution by 1636. This court became the main agency used by Wentworth to deal with dissenting voices. It was swift and effective, having the power to impose large fines, though it did not have the death penalty available to it. The court was used against Richard Boyle, Earl of Cork, over his ownership of church lands and against the Galway jury in relation to the Connacht plantation. But these were only the tip of the iceberg of business dealt with by a court that met more than twice a week.

The second institution on which Wentworth relied, the Court of Wards and Liveries, was again an older body; it had been established in 1615 and revamped by the 1622 commission. Its main function was to raise revenue for the crown by exploiting feudal duties such as wardship, liveries and alienations. Under Wentworth the existing system was tightened, including the collection of considerable arrears. The network of officials who monitored royal rights in land was enlarged, and inquisitions into alienations and wardships became more common. The quest for information, and with it a firmer grip on royal rights, was a marked feature of this aspect of Wentworth's government. Moreover, the workings of the Commission for Defective Titles drew more property into the net of the courts as new grants under the commission imposed new feudal duties on property that had been previously exempt, a fact that annoyed the New English settlers in the plantations who previously had held their property on favourable conditions. The result of all this was that the court generated an average of £7,000 a year between 1630 and 1640, a considerable rise on previous revenues for the body. This came at a considerable cost. It was a political irritant to both Catholics and Protestants, who found themselves increasingly drawn into the control of the court to their financial disadvantage.

## REACTIONS

Contemporaries left few traces of their reactions to Wentworth's ideas and actions before his trial in 1641 when their indignation flowed in full spate. Nevertheless, it is possible to trace in the writings of two individuals their reactions to Wentworth's constitutional experiment.

The first is the Irish Auditor General, Sir James Ware. Before the 1630s Ware had been involved in tracing the succession of Church of Ireland bishops in a project akin to that of Archbishop James Ussher. In 1633 he shifted direction and produced a collection of documents on the history of Ireland dedicated to Wentworth, declaring: 'These histories do afford the knowledge of former times and the good use which may be made of them by any who have leisure, desire and ability to polish a lasting structure of Irish affairs.' One of these texts was particularly important 'for matter of history and policy'. This was Edmund Spenser's *View of the present state of Ireland*, originally written in 1596 but not published until 1633. It was unusual since all the other texts in Ware's collection were medieval, whereas this was almost contemporary. If it was intended as a source for 'policy', it appears to be rather out of date, urging as it did a military conquest of Ireland that was long over. Moreover, the language was toned down by Ware, and a number of passages reflecting on people still alive were removed. Reviewing the events of the 1590s are not the reason for the publication of the *View* in the 1630s. Rather, it was aimed at justifying the two planks of Wentworth's approach to Ireland.

First, in contrast to Davies's advocacy of the conquest of Ireland by the common law, Spenser argued that the English system of common law would not work in Ireland,

> for they [the Irish] were otherwise affected, and yet do so remain, so as the same laws (me seems) can ill fit with their disposition, or work that reformation that is wished. The laws ought to be fashioned unto the manners and conditions of the people, to whom they are meant, and not to be imposed upon them according to the simple rule of right, for then . . . instead of good they may work ill and pervert justice to extreme injustice.[6]

Here is Wentworth's constitutional exceptionalism writ clear and given the cultural authority of the poet Spenser. This exceptionalist argument was further developed by Spenser in his discussion of the office of Lord Deputy, another area of particular interest to Wentworth. Spenser's view of the Lord Deputy's authority was 'that it should be more ample and absolute than it is, and that he should have uncontrolled power to do any thing that he with the advisement of the Council should think fit meet to be done'.[7]

Secondly, Spenser's work provided an explanation for Wentworth of how the situation in Ireland could have grown so out of control. For Spenser, the weak point in the Irish polity was the Old English, who were once English but had temporised with the Irish enemy. In relation to the medieval settlers, he commented how 'through greatness of their late conquests and seignories they grew insolent, and bent both that regal authority and also their private powers, one against another, to the utter subversion of themselves'. More importantly, Ireland led settlers to allow laws to be slackly enforced, so that they 'grow more loose and careless of their duty, so that they become flat libertines and fall to licentiousness, more boldly daring to disobey the law'.[8] This was exactly the situation which Wentworth had described among the New English settlers in the 1630s. To redress this seemed to require the sort of agenda that Spenser had proposed, including plantations. Ware's publication of Spenser's *View* can be seen as providing a justification, drawn from the practical experience of a distinguished sixteenth-century settler, of the Wentworthian plan for reform of Irish law and curtailing the licentiousness of the settler community.

If Ware provided Wentworth with historical justification for his actions, another writer, the lay Catholic Michael Kearney, in 1635 produced a very different commentary on the Lord Deputy's activities in a preface written to an English translation of Geoffrey Keating's *Foras feasa ar Éirinn*. Kearney's work was a direct attack on Spenser's *View*, citing it as an example of a Machiavellian project of 'plantations, displantations, transplantations, translations, dispersions and scattering' designed to undermine the position of native Irish Catholics. Kearney drew particular attention to Spenser's antipathy to the Old English, who were 'hated and undervalued' despite the fact that they were 'tractable and ameasurable to the civil government and common laws of England'. Kearney had a clear view of loyalty to the crown, claiming that Catholics had to be loyal to both king and pope, and asserted that they would never 'forsake the anciently professed Catholic Roman religion nor their true allegiance to the imperial crown of England'. Reflecting on policies implemented since the reign of Elizabeth in respect of language, education, religion and wardship, and most especially 'the hateful confiscations usually made of their lands and goods', Kearney pointed out that, in a contemporary context, these policies 'did undermine their very hearts'.

This was no mere catalogue of past wrongs: they were issues of current concern in the 1630s. The immediate context was the parliament of 1634 and the failure of the Graces. The proposed plantation of Ormond, with the support of James Butler, twelfth Earl of Ormond, would have serious consequences for the gentry in the Tipperary region where the account was written. The colonial process as projected by Spenser and implemented by Wentworth was not only a threat to Irish land titles, but fundamentally undermined the honour and respect which Old English Catholics, in particular, believed was their entitlement. In contrast, those who had recently arrived in Ireland along with Wentworth and had 'received advancement in honour and riches beyond their merits or deserts' threatened to turn Ireland into a skeleton of its former self, 'a withered stump of a tree left without fruit, flower, leaves or bark'. Although the 1630s seemed to be peaceful, Kearney's analysis of the challenge to the 'ancient constitution' posed by the social, political and religious changes then being implemented, reveals an undercurrent of opposition to the policies of Wentworth and his administration.[9]

**REMAKING RELIGION**
Given the radical overhaul that most of the institutions of state received under Wentworth, it would have been strange if the church had escaped. As in other areas of Irish life, two aspects of the Church of Ireland fell under scrutiny: belief and structure. In so far as the doctrines of the Church of Ireland had been codified in the seventeenth century, that had been done in the 104 Irish Articles agreed at the convocation of 1615. These articles drew on existing confessions, including the Thirty-Nine Articles of the Church of England, the *Book of homilies* and the Lambeth Articles of 1595, which Queen Elizabeth had refused to agree to. They also drew on the European Protestant inheritance of the doctrine of John Calvin. While the Church of England had certainly been Calvinist in inclination before the 1620s, its articles of belief were vague on certain matters. The Irish Articles of 1615 left no one in any doubt as to what side of the theological discussion that church stood on. Article 12 was clear on the crucial issue of predestination or election: 'God hath predestined some unto life and reprobated some unto death', a world away from the vaguely worded Article 17 of the Thirty-Nine Articles. Article 80 of the Irish Articles went yet further in identifying the pope

as 'that man of sin' foretold in Scripture, or Antichrist. What this reflected was a church by the 1630s theologically far removed from its English sister: a church inclined to the godly end of the spectrum and which emphasised the common heritage of Protestants of different traditions in opposition to Catholicism. As Henry Leslie, the future Bishop of Down and Connor, said in a sermon at Drogheda in 1622, 'Contention extinguishes the very life of religion which is brotherly love and therefore they who make so much ado about ceremonies had need to take heed that in the meantime they lose not that which is most precious. . . . Let us labour to reconcile ourselves and at length to embrace unity.'[10] In these circumstances, it was easy to accommodate those Scots of a Presbyterian disposition, even radicals such as Robert Blair at Bangor in County Down, into the Church of Ireland.

The existence of the Irish Articles of 1615 had an implication other than the straightforwardly theological. Politically they appeared dangerous, since in 1629 they had been used by the opposition in the English parliament in their 'Resolutions on religion' and hence could be seen as a rallying-point against the king's religious innovations, which seemed to be moving the church away from Calvinism. More importantly, they implied that the Irish church was somehow distinct from its English counterpart. This seemed a confusing situation. Both churches used the same liturgy and spoke the same religious vocabulary. The Dublin printing-presses produced almost no devotional literature in the early seventeenth century, leaving English published works to fill the gap. As a result, the spiritual language of Protestants in England and Ireland was indistinguishable. Moreover, while the Irish church granted dispensations, appeals from the Irish ecclesiastical courts continued to be heard in the English High Court of Delegates, implying that the Irish church was inferior to that in England. This theological and administrative confusion was exactly the sort of situation that Wentworth disliked and specialised in reforming.

The first strand in the Irish church's arrangements which seemed clearly in need of reform according to Wentworth was its theological formulations. From the 1590s an alternative set of propositions about the nature of God's grace and the prospects of salvation for people had been circulating in England. Such views gave much greater weight to free will against the determinism of Calvinism and declared that

Christ died for all rather than for the elect. Thus the centre of worship was the sacramental worship of the wider community rather than godly preaching intended to gather together the elect. This high view of ministry and the sacraments, together with an appropriate setting for their celebration, seemed to some to be flirting with Catholicism, but by the early 1620s it was gaining hold at the court in London and Charles I was a firm advocate. As might be expected following his appointment as Archbishop of Canterbury in 1633, William Laud, was a strong proponent of this Arminian view, as it became known, as was Wentworth. In practice it was these two men rather than the king directly who moved to reform the Church of Ireland.

In the eyes of Wentworth, the Irish church with its Calvinistic ideas seemed backward and in severe need of modernisation. The first task was to provide a framework for reform, a framework conveniently provided by the Thirty-Nine Articles of the Church of England and the Church of England canons of 1604. In the latter case this was a significant new departure, since Ireland had previously not had any codified body of canon law. Much had been done by custom and precedent, so that there was considerable variation in, for example, the way in which parishes were administered. The context in which reform was to be achieved was the convocation which met in tandem with the Irish parliament of 1634–6. In the event, this proved not to be as simple as Wentworth had anticipated. The lower house of clergy and upper house of bishops both resisted the adoption of his new framework. There was a wide range of motives at work here. Some, such as James Ussher, Archbishop of Armagh, were motivated by a defence of the Calvinist consensus developed by the 1615 Articles and a fear of the apparent Catholic tendency associated with the new theological practices. Others were less theologically minded and resisted in defence of the perceived constitutional independence of the Church of Ireland and in opposition to attempts to impose uniformity. The grounds of the debate were clearest on the proposal to adopt the English canons of 1604 in the Irish church. These were outrightly rejected. A committee was duly appointed to draft a set of Irish canons; and when these were not to the Lord Deputy's liking, particularly on the issue of subscribing to the Thirty-Nine Articles, Wentworth himself intervened to improve the committee's draft. In the end opposition to the adoption of the Thirty-Nine Articles collapsed in the face of Wentworth's unremitting exercise of viceregal power (although the 1615 Articles were not revoked), but the 1604 canons were not adopted. Instead a new set were drafted, but these were almost entirely based on a number of English precedents. The result may, at best, be called a draw between Ussher and Wentworth, but in practice power was moving in the direction of the latter. From 1635 Ussher effectively withdrew from the running of the church, leaving it in the hands of Wentworth's enforcer, John Bramhall, Bishop of Derry.

In implementing this pattern of reform, the first problem was to recruit clergy with suitably reforming views who could be trusted to oversee change. In the eyes of the reformers, many of the Irish clergy were deeply suspect, and the main recruiting ground for the new elite was to be England or, in a few cases, Scotland from the ranks of those who sympathised with the reform programme there. Fifteen Church of Ireland bishoprics had to be filled in the 1630s. Almost all the appointees came with impeccable credentials. John Atherton, Bishop of Waterford and Lismore from 1636, was a staunch supporter of the new order, and William Chappel, promoted to Cork and Ross in 1638, had been tried out as Provost of Trinity College Dublin before his elevation. George Webb, appointed Bishop of Limerick in 1634, was a former chaplain to the king, and Henry Tilson in Elphin and Robert Sibthorp in Kilfenora were associated with the Lord Deputy. There was also a group of Scots loyalists, Henry Leslie of Down and Connor, Archibald Hamilton in Cashel, and John Leslie in Raphoe. However, there are hints that all was not perfect. Robert Ussher, a cousin of the Archbishop of Armagh and no lover of reform, was appointed to Kildare in 1635, and Lewis Jones, appointed to Killaloe in 1633, was later accused of being favourable towards the Covenanters in Scotland in the late 1630s. At the level of cathedral deans, the position is less clear. Twenty-five deaneries were filled in the 1630s, some more than once, and a few were exchanges. Some of these deans would later go on to be bishops, such as William Chappel, Dean of Cashel in 1633, or Henry Tilson, Dean of Christ Church, Dublin. Others came from Wentworth's immediate circle or directly from England, including George Horley, Dean of Ross in 1637, who came from Westminster. Michael Wandesford, Dean of Limerick in 1635, was the brother of Wentworth's Master of the Rolls and later Lord Deputy; Robert Forward in Dromore in 1638 was one of Wentworth's chaplains; Thomas Grey in Ardfert was also patronised by Wentworth, and Peter

Wentworth, Dean of Armagh in 1635, may well have been a relation of the Lord Deputy. In only a few cases was the reform as thoroughgoing as at Christ Church Cathedral in Dublin, where between 1632 and 1635 the entire chapter was replaced, with a single exception. Two members had died, but the rest resigned, presumably under pressure. Four of the new members were brought from England, but most of the new chapter were recruited from among the Lord Deputy's chaplains and hence were familiar with the new style of churchmanship. These appointees were clearly to be used as a pool from which to supply the wider church. Four members of the chapter became bishops before 1640, and others were appointed deans elsewhere.

As part of this process of introducing new personnel, there emerged a number of key reforming individuals. Most important was John Bramhall, who held the lucrative bishopric of Derry, and was the main architect of church reform in the 1630s. Bramhall's strategy was to ensure conformity with the new Articles and canons of 1634. Other bishops followed suit, prosecuting nonconformity in the Court of High Commission. Not surprisingly, the force of this was felt most where nonconformity was strongest: in Ulster. In Down diocese Henry Leslie summoned five nonconforming ministers of strongly Presbyterian backgrounds to a 'conference' associated with his visitation in 1636 at which the issues of kneeling when receiving the sacrament, the use of the Book of Common Prayer, holy days and the sign of the cross at baptism were given full vent. Leslie was tempted to make some concessions, but the arrival of Bramhall half way through the debate put a stop to that. The increasing pressure placed by Bramhall on the diocese of Down led the principal Scottish ministers and some 150 of their followers to take ship for North America, although, thanks to a leak, they had to return to Ulster, from where many of the clergy made their way to Scotland. Presbyterianism seems to have been identified as the most significant problem in the Irish context because of its evangelical nature. Religious revival had broken out in Ulster in 1625 at Six Mile Water in County Antrim, producing religious fervour that was difficult to control.

Catholicism, on the other hand, was equally nonconformist and probably more dangerous because the church was much better organised in the 1630s than it had been even a decade earlier. On the evidence of episcopal reports to Rome, there seems to have been a good deal more activity in Catholic Ireland. Bishop Egan of Elphin reported that he had forty-two parish priests in 1637, compared with thirteen in 1625. From Waterford Bishop Comerford reported an increase of nineteen parish clergy and five religious between 1630 and 1639. There are also reports of mass-houses being built. While Wentworth had no love for Catholicism, he allowed the *de facto* toleration that made this expansion possible. Part of the explanation for this state of affairs may be that the Lord Deputy did not perceive Catholicism as a serious short-term threat. In the 1630s the potential authority of the church was weakened by disputes between secular and regular clergy, especially the Franciscans, about their roles in the newly reorganised ecclesiastical structure. In Dublin this resulted in excommunications of a number of secular clergy, such as Paul Harris, for their preaching and writings against the regulars, whom they regarded as usurping the rights and payments due to parish priests. Another part of the rationale for the Lord Deputy's apparent toleration seems to have been purely a political one, Wentworth considering that it was not wise to launch an attack on Catholicism until the Church of Ireland was adequately reformed.

While the internal Church of Ireland reform was to be spearheaded by a number of bishops, the evidence for the impact of the theological shift in the practice of worship in Ireland is limited. In the case of one of the power houses of reform, Christ Church Cathedral, Dublin, the evidence is unambiguous. According to a Dublin diarist in June 1633, 'The communion table at Christ Church was set up after the manner of an altar, north and south, and upon the Sunday following viz 23 June the epistle and gospel and ten commandments were read there by Mr Atherton, prebend of St John's.'[11] Previously the communion table had stood in the middle of the choir, but it was not fixed, raised up or paved around. The effect for the congregation was to orientate them away from the pulpit and reading desk—the focus of Calvinist preaching—to the sacramental activity of the altar. The physical setting of the communion table was improved, and new communion silver was acquired. The church itself was extensively repaired and the role of music in the liturgy expanded. The precincts of the cathedral were also cleaned and some of the worst eyesores removed. In the prebendal churches associated with the cathedral there was innovation. The Dublin parish of St John saw the emergence of a strong sacramental tradition. During the 1620s, when churchwardens' accounts first become available, the parish of St John celebrated communion on five occasions a year, rising to ten by 1633. The Laudian reforms of the late 1630s resulted in the communion table being railed in and raised up and the area around the chancel improved to create a symbolic distance between clergy and people. All this was done without local opposition. The limited evidence available for other cathedrals and churches does not suggest much in the way of innovation. At Elphin the Laudian precentor, James Croxton, reported in 1634 that he had celebrated Easter with 'due ceremony', and later in Kilkenny he introduced confession in the Laudian manner.[12] In Cork and Kildare the cathedrals showed little inclination to change their traditional forms of worship and neither did the other Dublin cathedral of St Patrick. The closest that St Patrick's came to this sort of innovation was the clash between Wentworth and the earl of Cork in 1633–4 about the location of the Boyle funeral monument within the cathedral. Boyle wished to place it at the east end of the church, while Wentworth believed that this showed disrespect to the sacred space where the communion table should stand, and Boyle was forced to back down. There are only hints of lay resistance to the religious innovations of the 1630s. As the godly settler Sir John Clotworthy in Ulster wrote in 1635, 'We want no addition that the wit of man can invent to make the worship of God pompous in outward but penurious in inward part.'[13] It therefore seems unlikely that liturgical reform struck deep roots in Ireland.

The final, and perhaps the most intractable, problem was to provide the finance for church reform. The church was, in practice, funded by its endowments of land; yet, as Wentworth soon discovered, the difference between theory and practice was great. This problem was not unique to Ireland. In Scotland a similar situation had been solved by the Act of Revocation of 1625 that had restored land to the church. In Ireland the visitation of 1634 had indicated the scale of the problem. In 1634, of 959 rectories returned in the visitation outside Ulster, where the parish structure had been remodelled at the plantation, some 594, or 62 per cent, were in the hands of laymen. More worryingly, where comparison can be made with the visitation of 1615, the situation had deteriorated. In 1615 some 56 per cent of rectories were impropriate. This problem of extracting an income from an ecclesiastical living seemed to reflect itself in other ways. The number of parish clergy outside Ulster, where financial provision for clergy had improved, increased between 1615 and 1634, up from 393 to

486, but a growing proportion were non-resident, a third in 1634 as opposed to 20 per cent in 1615. Moreover the Catholic Earl of Clanricard had mortgaged over £4,000 worth of parsonages in Connacht, and in Meath nearly half the livings were impropriate, half of these being in the hands of Catholics, such as the Earl of Westmeath. This situation, all in Ireland agreed, was not sustainable. Even Ussher initially worked with Laud to tackle it. Clearly there was need for a programme for the proper endowment of clergy through the restoration of impropriations, and for a restraining hand on leases and alienations of church land so as to curb pluralities and enforce clerical residence. The main plan of attack was provided by John Bramhall, Bishop of Derry. The parliament of 1634 provided a legislative framework of three acts for placing controls on the leasing of church property, reclaiming impropriations, and a special act to deal with the situation in Ulster which had arisen from the conditions of the plantation. Such legislation was not sufficient on its own; it needed also a campaign to ensure that it was enforced. Great men who had benefited from church property which they had acquired by legal or other means found their actions under scrutiny. By a combination of purchase, pressure and legal proceedings, Bramhall reported in 1639 that Ulster diocesan finances had improved by £14,500 over the previous six years. The income of the Archbishop of Armagh alone had risen from £1,800 in 1629 to £3,500 in 1639. This may have been a rather better result than could be expected in other parts of the country where those holding impropriations had shaky titles and were prepared to negotiate. In Dublin the campaign started later and followed an abortive attempt in the early 1630s to sort out the mess of reversionary leases in which the Christ Church property was entangled. A number of prosecutions were taken about the cathedral lands, but not much progress was made before the crisis of 1640.

Undoubtedly the highest-profile case was that of Richard Boyle, Earl of Cork, which dragged on for four years. Wentworth, who was doing for the southern dioceses what Bramhall had done for those in Ulster, was determined to make an example of the earl. Boyle read the writing on the wall and had surrendered a number of his impropriations. However, in early 1634 his relationship with Wentworth was soured by the dispute over the tomb he proposed to erect for himself in St Patrick's Cathedral in Dublin. Tensions between the two increased, and in 1634 Boyle was summoned before the Court of Castle Chamber to justify his possession of the collegiate church at Youghal. Boyle tried several stratagems to have the case dropped, including trying to have it moved to England, but these failed. Wentworth's connections prevailed on him to accept that a settlement would be better than pressing the case to its logical conclusion. In April 1636 Boyle was summoned before the Lord Deputy and a deal was struck. This involved a fine of £30,000 which was eventually reduced to the £15,000 that Boyle offered, payable over three instalments. Yet that was not the end of the earl's problems, for the Bishop of Waterford and Lismore, John Atherton, took up the question of the manor of Ardmore detained from him by the earl and this was not settled until July 1637.

The attempted reform of the church by Wentworth and Bramhall marked a significant shift in the approach of the administration to the question of religion. Before the 1630s the debate had focused on the issue of strategy for reform. It had assumed that the problem was the conversion of an obdurate group of native Irish and Old English Catholics. Furthermore, it assumed that conversion would be carried on by a single Church of Ireland which had tended to fudge precise questions of ecclesiastical organisation in favour of a comprehensive Calvinist theology. However, the church had failed to make up its mind as to how to achieve this aim, with the result that there was vacillation between coercion and persuasion, the former being most associated with the Irish bishops and the latter with the London government. What Wentworth did, as in other areas of Irish government, was to change the question. The problem was not now conversion but reform, with the link between Dublin and London being not the problem but the solution. Strategies based on English experience and theological outlook came to dominate the workings of the Irish church. This was not so much a blueprint for mission as for anglicisation. As Wentworth himself put it in 1638, the Church of Ireland he had created 'hath ever been reformed by and to the Church of England'.[14] However, this was less a takeover than a realignment of structures within a wider context. The Church of England was a model that could be used for adjustments within the Irish church rather than subsuming it. Indeed, the process of reform of the Irish church would, it was thought, serve as a blueprint for further reform in England. As with the common law, in Wentworth's view a 'one solution fits all' strategy had to be tempered with local approaches to meet local difficulties. As a consequence, Wentworth, with a studied impartiality, succeeded in alienating almost every group in the Ireland of the 1630s.

## THE IMAGE OF IRELAND

Land, institutions and religion were all important in the mind of Thomas Wentworth, but equally important was the ability to articulate the power that they represented in a form which could be more widely understood and used to impress. Ireland might be one of the king's dominions, but unless it had the trappings of a kingdom, it was meaningless. The plan to establish a mint in Ireland was one example of the creation of a kingdom distinct from that of England, and a building for the mint was under construction in 1635 although, like the project itself, never completed. The messages of the new administration and its rulers are perhaps most clearly seen in the buildings it erected and the ceremonial with which it surrounded itself. Wentworth's own large, unfinished house at Jigginstown in County Kildare was a testimony to the scale of the Wentworthian vision and its innovation, since the structure is the first employment of brick on a large scale in Ireland. He explained its grand scale as not being the prompting of self-aggrandisement, but rather the creation of a royal residence for the king when he would visit his Irish kingdom. Wentworth also carried out works to improve Dublin Castle and make it a fit centre of power, although the evidence does not allow us to reconstruct what these were. Such activity may have inspired what seems to be a significant improvement in the material culture of the Irish gentry in the 1630s. Dublin certainly boomed, with the well-travelled James Howell noting in 1639: 'There is a splendid court kept at the castle and except that of the viceroy of Naples I have not seen the like in Christendom. . . . Traffic increaseth here wonderfully with all kinds of bravery and buildings.'[15] Certainly in the freemen's rolls of Dublin there was a growth in the number of people practising luxury trades, such as goldsmiths, as well as those in the building trades in the city during the 1630s.

Wentworth not only reconstructed state buildings, but paid attention to the rituals and practices that went on in them. He established rules for the ceremonial of a viceregal court in Dublin, since without this 'the king's greatness, albeit in the type, [would] become less reverenced than truly it ought to be'. To see the Lord Deputy was to see the king represented in his person. Objecting to the comments of a lawyer in 1639, Wentworth claimed that he had 'traduced his [Wentworth's] person and in him His Majesty whose character and image he was'.[16] Built around the quasi-royal court was a smart centre of sociability. Part of this was the creation of a theatre in Dublin which linked play-going and court civility. The performance of small-scale dramatic productions had been known in Dublin Castle since the beginning of the seventeenth century, and Wentworth reorganised and increased the number of such performances in order to improve the status of his court. In 1638 theatre in Dublin was formalised with the appointment of John Ogibly, a Scottish dancing master who had come to Dublin with Wentworth in 1633, as master of the revels. A playhouse had been opened in Werburgh Street by the middle of 1636, probably based on the design of the Cockpit Theatre in Drury Lane in London. Wentworth also attracted to Dublin James Shirley, a well-known court dramatist in London, and a troupe of English players and musicians. The repertoire, perhaps not surprisingly, included London favourites such as plays by Ben Jonson and John Fletcher, but Shirley also wrote plays for the Irish stage with political and religious messages. *The royal master*, first performed in 1637, has at its core a plot about loyalty and the restoration of order in a disordered polity with the removal of malicious ambition from the body politic and its replacement with royal service. It is difficult not to see this as a reflection of the Wentworthian agenda. Interestingly, it drew support from a number of groups in Ireland, including the Old English gentleman Richard Bellings, who wrote commendatory verses for it. Even more clearly, Shirley's *St Patrick for Ireland*, probably first performed in late 1639, set out the religious agenda by remodelling St Patrick as a Laudian bishop who duly blessed Ireland and its monarch. By contrast, the soldiers in the play, shown as Irish kern, were guilty of rape and the murder of members of their family. The rituals of theatre may have been entertaining, but they also contained powerful political messages.

Rituals spread out from Dublin into the surrounding countryside, following the Lord Deputy. As Wentworth went on viceregal progresses around the country he was met with formal set-piece entrances as he arrived at towns. These occasions were heavily laced with symbolic meaning in an attempt to create an enduring image of his kingdom. In 1637 he went on a progress throughout south Leinster and Munster which was accompanied by a series of set-piece civic receptions. He passed through Carlow, Kilkenny, Clonmel and Limerick, and there were formal entrances on each occasion. The Lord Deputy was met by civic dignitaries, many of whom were likely Old English, at the outskirts of the city or town and presented with a formal oration before entering through a triumphal arch. At Limerick there was also a sophisticated pageant with two triumphal arches and festal water transport. Entrances on such a scale had not been known in Ireland since the Lord Deputyship of Sir Henry Sidney in the 1570s. They succeeded in making the power of the state visible in the drama of the entrance. Equally the town in question put itself on display and also tried to articulate its own local power and solidarity against that of the Lord Deputy. Thus Wentworth was always met on the edge of urban authority and by implication only entered the town by invitation of the ruling elite. The display of such symbolic power by both the state and local power groups in Wentworth's Ireland constituted the complex negotiation of what the Lord Deputy might achieve in the real world of power politics.

## LEGACY

Wentworth's achievement was that he created new ways of thinking about the governance of Ireland. Before his arrival in 1633 Ireland cannot really be thought of as a kingdom with a centre in Dublin and peripheries along the north, west and southern parts of the country which were being drawn into conformity with the core. The centre of Dublin was too weak to exert much of a centralising role. Rather, the country might be thought of as a series of micro-societies or a dispersed constellation of centres, presided over by great lords, mostly Old English or New English, and held together by the consumption of symbolic goods of which the most important was the law. Law was welcomed because it gave stability and legitimacy to local society rather than because it reflected the power of the centre. The precise terms of that law, whether English common law or a specially designed Irish variant, was left an unresolved question. In practice, local law was what the gentry when sitting in local courts said it was, perhaps guided by new manuals being prepared for them such as Richard Bolton's *Justice of the peace for Ireland* (1638). Central authority was thus mobilised by local interests when it suited and ignored at other times. Dublin was, in theory, powerful but in practice severely constrained in the exercise of that power. More practically, inter-regional trade provided concrete evidence of linkages between different parts of Ireland without emphasising centralising tendencies. Wentworth's contribution to this world was to create a centre in the court at Dublin Castle from which the Lord Deputy would sally forth on grand journeys around the kingdom, making the presence of the central power visible in the provinces. In a less spectacular way, the improved efficiency of government administration based on executive institutions located in that court achieved the same end. Ireland began to be knit into something vaguely approaching coherence, with the Lord Deputy and his administration at the core.

It is conventional to assert that the Wentworthian experiment did not last. It is certainly true that in the 1630s he had done more to highlight problems than to find solutions. The fall of Thomas Wentworth, now Earl of Strafford and Lord Lieutenant, in 1640 and the outbreak of war in 1641 postponed the realisation of some of the ideas that Wentworth had propounded, but it did not destroy them. Some aspects of Wentworth's view of how society was to be ordered were resurrected in 1660 when the time came to rebuild a royalist world after the Cromwellian interlude. In part this was the result of the continuity of personnel. The Archbishop of Armagh in 1660 was John Bramhall, who as Bishop of Derry in the 1630s had been one of the main shapers of ecclesiastical policy. The Archbishop of Dublin was James Margetson, who, as Dean of Christ Church Cathedral, Dublin, in the 1630s had implemented Laudian reform there. Perhaps even more importantly, the new Lord Lieutenant, appointed in 1662, was James Butler, Duke of Ormond, an unrepentant admirer of Wentworth. Indeed, Wentworth had appointed him as a Privy Councillor in 1634 and lord lieutenant of horse in the newly reorganised Irish army in 1638. As a reminder of his patron, Wentworth's portrait hung in Ormond's great castle in Kilkenny throughout the late seventeenth century. By then Wentworth was long dead, but some of his modernising ideas about how Ireland might be governed certainly were not.

# Part II

The Breaking of the Old Order

# 5
# Destabilising Ireland, 1639–42

At the point when it seemed that Wentworth's vision for the evolution of Irish society might just triumph in the short term, events elsewhere intervened. In Scotland opposition to Charles's liturgical innovations in the church had been building since the latter part of 1637. This resulted in the popular National Covenant, subscribed at Edinburgh in March 1638, opposing the changes in the church through a tradition of forming contractual defence bodies dating back to the 1580s. The king refused to compromise and threatened to invade Scotland. In response, the Scottish aristocracy and radical Presbyterians combined in a body of Covenanters. In 1638–9 the Covenanters drew up a new constitutional blueprint for the kingdom which the Scottish parliament ratified piecemeal between 1639 and 1641. Provincial government was also reorganised through a set of gentry-dominated committees that organised the recruitment, training and provisioning of a national army. The result of this military standoff, the First Bishops' War, was that hardly a shot was fired, the king's commanders lost their nerve, and peace was made in the Treaty of Berwick.

For Wentworth this Scottish episode posed considerable problems. The most important of these was finance. As part of his military preparations for war, the king proposed to use Irish troops, led by the Catholic Earl of Antrim, to pin down the Covenanters in the western Highlands. Wentworth was commissioned to raise a force of 10,000 men to support Antrim's army; of these 8,000 would be raised in Ireland. This, with other military commitments necessitated by the strengthening of security in Ulster against the Scots, placed considerable strain on the Irish exchequer, and the only way of raising the necessary funds was by summoning parliament. Wentworth, created Earl of Strafford and elevated to Lord Lieutenant of Ireland in January 1640, was so confident of his ability to control such a parliament that it was proposed it would meet in March 1640, vote the king the necessary supply, and by so doing act as a model of loyalty to be emulated by the English parliament which was scheduled to meet in April. Wentworth was overly confident. In 1639 he had opposed the calling of an English parliament, realising how difficult it would be to manage. Yet by 1640 he advised the king to take the offensive against the Scots, a view which supported the king's own, confident that he could persuade both the English and Irish parliaments to provide the necessary funding. Events were to prove how wrongly Wentworth had read the situation. Such misreadings were compounded by the fact that he fell ill in the middle of 1640 at the height of the ensuing crisis, and his absence from English and Irish politics at this point undoubtedly diminished his considerable authority and contributed to the situation running out of control. In addition, Wentworth's rivals in the English Privy Council were becoming restive. Many of these men had wished to acquire Irish land and offices in, for example, places such as County Londonderry, but had failed to do so thanks mainly to the Lord Lieutenant's actions. For such men, an adverse Irish reaction to Wentworth's rule would be a welcome development.

## THE PARLIAMENT OF 1640

The Irish parliament met on 16 March 1640. On the following day the Dublin theatre staged a play by the Old English lawyer, and later member of the Confederation of Kilkenny, Henry Burnell. Burnell's *Landgartha* was a thinly disguised political allegory which on the face of it was a story about virtuous Norwegian women, led by Landgartha, who after the expulsion of the tyrannical King of Sweden by Reyner, King of Denmark, were left in Norway to be 'the law-makers to yourselves'. Landgartha was subsequently seduced and betrayed by Reyner, who understood too late the reprehensibility of his actions after her loyalty had been displayed in a civil war. The betrayal of the loyal Landgartha might well be interpreted as the betrayal of the Old English by a Charles/Reyner figure. This equation allowed Burnell to expound a set of political principles about how society should be organised, based on ideas of the virtue and honour so greatly admired by the Old English. Landgartha's final speech set out a view of the relation of kings to their subjects which urged monarchs to treat their subjects with love so that the tie between them could never be broken. It urged that the women—or the Old English —should be the natural law-makers for the kingdom. Such sentiments were clearly aimed at Wentworth's administration and the king and were intended as an opposition manifesto for the parliament.

The House of Commons which met in March 1640 comprised 240 members of whom seventy were Catholics, an appreciable reduction on the number of Catholics in 1634 largely due to Wentworth's manipulation of the constituencies in an attempt to secure a government majority. Of those Catholics, the vast majority were of Old English extraction, although a number with native Irish backgrounds also sat in the Commons. Such an analysis, however, conceals as much as it reveals. Religion was certainly a divisive issue between the various groups, but, as the experience of the Graces had shown, it was possible for Catholics and Protestants to co-operate on some political matters of common interest. Moreover, at the higher social levels there were, by 1640, significant marriage connections and bonds of debt between Old and New English. Again, the handful of those M.P.s with native Irish backgrounds had good cause to be described as culturally Old English if measured by their political actions and affiliations. They were all members of local landholding elites and held offices within county government. As such, they belonged not to a marginalised group but to an active political network. Among the Protestants within the parliament there were also diverse interests. Strafford's followers, particularly those he had brought with him to Ireland, formed one clear interest block. A second faction centred around Ireland's most powerful Protestant landowner, Richard Boyle, Earl of Cork. In the late 1630s Boyle attempted to patch up his relations with Strafford and secure his church land in Munster. Despite this, by the beginning of the parliament tensions were already resurfacing again between the two men and would prompt hostility against the Lord Lieutenant at his trial. A number of other factions can be identified, clustering around magnates such as Lord Lambert from Westmeath and Sir William St Leger in Munster. In addition, there were a number of Scots M.P.s in the parliament who had their own grievances against the Lord Lieutenant, most notably the imposition of the 'black oath' on Ulster Presbyterians in late 1639 in an attempt to divide them from the Scottish insurgents implicated in the Bishops' Wars.

Within the Lords it was a similar story. The attendance of the peers was rather smaller than in earlier parliaments, some forty-three temporal peers for the first session, thirty-nine for the second and twenty-four for the third, out of a possible sixty-nine peers. In some cases illness or attendance at parliament in London account for absences, but in others it seems that certain peers were simply not summoned, Wentworth fearing opposition. The Lord Lieutenant had also gathered proxies from peers who were absent but who might support him, although over time this tactic became less effective as the Lords refused to accept the proxies of non-resident peers. Almost all the peers had previous parliamentary experience, either in the Lords or Commons, and this may suggest why such a large proportion of those present, some twenty-three, became very active in parliamentary business. All of these had links with members of the Commons which probably helped facilitate the choreography between the two bodies. Of the activists, about half were Catholic peers, although religious divisions were transcended because of dislike for Wentworth arising out of his tampering with aristocratic power bases. There were exceptions such as Lords Lambert, Mayo and Ormond. On an even wider canvas, events would show the peers to possess a remarkably similar constitutional outlook, albeit one tempered with local and family interests. The Irish peers had extensive marriage connections with their English counterparts, and many held English titles also, although, with the exception of the Earl of Clanricard, their English titles were always of a lower rank than their Irish. However, this does suggest that the Irish peers can certainly be said to have been well informed about political and constitutional matters elsewhere.

The atmosphere within the Irish parliament during its next four sessions changed dramatically over time. This reflected the shifting configuration of power in England and the ability of different Irish groups to galvanise support for their position in the Commons. At times the various factions might coalesce and at other times act independently. Thus over some issues the Commons appeared united, while on others divisions emerged. The first session of the parliament from 6 March 1640 to 17 June was dominated by the Lord Lieutenant's supporters. Within days of its meeting the parliament had begun the main government business of securing four subsidies of £45,000 each to support the king's war effort against the Scots, and in particular the Irish army for service in that war. By early April, when Wentworth left Ireland for the meeting of the Short Parliament in England, leaving Christopher Wandesford as his deputy, all seemed well. The main way of managing the parliament had been the committee system, which took most of the major decisions. In the first session of parliament a high proportion of the leaders of these committees held government office and hence the viceroy controlled them easily. Having dealt with the main government business, parliament was prorogued to meet again in June to deal with more contentious issues such as the proposed plantations in the province of Connacht and County Tipperary.

By the time the parliament reassembled the political atmosphere had changed. The meeting in London of the Short Parliament—so called because it only lasted three weeks—had collapsed in disorder as the Commons refused to grant the king the finance necessary to deal with the Scots. Moreover, in Ireland economic conditions were deteriorating as a result of bad harvests, while Ulster's trade with Scotland was increasingly affected by the disturbed state of affairs. Parliamentary management was weakened by the absence of Wentworth, who was still in England. What characterised the latter part of the first session of the parliament was not outright defiance of the government, but rather the infliction by a growing opposition of serious embarrassment on the government over a variety of issues. The legislation for the Connacht plantation was sidelined, and the collection of three of the four subsidies was stopped on procedural grounds, although the first was to proceed. The resolution of this matter resulted in the collection of the remaining three subsidies in such a way that their value was much reduced, raising less than a quarter of what was intended. In consequence, the parliament was prorogued on 17 June 1640 to meet again on 1 October. Given the large Protestant majority in the Commons, the message seemed clear: Catholics and Protestants were co-operating to destabilise Strafford's government. The limited nature of the opposition's obstruction of parliamentary business suggests that it was hastily improvised. Significantly for later events, many activists in this Catholic opposition were to become members of the Catholic Confederation set up in 1642 and most were to be involved in the moderate wing of that body.

By the time the second session of the Irish parliament met in October 1640 the political landscape had been transformed. In late August the Scots, whose impatience at Charles's recalcitrance in reaching a deal after the First Bishops' War had been stretched to breaking-point, marched into England, where they defeated the English army at Newburn and seized Newcastle-on-Tyne before concluding the Treaty of Ripon on 21 October 1640. What was even more worrying was that it seemed a number of English peers and gentlemen had been plotting with the Scots Covenanters for some time. The Second Bishops' War, as this became known, was not just a military incursion, it was a virtual *coup d'état*. The king's will and authority were now being openly challenged. Moreover, a cycle of violence that proved difficult to control had been initiated. Charles was forced to summon a parliament at Westminster—known as the Long Parliament since it would continue to meet throughout the 1640s—on 3 November 1640. Once convened it quickly declared that it could only be dissolved by its own resolution and not by the king. With Charles bankrupt, both financially and politically, parliament effectively assumed the reins of government in England and began its attack on the perceived abuses of the king and his 'evil counsellors' over the previous twelve years.

## THE FALL OF WENTWORTH

In this charged environment, the Irish parliament reassembled on 1 October 1640. In late October and early November the Irish House of Commons seized the initiative, probably encouraged by the opposition in the English parliament. On 7 November the Commons adopted a petition of remonstrance, which was an indictment of Wentworth's government of Ireland and, following the model of Scottish commissioners then in London after the Bishops' War, appointed agents to take their petition to the English parliament, which had assembled on 3 November. As if to demonstrate the unanimity of the Commons, commissioners were drawn from diverse backgrounds and included Sir Donagh MacCarthy, a Catholic native, and Sir Hardress Waller, a devout New English settler and later regicide. Attempts to prevent the agents leaving Ireland were circumvented, and by 19 November the substance of the Irish petition was in London. Already there was a close connection between the Irish opposition and their English counterparts. Indeed, one member of the English parliament, Sir John Clotworthy, was an Antrim settler and implacable opponent of Wentworth for what he regarded as the Lord Lieutenant's laxity against Catholicism. It was Clotworthy who was a key figure in the process leading up to the impeachment of Strafford, and he was one of a committee of five of the English Commons that recommended that the Lord Lieutenant be charged with high treason. His role may have been even greater than this evidence suggests. In 1640 it seems that Clotworthy had strong links with the Scots; he certainly travelled to Scotland. It was later alleged that he may have been fomenting trouble in Scotland for his own ends so as to destabilise Wentworth's regime in Ireland. However, Clotworthy was not the only link between the Westminster parliament and that of Ireland. William Jephson, a Munster settler, was a member of the English House of Commons, as was Lord Dungarvan, Cork's eldest son; other of Cork's relations were members of the English peerage and had seats in the House of Lords at Westminster. Moreover, Cork's dealings with Wentworth had been stormy in the past. Although he had attempted to patch these up in the late 1630s as part of a wider deal over Cork's Munster property, the new-found friendship crumbled rapidly as Strafford embroiled Cork in his trial as an example of the perpetrators of shady dealings that he had to deal with in Ireland. The Earl of Cork, with his usual concern for his own wealth and status, turned against the Lord Lieutenant and testified against him. Strafford was arrested on 11 November and the initial charges were brought against him thirteen days later.

When the Irish parliament reassembled for its third session in January 1641, its main aim was to provide material for the articles of impeachment against Strafford. In February information on the tobacco monopoly, which Strafford had instituted in Ireland, and other administrative innovations of the 1630s was sent to England. By then the English process was moving with some speed. On 30 January 1641 the formal articles of impeachment of Strafford were sent by the English House of Commons to the Lords to be read to the Lord

Lieutenant. This was not a straightforward document. Since no single act of treason could be laid at the Lord Lieutenant's door, it was necessary to argue on the basis of a series of arbitrary actions, none of which was treasonable in itself and all, arguably, within the powers of the holder of the office. Sixteen of the twenty-eight items related to Irish affairs.

The formal trial began on 22 March. A number of Irish witnesses were called. Initially, at least, the prosecution went well, although some of the problems which seemed so acute in Ireland did not raise the hackles of English peers in the same way. Some English peers may even have agreed with the third article against Strafford, which alleged that in 1633 he had declared in public 'that Ireland was a conquered nation and that the king might do with them what he pleased'. Strafford managed to rebut successfully almost all the charges against him, pointing out that even if they were true none was treasonable. His mastery of the detail of specific events, his impugning of the morals of witnesses against him and his oratorical skills all represented key elements in his defence. In effect, the case against him collapsed. Strafford may have won the legal battle, but he lost the political war. The English parliament was left with no alternative but to declare Strafford guilty of treason by passing a bill of attainder. This was supported by popular agitation in the form of a petition from the city of London with some 20,000 signatures. The bill was read for the first time on 26 April and received the royal assent on 10 May. On 12 May 1641 the Irish Lord Lieutenant, Thomas Wentworth, Earl of Strafford, was executed on Tower Hill in London. Ironically, he was attended on the scaffold by the Calvinist James Ussher, Archbishop of Armagh, whose power he had eclipsed in Ireland. Wentworth's fall had been achieved not by the English parliament alone but with the active co-operation of the Irish parliament. This had two very significant effects. First, it inextricably linked events in Ireland with those in England. The agents who had taken the remonstrance from Ireland remained in England to lobby for Irish interests and to act as the representatives of the Irish parliament in its dealings with the king, whose relations with the London parliament were fast degenerating. Secondly, while the outcome of the co-operation between the two parliaments may well have been satisfactory for both sides on this occasion, it created a precedent which was potentially dangerous. Parliament in London had impeached an Irish official and thereby demonstrated its ability, and willingness, to interfere in Irish affairs, formerly held to be a matter for the crown alone. That would have long-term repercussions.

## UNDOING THE WENTWORTHIAN EXPERIMENT

In the spring of 1641 the Irish parliament made important strategic decisions. As the fall of the Lord Lieutenant now seemed assured, the parliament moved to fill the power vacuum which that created to ensure that the Wentworthian experiment in rebalancing the Irish constitution could never be repeated and the *status quo* returned. The most immediate way of achieving this was by removing from power those associated with Wentworth's experiment. In the view of many, his supporters were the root of the problem. In the rhetoric of royalism, it was not the king who was to blame for the problems of the 1630s but his 'evil counsellors' appointed by Wentworth to positions of authority. For a group of O'Reillys writing to the Lords Justices in the aftermath of the rising of 1641 the problem was the 'rigorous government of such placed over us as respected more the advancement of their own private fortunes then the honour of His Majesty or the welfare of us his subjects'. This had the effect of 'dissolving the bond of mutual agreement with hitherto hath been held inviolate between the several subjects of this kingdom'.[1] As politics was still a very personal matter and offices were major sources of social distinction and financial security, the power of appointments and preferment cannot be exaggerated. Thus the appointment to office by the Lord Deputy was nothing less than investment with the power to structure society as a whole. Lords Deputy could thus manipulate office to build arbitrary webs of influence which were a constant source of anxiety to those who were not part of them. A case in point was Wentworth's introduction into the Irish standing army of the practice of purchasing commissions rather than relying on the tradition of the gentleman soldier to command the force. The appointment of unsuitable men in church and state resulted in an inability to command the moral authority that proceeded from an adherence to duty and honour which was required in the government of Ireland. The result was, as the Old English priest John Lynch described it in the 1660s, 'to make Ireland a theatre and area of slavery'.[2] The point was well made in the elections to the parliament of 1640 when prominent peers, such as Clanricard, were informed that their attendance would not be necessary. In the Commons, borough constituencies were reduced by threats to revoke charters, while in the counties pressure was applied to Privy Councillors to manipulate elections, which were often held at irregular times and in unusual locations to procure the election of supporters of the Lord Deputy.

Such unacceptable advisers clearly had to be removed after Wentworth's fall. The death of his deputy, Christopher Wandesford, in December 1640 dealt with one immediate victim, but there were to be others. The mechanism that the parliament adopted, probably in imitation of the actions of the London parliament, was impeachment. This was a risky strategy, since no Irish officials had been impeached in living memory and the techniques for doing so were imperfectly understood. Nevertheless, in March 1641 the Irish House of Commons drew up articles of impeachment against Bishop Bramhall, the architect of ecclesiastical reform, Lord Chancellor Bolton and Lord Chief Justice Lowther, associated with the Court of Castle Chamber, and Wentworth's secretary Sir George Radcliffe. The process ran into trouble almost immediately on procedural grounds. Bolton argued in his defence in the House of Lords that Poynings' Law restricted its right to impeach. The argument was stopped by the prorogation of the parliament on 5 March but was taken up again in May 1641 when the parliament resumed. Attempts were made to try to find precedents, but without success. However, the argument on the judicial powers of the parliament eventually reached stalemate, and the case for impeachment had to be dropped.

In these impeachment proceedings one prominent figure was absent, namely John Atherton, Bishop of Waterford and Lismore, who had been the driving force of successful practical Laudian reform at Christ Church in Dublin and a strong supporter of the Lord Lieutenant. His was to be a different fate. Atherton's life had been dogged by scandal. In the middle of the 1630s he was said to be troubled by the ghost of the recently deceased Susannah Leakey, Atherton's mother-in-law, in Somerset, who had accused Atherton of infanticide, the child's mother being Atherton's wife's sister. In June 1640, in addition to charges of incest and infanticide, allegations of sodomy and adultery were added to the list of accusations. Throughout the summer more evidence, mainly of adultery, was collected against him. Some of this he admitted, but he denied buggery, which was a capital crime. On 27 November Atherton was found guilty of buggery and condemned to death. The timing was fortuitous, as proceedings for the impeachment of Strafford were just beginning and the activities of Atherton, as Sir John Clotworthy pointed out, did not reflect well either on episcopacy or on the way in which Ireland was run, given that such a man could become a bishop. Whether Wentworth's opponents had a more active hand in Atherton's downfall is possible but not known.

Having dealt, as they thought, with the Wentworthian cabal, parliament turned its attention to the second prong of ensuring that constitutional change could not proceed as it had done in the 1630s. This attempt to define, in a permanent form, the constitutional framework for Irish governance was the task of the fourth session of the Irish parliament, which began in May 1641. At least some of the issues that the parliament had to deal with were clear from the remonstrance of November 1640, which had laid out the Irish grievances against Wentworth. These ideas were taken up and developed in a set of twenty-one queries which the parliament formulated in January 1641, to provide material for the articles of impeachment of Strafford. The queries ranged from the most basic 'whether the subjects of this kingdom be a free people and to be governed only by the common laws of England and the statutes in force in this kingdom?', through the power of proclamations and martial law to bind subjects, to much more complex issues about the oaths which judges were to take and details of the workings of the courts which Wentworth had operated through the royal prerogative, such as the Court of Castle Chamber.[3] In short, they were an attempt to define the limits of executive authority. These queries were debated again in February and were sent to the House of Lords to be presented to the Irish judges, who were expected to provide answers that would set guidelines for the governance of Ireland in future. The queries placed the Irish judges in a difficult position, the more so since the queries were asked of the judges not in ignorance of the law but in full knowledge of the answers. If the judges were to answer the queries in the affirmative, which was parliament's aim, then they would expose their own negligence in failing to make Wentworth and his executive answerable to the law. Thus, had the judges admitted their failure to maintain the legal code, they would have laid themselves open to actions against them. Moreover, they regarded the answers to some of the queries as trespassing on the royal prerogative, thus leaving themselves open to incurring royal or parliamentary wrath.

The replies from the judges were not forthcoming until 25 May, and then only with some coercion. They were disappointing because they systematically evaded the major points at issue. The replies did not reach the Commons until 29 May, when, in a grand committee, they commissioned Patrick Darcy, M.P. for Bannow in County Wexford, to produce a reply to the judges' queries which would take the form of an address to the House of Lords. In reality, this was not the task of Darcy alone, for it was too complex and written in too short a time to be the work of one man. It seems that he had a consultative committee of lawyers working with him. The result was, rather, a composite argument, or more precisely a series of arguments with a common thread. The effect of this (subsequently published at Waterford in 1643 as *An argument delivered . . . by the express order of the House of Commons*) was to define the constituent elements of legal authority in Ireland. Darcy began with a well-worked theme: the power of the king which was the cement of the social order. Thus the sort of relationships in which the king was enmeshed reflected the social order: 'The trust between the king and his people is threefold; first as between sovereign and subject; secondly as between a father and his children . . . thirdly as between a husband and wife, this trust is comprehensive of the whole body politic.' For anyone to contrive a breach of that trust was a dangerous act. It was, claimed Darcy, the working out of that trust that led subjects to 'maintain the just prerogative of our gracious lord King Charles and his posterity, whom we pray to God to flourish on earth over us and ours'. The imagery was not peculiarly Irish. The idea of the king as father was ultimately Biblical, and it had appeared in Bonaventure Ó hEodhasa's early seventeenth-century Irish catechism, produced in Louvain. However, the imagery is significant, since it placed monarchy in a social setting. Marriage, for instance, was certainly regulated by legal contracts and hierarchical rules, but relationships between husbands and wives were, as seventeenth-century clergy realised, ultimately worked out as a series of compromises, though without compromising the essential inequality in decision-making power, to make a workable relationship. As Darcy developed his argument, it was not the function of kings to change the law but rather to defend it. It was the role of kings 'to observe and maintain the law, the judge by his oath

. . . is bound to do right between the king and his people and that right strengthens the king's prerogative'. Thus proclamations, as used by Wentworth, or even royal letters patent could not alter the law, and those that did so were 'absolutely void'. The emphasis on the importance of judges as arbiters between king and people was an attempt to expose the failure of the Irish judges to respond to the growth of executive authority.

Secondly, Darcy turned to the working of the law itself. The move was a significant one because it equated the system of law with the form of government, so that law, rather than the executive, would define the division and distribution of state power. 'This kingdom', he argued, 'was governed and ought to be so by the law of England, as the law of the land, which law, as it was always here received, consists of three parts. First the common law. Secondly, the general customs of England. Thirdly the statutes here received.' This argument concerning the shape of law was drawn straight from the English jurist Sir Edward Coke's *Institutes* of 1628, which allowed Darcy to use English case law to construct his own Irish argument and thereby turn the tables on the judges, who in their replies to the queries seemed to suggest that legal systems were not transferable. According to Darcy, the law, again based on Coke's arguments, was the prerogative of parliament, which 'is the supreme court, nay the primitive of all other courts; to that court belongs the making, altering, regulating of laws and the correction of all courts and ministers'. Thus Darcy linked the laws of Ireland and England in a way that involved the working out of the 1541 act, which had declared that the crown of Ireland was 'united and knit to the imperial crown of the realm of England', or, in Darcy's words, 'Ireland is annexed to the crown of England' and the two peoples and judicial systems were effectively one. This allowed Ireland in 1640 to appropriate the English common law.

It was equally important that these arguments gave the customs of the realm a clear status. Custom stood at the interface between statute law and everyday life and was sanctioned not by the king or executive authority but by tradition. Sir John Davies, the Irish Attorney General, in his law reports had defined custom as follows: 'When a reasonable act once done is found to be good and beneficial to the people, and agreeable to their nature and disposition, they do use it and practise it again and again, and so by often iteration and multiplication of the act, it becometh a custom and being continued, without interruption, time out of mind, it obtaineth the force of law [which is] the most perfect and most excellent, and without comparison the best to make and preserve a commonwealth.' Thus both parliament and the common law drew their force from custom.[4] Since custom was greater and more binding than even statute law, it was of central importance in underpinning the Old English political position. It appealed to the past as a way of cohering the Old English sense of themselves. It also allowed at least the possibility of the introduction into the constitutional debate in the longer term of the sort of ancient constitution that the historian Geoffrey Keating had constructed for the Old English. Moreover, by defining custom as English custom, Darcy identified the Old English as a civilised group who were not tainted by the sort of barbaric activity that sixteenth-century commentators had attributed to the native Irish. Thus, as Darcy commented, the Irish custom of gavelkind had not been outlawed as a result of a judicial decision by Sir John Davies, but because it was not a civil custom. To defend custom and the past, as Darcy seemed to be doing, also appealed to the Old English sense of honour that had been clearly shown to be part of that group's view of itself in the 1620s over the Graces episode. Moreover, the resort to English custom provided a common ground on which links could be built with settlers.

At the same time as appropriating custom and the common law, Darcy repudiated the idea that the Westminster parliament had the power to legislate for Ireland. While some English statutes had force in Ireland, 'no other statutes or new introducing law [had such force] until the same be first received and enacted in the parliament of this kingdom'. Consequently, those in Ireland might use the machinery of the law in England, while protecting themselves from its problems. In addition, Darcy re-emphasised how the strengthening of the Irish parliament weakened the power of the executive government favoured by Wentworth. This was an argument which even New English settlers could support.

The subtleties of Darcy's argument may not have been as clear as they later became because of the way in which it was presented—in the form of comments on the queries to the judges rather than a coherent prose narrative. By July, however, parliament had clearly got the message and in a series of declarations on the queries pronounced that the subjects of this His Majesty's kingdom of Ireland are a free people, and to be governed only according to the common law of England and the statutes made and established by parliament in this kingdom of Ireland, and according to the lawful customs used in the same.[5]

The importance of this argument lay not so much in its content as its timing. Parliament had, after all, not been a significant feature of Irish political life in the late sixteenth and early seventeenth centuries, but now was being given a key role in the governance of Ireland. This development stemmed from the growing power of the English parliament, buoyed up by its success in the attainder of Strafford, and the corresponding weakness in the position of the king, the traditional locus of Old English power. All this was clear from rumours in Dublin in June and July 1641 that the English parliament, dominated by John Pym and his 'godly' faction, was about to introduce anti-Catholic legislation that would impact directly on Ireland. Not only was the role of the Irish parliament being enhanced to prevent the rise of executive government, it also prevented the interference of the English parliament in Irish affairs.

The second strand in this reshaping of the governance of Ireland was in legislative change. Wentworth's actions had demonstrated the way in which Poynings' Law could be used by a viceroy to control parliament. In order to prevent this occurring again, an act of explanation of Poynings' Law was demanded. This, it was intended, would reinstate its original function of ensuring that the monarch was directly involved in the government of Ireland as a protector against the actions of a viceroy and that the king would be prevented from excessive delegation of royal power to a viceroy. While for the Scots in 1640 the political problem was the king, in Ireland the same king was seen as the solution to their political problems. What was at issue here was not the restriction of Poynings' Law in respect of the initiation of legislation by parliament, but rather the opening of lines of constitutional communication with the King of Ireland. The campaign for such a change was clear in the parliamentary sessions of early 1641, when all government legislation was rejected as the Commons tried to seize the legislative initiative based on the belief that it had the right to initiate legislation. The agents of the Irish parliament in England were ordered to request as part of their grievances to the king that a bill of explanation of Poynings' Law be prepared. In April the king, now under growing pressure from the English parliament, acceded to the petition for grievances in return for promises of money. A week later bills were prepared and approved by the Irish parliament for transmission, and these were accepted by the Irish committee of the English Privy Council.

Faced with these challenges, the Dublin Castle administration, headed in the spring of 1641 by two conservative Protestants (Sir William Parsons and Sir John Borlase) who were succeeded in June by the 'godly' Robert Sydney, Earl of Leicester, was growing increasingly nervous. The assumptions, established by Wentworth, which guided its actions were increasingly under threat. However, the strength of the opposition was weakening. The execution of Wentworth had removed the common enemy that held the various interests in the parliament together. In June 1641 it was complained that some of the Protestant party in parliament felt that things had gone too far and that the Catholic interest was 'pressing too near upon the honour and power of the government' and the financial rights of the king. A split between Catholics and Protestants in the parliament seemed imminent.[6] While the opposition had been vocal, it had actually achieved little. Legislation that it wanted had not been passed, and the assumption that the king would support its position was a rash one. Charles might have been prepared to agree to an act of explanation of Poynings' Law, but he rejected the demand that the Irish parliament be allowed to transmit its own draft bills to him without the approval of the executive. On 7 August the Dublin Castle administration moved and procured a dissolution of parliament until the following November. How desperate a move this was may be judged by the financial context. The exchequer was now empty, despite the subsidies, and consideration was being given to borrowing from members of the Privy Council to keep government afloat, although the projected loan of £6,500 would have been insignificant. To dissolve parliament and thereby abandon hope of taxation was a truly desperate move.

## POLITICS WITHOUT PARLIAMENT

The prorogation of the parliament in August 1641 did not curtail the political debate; it simply moved it to another context. The Scottish Bishops' Wars of the late 1630s had demonstrated the effectiveness of extra-parliamentary activity in forcing concessions. Such extra-parliamentary activity was building in Ireland in the late 1630s and early 1640s. Perhaps the earliest indication of this emerged in Ulster during the late 1630s. A number of problems here had combined to produce discontent. Economic conditions had deteriorated considerably as a consequence of poor harvests in 1638 and 1639, as can be seen in the declining customs returns. In addition, Wentworth had quartered in Ulster an army raised in Ireland for service in the Bishops' Wars in Scotland, an army which was largely Catholic. As if that were not enough, Wentworth attempted to impose conformity on Ulster, with its strong Scottish links, in the wake of the Covenanter disturbances in Scotland. He ordered that closer watches be kept on movement between the two countries and sent supplies of arms to government forces in Ulster. In the autumn of 1638 he learned with increasing concern about growing links between the two areas. By early 1639 he decided to impose an oath on the inhabitants of Ulster, the 'black oath', abjuring the Covenant, that he thought would not only flush out the dissenters but be a propaganda weapon for the king in his contest with his Scottish subjects. Initially there seems to have been little opposition to the oath, which was to be administered by the army, but by August 1639 local discontent was evident. As a result of this, men from Antrim and Down left for Scotland, creating a problem for the harvest in the autumn. Both the army and Church of Ireland clergy were coming under attack from women 'with their laps full of stones and men armed with swords', and there were rumours of insurrection.[7] In the event, the scare passed with the recall of Wentworth and the scrapping of the oath, although rumblings were heard in Ulster into 1641. That episode was significant in demonstrating the importance of popular resistance in curtailing government action.

Further signs of conspiratorial discontent were manifest early in 1641. According to one Ulster peer, Lord Maguire, he was approached in late January or early February 1641 by Rory O'More, an Armagh landowner, who proposed staging a rising. A few others seem also to have been involved, but none of these was to be active in later plotting. There was a good deal of discussion and a plan was made to meet again in May, but nothing seems to have developed, since, according to Maguire, by August no further action had been taken. The motives which drew these men together were varied. There was clearly general discontent with Wentworth's actions, and in particular his policy of plantation. Yet there were probably other forces also at work in creating discontent. Native Irish landownership, in particular, was under threat from wider pressures than plantation. Sir William Petty later estimated that the number of Catholic landowners in 1641 was about 3,000, of whom 2,000 were probably Old English. Even those native Irish who had benefited from the Ulster plantation were under strain. In County Cavan the amount of land held by native proprietors had decreased from 20 per cent in 1610 to 16 per cent in 1641. In County Armagh the fall was from 25 per cent to about 19 per cent over the same period. Maguire claimed that his motivation for joining the plot was the scale of his debts. The growing demands of taxation in the subsidy of 1640 had certainly not helped his precarious situation. Others who would later become plotters, such as Sir Phelim O'Neill, also had considerable debts, he having mortgaged land for at least £13,066 by 1641. The economic conditions of early 1641 did not inspire much confidence for any real reversal of these conditions, with further harvest failures, falling royal revenues and the demand for payment of the royal subsidy. More specifically, the recall of Wentworth in February 1641 and his replacement with Lords Justices who were known to be of a strongly anti-Catholic cast of mind may have energised a plot. Certainly as early as the end of December 1640 there were rumours in Dublin of an anti-Catholic clampdown, possibly inspired by the perception of Westminster's Long Parliament as a body dominated by John Pym and his 'godly' faction. In practice this clampdown never occurred, which may partly explain why the plot lost its momentum. Another factor may have been the quickening tempo of parliamentary activity, since the plotters were all members of parliament. The episode is important nonetheless, since it provided a structure on which later plots could be built.

In the late spring of 1641 another plot emerged in Ireland. This seems to have been inspired by a number of Irish Catholic colonels who were in the service of the army of Spanish Flanders and who arrived in Ireland to recruit from Wentworth's Catholic army raised for service in Scotland, which London had now decided to disband, for service in Europe. The colonels' mission was still-born, since in July the Commons, fearing a weakening of Ireland and a strengthening of Spain as a result of their activities, stopped the recruitment. This left a number of men with military experience unpaid in Ireland. What inspired them to begin to plot is unclear. It may have been their concern about the new rumours now circulating in Dublin in the late spring of 1641 of a clampdown on Catholicism by the Long Parliament. Moreover, there were also rumours that the Scots, fresh from their triumph in the Bishops' Wars, were intending to crush Catholicism, by force if necessary. It seems that in this lay the germ of the idea that the insurgents should seize Dublin Castle. However, little came of this, and by September 1641 the colonels' plot had collapsed, although some of those involved in it joined a third plot then taking shape in Dublin.

The broad outline of this third plot seems to have been decided in June or July of 1641. Its architects appear to have been a number of malcontents from previous conspiracies, including Lord Maguire, Rory O'More and possibly a few of the recruiter colonels. Initially it seems to have lacked direction, and motives were confined to generalised grievances about plantation and the treatment of Catholicism. Their sense of grievance and foreboding may have been worsened by the appointment in June 1641 as Lord Lieutenant of Robert Sydney, second Earl of Leicester, a man with a reputation as a Puritan sympathiser. The plot received a major boost with the prorogation of the parliament in August. There were now a number of disillusioned M.P.s who had lost confidence in the parliament as a way of achieving progress by constitutional means and were finally deprived of that forum for their views after the prorogation. Any parliamentary advance that had been made looked as though it was to be outflanked by the increasingly radical Long Parliament in London. Such constitutional concerns were clearly in the mind of some of those later involved in the rising. In January 1642 Viscount Gormanston, by then with the insurrectionists, explained that his motive for becoming involved in the Irish war was his objection to the fact that the English Puritan parliament had invaded the royal prerogative and 'they teach that the laws of England, if they mention Ireland, are without doubt binding here . . . and what may be expected from such zealous and fiery professors of an adverse religion, but the ruin and extirpation of ours?' and this had informed policy in Dublin.[8] A number of M.P.s, including Sir Phelim O'Neill, Rory Maguire and Philip MacHugh O'Reilly, seem to have joined the plot at this stage. O'Neill, whose family had benefited from the Ulster plantation, had been active in the parliament. He had sat on ten

Commons committees in June and July, and Philip O'Reilly and Rory Maguire sat on twelve and nine committees respectively. Both O'Reilly and Maguire sat on key committees, such as that on the tobacco monopoly, the committee on the agents in London, and the committee which drew up the charges for the projected impeachment of Lord Chancellor Bolton. In the House of Lords, Lord Maguire had attended regularly, and it was he who put the motion for the impeachment of Bolton to the house. The recruitment of these men gave the plot new life, and it seems that it was O'Neill, borrowing ideas from the earlier colonels' plot, that gave the conspiracy its final shape. O'Neill personally seems to have been unenthusiastic about the practicability of seizing Dublin Castle without trained men and equipment. He was in touch with other military commanders, including Owen Roe O'Neill, then serving with the Irish force in the army of Spanish Flanders, but Sir Phelim does not seem to have envisaged that Owen Roe would play an active part in the rising. The fact that Owen Roe did not arrive in Ireland with a force until well into 1642 is consistent with this view. The final plan was agreed at a meeting at Glaslough, County Monaghan, on 5 October 1641. It involved a rising on 23 October to seize Dublin Castle.

On the evening of 22 October 1641 Sir Phelim O'Neill, member of the Irish parliament and justice of the peace for County Armagh, arrived for dinner with the governor of Charlemont Castle in Ulster, which suggests that the two were on good terms. On entering the castle, he was followed by an insurgent force, and, drawing his sword, he seized the castle in the name of the king. It was clear that this was carefully planned. Using the network of Ulster families as an organising framework for the rising, each group seized castles in its own area. The Quinns seized Mountjoy Castle in County Tyrone, the O'Hanlons took Tandragee in County Armagh, and the Magenisses and MacCartans invested Newry, while the MacMahons focused on key sites in County Monaghan. A rising organised by kinship certainly explains why, at least in its early weeks, war was concentrated in regional pockets.

O'Neill had effectively pre-empted the plan to rise in Dublin on the following day. His motives are unclear, but it seems likely that he hoped a surprise strike would allow him to march quickly on Dublin and, like the Scots in the Second Bishops' War, put himself in a powerful negotiating position. That tactic depended on the element of surprise, but this was lost later the same evening when Owen O'Connolly, a servant of the Ulster landowner Sir John Clotworthy and foster-brother of one of the plotters, was arrested in a drunken state in Dublin and under interrogation revealed the plot to seize Dublin Castle the following day. The conjunction of this revelation and news from Ulster that a rising had actually begun conflated the two events, and a wave of panic and fear spread through the city. As Richard Bellings, later secretary to the Confederation of Kilkenny noted, 'some proposed to themselves all the horrid things which they read or heard to have been acted in the sack of a town' and others 'felt their hearts shrink with fright and astonishment. . . . The concourse was great in the streets, as is usual in a populous city upon far less occasions, and their own numbers did fright them.' There was 'a bare face of terror'.[9] Lord Maguire, Colonel Hugh MacMahon and about thirty others were apprehended and imprisoned, and while this effectively ended the unrealistic plot to seize Dublin, it did little to calm fears.

## THE PROBLEM OF WAR

Over the next few weeks law and order in Ulster collapsed. Many of those who were the key figures in county administration, such as sheriffs and justices of the peace, were either dead or among the insurgents. In other cases the scale of the rising was such as to leave them powerless to act. As one Scotsman travelling through Ulster to Dublin in November 1641 observed, 'The most woeful desolation that was ever in any country in the sudden is to be seen here. Such is the sudden fear and amazement that has seized all sorts of people that they are ready to run into the sea.'[10] There was further reason for the fear. Poor military organisation and a dramatically heightened sense of anxiety, combined with the dislocation resulting from harvest failures and food shortages, led to social breakdown, with resulting massacres of settlers, some conducted in order to settle old grievances. Just how many were killed can never be known. The depositions taken after the outbreak of the rising produced dramatically exaggerated and conflicting accounts. A great deal of hearsay was collected from people who had not witnessed anything but had heard rumours second- and third-hand. As time passed stories became increasingly exaggerated and the number of accounts grew, and the estimates became more a matter of politics than accurate calculation. In 1646 Sir John Temple's history of the rebellion estimated 300,000 dead in the first two years of the rising. The Rev. Devereux Spratt, the Restoration incumbent of Tipperary, believed it was 150,000. More realistically, Sir William Petty's account of Ireland, written in 1672, reckoned the number massacred at 37,000. In County Armagh estimates from the depositions of the number murdered ranged from 527 to 1,259, depending on the level of credulity of the accounts, or between 10 and 25 per cent of the settler population. Armagh, however, was probably an extreme case, since there settler and native numbers were more closely balanced than elsewhere, which gave rise to greater tensions.

The speed of the rising and its violence shocked most of the Old English and the settlers. Most were unprepared for anything like this. There had not even been rumours of disaffection in Ulster for the previous ten years. In the muster of 1630 Ulster settlers were less well armed than they had been previously. Whereas in 1619 one Ulster settler in eight owned a musket, there was only one between thirty-three in 1630. Even military garrisons were poorly equipped by the late 1630s. Moreover, by the 1630s settlers had begun to abandon the heavily fortified castles which they had constructed in the early stage of the settlement in favour of Jacobean-style manor houses. Sir Toby Caulfield's new house at Castlecaulfield in County Tyrone was constructed with almost no defensive features and sported large windows, a liability in a siege. The folly of this innovation in the light of later events was well expressed by one Kerry gentleman begging for refuge with the Earl of Cork: 'My house I built for peace, it having more windows than walls'.[11] Settlers retreated, as one might expect in a paternalistic society, into the protection of local landlords. In Ulster the military response to the rising was mainly a local one, with individual landlords raising armies. Those to the west of the province created a body known as the Laggan force under Sir Robert Stewart, while to the east, Viscount Ards assembled his tenants into a force and armed them as best he could. Others simply formed local bands to protect themselves. One of the Earl of Ormond's corespondents commented in December 1641 that it was impossible to organise a concerted response to the rising in County Down because local communities would not co-operate 'when their own interests did not evidently press them to it'.[12]

Moments of political instability enacted in public, rather than in the privacy of conspiracies or councils, saw the meeting of a multitude of priorities and temperaments. As the local government system crumbled around them, settlers turned to those who had risen for some explanation of their actions. They found many different versions and motivations. In Donegal, for instance, one of those involved in the early weeks of the rising, Turlogh Roe O'Boyle, had a long history of conspiracy. Although he had received land in the plantation scheme, it was claimed that in 1628 he was in contact with Spain and was involved in a plot for a rising in Donegal, for which he was imprisoned. It is this radical tradition which is present in Uilliam Óg Mac an Bhaird's poem of 1641 urging those in rebellion to unity and religious purity in order to reverse 'oppression, misfortune and tyranny' by 'a foreign crew'.[13] Others seem to have had more personal grievances, using the breakdown of law and order as a way of settling old insults, perceived injustices and the cancellation of debt by destroying books and other financial records. Others simply and opportunistically took to robbery as a way of becoming rich.

The accounts which settlers received from those who attacked them were often contradictory. Some were told the rising had been planned for two years, some talked of a seventeen- or eighteen-year plan, some talked of a complex organisation, while others said nothing about a plan at all. One woman claimed that she had been told that Wentworth had plotted the insurrection. Others alleged wider interventions, claiming that English noblemen were involved and that the Tower of London and Edinburgh Castle had been taken. Others again said the that the king was dead (some claimed executed by the Scots) and his heir turned Catholic, while still others thought the queen, the Catholic Henrietta Maria, had been seized by London Puritans and would be executed as her chaplain had been. Many mentioned their fear of the intentions of the London parliament with regard to Catholics. One dominant rumour was near universal: the rebellion was not against the king but for him in support of the royal person against evil counsellors. This allegation gained credence when on 6 November Sir Phelim O'Neill produced a document which he claimed was a commission from the king for his action. The fact that this document was forged is not the point. It was believed by the rebels that the king would have supported the rising if he had been allowed to do so. The forged commission was a master-stroke of propaganda, for even the illiterate responded to the document because of its royal seal—snipped from a land grant—and the Catholic Bishop of Derry claimed that it was invented not to convince the gentry but 'the common sort of people'.[14] At a more sophisticated level, the insurgents may have had an eye to potential support from the loyal Old English of the Pale. The forged commission was only one element in the propaganda war which was designed to provide some coherence to the rising in its early months. O'Neill also deliberately manufactured rumours and wrote letters to himself, said to come from prominent gentry, pledging support for the rising. He encouraged the discovery of prophecies said to relate to current events and even went so far as to produce a machine which he claimed made gunpowder in order to convince insurgents that he had access to supplies.

In the face of this considerable confusion, both sides turned to where they thought they could find most security: in their religious beliefs. Religious divisions that had been acceptable and accommodated in times of stability came to the fore as social order collapsed in the atmosphere of uncertainty, and a whole range of grievances came to be expressed in religious language. Catholic insurgents tore up Protestant Bibles in acts of desecration and refused to allow Protestants to be buried in consecrated ground for fear that they would pollute it. Older Protestant burials were disinterred. Religious ceremonies and use of iconic imagery were prominent in the early stages of the rising. Irish Catholic soldiers going into battle carried prayers, often of a charm-like quality, promising them a quick passage to heaven, and others wore devotional objects, such as St Francis's girdles. This marshalling of religion to support each side's position drew on the doctrine of providence, the idea that God not only existed but was actively at work in the world supporting His chosen people. In the same way as those engaged in contemporary European religious wars, the Catholic insurgents were firmly convinced that God fought with them and that it was no sin to kill a Protestant. The logical consequence of this argument was that the devil fought for Protestants, and, in one case in County Antrim, insurgents actively associated settlers with witchcraft. Protestants too believed that God was on their side, and in the stories they told in the depositions of their experiences in the rising there were providential narratives of supernatural assistance and strange coincidences that were ascribed to God's plan. Both sides saw God's hand at work in unusual occurrences in the natural world. In Armagh, rivers were said to have run red as if made of blood, fish disappeared from rivers, and at Portadown, in a spectacular turn of events after the massacre at the bridge, ghosts appeared on the river calling for revenge. The same was reported as having happened at Belturbet in County Cavan. The months of late 1641 were profoundly disturbing times for all those living in Ulster. War was spinning out of the control of military officers who had little experience of command, and looting, revenge and gratuitous violence came to dominate these months, much to the concern of the gentry and clergy. This situation was made worse by wild rumour, at least in part encouraged by Sir Phelim O'Neill. The problem of how to restore order to this world was a difficult one to resolve.

The war which began in Ulster in October 1641 was premised on a swift action to put the insurgents into a position of power from which they could negotiate. As such it required that the war shift out of Ulster. The rising there found an imitator in Wicklow within weeks. There the instability caused by Wentworth's land settlements had fomented discontent which was galvanised into action by the Ulster rising. The Ulster insurgents themselves moved west into Counties Leitrim and Mayo, but the main driving force was towards Dublin. The army marched south through County Louth, arriving at Drogheda by the end of November, where they laid siege to the town. The long period required to march this short distance reflects the poor military organisation of the insurgent army and the fact that they met with a less than enthusiastic reception from the Old English gentry of the Pale. The Old English were in a difficult position. On the political front, a number still sat in parliament, which had been briefly resumed on 16 November 1641. They had been instrumental in forming a parliamentary delegation to meet the insurgents to discover the reasons for their actions, with the aim of defusing them, but this plan was still-born since parliament was prorogued the following day. Militarily their principal problem was defence. The capacity of the Ulster insurgents to penetrate as deeply into the Pale as Drogheda, just thirty miles from Dublin, gave cause for considerable concern, and the sort of popular discontent characteristic of Ulster was beginning to appear in Pale counties such as Meath, which resulted in gentry defecting to the insurgents as a result of popular pressures. Moreover, the Dublin Castle government either would not, or could not, defend them. At the end of November a government force sent to relieve the siege of Drogheda was soundly defeated at Julianstown, to the south of Drogheda, through a mixture of incompetence and disorganisation rather than by superior military power.

As many Old English saw it, the explanations for the government's inactivity and incompetence were not entirely innocent. Relations between Old English Catholics and the administration had rapidly worsened in the summer and autumn of 1641. This was part of a more general deterioration in confessional relationships in Ireland over this period, fed by rumours of what the London parliament was intent on doing and the weakening of the king's ability to afford them any guarantees. Most were unwilling to join the rebellion and remained M.P.s until they were finally expelled from the Commons in June 1642. However, they distrusted the Lords Justices, who had reputations of being of a 'godly' persuasion and decidedly anti-Catholic. What was seen as proof of that suspicion appeared with the rising. In response to the rising on 23 October 1641, the Lords Justices issued a proclamation accusing 'evil affected Irish papists' of disloyalty. Those gathered under the Old English political umbrella of loyalty reacted strongly. According to Sir William St Leger, the President of Munster, 'I did read this proclamation to [Donal] O'Sullivan. At the reading of the words "ill-affected Irish papist" I did never in my life observe more venomous rancour in any man's face than was in his.'[15] The Old English vehemently pointed out that, although Catholic, they were loyal to the crown. Two days later the Lords Justices issued a corrective, but by this stage the damage was done. Appeals for arms by the Old English gentry went unheard, and the actions by some commanders of the Dublin army, particularly Sir Charles Coote and his burning of Mr King's house at Clontarf in December, created further grounds for grievance.

The Lords Justices, according to Richard Bellings's later account, exacerbated the situation simply because they could not cope with the fast-changing crisis. The Irish government, Bellings argued, was composed of 'some new mean men not long before made Privy Councillors' with neither the experience of authority nor the ability to govern. Indeed, Bellings went on to accuse the Lords Justices of outright duplicity in goading the Old English into rebellion. They prorogued the parliament on 17 November 1641 without royal authority, thus depriving the Old English of the opportunity to fulfil their duty to advise the king. Moreover, they publicly slandered Richard Butler, Viscount Mountgarrett, forcing him into the insurrection against the Dublin administration, though not, as he emphasised, the king. Bellings concluded from this experience that the Dublin Castle administration was unfit to govern and could not be trusted with the king's Irish subjects. The Lords Justices seemed rather to 'discountenance the further interests of their master' and in return created a 'most unnatural and lamentable war'.[16] In the view of the Old English, these men failed to command the moral authority, which proceeded from an adherence to duty and honour, necessary to govern Ireland. In this context, the Old English had little option but to forge some form of alliance with the insurgents. In early December representatives of the Old English community of the Pale met their Ulster counterparts at Knockcrofty in County Meath and agreed on a loose alliance. The basis of this arrangement was loyalty to the king and the familiar refrain of the defence of ancient liberties. A week later they met again, now on the symbolic Hill of Tara, and cemented the union. In some ways it was a realisation of what Geoffrey Keating had seen in the aftermath of the Graces, the emergence of the idea of an Irish people, though he had no thoughts of a rising. In this case bonds of marriage, parliamentary links and the concerns of landowners generally formed common ground on which to meet. These actions of December and January were not new developments, but rather the culmination of a series of defections to the Ulster insurgents over the previous month, while at the same time trying to maintain lines of communication with the king. The Earl of Ormond took a positive view of these events, thinking that they would moderate the demands of those in arms. It was not that simple, however. For some Irish Catholic peers of Old English background, such as the Earl of Roscommon, Baron Howth and Viscount Taaffe, loyalty to the crown was too strong an imperative and they refused to join an alliance. Others, such as Patrick Barnewall, Baron Dunsany, whose instincts were to remain loyal, were treated with suspicion by Dublin and arrested.

By the end of 1641 the Irish war had almost ground to a halt. The Ulster forces were bogged down at Drogheda in a siege that would not be relieved until March 1642. To the west the drive through Leitrim and into Connacht had also ceased as the insurgents failed to penetrate the lordship of the Catholic and staunchly royalist Earl of

Clanricard, recently returned from England. It is true that the rising had spread to other parts of the country. By the end of 1641 disorder was widespread throughout most of Leinster, but it was the early part of 1642 before trouble appeared in most parts of Munster, largely as a result of activity spilling over from County Tipperary. However, in the main this was not the sort of military action that the planners of the rising had envisaged. Rather, it was the consequence of local disputes, and the resulting pattern of violence was rather similar to that in Ulster in November of 1641. Religious feelings were exacerbated and Bibles burnt; houses were raided, often by people well known to the victims. Random murders took place. The pattern was not neat. In certain places older relationships continued to work, and some Catholics warned their Protestant neighbours of attack and occasionally preserved their goods for them. In County Meath one wealthy 'British Protestant', George Booth, entrusted his goods to a Catholic friend, Thomas Geoghan, for safe-keeping. Others used pre-existing social contacts as pretexts to gain admission to certain houses. In Meath John Ware was murdered in a drunken brawl with those with whom he was dining, and in Tyrone a justice of the peace opened his house to O'Donnellys who told him they were coming for a warrant to search for stolen sheep. On the other hand, settlers drew on pre-existing networks of good neighbourliness and friendship with the Catholic Irish and as a result managed to continue to live on their property behind enemy lines.

Sir Phelim's plan for a short, sharp war on the Scottish Bishops' War model, if that is what he intended, had failed. That would have long-term consequences, since war, in various forms, dragged on in Ireland for another ten years. This persistence of low-grade violence and the lack of institutions to deal with it was a source of considerable concern to many of those living in provincial Ireland. Most Catholic clergy attempted to curtail the violence at local level. While they certainly had a concern for order as such, most were more worried that unrestrained violence would damage their providential relationship with God, whom they regarded as the ultimate arbiter of the war. This was true not only of clergy but of some military commanders as well. Sir Phelim O'Neill was recorded as saying that he feared God would not bless the insurgents' efforts 'because of those murders and cruelties'.[17] In early 1642 the insurgents in Leitrim were engaged in re-creating the local government structure with their own justices of the peace. In other parts of the country local associations were set up in an effort to manage the problem of war. At a higher political level, the Earl of Clanricard sought to open lines of communication with the leaders of the rising in the hope of bringing about an early peace. Neither of these strategies, local or national, would prove effective, and the problem of order remained one for which a solution would have to be found. That was a task the insurgents had to turn to next.

# 6

# The Quest for a Settlement, 1642–51

W hen contemporaries later reflected on what had happened in the last months of 1641, they were taken aback by two aspects of events. The first feature that struck them was the speed with which it had all happened and the fragility of the relationships that had broken down. As Richard Bellings, later secretary to the Catholic Confederation of Kilkenny, commented, the rising had come into a world in which the inhabitants of Ireland '(setting aside their different tenets in matters of religion) were as perfectly incorporated, and as firmly knit together, as frequent marriages, daily ties of hospitality and the mutual bond between lord and tenant, could unite any people'. Even the vitriolic settler Sir John Temple admitted that the English and Irish were consolidated 'into one body, knit and compacted together with all those bonds and ligatures of friendship, alliance and consanguity as might make up a constant and perfect union betwixt them'.[1] Yet all this, forged over forty years, had collapsed within weeks under pressure of violence on an unprecedented scale in recent memory.

The second thing that struck contemporaries was the confusion that characterised events as the rising unfolded. Order and hierarchy seemed to break down rapidly, and power passed from the gentry to the lower social orders. A Gaelic Irish peer, Lord Muskerry in Kerry, described in March 1642 to Lord Barrymore how events spiralled out of control in Munster, led by the lower social orders. He stressed that he 'did abhor their insurrection', but that 'I have [seen] such burning and killing of men and women and children without regard of age or quality that I expected no safety for myself' and was forced to join the rising.[2] Blame for the breakdown of law and order resulting from the actions of insubordinate peasantry became a common motif of writing about the 1640s, both in Ireland and in England. In November 1641 a number of the O'Reillys wrote to the Lords Justices apologising for 'the mischiefs and inconveniences that have already happened through the disorder of the common sort of people'.[3] After the war Nicholas Plunkett, who was heavily involved in its events, reflected that the rising had been 'only the act of a few persons of broken and desperate fortunes' supported by 'a rude multitude'.[4] More worrying was the sense that what had begun with relatively modest aims was fast becoming a radical movement. The O'Reillys in 1641 had stressed that those involved in the rising did not want to overturn the Ulster plantation scheme, which would, after all, have cost some of the leading insurgents their estates. Rather, they sought to redress political grievances which had originated in the 1630s. By February 1642 a document entitled the 'Demands of the Irish' sought that the crown and its ministers unwind the plantation schemes back to the Elizabethan era, restoring the land to the 'very nearest of kin' of their original owners. It called for the expulsion of the Scots from Ulster, the establishment of Catholicism as the state religion, the surrender of all churches to the Catholics, the appointment of a Catholic Lord Deputy, surrender of all garrisons to Catholic commanders, and the passage of an act of oblivion for all involved in the insurrection.[5] This was a long way from the conservative requests for reform articulated in the previous November. It was, in short, a demand for social revolution and potential political disorder.

## CREATING ORDER

For contemporaries, such uncertainty and confusion seemed to suggest that Ireland was being drawn into a dangerous vortex, although in fact things turned out not to be as dramatic as they imagined. As the war developed it proved to be a low-intensity affair. Many had predicted worse. The Earl of Ormond, with limited military experience, clearly expected an attack on Dublin and in November 1641 ordered that all crops within a ten-mile radius of the city be brought into the city or burnt to deprive a besieging army. This was a dramatic miscalculation of the insurgents' military strength, but it had a significant impact on the food supply of the city. As the military campaign rolled out into 1642 and 1643 it became clear that the insurgents' forces were less well supplied and organised than might have been expected. The war began to move in favour of the government forces. In March 1642 the siege of Drogheda was raised, and in April Ormond defeated the opposing forces at Kilrush, County Kildare, which allowed him to take Athlone on the River Shannon and open up the hinterland of Dublin. In Munster Murrough O'Brien, sixth Baron Inchiquin, won the battle of Liscarroll, County Cork, in August 1642. In Ulster the war was more a series of guerrilla offensives, although in 1643 Owen Roe O'Neill defeated the settler commander, Sir Robert Stewart, in a set-piece battle at Clones in County Monaghan. With such minor exceptions the military side of the war was going well for the settler forces. In the short term, there was one bright light. In March 1642 the London parliament passed the Adventurers' Act, which, in return for immediate money, promised 'adventurers', mainly London merchants, that they would be paid in Irish land at the end of the war. The hope of military and financial assistance was raised, but the long-term implication of the move was to reshape the entire structure of Irish society as it led to the introduction of new settlers in the 1650s with different priorities to those of the longer-established landholders.

If military affairs were not the disaster some had feared, the economic consequences of war seemed more problematic. The economic difficulties that had been obvious in the early weeks of the rising were made much worse by the spread of hostilities. Problems caused by harvest failures in the late 1630s escalated into a financial crisis with the outbreak of war and as trade collapsed. The transformation of the balance of trade from surplus to deficit meant that imported coin in Ireland, in effect the only form of money since Ireland had no mint, soon became inadequate for even normal transactions. In consequence, rents remained unpaid and markets ground to a halt. However, by the middle of 1642 there were signs that the economy was adjusting to war conditions. Rents stabilised, albeit at a lower level than before the war, and the harvest of 1642 was unusually good. The Dublin administration also took the unusual step of trying to stabilise the commercial crisis that war had created by issuing an Irish coinage in 1642 and 1643, using silver plate called in by proclamation. Financial problems were to worsen into 1643 with the outbreak of civil war in England, which made trading with ports there difficult. Moreover, this was an economy which now had to support a significant military force that had not been there before. The financial requirements of the Earl of Ormond's government army by 1642 were more than seven times the income of Ireland in 1640. The gap between income and expenditure was met by voluntary loans and with substantial contributions by Ormond himself, but this was clearly not sustainable. Economically, Ireland was certainly in a difficult situation; yet it was not the complete collapse that some had feared.

The most dangerous threat that war posed to all the parties in Ireland was political. In the context of war, the most pressing matter was to replace confusion with order and to establish rules for the management of war and the construction of peace. From the insurgents' point of view, the first steps in this direction were taken by the Catholic hierarchy, who, while they supported the rising, abhorred the social dislocation it brought. At a synod at Kells, County Meath, in March 1642 a declaration was issued calling for the creation of a council of ecclesiastics and laity with the conservative agenda of enforcing law and order. Two months later a national synod at Kilkenny provided a forum to discuss the options for achieving this. The clergy decided on an oath-bound association with a general council, created to rule until a general assembly would meet. The oath was to be administered by Catholic parish clergy at mass. The scheme was fleshed out in early June 1642 by a group of gentry who seem to have been elected on the basis of the old parliamentary constituencies. A Supreme Council of twenty-four, elected from a General Assembly, was to act as the executive. It had at least twelve members resident at Kilkenny at any one time. The General Assembly, which met on nine occasions in the 1640s, was elected using the older parliamentary boundaries and the pre-1640 franchise, but excluding Protestants. The first formal General Assembly met in October 1642, a meeting which lasted four weeks. This structure was to govern most of Ireland for the next seven years in parallel with the Dublin-based administration.

There are two significant features of this new body: its form and its function. The form of the government of Ireland was to be that of a confederation, held together by an oath. Confederation for constitutional and confessional purposes was not unusual on the edges of contemporary Europe. It had been reinvigorated by the Protestant Estates in Moravia, Austria and Hungary against imperial power in 1608, and was subsequently used against territorial integration in Bohemia, Moravia, Silesia and the two Lusatias in 1619. However, one does not have to look that far beyond Ireland to find models that the Irish Confederates could have followed. Most obviously, the Covenanter movement in Scotland had used the National Covenant of 1638 as a basis for establishing what was, in effect, an alternative government. It may not even be necessary to go as far as Scotland. In March 1642 the gentlemen of Leinster and Munster formulated an oath as a way of providing coherence for local society. The text of the oath is almost identical with that of the English protestation oath of 1641, substituting 'Catholic' for 'Protestant' where required, along with other similar changes. The parallels should not be pushed too far. The Irish Confederation was seen as a temporary expedient rather than a permanent government and was not underpinned by the sort of radical covenant theology that was evident in the Scottish National Covenant. As such it had much less of an impact than similar bodies in Scotland and elsewhere.

What is striking about the form of the new body is that it was intended to be a comprehensive one. Here the assembly took its lead from the Catholic clergy, whose draft of the Confederate oath emphasised that there were to be no divisions between the Old English and Irish. At the first General Assembly the Confederation defined itself by resolving:

> For the avoiding of national distinctions between the subjects of His Majesty's dominions, which this Assembly doth utterly detest and abhor, and which ought not to be endured in a well-governed Commonwealth it is ordered and established . . . that every Roman Catholic, as well English Welsh as Scotch, who was of that profession before the troubles . . . shall be cherished in his life, goods and estates by the power, authority and force (if need require it) of all the Catholics of Ireland, as fully and freely as any native born therein.

Moreover, 'there shall be no distinction or comparison made betwixt old Irish and old or new English, or betwixt septs and families, or betwixt citizens and townsmen and countrymen joining in union'.[6] This extension of the clergy's insistence on coherence between Old English and Irish represented an ingenious solution to the problems of the early seventeenth century. By redefining the political nation in religious rather than ethnic terms, it appeared to solve the problem of how to deal with fractures within the world of the ruled. It also allowed English Catholics with Irish interests, such as the Earl of Castlehaven, to become part of this new order. It aligned political assumptions and institutional arrangements with religious allegiances. Moreover, it reflected popular attitudes that used Catholicism as a defining feature of loyalty. In the early stages of the rising some Irish had attempted to impose local confessional unity in their own regions. In Longford, for example, they declared that 'none should live in Ireland but such as would go to mass', and in one Monaghan case it was claimed that some Protestants 'could not be Christians unless they were so christened anew'. Threats were made to force Protestants to conform to Catholicism, and, more practically in a state of warfare, it was claimed in Longford that soldiers 'could give quarter to them that were Catholics but not to the heretics'. Others converted to Catholicism to save their goods or lives.[7] By insisting only on a self-definition of Catholicism, and since parish priests administered the oath at mass, the lowest common bond within Catholicism, it also held together the different types of Catholicism in Ireland that had proved divisive earlier in the century. Thus the worlds of traditional religion, which some of a Counter-Reformation cast of mind regarded as merely superstition, and its more European form, characteristic of the Old English world, could be joined. The sort of debates that had split parish clergy from those in religious orders over rights to parochial dues and the control of bishops in the 1630s were also reduced in significance, although they were far from being solved and the effects of these divisions were still apparent at the end of the century.

This attempt at comprehension produced some features that were less than desirable. The first was that both the General Assembly and the Supreme Council lacked a strong leadership underpinned by social authority, having no coherent group among their membership from the upper social strata. In the early 1640s many Old English peers either fought against the Confederation or tried to remain neutral. A 1644 listing of the members of the General Assembly recorded thirteen bishops, eighteen peers and 166 members of the lower house. A second list of 1647 records eleven bishops, sixteen peers and 292 commoners. Among the Supreme Council the peerage was better represented, with seven peers out of thirty-six serving members before 1645. All this suggests that the Confederation was truncated in social terms. The expectation was that the Confederation, as a political body, would produce a coherent structure for the governance of Ireland, yet it lacked members with sufficient personal influence and scope for patronage to fulfil those expectations. Consequently, its capacity to bind its members together was exceedingly fragile and vulnerable to challenge. Such challenges soon appeared. Within the Confederation there were a number of fracture lines. On the issue of war, for example, moderates such as Patrick Plunkett, Richard Bellings, the secretary to the Supreme Council, and Viscount Muskerry advocated conciliation, while others proved to be more hardline. In another context, the question of the fate of the lands of religious houses confiscated at the Reformation and redistributed mainly to Old English beneficiaries, there were conflicting voices. Such fractures were to become very apparent in 1646 and 1647.

The second important aspect of the Confederation was its function. Its aim was to provide a civil administration which would reverse the breakdown of order and oversee the re-creation of an older, more stable, world. For some, the rapid disintegration of the social order was almost as frightening as the violence that accompanied it. As the Confederation declared at its first meeting, 'No family, city, commonwealth, much less any kingdom, may stand without union and concord, without which this kingdom for the present standeth in most danger.'[8] The Confederates were clear that they were not a parliament since they had not been summoned by the king. However, the subtleties of this position were not appreciated by many who referred to it as a parliament. Over time, however, the assembly was forced to assume royal functions. It dispatched ambassadors to seek funding to realise its aims, and in order to maintain economic activity it was forced to issue £4,000 worth of its own coinage in 1642 despite the minting of coinage being a function reserved to the king. Moreover, it acquired many of the trappings of government in the early seventeenth century, the most important of which was a printing-press, located initially at Waterford and later at Kilkenny, by which its legislation, proclamations and propaganda could be disseminated. It was a parliament in all but name, but it was careful not to take the name so as to maintain its royalist credentials.

The relatively simple domestic political agenda of the Confederation was made complex by forces outside its control. It was propelled unwillingly into other spheres of action in the course of 1642 as new influences entered the Irish war. Undoubtedly the most important consideration was the outbreak of hostilities between king and parliament in England in August 1642. Most immediately this affected a Scottish military force based in Ulster. When Charles I learned of the outbreak of the Ulster rising in October 1641, he was in Scotland and immediately asked the Scottish parliament to provide a force for the suppression of what was perceived as rebellion. However, it was not until April 1642 that a Scots force arrived at Carrickfergus, County Antrim, under the command of Robert Monro, a man of considerable military experience in the Swedish war. The main reason for this delay was the constitutional machinations involved in raising such a force. The Scottish Covenant claimed, and the Treaties of Berwick and Ripon established, that Scotland was an independent, sovereign kingdom, whereas Ireland was perceived as a dependency of the English crown. Thus any Scots intervention in Ireland required an international treaty. The details of this treaty were important for the future actions of that army. Some 10,000 men were to be raised in Scotland, paid at English rates by the English parliament and to remain distinct and not to be quartered with other soldiers. In addition, the commander of that force was to receive instructions from the chief governors of Ireland as the king's representative. Thus it was constituted as a Scots army, paid by parliament and commanded by the king. Being a Scots army, it immediately began to set up the structures of Presbyterianism in Ulster in order to export the Scottish Covenanting revolution. As a parliamentarian army it would, after the outbreak of civil war in England, establish a parliamentarian presence in Ulster which would be important for the future, although fluctuations in the king's and the parliament's attitude to this army, especially in 1644, meant that its position was rather uncertain. Moreover, the treaty authorising and dispatching the force had not addressed its relationship with the existing settler army in Ulster, and this was to be a source of considerable friction.

The settlers had a rather different agenda to that of the recently arrived Scots, and while the settlers wanted military supplies they were unwilling to surrender territory or command.

Secondly, the Irish war was also drawn into the wider world of European hostilities. Pope Urban VIII, under pressure as a result of developments in the Thirty Years' War, gave his blessing to the Irish Confederate war, sending some £7,000 for the war effort, which was enough to keep the Leinster army in the field for eight months. In July 1643 a papal envoy, Pier Francesco Scarampi, arrived in Kilkenny. More important was the arrival at Doe Castle in County Donegal in early July 1642 of Owen Roe O'Neill with a force gathered from the Irish contingent in the army of the Spanish Netherlands. Born in Armagh in the 1580s, O'Neill had gone to Flanders as a soldier in 1604 or early 1605. He therefore brought considerable military experience to the chaotic insurgent force in Ireland, and he was appointed commander of the Confederate army when the General Assembly met. Two months later this force was reinforced by the arrival of another continental soldier and O'Neill's future rival, Thomas Preston, with men and arms at Wexford. What Owen Roe anticipated he would find in Ireland is not clear, but some of the correspondence of another inhabitant of the Low Countries, Hugh Bourke, the commissary of the Franciscans in Germany and the Low Countries, suggests that he thought it was a war about religion and its institutions. 'This is a war', declared Bourke in early 1642, 'waged solely for God and the defence of the Catholic church, [and] the kingdom and monarchy of Christ's vicar on earth'; it was a war intended to secure Catholicism 'to the very last man'.[9] Owen Roe's perception of events was probably similar, especially since he had lived most of his life exposed to the full rigours of continental Counter-Reformation Catholicism. Thus, as events developed in the 1640s, Owen Roe operated on a rather different agenda to that promoted by the majority of the Confederation, many of whom were prepared to make accommodations even in the area of religion. Owen Roe took his political lead from the papal nuncio, Giovanni Battista Rinuccini, who had succeeded Scarampi with full legatine powers, and this had devastating consequences for the unity of the Confederate cause in the late 1640s.

These interventions from outside Ireland might have been assumed to have given the contending parties in Ireland distinct military advantages in the form of subventions and military skills to wage war. In practice neither of these advantages materialised. In England Charles's involvement with the war there meant that there was little to spare for the Irish sphere of operations. Before 1643 some 10,000 men were sent to Ireland, but this quickly came to a halt with the outbreak of hostilities in England. Between October 1643 and the end of the English Civil War some 9,000 English troops were recalled from Ireland. In fact the king hoped that a truce could be reached in Ireland so that he could draw on Irish men and money to support the royalist effort in England.

Money, as both parties in the Irish rising discovered, was the sinews of war. Neither had any experience of war financing. In the sixteenth century the Nine Years' War had been funded directly from the London exchequer and by massive debasement of the Irish currency. In the 1640s both sides resorted to issuing their own coin, collecting existing taxes and borrowing. However, the nature of war made such a task difficult. The government forces maintained control of the main ports, including Dublin, Cork and Derry, which meant that the Confederates had no access to the customs which composed about a quarter of pre-1641 revenue. Equally, they had no access to the main source of loans: the wealthier merchants. As a result, they were forced to borrow modest amounts from smaller merchants. Borrowing on a wider scale was also difficult for the Confederation because of its uncertain constitutional position. Conversely, the Dublin administration was deprived of royal rents and composition payments from land now under Confederate control, which had accounted for about half of royal revenue. Both sides resorted to levies on the territories they controlled, but economic and administrative conditions made these difficult to collect and the Confederates soon discovered that the maintenance of a bureaucracy in Kilkenny was an expensive necessity in addition to keeping an army in the field. The result was that by the middle of 1643 the ability of either side to wage a military campaign was much reduced. It was clear that the war, although by mid-1643 militarily successful for the settlers, could not be satisfactorily concluded for want of men, money and supplies. The unsatisfactory possibility of a stalemate emerged. There was little choice but to attempt to find a political settlement to end the war. The process of negotiating a truce to allow peace talks to begin commenced with a royal commission of April 1643 to the commander of the Irish army, the Earl of Ormond, to negotiate a cessation of the war, initially for one year, taking effect on 15 September.

## THE CESSATION OF 1643

The cessation of arms agreed in September 1643 was forced on all the parties by economics and wider political considerations. Nevertheless, it was not welcomed by all. Since this was a truce rather than a peace, armies could not be stood down, although they could be reduced significantly to match available resources, and this meant that supplies were still needed. The outbreak of the English Civil War in August 1642 meant that the king was in no position to support the Irish army. Whether parliament might do so was another question. Some felt that the Irish war, which had been going well in early 1643, should be continued and the problem of rebellion finally solved. In Ulster Robert Monro's force, paid by the parliament in London, refused to accept the 1643 cessation on parliament's instruction, since they feared that an Irish cessation would release troops for the royalist cause in England, then waging a successful war, and insisted that the Ulster war continue.

More serious were the ideological problems that emerged from the cessation. The effect of the rising had been to galvanise the more radically inclined Protestants in a powerful anti-Catholic crusade. Faithful Teate, a Church of Ireland minister from Cavan and in 1642 Provost of Trinity College, led an anti-Catholic preaching crusade in Dublin. The implications of some of the things said were dramatic. One sermon in Christ Church Cathedral in late 1642, preached by Steven Jerome, portrayed the rising as God's punishment for the marriage of Charles and his Catholic queen, Henrietta Maria, who, in an Old Testament parallel, was said to be the daughter of Jezebel. For the preacher, English royalists and Catholic Confederates were birds of a feather. Jerome had many sympathisers. His sermon cost the Chancellor of Christ Church, who had organised it, his living and university degrees (he later re-emerged as a Baptist peacher). Some of those who were part of John Rogers's separatist congregation at Christ Church in the 1650s identified their experience in Ireland in the early 1640s as the factor that had awakened their latent radical religious sympathies. At a higher social level, some saw the 1643 cessation as temporising with Catholics, which they felt would bring further judgments of God on Ireland, and objected strongly. As a result, four Privy Councillors who opposed the cessation were imprisoned in July

1643 in order to silence them. The war and its conduct had an important psychological and practical impact on the inhabitants of Ireland, forcing them to think radically about how society should be organised and about the relationship between the various groups on the island.

Two ways of thinking about how Irish society should evolve were beginning to take shape. The first was a world associated with a providential mind, which identified itself with a radical, godly agenda and was built around a covenant, an idea which from the 1640s would be associated with radical religious bodies in Ireland. Ideologically this made for a coherent social order, but, in contrast to the long chains of authority linking the ruler and the ruled, a covenanted society was a more fragmented affair, composed of voluntary associations held together by an agreement or oath. Such groups then created contractual bonds with a reformed godly ruler, constructed on the model of the Old Testament king. This was the sort of world associated with the Scottish Presbyterian revolution of the late 1630s. By the early 1640s the Covenanter drive to export that revolution had become inextricably associated with the position of the Scots in relation to the English Civil War. In September 1643 a rather unwilling Long Parliament and the Scots entered an agreement which was set out in a document, the Solemn League and Covenant. The point of that arrangement was not to dispose of the king but rather to overcome the problem of lack of trust in him by forcing him to take the Covenant and thereby circumscribing his actions. By 1644 the Covenant was being tendered to those inhabitants of Ireland who supported the parliamentary cause, often in return for military supplies. Descriptions of the taking of the Covenant record large crowds raising their hands to heaven to swear the oath as the document was read out. Such oath-taking was dramatic because participants knew, however crudely, that something important was happening in a ceremony in which the personal and moral relations of an older, hierarchical society were dissolved and new social bonds were created by the oath.

This Covenant served a number of functions for those in Ireland. First, in Ulster the 1643 Covenant became one of the most potent symbols of belonging to Scottish Presbyterianism among the settlers. Something of the impact of the Solemn League and Covenant in the popular Ulster mind can be attributed to the circumstances of its introduction. Simply on the grounds of chronology, its appearance virtually coincided with the formal establishment of Presbyterianism in Ulster. A few radical ministers, such as Robert Blair at Bangor and John Livingston at Killinchy, had established a form of Presbyterian discipline in Ulster before 1640. However, such experiments were isolated, and no structure of presbyteries or other Presbyterian forms of church government existed in Ulster before the foundation of the first presbytery at Carrickfergus on 10 June 1642 by the soldiers of Robert Monro's expeditionary force. In contrast to the situation in Scotland, Presbyterianism in Ulster could not call on any state backing or tradition of development, and in that sense the Covenant served as a foundational statement of belief and order.

The circumstances and method of the introduction of the Covenant into Ireland had important implications for the social shape of religious change in the 1640s. Since Presbyterianism became a way of regulating a disordered community in the 1640s, its structures and effectiveness became deeply intertwined with the structures of local communities. In this it was rather different to Scotland, where the kirk session was, in many respects, a branch of central government, although the boundaries between secular and spiritual jurisdictions were always contested. In Ireland the Presbyterian discipline evolved from within the community and relied on community pressures rather than on any official sanctions such as the established Church of Ireland could call on. This association of Presbyterianism with the community, and especially in the disturbed period of the 1640s, led at least some Presbyterian sessions to claim authority not just over those who voluntarily adhered to its discipline but rather over the entire community. In doing so it operated as an established church, but without the limiting and supporting power of the state in the manner of Scottish Presbyterianism. In the Presbyterian session book for the congregation at Templepatrick, County Antrim, for September 1647 there is a note that a Lieutenant Wallace 'hath some Irishes under him who comes not to the church[;] the session ordains W[illia]m Mc Cord to speak [to] the lieutenant that either he will put them away from him or else cause them to keep the church'.[10] For the local Presbyterian church, coherence within the community who lived in a particular place and the control of the session was paramount, since it was the local organising body, the session, which in the 1640s provided a way of organising the local community. The local native Irish were drawn in not so much by conversion as by the impact of local administrative structures. This goes some way in explaining why Ulster Presbyterianism regarded itself as effectively the established church in the northern part of Ireland.

How much support the Covenant, and the parliamentary cause, really had in Ireland is difficult to determine. In Ulster one of the driving forces in the rapid spread of the Covenant was the hope on the part of the army that adherence to the parliamentarian cause would bring supplies for a settler army that had been ignored by Dublin and London. Even the Scots force in Ulster under Monro were unenthusiastic about the Covenant until their demands for supplies were met in the spring of 1644. However, there were other motives which made the Covenant attractive. It provided a structure around which local order could be re-established in a society in which the structures of local administration had collapsed in the face of disorder. War had rendered ineffectual the normal mechanisms of local administration, producing a powerful localism that was difficult to break. Those who had seen the beginnings of Presbyterian discipline before the rising also witnessed its collapse. John Livingston, the minister at Killinchy in the 1630s, observed on his return to Ireland in 1642: 'I found ane great alteration in Ireland. Many of those who had been civil before became [in] many ways exceeding loose; yea sundry who, as was conceded, had true grace were declined much in their tenderness.'[11] In this situation, the Covenant and the structures of order that it introduced were of considerable importance in organising local society. Indeed, the importance of the Covenant in creating oath-bound communities of interest was recognised by the Marquis of Ormond in 1644 when he advocated a 'counter-covenant' using oaths already in use in England. One element of this bonding was the association of a Covenanter settler interest with anti-Irishness. As one early historian of Presbyterianism, Patrick Adair, recorded at Enniskillen, 'The Irish, who were protected, hearing the Covenant was coming that way, fled, because they heard that the Covenant was to extirpate all papists and was against protecting them', which may well reflect local perceptions.[12] At least one man, probably a Scottish minister who served in the Church of Ireland, saw the Covenant as a bond 'to defend and maintain the just laws and liberties one of another against the common enemy', with no implications for the form of church government.[13] Some Scots, such as Robert Stewart, the commander of the Laggan force in east County Donegal, had reservations about the constitutional implications of a Scottish document being imported into Ireland, but such objections were quickly swept away in the face of popular pressure for its adoption. In this way the Covenant and the position of the English parliament against the king came to be identified with local interests, rather than specifically Presbyterian ones, and hence made significant inroads into Ulster society.

The Covenant and the parliamentarian cause also found support in some areas outside Ulster. In Munster Lord Inchiquin was confronted with the practical dilemma of providing supplies for his force, which he felt should have been pressing its military advantage against Catholics rather than ceasing its activities. It seems that this problem of supplies for the army, which he hoped would be dealt with by the London parliament if the Covenant were taken, and the desire to prosecute the war were the main motivating forces in allowing the Covenant to be taken in Munster. However, Inchiquin was not pleased at the scale on which it was tendered and tried to formulate his own oath to replace it. There may also have been more personal considerations, such as the king's failure to appoint Inchiquin President of Munster when the office fell vacant in 1644. While Inchiquin was prepared to accept the possibility of supply from the English parliament, he was more reluctant to involve himself in the ideological battles associated with the English Civil War, though some in Munster were clearly inclined towards parliament. For Inchiquin, the primary war was against the Confederation, whom he regarded as the king's enemies, and the war needed to be prosecuted by whatever means were necessary. Hence the Covenant and the parliamentary cause were simply means to a military end.

The second sort of society which was on offer was preferred by most of those in Ireland in the 1640s: a return to the world of monarchy and its associated social structures. To achieve this, the cessation of 1643 between the government forces and the Confederation had to be transformed into a peace treaty. That transformation had taken place by March 1646 when the first Ormond peace was agreed between the Lord Lieutenant and the Confederation, but it was not an easy process. The Marquis of Ormond (appointed Lord Lieutenant of Ireland in November 1643), for instance, clearly found negotiation with the Confederates distasteful, despite the fact that many of them were his relatives. At least once, in 1644, he threatened to resign the chief governorship. In the spring of 1644 Confederate agents travelled to Oxford to put their case to the king, and at the same time the Dublin Privy Council sent four members to the king to offer their advice. A third delegation, composed of Protestants, also made its way to the royal court to set out its vision of the future. However, it was the eighteen points of the Confederate proposals that were to dominate the discussions. The outline of the Confederate position was derived from Patrick Darcy's *Argument*, first drafted in 1641 for the House of Commons, but printed for the first time in 1643 by Thomas Bourke, printer to the Confederation at Waterford. The use of this text is clearly significant in linking the Confederate argument about the nature of Irish government with the commission of a legitimately summoned parliament, as the assembly of 1641 was. From this flowed the eighteen propositions that centred on the removal of religious and civil disabilities on Catholics and the reform of government. These articles dealt with plantations and landownership, the repeal of penal laws, the erection of Catholic educational institutions, the opening of government office to Catholic 'natives', reorganisation of the army, a declaratory act repudiating the jurisdiction of the English parliament in Ireland, a new parliament with the suspension of Poynings' Law, restrictions on the viceroy and limits on Privy Council jurisdiction. There was little that was new in this. The position of the parliament had been discussed from every angle since 1640. Many of the other proposals, such as the ownership of churches by Catholics, a Catholic university and access to higher offices for Irishmen and Catholics, bore a chilling resemblance to the demands tabled by the Earl of Tyrone at the height of the Nine Years' War against which Sir Robert Cecil had written 'Ewtopia'.[14] Whether any new light could be shed on such well-chewed-over difficulties was highly problematical. By contrast, the Protestant articles for the negotiations were more traditional. They sought a complete Confederate surrender and the reinforcement of the Protestant confessional state, as well as the enhancement of the plantation programme, a settlement that was similar to that envisaged by the English parliament for Ireland. In the summer of 1644 the peace talks moved from Oxford to Ireland, leaving the Lord Lieutenant, the Marquis of Ormond, with considerable latitude to fashion a deal. There were two overarching principles underpinning the king's position: first the need to establish universal royal authority in Ireland, and secondly that this be done within the existing rule of law. These principles were to be employed flexibly, but at the same time the opening of peace talks between the king and the Westminster parliament at Uxbridge could not be jeopardised, though they did in fact fail in early 1645, owing to allegations that the king was soft on the Irish Catholic rebels. Thus, as the king repeatedly told Ormond, one of his tasks was to safeguard Protestant subjects.

The most immediate problem, that concerning pardons for those in rebellion, was relatively easily solved. A clause was included in the peace treaty offering an act of oblivion for all those involved in war (despite Ormond's attempt to issue individual pardons and hence fragment the Confederation), thereby bringing Confederates within the king's peace. Greater difficulties were encountered in respect of the demand that Catholics be admitted to offices of state, since the king proved reluctant to allow the main offices of state to be opened to them. By July 1645 this impediment too had been overcome by a resolution that civil and military appointments would be agreed later with the king. In effect, this granted royal authorisation to the Confederate government even after the dissolution of the Confederation, which would be the result of a peace treaty. The issue of the freedom of the Irish parliament, one of the key demands of the Confederates, was more problematic, since to declare that the London parliament had no authority in Ireland would have important implications for the Adventurers' Act of 1642. In effect, it was left to the Irish parliament to declare its own mind on this when it met. The issue of the workings of Poynings' Law was doomed to remain unresolved.

The most acrimonious area of the peace negotiations was that of religion. The king was initially not prepared to alter the penal legislation against Catholics, but by early 1645 his worsening military position obliged him to take a more conciliatory tack in return for support. He was prepared to concede that Catholics might erect churches where they were in a majority. The more complex subject of a national church, which involved both political and spiritual issues as well as relations between crown and church, was more difficult. Ormond refused to consider the repeal of the Act of Supremacy, arguing that to do so would abrogate and deliver over to the pope the king's royal right to govern, which came from God. Thus matters of religion and royal authority lay behind more prosaic issues such as the control of church buildings and the appointment of bishops. A peace treaty was only achievable by laying these matters aside for resolution later. Ultimately they would be the cause of the collapse of the settlement.

Overall, what the king and Confederates were striving towards in 1644 and 1645 was a peace they could regard as an honourable one. What all parties wanted was a return to the royalist world of the 1620s where concessions could be arranged between all parties and royal authority over people and institutions could be restored. The wars of the 1640s were not, in the eyes of royalists at least, wars of conquest. Yet the king could not break the bond between crown, church and nation as some of the radicals in the Confederation and the Covenanters in Ulster demanded that he should. The result was that the Irish polity under a king would have to remain a Protestant one, albeit with some guarantees of toleration for Catholics.

This process of negotiating a peace was made more complex by unstable and unpredictable forces at work in Ireland. The first of these was the murky world of ecclesiastical politics symbolised by the presence of a fully accredited papal nuncio, Giovanni Battista Rinuccini, in Ireland. Rinuccini had arrived in Ireland in October 1645, in succession to Scarampi, as the result of a mission in late 1643 by Richard Bellings, secretary to the Confederation, to European political powers in an endeavour to raise funds for a financially bankrupt Confederation. Bellings's mission was singularly unsuccessful. While the major European powers showed an interest in Irish developments, and some maintained ambassadors at Kilkenny, they were more concerned with recruiting Irish soldiers for the Thirty Years' War after the 1643 cessation than with funding an Irish campaign. Of the £70,000 raised, £56,000 came from the pope, £6,400 from France, and £5,000 from Spain. Thus the only significant contributor was the papacy, and this support came with the unwelcome price of the appointment of a nuncio to Ireland to look after papal interests there. As the negotiations for peace developed Rinuccini became increasingly unhappy. The problem stemmed from Rinuccini's attitude to religion. For the nuncio, religion, both in its political and devotional senses, lay firmly in the public sphere, a view shaped by his Italian experience as Archbishop of Fermo. He was convinced of the importance of public events and spectacle, and when taking part of the washing of the feet at Limerick on Holy Thursday 1644, he noted of the public ritual 'that it will be a sufficient stimulus for them [the inhabitants of the town] to have seen this spectacle once to make them cling to the Catholic religion and defend it forever'.[15] By contrast, for many of those on the Old English side, religion was, in essence, a private affair. As Sir Robert Talbot said, 'it is indifferent to him to have mass with solemnity in Christ's [Church Cathedral] or St Patrick's Church as privately by his bedside'.[16] This tradition of the domestication of religious practice was well established by necessity in Ireland before the 1640s, with mass usually being said with little pomp in private houses, often the house of the landlord. As Rinuccini railed, 'even the lowest artisan wants to hear mass at his bedside, often to our great scandal on the very table from which the altar cloth has just been removed, playing-cards or glasses of beer together with food for dinner are at once laid'.[17] The problem was that Rinuccini's agenda was set in Rome, not in Ireland. For Rinuccini, clearly nothing but a full establishment of Catholicism as the state religion was acceptable, while many of the Confederates were prepared to settle for less. It was not that these views were new or peculiar to the nuncio. Many of the Irish bishops also held them, but they had been circumspect about expressing them. The difference was that Rinuccini articulated such views in a forceful way, backed by papal authority and finance.

The second unstable element in the negotiation process was the king himself. Charles's position in England deteriorated rapidly during the First Civil War after 1643. Although royalist principles had governed the negotiations for a peace in 1644, by 1645 he was desperate for military support from Ireland and was prepared to abandon principles. The failure of the negotiations with the parliament at Uxbridge in February 1645 meant that the king no longer had to present himself to an English audience as taking a hard line with Confederates. Towards the end of June 1645 the Earl of Glamorgan, an English Catholic royalist with Irish connections, arrived in Ireland with secret instructions from Charles to make the best possible deal with the Confederates in order that he might obtain Irish troops. Ormond, the Lord Lieutenant, was not told of this arrangement, but was informed that Glamorgan was in Ireland to conduct private business and to assist the Lord Lieutenant in making a peace. In August Glamorgan set out for Kilkenny as part of the peace negotiation team. Within three weeks he had negotiated his own treaty. The terms were sweeping. It provided for a complete toleration for all Catholics, exemption for Catholics from the jurisdiction of Protestant clergy, and the confirmation of the treaty by parliament, although the king was to give his word that the concessions would be honoured. In return, the Confederation would provide 1,000 men under the command of Glamorgan for the royalist cause in England. The Confederates formally agreed to the provision of troops in September 1645. These terms were manifestly unacceptable to Ormond and the Dublin council, so the treaty was to remain secret. Moreover, the papal agent in Ireland, Scarampi, thought it did not provide sufficient guarantees for Catholics, even though it did meet exactly the negotiating demands of the Confederates.

The arrival of Rinuccini at Kilkenny in November 1645 increased demands for more concessions on the position of Catholicism in line with his conception of the role of religion. The nuncio insisted that the Lord Lieutenant be a Catholic, that Catholic bishops be allowed to sit in parliament, that a self-governing Catholic university be established, and that the Confederation should not be dissolved until the king formally ratified the religious concessions. It seems that Glamorgan on behalf of the king agreed to these more radical proposals. The details of the secret treaty leaked when a copy was found in the baggage of Malachy O'Queely, Archbishop of Tuam, who was ambushed and killed by the Scots army in Ulster near Sligo. The copy of the treaty made its way to London, where it was printed as evidence that Charles was secretly conspiring with Catholics. On 26 December Glamorgan was arrested for treason and imprisoned in Dublin. Glamorgan expected his imprisonment would be short, and he was right. The circumstances behind his release on 22 January 1646 are unclear, but it was on Ormond's own initiative, and Glamorgan went to Kilkenny, where he remained for two years and continued to play a part in the Confederate royalist cause. The king repudiated the treaty, although it is fair to say that he did not have detailed knowledge of what Glamorgan had agreed on his behalf. What gives some credence to the view that he might have accepted the terms is the fact that the queen, Henrietta Maria, and her emissary, Sir Kenelm Digby, had agreed a treaty with the pope in November 1644 (although the king had not been a party to it) which contained even greater concessions to Catholics than those in the Glamorgan agreement. Glamorgan accepted the papal treaty and perhaps hoped its ratification would make his Irish agreement unnecessary. He argued that the king's repudiation of his deal was made under duress. While the Confederation accepted this, Rinuccini did not. In his letters to Glamorgan the king was more circumspect, informing him that the royal trust in him had not been diminished by events and promising revenge for the earl's treatment. What the Glamorgan episode demonstrated to contemporaries was the uncertain nature of the king as a focus for holding a kingdom together. Glamorgan's intervention almost wrecked the official negotiations. It also highlighted the success of the parliamentarian forces in England, and in Ireland as the Covenant spread in 1644 and 1645, as a potentially destabilising factor in Irish affairs. The ability of the Confederation to deal with this by an offensive strategy was severely limited by financial constraints. While taxation might support a defensive strategy, it would not extend much further. Such pressures certainly focused the minds of those attempting to finalise a peace treaty.

The first Ormond peace was agreed between the Confederates and the Lord Lieutenant on 28 March 1646. French diplomatic support and money helped to ensure that Rinuccini's papal and pro-Spanish contacts were marginalised, and a royalist coalition was created around the king, which the French backed. The treaty was a long and complex document which fudged many issues. Religious matters, for instance, were simply dismissed with a reference to 'His Majesty's gracious favour and further concessions', which, in the light of the Glamorgan episode, might have meant anything.[18] On the role of parliament again there was little that was positive, but again some improvements were possible. It did contain certain concessions, most notably the general pardon and guarantees of the position of the Old English in political life. The peace was not to be published immediately, and Rinuccini clearly hoped that if the king would ratify the treaty between the pope and the queen, that would make the Irish treaty irrelevant. In the event, developments in England ensured that that did not happen.

## THE AFTERMATH OF 1646

Whatever the first Ormond peace may have said, the messages conveyed by the ritual surrounding its proclamation seemed to offer the comforting hope that the old world of monarchy and its attendant social order was to be restored. When Ormond entered Kilkenny for the proclamation of the peace there, it was through triumphal arches, like those erected for Wentworth's progress in the 1630s, on which were written Ormond's genealogy and accounts of his noble actions. It seemed as though the traditional order with its sense of honour and lineage was about to be restored. However, the peace did not please everyone. The sort of conflicting tensions that existed in Kilkenny are clear from the political overtones of theatrical performances available in the city. Henry Burkhead's *Cola's furie*, probably written in later 1645 and on sale in Kilkenny in 1646, charts the war between the Lirendeans and the Angoleans, who are clearly the Confederates and the English. It deals with the period up to 1643, and most of the characters are readily identifiable with contemporaries involved in the war. The villain is Sir Charles Coote (Cola), the hero Abner (Thomas Preston); and while some of the government, such as Oeisus (Ormond), appear as moderates, others are bloodthirsty and inclined to parliament. The play is essentially a justification of the Old English political position, which was deeply royalist, but says almost nothing about the role of religion in these wars. By contrast, *Titus, or The palm of Christ's courage*, staged by students in the Jesuit school at Kilkenny in 1644, conveyed a message in which religion was central. In this play Titus triumphs over the efforts of the King of Bungo to deflect him from the true faith and demonstrates the power of Christian fortitude over political expediency and oppression. In the world of the church and *Titus*, religion was central to any political deal.

Some in the radical party in the Confederation, dominated by Rinuccini and supported by Owen Roe O'Neill and his forces, found much to dislike in the 1646 Ormond peace. A few were opposed on principle, but for Rinuccini it was the religious provisions that were the stumbling-block, as the Kilkenny Jesuits' play had predicted. In August 1646 Rinuccini summoned a synod of the clergy at Waterford, declared that those Confederates who supported the Ormond peace had broken the oath of association of the Confederation, and excommunicated anyone who assisted in the implementation of the peace. There is little doubt that he had popular support. The Dominican poet Pádraigín Haicéad wrote at least one vitriolic poem on the peace, describing it as a betrayal of Ireland by dealing with Luther's followers and as a deviation from the path of true religion.

Having seized the initiative, Rinuccini moved to Kilkenny to dictate terms to the Supreme Council, backed by Owen Roe O'Neill's army, which had marched south after defeating the Scots force at Benburb in June. It was this army which, now commanded by Thomas Preston and funded by a loan from the Spanish ambassador to the Confederation, after Rinuccini's putsch marched on Dublin and the Marquis of Ormond. The military campaign was a fiasco and failed to make any impact on the city before winter set in. The General Assembly met in January 1647 and under Rinuccini's influence formally rejected the peace, although it was clear that it still had supporters, and changed the oath of association. This was a move that clearly broke the social rules of governance. Peace treaties were matters for the ruler, not the ruled, and by appealing to the assembly over the head of the Supreme Council, Rinuccini managed to offend the council members he had not already alienated. Despite meeting for four months, the assembly had failed to weld the body together after the splits caused by the peace.

For all this disputation, the peace solved little. What should have held it together was the person of the king, but in May 1646, a little more than a month after the agreement of the peace, Charles surrendered to the Scots at Newark. As the peace treaty collapsed under Rinuccini's fulminations and military attack, Ormond abandoned any attempt to save it, despite the effort of the Marquis of Clanricard to salvage a modified deal. Instead Ormond applied his energies to building as secure a loyal constituency in Ireland as he could. The first sign of this was his decision in June 1647 to surrender Dublin to parliamentary commissioners who had arrived earlier that month at the city with a force of 2,000 men. In July Ormond left Ireland to consult with the king, now in the hands of parliament, in England, where it seemed a new alignment between king and parliament was being constructed in late 1646 and early 1647. The parliamentary army, under the command of Michael Jones, having arrived in Dublin, together with the Scots in Ulster and Inchiquin in Munster, comprised a significant military force which took advantage of its position in the summer of 1647. It defeated the Confederates at the battles of Dungan's Hill near Trim, County Meath, in August and Knocknanuss near Mallow, County Cork, in November, and sacked Cashel, County Tipperary, in September. All this convinced the Confederation that it could no longer prosecute the war itself. It claimed its exchequer was empty, customs receipts were at an all-time low, demonstrating the collapse of trade, and borrowing had become almost impossible because of a scarcity of lenders. In Tipperary Inchiquin's offensive in the autumn of 1647 destroyed large quantities of grain in an important corn-producing region, prompting fears of famine. The Confederates decided that external support was necessary, and in early 1648, after a good deal of acrimony, Confederate envoys were sent to France, where Queen Henrietta Maria was now living, and to Rome to seek support. Rinuccini demanded the right to veto the religious terms on which any support would be given.

Parallel with these developments, the king hoped to exploit growing tensions between the army and parliament in England after the First Civil War. This was a British Isles strategy which involved a treaty with the Scots, the Engagement, by which Charles accepted the Covenant and began to assemble a coalition which would make a second civil war possible. The Irish strand in this arrangement was a peace with the Confederation which would supply the king with further forces. This was to be achieved by Ormond, who was instructed by the king to reach a peace guided by instructions from the queen and the Prince of Wales and ordered not to hesitate in concluding a deal for lack of authorisation from Charles personally. Ormond's first reaction to this strategy was to open negotiations with Inchiquin in Munster as a potential recruit to the royalist cause. He then left for Paris and the queen, arriving there in late February 1648.

In Paris the strands of the plan began to weave together as the queen commanded the Confederate representatives in the city to reach a deal with Ormond, notwithstanding the fact that they had already broken one peace agreement. One other element in the wider plan to assemble a royalist coalition fell into place in May 1648 when Inchiquin, rather unwillingly, reached a truce with the Confederation under Ormond's influence. While a deal with Catholics ran counter to Inchiquin's natural instincts, he understood the value of such an agreement as part of the opposition to the king's enemies in England. Personal influence may also have played a part. In the spring of 1647 Inchiquin had been forced to play host to the new Irish Lord Lieutenant appointed by the English parliament, Viscount Lisle. The encounter had not been a happy one, and Inchiquin was convinced that Lisle wanted to remove him from the post of President of Munster. Moreover, Lisle, advised by a number of Irish Protestants, was pressing parliament to institute another round of plantations and to remove Ormond. Neither was a scenario that Inchiquin wanted. To Rinuccini all this seemed to smack of a conspiracy against his authority and a religious deal with Ormond. On 27 May 1648 he excommunicated the supporters of the truce. His action placed strains on the loyalty to the Confederation which irrevocably split it. The moderates appealed to Rome against the excommunication, while Rinuccini's supporters refused to attend the General Assembly that met in September.

By the time the General Assembly met in September 1648 the situation was serious. The king and the Scots had gone to war against the parliament in May, but the Second Civil War, though bloody, was short and by August it was over and the king defeated. The problem of what would become of the king was now an urgent matter, and some were considering radical solutions, realising that it was impossible to reach agreement with Charles. Ireland remained the king's only hope of support and indeed survival. In this context, Ormond arrived in Cork on 30 September 1648 to organise the royalist campaign there. Through the autumn negotiations went on between Ormond and the Confederates for a settlement that would allow the formation of a royalist front with Inchiquin against the Westminster parliament. Ormond argued for a slightly modified form of the 1646 peace, but the Confederates held out for more, asking that there be free exercise of Catholicism, that the traditional immunities be given to clergy, and that they would continue to hold the territories and churches they held presently. An accommodation was reached by agreeing that they could have these terms, but reserving the king's right to revise these after a parliament in the future.

## THE SECOND PEACE AND ITS CONSEQUENCES

On 17 January 1649 Ormond and the Confederation agreed a peace treaty which united both sides in support of the king. What may have focused minds on this matter was the news which reached Kilkenny on 29 December 1648 that King Charles I was to be put on trial for his life by the English parliament, from which the moderates had been purged. This solved at least one problem of the Irish war which many thought insurmountable: the division among those who had a common agenda of royalism. The threat to the king, the great connecting principle of Irish society, and his eventual execution on 30

January 1649 marshalled the link between allegiance, honour and traditional assumptions about hierarchy in support of the monarch in a way that overcame other divisions. More practically, the nature of the settlement in seventeenth-century Ireland meant that few could rely on inheritance for their land or status. That had been granted directly by the king, and the execution of the monarch had the potential to set in motion a social revolution that few wanted. Under the terms of this second Ormond peace, the Confederation was dissolved and twelve commissioners of trust were to be appointed who would act under Ormond as Lord Lieutenant for Charles II, proclaimed as king in Ireland after his father's execution. The Scots in Ulster also became part of the new arrangement under the terms of their earlier agreement (the Engagement) with the king. Rinuccini, outflanked and having failed to exert any influence at all on events, left Ireland from Galway on 23 February 1649, and with him went papal influence in the politics of the 1640s. Owen Roe O'Neill, who represented the military wing of the nuncio's ambitions, found himself without direction and attempted to forge a series of agreements with some of the most unlikely allies, including Ormond, before death removed him from the political configuration in November 1649.

The effect of the second Ormond peace was to change the shape of war in Ireland. The focus of Irish efforts was now support for the king rather than the question of a specific Irish settlement. This transformed the Irish war from a civil war into a part of a British Isles conflict. As such, the new English Commonwealth could not afford to ignore royalist forces such as the Scots to the north or the Irish to the west. The intervention of Oliver Cromwell in the Irish war in August 1649 was to be decisive. He arrived with a force of 12,000 men to supplement the 8,000 parliamentary soldiers already in Dublin, and, more important, he had a train of modern artillery that was skilled in siege warfare. Whereas the first siege of Drogheda in 1642 had lasted several months, the Cromwellian siege in September 1649 was over in days thanks to the destructive impact of Cromwellian cannon. While Ormond's strategy was to draw Cromwell north to Drogheda, the short campaign there culminating in the siege was quickly over and left the parliamentarian forces free to concentrate on the campaign against Ormond and Inchiquin in the south of the country. By 11 October Cromwell's forces had taken Wexford with the same tactics used at Drogheda, and by the end of the year Waterford had also fallen. By March 1650 Kilkenny was under Cromwellian control. The main thrust of the reconquest having been achieved, Cromwell left Ireland in May 1650 to deal with the problem of the Scots.

Under the weight of military failure, the political alliances which had been created by the second Ormond peace began to buckle. Most of the difficult issues had been papered over in the peace, and the fault-lines re-emerged in 1649 and 1650. In December 1649 the Catholic bishops met at Clonmacnoise in an endeavour to present a united front around which royalism could rally. The end product was a printed declaration of loyalty, calling for an end to dissensions, which was to be sent to all parishes. Under the surface there were still deep divisions, even among the bishops, continuing their actions under Rinuccini. Some had difficulties supporting a call for loyalty to Ormond, and the meeting broke up in an acrimonious debate about the validity of Rinuccini's censures in 1648. In the course of 1650 some Irish Protestants, as well as the Scots in Ulster, drifted away from the royalist coalition because of its Catholic dominance. By the middle of 1650 the splits in the royalist coalition were apparently irreconcilable. The Catholic bishops meeting at Jamestown, County Leitrim, declared that Catholics could no longer accept Ormond as their leader and called for the revival of the confederacy. It was a desperate and unrealistic measure, but a committee of bishops was set up to implement it, dominated by those who had supported Rinuccini in the debates of the previous four years. Using similar tactics, they excommunicated Ormond on 15 September 1650. Yet Ormond retained support among the Catholic laity, and it was they who tried to broker a deal. At a meeting at Loughrea, County Galway, in November a compromise was agreed whereby Ormond would leave Ireland, delegating his authority to the Marquis of Clanricard, a move which at least preserved some vestige of royal authority in Ireland.

On 11 December 1650 Ormond, together with Inchiquin and Richard Bellings, the former secretary to the Confederation, left Ireland for France to join the royal court in exile. Ireland might now be considered part of the English Republic by right of conquest. Ormond's replacement, Clanricard, valiantly tried to muster support for the Irish campaign from Charles, Duke of Lorraine, who had effectively lost his duchy through the Treaty of Westphalia which ended the Thirty Years' War on continental Europe in 1648. However,

Lorraine soon found himself besieged by envoys from Ireland, one demanding terms acceptable to the papacy and the other demanding terms acceptable to the king. Given the success of the Cromwellian campaign, all these proposals and debates and all the efforts to forge an agreement were in reality nothing more than insubstantial smoke, but it was the sort of smoke that had blurred the vision of many in Ireland throughout the late 1640s.

## REMEMBERING THE 1640s

The 1640s were, in many ways, a pivotal moment in the history of seventeenth-century Ireland as in England and Scotland. How individuals behaved in that decade would be remembered and discussed in the latter half of the century. In the 1650s the Confederates in exile in Paris and Rome debated endlessly the justness or otherwise of Rinuccini's censures of 1648. The Irish Franciscan Paul King argued in favour of the censures in a pamphlet published in Paris in 1649 and drew a vitriolic reply from John Callaghan in his *Vindiciarum Catholicorum Hiberniae* published in the following year. The dispute melted into a wider range of controversies, including that between Jansenists and anti-Jansenists in Paris. Others joined the paper war, including the former secretary to the Confederation, Richard Bellings, and the Cork Franciscan John Punch. The final monumental justification of Rinuccini's position, the *Commentarius Rinuccinianus*, compiled to defend the nuncio, remained unprinted. In the 1660s how one behaved in the 1640s was again raked over in the courts of claims which determined guilt or innocence in an effort to create a new land settlement. In the early 1680s, at the sensitive time of plots and towards the end of the lives of those who had been involved in the events of the 1640s, the Earls of Castlehaven and Anglesey and the Duke of Ormond again tried to blacken the reputations of others by recalling in print the events of that decade. The *Memoirs* of the Catholic Earl of Castlehaven, who had fought alongside the Confederates, were published toward the end of 1680. This drew a reply from Anglesey. In the course of this reply he alleged that the cessation of 1643 and the peace treaties of 1646 and 1649 were 'highly dishonourable to the crown of England', a claim that cast aspersions on the then Lord Lieutenant, who was by now Duke of Ormond. This historical debate quickly turned into a political row which attracted the attention of the Privy Council and the king himself. Anglesey was disgraced and Castlehaven's *Memoirs* branded a 'scandalous libel'.[19] What had happened in the 1640s still had the power to excite passions a generation later.

The memory of the 1640s was not allowed to die with those who had been involved in the events of the decade. In 1642 the Irish Privy Council ordered that 23 October, the anniversary of the outbreak of the rising, should be observed as a day of thankfulness for deliverance from the Irish rebellion. At the restoration of the king in 1660, parliament authorised a liturgy for use on that anniversary which gave thanks for deliverance from the Irish and called for repentance for the sins of the nation. There were formal set-piece sermons preached before parliament, if sitting, and also in more humble parish churches. As one County Cork rector described the event in 1673 in his parish,

> I appointed a solemn day of public thanksgiving for that signal deliverance of us from that general intended massacre of the whole body of the Protestants in Ireland; on which day I solemnly rejoiced before the Lord and in His word, for general and particular, temporal and spiritual preservations. I set [forth] of the horridness of the plot, the greatness of their sin of rebellion and God's great mercy.[20]

Such formal celebrations attracted their popular counterparts in bonfires and bell-ringing and, in one case at Athlone in 1685, an improvised pope-burning ceremony. In the late 1680s such events were to be flashpoints with the new Jacobite regime. In 1686 in Kilkenny bonfires were put out, windows broken, and one man was shot for making a bonfire. In 1687 and 1688 celebrations were also curtailed, and bonfires in Meath were extinguished. What fed sermons and popular agitation was the political writing that went on about what had happened in the 1640s. Some of this was contemporary propaganda, such as Henry Jones's *A remonstrance of the diverse remarkable passages concerning the church and kingdom of Ireland* (1642), which sought to demonstrate that the rising was 'a most bloody and anti-Christian combination and plot hatched by well nigh the whole Romish sect . . . against this our church and state' and drew a Confederate reply.[21] Much writing in this area, like Edmund Borlase's *History of the execrable Irish rebellion* (1680), was unexciting stuff, doomed to the scholar's study. Other works were more scintillating. One pamphlet, by an author known only by the initials R.S., defending the Irish against attempts of massacre in the 1640s and detailing the massacres carried out by the settler forces was deemed sufficiently dangerous to be publicly burnt in 1663. Most influential in the long run was Sir John Temple's *The Irish rebellion*, first published in 1646 and reissued in 1679 and 1698, with a failed attempt to reprint it in 1672. This extraordinary work was thrown together rather than written by Temple, the Protestant hardline Master of the Rolls in Ireland, who opposed the cessation of 1643. The book reprinted many of the depositions taken after the outbreak of the rising in Ulster, dwelling in detail on ripped bellies, ghostly apparitions and gruesome murders. As such it was part history, part godly providential narrative and part lurid massacre literature from which readers could draw what they wished to confirm them in their own prejudices. Moreover, its stories were not confined simply to the book-buying public, since they were incorporated into sermons and other pamphlets. Temple's history of the rising provided the raw materials from which Protestant memory, shaped by reading and ritual surrounding the wars of the 1640s, would be created in later generations. Its impact would ensure that the accommodations that had been made between Protestant and Catholic before the war would later be more difficult to achieve.

# 7
# Cromwellian Reconstruction, 1651–9

In so far as the wars of the 1640s came to an end at a specific point in time, that point was 27 April 1653, when the last of the royalist forces, under the command of Philip O'Reilly, surrendered to the parliamentary army at Cloughoughter Castle in County Cavan. In reality, the war had been long over. The Cromwellian campaigns of late 1649 and the early 1650s had transformed Ireland from a royalist stronghold into a parliamentary one. By May 1650 the Cromwellian forces controlled almost all the territory east of a line from Derry to Macroom in County Cork. By the end of the year only Connacht held out. Galway did not surrender until May 1652, but by then the serious military action was over. What was left was a guerrilla war that was to drag on through the 1650s with little prospect of doing any real damage to the Dublin administration but which served as a constant irritant. Prisoners of war were transplanted to the West Indies as a way of removing potential problems, although such transportation seems to have ceased by 1655.

## LEGACY

The wars of the 1640s left a legacy of considerable destruction. Some of this was the result of armed combat, but more important was the economic and social dislocation that accompanied war. The Civil Survey, made in the middle of the 1650s to record the ownership and condition of land as part of the Cromwellian land settlement, makes it possible to see something of the sort of destruction that war had caused. Civil Survey estimates of the value of buildings in north Kildare, for instance, show a drop from about £126,000 in 1640 to £4,350 in 1654. Some devastation, such at that at Maynooth, could be spectacular: the castle fell in value from £3,000 in 1640 to £500 in 1654. In County Wexford damage was greatest in the northern part of the county. Of the twenty-one castles and twenty-six mills in the three northern baronies, seventeen and twenty-two respectively were in ruins as a result of the Cromwellian campaign of 1650–52. In the southern part of the county, of sixty-eight castles and twenty-seven mills, just three and eleven respectively were destroyed. Clearly, Irish capital was being seriously depleted. A slightly different measure is that of the yield from church tithes. In Counties Armagh and Down between 1640 and the middle of the 1650s tithes were reduced by 30 and 32 per cent respectively, although in County Antrim the fall was only 25 per cent. Yet a third measure of the impact of war, rental incomes, also reveals the considerable economic shock of war, but with a wide geographical variation. In Ulster the rental of the Brownlow estate in County Armagh fell from £782 per annum in 1635 to £488 in 1659, and even by the 1670s it had not recovered to the 1635 figure. The same was true of the Countess of Huntingdon's property in Counties Fermanagh and Tyrone. In Munster the Purcell estate in County Tipperary had a valuation of £878 in 1640, which had declined to £863 by 1663, and on the Earl of Thomond's estate in County Clare it was not until the 1680s that rentals again attained the 1640 level. On the Perceval estate in Cork in 1677 rent levels were still between 10 and 20 per cent short of the 1641 level.[1] The effects of war were not evenly distributed over Ireland. In the more commercialised east, commercial crisis had joined with a military one to wreck its own form of havoc, but in the north and west, which depended for survival on cattle rather than grain, the effect may have been less dramatic.

Perhaps the most significant impact of war was on the towns. The Cromwellian campaign with its devastating use of cannon, which hitherto had not been a feature of Irish military campaigns, caused considerable destruction. In New Ross 43 per cent of the tenements of the town were still waste in the middle of the 1650s, while at Kilmallock, Kilkenny and Limerick 26 per cent, 14 per cent and 12.6 per cent of the tenements respectively were destroyed.[2] In the case of Limerick, the destruction rate was much lower than New Ross, but, unlike New Ross, it spanned the entire range of property valuation. While the sort of destruction characteristic of Limerick was probably the result of Cromwellian cannon, that at New Ross was probably caused by the more prevalent form of military destruction, carried out by quartered soldiers who tore down buildings for firewood and looted shops and property abandoned by those who fled the town for England.

Most dramatic and shocking for all was the plague which arrived in Ireland at Galway in 1649 and by 1650 had spread into Munster, where it hit Waterford. By the summer of 1651 the plague had reached Dublin, spreading as it did most effectively in the summer. It returned to the city in the summers of 1652 and 1653. Only Ulster seems to have escaped. A sense of the impact this rampant spread of disease had on contemporaries is clear from Sir William Petty's calculations made in the later seventeenth century that the Irish population in 1652 was some 40 per cent below its pre-war total and most of that fall had occurred between 1650 and 1652. At its height Petty suggested that the pestilence killed 1,300 a week in Dublin alone. These contemporary estimates are probably grossly overstated, reflecting the fear that these epidemics generated rather than the reality of population loss. A population decline of about 10 per cent in Dublin is probably a more reasonable estimate, with perhaps 20 per cent in the western towns where the plague hit first. In the countryside population falls may have been of a similar order, but here war, as much as plague which tended to be an urban phenomenon, may have been largely to blame.

The responses to all this were varied. Among the defeated, despair was almost universal. For those political commentators writing in the Irish language, whether Old English or native Irish, the sense of trauma is marked. For Dáibhí Cúndún, the author of the poem *Is buartha an cás so 'dtárlaig Éire*, the 1640s was perceived as an era without historical precedent in classical or Irish history. The poet resorted to the traditional explanatory motif of blaming Irish misfortunes on their own errors and misjudgments and ended with a stereotypical prayer for forgiveness. Éamonn an Dúna, again writing in the aftermath of the war, complained bitterly that he could comprehend a conquest of Ireland by those of noble birth but not 'by the odorous remnants of churlish craftsmen descended from harlot's monsters and rebels of whom nobody in Europe knew what dog had excreted them', and concluded that, with the execution of the king, Ireland had lost her head. Seán Ó Conaill's historical poem *Tuireamh na hÉireann* stressed the disjuncture between past and present in the early 1650s by creating a complex synthesis of the history of Ireland from Japheth, son of Noah, to the present. Ó Conaill attempted to explain the significance of history to Irish Catholics at this juncture and affirm the positive equation between Catholicism and Irishness which had been clearly articulated by Geoffrey Keating in the 1630s. As Ó Conaill put it, the turmoil of the 1640s was 'the war that finished Ireland'.[3] The themes of the importance of Catholicism, the need for repentance, and a clear break with the past are drawn together in the political poetry composed in the 1650s by Dáibhí Ó Bruadair. What all this verse articulates is a sense of oppression deriving from the contemporary political upheaval of the 1650s that was absent in the writings of the early seventeenth century. It seemed, for the defeated at least, that a new unwelcome era had dawned.

In this context, the Cromwellian regime that came to power in Ireland in the early 1650s had three main problems to tackle. The first might be described as a law-and-order problem; the second the more complex task of building a power base for the new regime; and finally the central challenge of reshaping Irish society in the form that the new regime thought it should take.

## CREATING STABILITY

The most immediate challenge for the new regime was the establishment of law and order in the aftermath of war and the creation of a workable system of government that could manage a transition to a peacetime administration. The framework within which law and order were to be created had been set out as early as 1642 with the Adventurers' Act which secured the money advanced by English-based 'adventurers', mainly Londoners, for the reconquest of Ireland on land that would become available when the war ended. Early in 1653 the 'adventurers' began drawing lots in London for the allocation of confiscated land. Thus some kind of new land settlement was inevitable. Moreover, soldiers from the Cromwellian army needed to be paid from an exchequer that had little money, and payment in Irish land was a convenient option. Some officials realised that even if only a small proportion of the 35,000 soldiers remained in Ireland, they would provide a reliable local governing elite for the new regime and could be trusted in a way that the older Protestant settlers were not. How much land would be needed to satisfy these various obligations was uncertain, but it was clearly a substantial amount.

The instructions from London which followed as the state tried to create a new social order through the manipulation of landownership were often imprecise and sometimes contradictory. In particular, there was the problem of how the blood-guilt of those involved in the rising was to be revenged. Many thought this their providential role and the reason they had won the Irish war, but more practically they needed to retain the loyalty of the bulk of the population so that the guerrilla war that characterised the early 1650s could be brought to an end. The memory of the 1641 rising was kept alive by some participants in the debate, and Henry Jones, former Bishop of Clogher and brother of the Cromwellian scoutmaster-general, produced extracts from the depositions recording murders and massacres taken after the rising for the parliamentary commissioners responsible for the government of Ireland and later arranged for these to be printed.

The first formal legislative attempt to establish a new landholding structure was the Act of Settlement of 1652. This classified the Irish opponents of the parliament according to their degree of guilt. It declared that it was not the intention of parliament to extirpate 'the entire nation', but that the lower orders, who had been misled by their leaders, and those at the upper end of the social scale would be treated according to their merits. Five groups were specifically exempted from pardon of life and estate: all who had been involved in massacres before 1642; all Jesuits and priests involved in the rising; 105 named magnates (headed by the Marquis of Ormond); all those guilty of the murder of civilians; and those who refused to lay down their arms within twenty-eight days. Protestant and Catholic officers alike who had fought against the parliament were to be banished, but their wives and children would be granted the equivalent of a third of their estates. Some 34,000 Irish soldiers chose to leave and enlist in continental armies. Catholics who had shown themselves well affected to parliament were to be given two-thirds of their lands wherever parliament should decide. To try those accused of murder a high court of justice was established in October 1652. Most of the trials were local events, although two high-profile cases, involving Sir Phelim O'Neill, who was executed in 1653, and Edmund O'Reilly, Catholic vicar general of Dublin, who was imprisoned and later banished, demonstrated that the new regime intended to deal severely with those who had fought against them. Yet the activities of the court were short-lived and had come to an end by the close of 1654.

The main instrument to be used against Protestant royalists was, as in England and Scotland, the confiscation of estates. All who had fought in the war were to forfeit their estates and be granted a third of their original holding. Those who had shown 'constant good affection' to the parliament were to surrender one-fifth of their estate. Over time this policy was ameliorated as the regime became increasingly identified with the longer-established Protestants in Ireland. In 1654 an act of oblivion for Munster Protestants was passed as a result of lobbying by local interests there. Subsequently Protestants outside Munster were allowed to compound for their estates, although the act of oblivion was not extended. The potential impact of such fines on many Irish landlords was severe. Fines compounding for delinquency were set at roughly the same level as for royalists in England—two or three times the annual income of the estate in 1641. This financial burden came at a time when landlord incomes were severely depressed. The impact of war in the 1640s had clearly reduced rentals, and these had not yet recovered in the 1650s as the Irish economy was only slowly rebuilt. Moreover, the levels of taxation in the monthly assessment in Ireland were higher than in Scotland, which was a further drain on landlord resources. The landlord's ability to manage debt was also much impaired. The large merchants, the main source of loans, were much less obliging than before the war. Old English Catholic merchants had been expelled from some towns, notably Galway, Cork, Waterford and Limerick, in 1644, and many had gone abroad to France and the West Indies. This had removed a number of potential lenders to indebted landowners. Others were unwilling to lend, since either their cash surplus was depleted by war or, for those who had benefited from conflict, a volatile land market allowed them to invest their money profitably in socially prestigious estates. In consequence, many Irish landlords in the 1650s were forced to sell land to meet their financial obligations, including those imposed by the 1652 act. The result was that a large number of new landed families entered the social world of Ireland in the 1650s. Others, such as the Marquis of Ormond, accumulated debts from which they never really recovered. The effect might have been much greater had not the collection of composition money been quietly dropped in the later 1650s as the administration of Henry Cromwell became increasingly reliant on those who owed the fines. The long-term social and political repercussions of such financial embarrassment were considerable. After the 1650s few Irish landlords had the power that their pre-1641 counterparts had wielded. Debt and reduced landholding effectively curbed their influence, so that they could not resist the power of central government and build up personal fiefdoms in the way that the Earls of Clanricard or Antrim had done earlier in the century.

The Act of Settlement thus identified royalist Protestants as at least as much a danger to the new state as the Catholic Irish. Something of this can be traced in subsequent events. In May 1653 orders were given for the transplantation of Ulster Presbyterians to Counties Kilkenny, Tipperary and Waterford. This was to prevent the situation that had arisen with the Covenanter violence of the 1630s in which Scottish disturbances had an impact in Ulster. The alliance of the Scots with the king in the Engagement, confirmed by Charles II's pledge in July 1650 to uphold the Covenant and Presbyterianism, may have been brought to a military halt by Oliver Cromwell at the battle of Dunbar in 1650, but that did not preclude further intrigue and conspiracy by those who held firm to the king, the Resolutioners. The Long Parliament may have been unenthusiastic about the Solemn League and Covenant, but the Scots retained its main purpose of limiting royal action rather than disposing of kings. The presbytery of Belfast, for instance, castigated the Westminster parliament about the killing of kings in 1649, and in reply parliament had commissioned their propagandist, the poet John Milton, to refute the imputations. The plantation plan for Ulster Presbyterians was never implemented, perhaps because of successful objections from Ulster landowners whose prosperity would be severely jeopardised by the move. The existence of these schemes highlights the fact that the new Commonwealth had a range of enemies in Ireland other than simply Catholics.

The Act of Settlement said little about the fate of the Irish insurgents in the 1640s, apart from making it clear that there would be land confiscation to meet the needs of the army and the 'adventurers' and to facilitate the strategic adjustments necessary to create a more favourable security situation. However, in late June 1653 the Council of State in England sent instructions for a more radical scheme requiring transplantation of forfeiting Irish proprietors to Connacht and Clare. This was to be completed by 1654, and land vacated was to be allotted to transplanted people and 'adventurers'. The Act of Satisfaction of September 1653 confirmed these provisions, adding the requirement that the transplanted Irish were not to be settled within four miles of the River Shannon or the sea. In effect, Connacht was being used as a way of containing any potential resistance to the social changes implied by the policy of land allocation.

Detailed planning for this scheme was carried out by the Dublin administration, staffed mainly by former army officers. Orders were given for three land surveys in 1653, since no national survey of Irish land existed. The first was the Gross Survey (which was little more than guesswork), then the Civil Survey (by inquisition), and finally a mapped survey, the Down Survey, masterminded by William Petty. By the end of 1653 the Gross Survey dealing with the land assigned to 'adventurers' and soldiers in the east of the country had been completed. Realists soon appreciated the magnitude of what had been taken on and the impracticability of achieving it within the agreed time. Moreover, there was considerable confusion about what was actually intended. The 1652 Act of Settlement had offered pardon to the 'inferior sort', targeting instead the leaders of the war. Whether those pardoned were to be transplanted or not was unclear. In addition, some landowners claimed the benefit of articles agreed at the surrender of Kilkenny and Galway which, they contended, entitled them to, at least, a portion of their estates. Again, some Old English Catholics from the Munster ports argued that they had been well disposed to parliament and were therefore covered by the 1652 act. Courts of delinquency were set up in each military district to deal with these questions, and certificates were to be issued to those who were to be transplanted. The certificates gave details of their allotment of land in Connacht as adjudicated by commissioners sitting at Loughrea. Floods of petitions came into these courts. The original date for completing the transplantation of May 1654 was extended to

March 1655, but by 1656 the practicalities were still not finalised. It seems that many went to Connacht but did not remain there, and the commissioners at Loughrea had little accurate information in the form of surveys or records to allow them to make enforceable decisions or to decide who was entitled to land.

A case in point is a number of those specifically exempted from pardon in the 1652 act, such as the Earl of Westmeath, who managed to obtain substantial estates in Connacht. In other cases transplanters could not claim estates, being already landowners in Connacht and waiting to move to smaller assignments. Others adopted traditional Old English tactics by disregarding local administrators and petitioning Oliver Cromwell directly. At least two of the Loughrea commissioners were dismissed for corruption. To deal with this situation a Court of Claims and Qualifications was set up in Athlone at the end of 1654. This, at least, had most of the Civil Survey available to it, as well as the records of the Kilkenny Confederation and the evidence of the depositions taken after the 1641 rising. It was also becoming clear that the amount of land necessary to pay off the Cromwellian soldiers had been woefully underestimated, and the administration began to encroach on Counties Sligo, Leitrim and Mayo, originally intended for those being transplanted, to make up the deficit. Similarly, part of County Clare, which had originally been assigned to transplanters, was reassigned to Cromwellian soldiers. Valiant attempts were made to sort out this confusion, including a restriction on the amount of land available for transplanters, but these had little impact.

Despite these practical difficulties, there were compelling ideological reasons for pressing ahead. In July 1655 Lord Deputy Fleetwood and the council issued new, more trenchant, instructions for transplantation. The context was the emergence of stories about the massacres of Protestants in the northern Italian territory of Piedmont, which resurrected the horrors of the 1641 rising. Such fears were not calmed by rumours that a regiment of Irish Catholics in France had been involved in the Piedmont massacres. However, such rumours proved ephemeral, and the arrival of Henry Cromwell to take effective control of the Irish administration in 1656 signalled a relaxation in the drive to remove Irish landowners and their followers to Connacht. While a great deal was achieved, including the important land surveys, in the end it was the sheer scale of the project and the administrative confusion which it generated that defeated the Dublin government. An act of June 1657 'for the attainder of the rebels in Ireland' in effect declared that the transplantation was over and, in a face-saving move, pronounced that it had been a success. Those who had not transplanted themselves by September 1657 were to forfeit all claim to benefit. The legacy of confusion was to prove advantageous to many at the Restoration. Undoubtedly the land rearrangements that were implemented introduced new elements into the Irish social mix. Some 1,043 'adventurers' eligible for Irish land under the 1642 Adventurers' Act and the Act of Settlement had allocated to them land in Counties Antrim, Down, Armagh, Meath, Westmeath, King's, Queen's, Tipperary, Limerick and Waterford, with Louth being held in reserve. Soldiers were to be settled alongside the 'adventurers' for security reasons. How many of those who drew their lands by lot, as the act required, actually settled, as opposed to selling their property to others, is not known. About 500 of those 'adventurers' who came in the 1650s had their property confirmed by the Restoration land settlement. Of the soldiers there were more. Some 33,419 debentures, or promises of land, were issued to soldiers, but only 11,804 were translated into land grants. The others preferred cash and sold their rights to officers or to *in situ* landholders or to those not from the army who wanted to acquire an estate cheaply. Of the roughly 12,000 soldiers who settled in the 1650s, some 7,500 had their property confirmed to them at the Restoration. These new elements, who would later describe themselves as New Protestants to distinguish them from the Old Protestants who had been in Ireland before 1649, would change the political face of Ireland after the Restoration.

The sort of land rearrangement that the Cromwellians planned for Ireland, and the language that was used about Ireland and its inhabitants, seemed to be of a traditional sort. Yet, at one level, it was a significant departure from what had gone before. In the early seventeenth century government had attempted to introduce some form of social regulation into the land settlements by requiring the building of infrastructure and in some places the introduction of settlers. War in the 1640s had destroyed a good deal of those physical improvements, and a substantial number of settlers fled to England. In parts of Ulster, for instance, up to half the surnames on the 1630 muster roll had disappeared by 1660. In the 1650s renewed immigration began as those from Scotland and England perceived economic opportunities in a recovering Ireland, although this migration was on a lesser scale than might have been hoped. William Petty estimated that between 1652 and 1672 the Irish population increased by 250,000, of which 160,000 were English or Scots settlers.

The Cromwellian settlement imposed no restrictions on settlement, which was driven by colonial spread rather than organised plantation. As a result, some areas fared better than others. In Ulster the establishment of Presbyterian congregations in the 1650s suggests a considerable influx of population spreading the limits of settlement further than they had been in the 1630s. This moving frontier reached as far south as Longford. In north Wexford the poll tax returns for 1660, when compared with the settler distribution in 1640, suggests an influx of settlers. This was probably true of south Wicklow also, where extended settlement was driven by the development of ironworking in that area. Again, to the north and west of Cork city, and to a much greater extent around Dublin, the pre-1640 population seems to have more than reconstructed itself. Across Counties Kilkenny, Tipperary, Limerick and Kerry the much thinner pre-1641 settlement failed to recover its earlier levels. In these areas Catholics of substance, called in the poll tax return 'tituladoes', survived in some numbers as substantial leaseholders. The result of this rather haphazard colonisation was that rather ragged frontiers began to appear in the Irish landscape between settled and more isolated areas. These constituted not simply border lines but regional societies which differed from the regions around them. South Ulster, for instance, emerged as such a border landscape where Irish continued to be spoken, patrons supported poets, banditry survived, and an older form of economic organisation persisted when much around it had changed. Parts of Connacht showed similar trends as a result of the emergence of new worlds, the persistence of old ones, and the appearance of transitional zones created by unregulated Cromwellian settlement.

While all this would seem to mark a new departure in Irish settlement, at another level the arrangements appeared to be of a traditional sort. Almost all accepted the need for a reconquest of Ireland, with the exception of a few radical English Levellers, and hence believed in a division of the spoils. Such traditional language was used by Oliver Cromwell himself, although tempered with more emollient language that distinguished between Old English Catholic gentry, who had been behind the war of the 1640s, and their followers who had been dragged in. The army officer Richard Lawrence, in his *Interest of England in the Irish transplantation stated* (1655), harked back to 1641 to prove Catholic Irish treachery and the sinfulness of Protestant Ireland through its corruption by the barbarism of the Irish, who could no longer be trusted in any new settlement. None of this was new; it was redolent of the sort of colonial rhetoric that had characterised sixteenth-century Ireland. Those Protestants who had been in Ireland before 1649 and had been royalists, the Old Protestants, were behaving in the same way as the Old English had done in compromising their position in sixteenth-century eyes. Again redolent of an older world, Lawrence, and indeed Oliver Cromwell, distinguished between the dangerous leaders of Irish Catholic society, the clergy, landowners and military commanders, and the followers. He argued that these leaders were the figures to be targeted by the land settlement rather than their peasant followers. Models for this sort of world were not difficult to find. A petition from officers in the Irish army in 1655 urged segregation of the Irish within Connacht and, in their demand for revenge, found justification in the world of the Old Testament which seemed to offer not only parallels to but precedents for the actions of the elect. In the course of time changing emphasis in Cromwellian policy forced Lawrence to modify his arguments. In his *England's great interest in the well planting of Ireland with English people discussed* (1656) Lawrence cast his proposals in a more practical light. Security, profit and the public good replaced arguments dawn from Biblical precedent. Catholics would still be corralled into Connacht, and an enlarged Pale between the Rivers Barrow and Boyne would be reserved for Protestants, but the remainder of the country, he argued, would be a mixed settlement in which Protestant landholders would be allowed to take Catholic Irish as tenants. The problem now was how to attract suitable settlers. Lawrence had begun to think like an Anglo-Irish settler rather than a sixteenth-century polemicist.

What was new about the world of the early 1650s was that views such as those articulated by Lawrence did not meet the sort of enthusiastic reception that might have been expected. Among some Old Protestant families, long established in Ireland, there was a pragmatic preoccupation with of the practicalities of everyday life. Vincent Gookin the younger, a Cork settler and member of

Cromwell's Barebones Parliament and the Protectorate parliaments at Westminster, challenged Lawrence's view of the world. Drawing on a wide range of classical authors, as well as Irish works by Sir John Davies, Edmund Spenser and Edmund Campion, Gookin in his *The great case of transplantation in Ireland discussed* (1655) reviewed the case advanced for transplantation of the Irish and found it wanting. He developed his arguments further in *The author and case of transplanting the Irish in Connaught vindicated* (1655) which was a reply to Lawrence. Gookin found practical economic reasons, well understood by an older settler, why transplantation was not a reasonable strategy. The removal of the Irish would result in a shortage of labourers to work the land held by settlers, with, as occurred in 1655, a consequent decline in income, tax revenue and a corresponding rise in agrarian violence. The sort of classical precedents which Gookin read led him to believe that if the Irish were corralled into Connacht, they would simply refuse to change their ways and therefore remain barbarous. Left in a mixed settlement, they could be reclaimed, particularly as their leaders had, he believed, either fled Ireland or been killed in the rebellion. Social and religious reform was now possible, especially since the power of the native Irish elite had finally been broken by the Cromwellian reconquest. This was, then, an optimistic, constructive approach to the problem of governing Ireland and not simply an apologia for English colonisation. Gookin condemned the arbitrary action of the army and insisted instead on the importance of justice, an idea derived from classical precedent, religious belief, and his experience of being brought up in Cork as a second-generation settler. This last circumstance had enforced coexistence between native and newcomer, regardless of what each thought of the practices of the other. The result was a view of Ireland driven more by practical considerations than ideological ones. It was a subtle and ambiguous reaction to the challenge of the 1650s. Yet, although it found advocates other than Gookin, it did not command universal support. Gookin's views would find little favour, for instance, with his neighbour and staunch supporter of the Protectorate Roger Boyle, Lord Broghill (and later Earl of Orrery). Nonetheless, the debate between Gookin and Lawrence demonstrates a diversity of opinion within Protestant Ireland which was to have long-term implications on the way settlers thought about their country.

## MAKING FRIENDS AND CONTACTS

In some ways the execution of Charles I and the Cromwellian conquest of Ireland simplified the task of governing Ireland. The removal of the crown from the political equation solved the problem of its relationship with parliament in Irish matters and ensured that the position of the Irish viceroy was perhaps more secure than it had ever been. From 1653 the Westminster parliament, in which there were now Irish members, effectively governed Ireland. In the Barebones Parliament of 1653, six members were summoned from Ireland, together with six from Wales, five from Scotland and 122 from England. After the ordinance of 1654 regulating the membership of the Protectorate parliaments, Ireland sent thirty members to London in 1654, 1656 and 1659. Yet the exact relationship of Ireland and England was never clearly defined. The Instrument of Government of 1653 assumed a union and Ireland was depicted on the great seal of the Commonwealth as part of one political entity, but bills for a formal union with Ireland, which were introduced into the Westminster parliaments in 1654 and 1656, failed to pass, and in 1659 there was a violent debate about the validity of a 'presumed' union. Moreover, the position of customs duties, law reform and proportionate taxation, all items dealt with in the Scottish union of 1654, were left unresolved in the case of Ireland. The workings of the Irish customs were a particular problem, resulting from the imposition of the English book of rates on Ireland and the farming of the Irish customs to a syndicate of English merchants in 1658. A group of Dublin merchants challenged the legal basis of the customs, but the case was stopped by the intervention of the English government. The failure of the Westminster parliament to grapple with these issues had important long-term consequences for the attitude of the Irish political nation towards the London administration after the Restoration in 1660.

Within Ireland the viceroyalty was initially placed in the hands of Oliver Cromwell, who was assisted by parliamentary commissioners. In 1650 two, later four, commissioners were named by parliament to deal with Ireland. All were English M.P.s. The title of Lord Lieutenant was abolished in 1652 and a new commission for Ireland appointed, although in 1654 the viceroyalty was restored with Charles Fleetwood, the former military governor and son-in-law of Oliver Cromwell, as Lord Deputy and a council of six, only one of whom was a survivor of the earlier commissions. All were English M.P.s. Since appointments were made in England, they reflected English needs rather than Irish priorities. Appointment to the Irish government was usually a reward for political loyalty in England, and none of those appointed in the 1650s had an Irish background. Thus most of the Irish government operated on assumptions formed in England and identified with political and religious groups based there, though this was by no means a new development. In these circumstances, animosities formed and played out in England often had significant ramifications in Ireland. Even more important, the newcomers lacked the network of kinship, patronage and influence that the Old Protestants had painstakingly constructed in the early part of the century. New links formed in the 1650s were more precarious and inevitably looser. As a result, governing Ireland in the 1650s involved a rather different process to that which had developed previously. The creation of many new property-owners as a result of the settlement, which conferred a new social authority on soldiers and 'adventurers', meant that political behaviour was often unconnected to pre-existing political structures. In addition, for the first time in the seventeenth century, the new landowners were not drawn from a social elite, a fact that Gaelic Irish poets such as Dáibhí Ó Bruadair commented on. Political management in this world was to be a difficult matter.

As with earlier viceroys, the commissioners' or Lord Deputy and council's approach to the government of Ireland was controlled by instructions from Westminster. These instructions focused on the standardisation and simplification of complex matters such as the administration of law and education across the entire Commonwealth. Thus the instructions issued to the Irish commissioners in 1651 bore a strong resemblance to those issued to their Scottish equivalents the following year. Furthermore, Lord Deputy Fleetwood was certainly in contact with his Scottish counterpart, George Monck, about developments in both countries.

If constraints from England in the shape of appointments and instructions represented one difficulty with managing Ireland, the second was finance. The main burden was the army, which between 1649 and 1656 cost almost £3 million to maintain, although the scaling down of the force after the war reduced costs. Even after 1658 the annual charge was some £336,000. Money came from two sources: English subventions and Irish revenues. Between 1649 and 1656 some £1,566,848 came from England, and £1,942,545 was raised from within

Ireland. England, itself with financial difficulties, was not in a position continually to support Ireland, and after 1655 the subvention was progressively reduced. By 1659 it was said that the payments might end altogether. The reduction in financial support meant that the Irish government was running an annual deficit of £96,000 in 1658. The main sources for income from Ireland were the customs and the assessment for the maintenance of the army, both of which were set at high levels and became contentious issues at Westminster. Customs income in particular depended on economic recovery in the 1650s; this, however, never really happened, and hence funding for government activities remained short. By the late 1650s there were signs of a resurgence of Irish trade, which was beginning to register an increase in customs revenue, but this was too little and too late to have much effect on the Cromwellian regime.

To contemporaries, the most significant area of reform was that of the law. Since the common law provided the framework within which authority was validated and exercised, the way that was to be shaped was of crucial importance to the Old Protestants in particular. The fate of the Court of Chancery, for instance, was intimately tied to the form of the land settlement, since Chancery was responsible for making land grants and thus consolidating new gains. Given that law and its operation had been closely bound up with monarchy before 1649, any reshaping of the system would provide important clues about how the Cromwellian regime thought about reorganising Irish society. There were even more complex legal issues to be resolved. Patrick Darcy's *Argument* of 1643 had raised practical problems about whether or not English common-law precedents applied in Ireland, apart from the even more basic question as to whether English statutes made before 1649 were operable in Ireland. Legal reform was not a theoretical matter, since the legal system, with its network of assizes and justices of the peace, was one of the most important points of contact between the government in Dublin and the Irish localities as well as the main mechanism for the resolution of local difficulties. In the immediate aftermath of the war, the law courts were suspended and the administration of justice was controlled by the army. By 1651 commissioners for the administration of justice had been appointed for Dublin, and their powers were soon extended to Leinster. These commissioners sometimes travelled to other parts of the country to try cases as an *ad hoc* replacement for assizes. However, large parts of the country, such as the entire province of Connacht, effectively remained under military law. Munster was served by the older presidency court, which was revived in 1649–50. Below this level, the revenue commissioners, who ruled over twelve revenue districts in the early 1650s, had significant judicial powers based on military law, and these replaced the pre-1649 local commissions of the peace. All these officials were drawn from the army or from the more recently arrived civil administration, and hence relations with the older Protestant inhabitants were strained. This was not simply a clash between military and civil jurisdictions but, perhaps more importantly, between different conceptions of social order. Appointment to the commission of the peace before 1649 was a mark of social standing, and the assizes were an important assembly at which gentry met, status was made visible and honour asserted. Hence assizes and membership of the commission of the peace were important and sensitive issues. In 1641, for instance, Hugh MacMahon of Monaghan had gone into insurrection because of offence given to him by a New English landowner who had refused to shake hands with him despite the fact that they were both justices of the peace. The commission of the peace was a contested area of life, and the replacement of justices of the peace with revenue commissioners was a significant insult. However, from the point of view of those who argued for legal simplification and reform, these new improvised courts had many attractions. They lacked the legal complexity associated with the older order, with its powerful lawyers, labyrinthine paperwork and hints of corruption.

It was 1653 before the parliamentary commissioners turned their attention to the more permanent structure of the administration of justice. Fleetwood, while asking for the restoration of the Court of Chancery, wanted a reduction in the number of courts from four (Chancery, King's Bench, Common Pleas and Exchequer) to two. He was perhaps hopeful of extending government control permanently over the legal system. Despite this, the plan that emerged from London in 1654 proposed to restore all four courts. It was the following year before any action was taken to confirm the restoration. At the same time, the commission of the peace came to be much more widely used. Hardly surprisingly, it was Old Protestants who wanted to be part of the local commission in view of its conveyance of status, and Henry Cromwell, then in the process of courting their support for his administration, was prepared to appoint them.

This restoration of the older legal system which marked the growing conservatism of the Cromwellian regime attracted little comment, although John Cook, a legal reformer who acted as a judge in the Munster presidency court, did complain about the return to older ways of doing business. It was more important that the legal system worked than that it be reformed, and from 1655 attention was focused on the supply of judges and law enforcement rather than reform. As with clergy, judges were recruited from England, attracted by the payment of state salaries—£1,000 a year in the case of the Lord Chancellor, although most other judges received £500. This had limited success, and there were always vacancies on the judicial bench. Some simplifications of the legal system were introduced, mainly in forms of procedure and the wording of writs, which expedited business so that the need for more radical reform of the older system was curtailed.

The social basis of these administrative and governmental arrangements was, at best, narrow. The failure of a large number of settlers to arrive from England in the short term meant that the army was the principal source of recruits to work the local government system, and most Irish towns remained under military rule until 1656. The army drew its support, in the main, from newly arrived soldiers, many of whom were religious radicals, mainly Baptists and Independents. These men had a rather different conception of society to that which had gone before, with its ties of obligation and power culminating in the king. Just as the hierarchical Church of Ireland reflected and moulded the older order, the newcomers' sense of religion as a voluntary society shaped their view of secular society also. Independent congregations, such as that at the former cathedral of Christ Church in Dublin, were held together by church covenants and local agreements rather than ecclesiastical hierarchy. In 1659 the Dublin Independents under Samuel Winter published their own forms of discipline and order in the *Agreement and resolution* of its ministers, which again emphasised the voluntarism of their society within a framework of order provided by the Solemn League and Covenant. As one Church of Ireland minister expressed it in the early 1650s, this was 'religion without direction'.[4] Such a conception of social order regulated by agreements and covenants had little in common with the Old Protestant ruling elite in Ireland, who were used to a central governing power that underpinned their position by its personal authority. It was this Old Protestant group who paid for the maintenance of an army that seemed to have little in common with them. The effect of this was to accentuate the alien character of the Cromwellian regime in Ireland. In short, the root of the failure of Fleetwood and his administration was their inability to translate the language of republicanism into a viable programme for action suited to the peculiarities of the Irish situation.

In July 1655 Henry Cromwell, son of the Lord Protector, arrived in Ireland. He came as a military commander, but within a month had replaced the hardline soldier Charles Fleetwood as *de facto* governor of Ireland. Although Fleetwood remained as Lord Deputy until 1657, when Henry Cromwell as appointed, he departed Ireland in September 1656, leaving Cromwell in charge. Henry Cromwell's arrival marked a change in priorities for the administration of Ireland. The threat of war between England and Spain and the need to integrate Ireland more fully into the Cromwellian Protectorate dictated that changes would have to be made to the strategy for governing Ireland. While Cromwellian administrators had expected to see some 36,000 settlers in Ireland, there arrived only some 8,000, leaving the regime vulnerable both at central and local level because of its narrow power base. Henry Cromwell's analysis of the problem of Irish governance thus identified the Old Protestants, with their experience of administration, rather than the more recently arrived religious radicals, as the key to achieving the stability of the regime. Thus, for instance, in the years after 1650 proposals for some sort of moderation towards Catholics, mainly for economic reasons as Gookin had suggested, were afforded a more receptive hearing by the Dublin administration.

Throughout 1655 and 1656 the Baptists, who had held power up to this point, fought a violent campaign in Westminster and Ireland to dislodge Henry Cromwell. Initially he was supported by the Baptists' religious opponents, the Independents, but such an alliance could not last. To replace one radical group with another, and one which had little support outside Dublin, did little to extend support for the regime. By 1658, however, it was the Old Protestants who were the principal supporters of Henry Cromwell. Increasingly they were appointed to the specialist committees for governing Ireland which emerged as divisions within the council made it difficult for the council to reach decisions. Old Protestants were also increasingly appointed to local offices, such as the commission of the peace. After

1656 military rule of towns was reduced and charters restored, so that borough government, for the most part, fell into the hands of Old Protestants in Ulster and Munster. In Connacht and Leinster, where Protestants were fewer, the new civil governments of towns tended to be held by military officers.

In religious policy, the Ulster Presbyterians and the former Church of Ireland clergy in Munster, organised by Edward Worth, former Dean of Cork, came to be more influential than religious radicals. Worth became Henry Cromwell's main adviser on religious policy, and in the late 1650s devised a religious scheme that emphasised uniformity rather than the toleration that had characterised religious policy in the early 1650s. To many this seemed the prelude to the creation of a national church of Presbyterians and former members of the Church of Ireland as an alternative to episcopacy. This appeared to be confirmed by the meeting of a convention of ministers in Dublin in 1658 to endorse the return of payment of ministers by direct tithes rather than state grants, which seemed to recreate the idea of an established church entitled to payments from all. Whatever doubts there had been about Henry Cromwell's relations with Independents, this action effectively severed all contact with them. The courting of those Presbyterians who opposed monarchy—the Remonstrants—had begun under Fleetwood as a necessary condition of ruling Ulster and continued apace under Cromwell, albeit with less success than the relations established with Worth. It was unlikely, for example, that Ulster Presbyterians would be prepared to accept the sort of compromise national church Worth was advocating in Munster. Nevertheless, by 1658 Henry Cromwell had established a firm foundation for the government of Ireland based on Old Protestant support. Indeed, developments in England with the Humble Petition and Advice of 1657 suggested that the pattern of alliances which had been established in Ireland with the pre-1641 elite was set to be adopted there. It may be no coincidence that Irish M.P.s at Westminster had a prominent role in these English developments. However, the death of Oliver Cromwell in September 1658 and the subsequent collapse of the Protectorate ensured that the possibilities of these initiatives would never be fulfilled.

## REFORMING MINDS AND MANNERS

Altering forms of government was an important priority in

Cromwellian Ireland, but that process was essentially a by-product of a much wider scheme. The overall project was nothing less than a radical restructuring of the principles on which society worked. Republicanism in the seventeenth century was a radical option not widely adopted in Europe. The absence of the person of the king as a focus for loyalty necessitated the encouragement of attachment to the idea of a commonwealth, and loyalty to that idea necessitated the promotion of what sixteenth-century political theorists called virtue and moral behaviour to a level that had not been demanded before. If monarchy required a sense of honour, a republic needed virtue. Order had to be created not through the complex web of patronage and honours that a monarch had at his disposal, but in other ways by nourishing public activism, social cohesion and morality. A republic was a fragile entity that relied upon the cultivation of piety and virtue in order to work. Failure to do that raised one further spectre: that God would judge the new order and find it wanting and would accordingly visit it with divine punishment. Hence the first element in a general reformation of society was religious reform. In 1647 the Church of Ireland and its liturgy were proscribed, and this was continued by instructing successive Lords Deputy to follow English practice regarding the ordering of religion. In the following two years the structures and influence of the Church of Ireland gradually collapsed as the Cromwellian power base extended throughout the whole island. What was to replace it was not yet clear. In many places Church of Ireland clergy simply remained where they were and operated covertly or adhered to the new order. That evangelisation was necessary was not in doubt among the religious radicals who held on to power in Ireland, but that evangelisation was not, at least initially, directed towards the Catholic Irish but to the military garrison itself. Between 1649 and 1655 religious policy in Ireland reflected this fact. In the early 1650s the religious idea of believer's baptism spread quickly through Ireland. While Fleetwood's religious background was Independency, he allowed the Baptist ideas, which had come to Ireland with the army, to spread. Two ministers who arrived in 1649, Thomas Patient and Christopher Blackwood, were largely responsible for the spread of Baptist doctrines among the army in Kilkenny and Waterford, and by 1653 Baptism was established in the main Irish towns with the support of army officers. However, Henry Cromwell's diagnosis of the dominance of Baptist radicals as a political problem led to their eclipse from political power from the middle of the 1650s. As a result, they lost a good deal of their influence and became little more than a small religious group, which had only modest support outside the ranks of the army.

The Baptists were not the only religiously radical group to arrive in Ireland in the 1650s. The Quakers also had a potentially powerful power base in the army, although their civilian converts, based mainly in south Ulster and Munster, were not particularly numerous. What most contemporaries feared was their socially radical theology. This required them not to pay tithes or to take oaths, and to denounce ordained clergy and not acknowledge superiors in the traditional language of deference or by removing their hats. Their conviction manifested itself in street preaching and disrupting traditional worship. Recognising the potential problem posed by the Quakers, Henry Cromwell moved to ensure that they never achieved the sort of influence that the Baptists enjoyed, and they survived as a small though very well organised and distinctive Protestant group into the Restoration.

If the Baptists and Quakers formed the radical wing of religious life in the 1650s, the more mainstream element was composed of Independents, led by Samuel Winter, Provost of Trinity College Dublin, and Presbyterians both of English and Scottish backgrounds. These two groups defined themselves around the Solemn League and Covenant of 1643 and emphasised the need for religious and ecclesiastical order against the more individualistic sectaries, although the Presbyterians and Independents disagreed on the extent of that organisation. In Ulster Presbyterianism had effectively restructured itself in the 1640s into something resembling its Scottish equivalent and had built strong connections with local communities to the point of setting up a parish structure. It effectively operated as an established church, with large-scale communion services involving whole communities. Independents and Presbyterians of English origin were less enamoured with these structures of control and tended to operate on a smaller scale, usually within voluntary associations of local congregations.

In the context of these diverse religious groups, exhibiting a range of ideas from the radicalism of the Quakers to the conservatism of the Ulster Presbyterians, the state had to formulate some method of making religious provision for the Irish localities in the absence of an established church. There was certainly a need to improve the quality of the ministry, and this was clearly linked to the financial arrangements for support of the clergy. Thus the existing fabric and resources of the disestablished church had to be made to work more efficiently. All this was aimed at the propagation of the gospel, not only to Irish Protestants of various sorts, but also evangelical activity directed at the Catholic Irish. The first strategy devised to achieve these aims was to encourage those Irish clergy, some formerly of the Church of Ireland, to come within the control of the regime by accepting payment from it. In addition, under an ordinance of 1650, prominent ministers from England were encouraged to settle in Ireland and were paid from the Irish exchequer. Some were paid up to £200 per annum, but £100 seems to have been nearer the norm. Clergy were normally recruited by personal and professional contacts between the commissioners and army officers and English godly clergy. Initially tests for orthodoxy were few, given the shortage of clergy, and this may have assisted the spread of Baptist activity. Only in Munster was there a committee, established by Oliver Cromwell in 1650, for the examination of ministers, and this operated throughout the 1650s. By 1652 clergy throughout the country had to produce recommendations which could come from a variety of sources, including the English committee for the approbation of ministers, laymen and Scottish presbyteries. These were vetted by an informal committee nominated by the Dublin administration. By 1656 this was formalised, possibly using the English model but without specific rules, and a proclamation of 1658 declared that no clergy should have a salary from the exchequer without approval from this committee. These approved clergy, some 376 of them over the 1650s, were paid from the Irish exchequer, since tithes had been abolished in 1649 and church land confiscated, although the legal basis of this confiscation was doubtful. By 1658 preachers' salaries cost almost £25,000 a year, but the income to the exchequer from church land and tithes was only £12,000. For an administration with financial difficulties, this situation could not continue. In 1658 measures were taken to reintroduce tithes and reorganise parishes or provide a subvention so that incumbents would receive a minimum of £80 per annum. Within a year the cost of ministerial salaries had fallen to £16,000 per annum.

This need to reform church structures, together with theological disputes among the sects, had the effect of making the Cromwellian church rather preoccupied with its own affairs. Some effort was made to preach the gospel to Irish-speakers, but it was very restricted. A number of ministers who could preach in Irish were active in Dublin, but there seem to have been few outside the capital. Only one can be briefly traced in Connacht, a prime area for evangelisation given the concentration of Irish there as a result of the land settlement. Moreover, very few godly works were translated into Irish for local consumption. The translation of the Old Testament made by William Bedell in the 1630s remained unpublished, whereas in Wales there were three editions of the Welsh New Testament between 1647 and 1654. The *Directory for worship* remained untranslated into Irish. Only one work was published in Irish during the 1650s in Dublin, a translation of William Perkins's *The Christian doctrine* by a former Church of Ireland minister Godfrey Daniel. This failure to engage actively in proselytism was curious. In many other seventeenth-century European countries where one elite replaced another, such as Bohemia, that process was matched by an intensive campaign of evangelisation to minimise future conflict. That this failed to happen in Ireland during the 1650s, as in the Dutch Generality lands after 1648, would have significant long-term consequences.

If persuasion had limited effect, coercion might have had more impact. Yet the Cromwellian regime was reluctant to meddle with tender consciences in matters of religion. The Act of Uniformity was repealed, and people were not compelled to attend any form of worship. However, Catholicism presented to even the tolerant Oliver Cromwell a special case since it was seen as idolatry and as such was condemned by scripture. This was the background to the act of June 1657 'for convicting, discovering and repressing of popish recusants'. This act required Catholics to take an oath abjuring the supremacy of the pope and denying the doctrine of transubstantiation on pain of sequestration of two-thirds of their property. The abjuration of papal authority was understandable in security terms, since it gave the papacy the status of a foreign power with whom the exiled King Charles II might attempt to deal. It was not a measure to be taken lightly, and as early as the following September Henry Cromwell was regretting the need for it.

The impact of all this on the organisation of Catholicism was dramatic. The structures that had been carefully built up in the early part of the seventeenth century collapsed. Archbishop O'Reilly of

Armagh reported that by 1660 each of the five dioceses of Dublin province had an average of seven priests, though in Armagh province the number was larger at twenty-two. Many other dioceses were little better off. There were thirty-two priests in Elphin in 1661 and fifteen in Killaloe in 1658. In the country as a whole there were probably no more than 500 or 600 Catholic priests, or about half the number recorded in 1622. The Catholic parish system was in chaos and the episcopate was effectively non-existent. Protestant domination of a whole range of national institutions became clear. Irish towns, including Dublin, came to have Protestants as a majority of their inhabitants for the first time in their history, and this dominance continued through the century. Restrictions were placed on Catholics becoming freemen in towns, although how widely these were enforced is not known. Urban government was confined in Protestant hands through the use of oaths of loyalty. While the constitutional settlement may have explicitly excluded Catholics from national political life, Protestant political control of the boroughs would have had the same effect, as the elections to the 1660 parliament demonstrated. In this the Cromwellian period marked a decisive shift in political control in Ireland.

The second element which was to be used to alter minds in the 1650s was education, which, in the view of contemporaries, was closely linked with promotion of religious reform. To be godly one must also be educated. The framework of educational provision had been well established in Ireland before 1649 as a result of legislation passed in 1537 and 1571 to create parochial and diocesan schools. The foundation of Trinity College Dublin in 1592 provided Ireland with its first and only university. The Ulster plantation scheme had also promoted education through the foundation of 'royal schools', and land in the plantation scheme was also granted to Trinity College. This threefold distinction between parish schools, diocesan grammar schools and university education was preserved through the 1650s. Parish schools were to continue functioning, but were now to be run not by clergy but by schoolmasters appointed and paid by government. Their remuneration was less generous than for ministers, usually being between £20 and £40 a year, and it was hardly surprising that few were attracted to the job. In 1659 there were only thirty-five state-paid schoolmasters in Ireland, mainly concentrated in the English garrison areas. Secondary education was to be conducted at a county level with schools supported by the income from confiscated lands. However, this assumed that there would be land left over after the settlement of the soldiers, a supposition that was entirely unfounded.

At university level, the advancement of learning was to be carried on at Trinity College in Dublin, and plans were devised for a second college, named after Oliver Cromwell, but this never materialised. The priority given to university education reflected the need for locally trained clergy. Trinity College had come close to collapse as a result of the war of the 1640s, and serious reform was required to allow it to undertake that role. The Provost, Samuel Winter, spent a good deal of his time in the early 1650s reorganising the college's land to increase its income. In the meantime the college was bailed out by the exchequer. In the longer term, the prospect for thoroughgoing reform was limited by the meagre supply of suitable scholars for fellowships. Many of those who occupied those posts during the 1650s were graduates of the college before 1640 and hence had distinct Church of Ireland sympathies. This meant that Provost Winter's position within the college was always precarious. In 1655 eight new candidates whose theological positions were closer to that of Winter, two being his sons, were proposed and five appointed. However, the task of attracting students for them to teach proved challenging. The number of admissions gradually rose from a very low level in 1654 to an average of twenty-seven a year between 1657 and 1659, about half of whom were born in Ireland. This was still far short of the number that had been admitted in 1640.

In general, the state made little practical impact in the sphere of educational provision. Rather more effectual were the efforts of private individuals who devoted their energies to educating the Irish. The most important of these was the 'adventurer' Erasmus Smith, who decided to promote the Gospel in Ireland by using income from his Irish lands to educate the young in the ways of godliness. He established some of his land in a trust, the trustees of which were prominent godly clergy and aldermen. The revenue they generated was to be used to establish and maintain schools. Five schools at Sligo, Galway, Tipperary and Antrim were to be set up, although in practice little was done before 1669 when Smith's estate was finally settled. A number of towns, including Dublin, also maintained schools which provided for local education.

The task of reforming minds was a difficult one, and, at least initially, many had to be content with a reformation of outward behaviour rather than attitudes. In the middle of the seventeenth century there seems to have been a shift in the approaches to social reform. Traditional belief in an unbreakable cycle of degeneration and renewal gave way to a new idea of progress or improvement in which moral change would be reflected in an ordered landscape and flourishing economic activity. These ideas were most associated with Samuel Hartlib and his circle in London. Hartlib had followers in Ireland also. Sir William Petty was probably the most significant, directing his talent for political arithmetic into analysing and prescribing for the illnesses of Ireland as well as the more practical task of mapping the country. The Boate brothers likewise turned their attention to Ireland in the mid-1640s, their work culminating in their *Ireland's natural history* (1652), which sought to reveal the benefits bestowed on Ireland by English settlers and thereby to suggest that there was a great deal more wealth to be extracted through reform of Ireland. A number of those who came to Ireland in the 1650s though less prominent than Petty or Boate showed a marked interest in the techniques of reformation. Myles Symner, professor of mathematics in Trinity College Dublin, who was certainly connected to Hartlib and his circle, displayed a strong interest in astronomy. Others, such at Robert Child in north Down, interested themselves in projects for improving individual estates. He urged the planting of fruit trees, draining of bogs and the introduction of new crops such as clover, hops and woad. Other longer-established inhabitants, such as George Rawdon at Lisburn, embarked on new schemes for soap production or the making of potash as a way of supplementing landed income. In purely economic terms, the impact of such changes in the 1650s was probably small, but in the longer term the enthusiasm for improvement, evident earlier in the social engineering scheme for the Ulster plantation, would have much more important consequences. Whereas previously in Ireland private individuals profited from new ideas under a system of monopolies, in the 1650s new men moved in to explore their world, carving out public spheres of science and political economy where none had existed before.

Despite these efforts to change hearts and minds, it was clear by the late 1650s that Ireland had failed to develop a radical tradition in the way that England had done in the 1640s. That does not mean that there were no home-grown products among the radical godly churches of the 1650s. Some of the state's preachers who were convinced radicals, such as Faithful Teate, had formerly been Church of Ireland clergy, and the former Chancellor of Christ Church Cathedral in Dublin, John Harding, became a Baptist and his son a Presbyterian. Some of those who were members of John Rogers's Independent church in Dublin in the early 1650s had been in Ireland in the 1640s. Yet what lay at the roots of their religious radicalism was anti-Catholicism which had been activated as a result of their experiences in Ireland in the early 1640s. This acted as a cathartic experience and seems to have brought a reconsideration of their religious position, leading them into the separatist churches. Anti-Catholicism alone was not enough to begin the process of radically restructuring a society. Among the Cromwellian governors, shifts in power in England and the limited ability of governors in Dublin to initiate policy all contributed to a general uncertainty about the form of the Irish state. Most of those involved in the government of Ireland before the mid-1650s were more interested in shifts of power in England than they were in developing the Irish polity. In particular, Fleetwood as governor of Ireland was an unfortunate choice who took his lead from London. In Ireland he found himself manipulated by too many English-inspired radicals to allow any coherent policy to emerge. On his arrival as Fleetwood's successor, Henry Cromwell had recognised the lack of a radical base in Ireland and adapted policy accordingly by locating and courting a coherent power base for the Protectorate, without which it had little chance of survival. The result was a more conservative shape for society. The radical, republican spirit which the Cromwellian intervention seemed to promise to breathe into Irish affairs after 1649 burned faintly and briefly before being finally extinguished in 1660.

## OTHER LIVES

As the 1650s moved on and Oliver Cromwell aged, many in Ireland became worried about the succession to the Lord Protectorship. Such concerns lay behind the offer of the crown to Cromwell in 1657. The Munster gentleman Roger Boyle, later Earl of Orrery, was a prime mover in that initiative. To have re-created monarchy, whoever the wearer of the crown was, would have been an important step in rebuilding a traditional type of society with its monarchial chains of authority and dependence. Concern about the succession may have been sharpened by the realisation that the royal court of the 1640s had not disappeared but had simply relocated itself first to Paris and then Bruges. Around the king there remained a significant number of Irishmen who had opted not to remain in Ireland under the Cromwellian regime. Indeed, at least some of tensions between the Earl of Orrery and the Duke of Ormond in the later seventeenth century stemmed from their different decisions about how they would pass the Interregnum. Ormond had chosen exile with the king, although in 1658 he was in England, gauging the possibilities for staging a royalist insurrection there. By contrast, Orrery had served the Cromwellian state. The men around the king in the 1650s were later to emerge as important in the Irish context. Of the six viceroys of Ireland between 1660 and 1690, four had been in exile with the king. The Archbishop of Armagh in 1660, John Bramhall, had also been at the exiled court, as had Sir George Lane, Viscount Lanesborough, later Secretary of State in Ireland. Charles II's Gracious Declaration of November 1660 required the restoration to their property of many, including Catholics, who had served him 'beyond the seas'. Most never scaled the dizzy political heights in Ireland, although Theobald Taaffe, Earl of Carlingford, served as an ambassador in Vienna, but many with native Irish names would become significant in local government and provide a local base for the Restoration regime.

The full significance of the careers of those who chose exile in the 1650s rather than remaining in Ireland is as yet uncovered, but given the importance of the offices some attained, their experiences in the 1650s were significant. At the simplest, proximity to the king created a bond forged in adversity which proved resilient. The Marquis, and later Duke, of Ormond is a good example of a man who forged close links to the king in these circumstances. Equally, enmities were also made. At the court in exile animosities developed between Ormond and Richard Talbot, who built up a powerful friendship with the king's brother, James, Duke of York. York's patronage of Talbot annoyed Ormond, and this skein of discontents would remain visible through late seventeenth-century Irish politics.

However, the political and cultural significance of exile may well be greater than the personal. For many, this was their first prolonged exposure to a wider culture. Ormond in the 1650s made the sort of

French contacts that he would exploit later in recruiting settlers for his estates. Moreover, it was probably the first exposure many had to Tridentine Catholicism and how that could work in a political settlement. Ormond certainly encountered this sort of world in his dealings with Cardinal de Retz in the 1650s, and in 1659 it was Ormond who conducted negotiations with Cardinal Mazarin about support for the future Charles II. More generally, those in France or the Spanish Netherlands in the 1650s had the opportunity to witness the practical outworking of the Treaty of Westphalia of 1648 that had brought the Thirty Years' War to an end. Crucially, while establishing political structures, the peace treaty also allowed for 'the free exercise of religion' in public and private, though at the same time it confirmed the power of the head of state. The model had obvious potential for application in the Irish context, and indeed seemed to echo the sort of position the Old English had advocated in the early part of the seventeenth century. Whether the European experience would have any lasting implications in Ireland was something that would have to be worked out in the messy world of Restoration politics.

# Part III

A New World Restored

# 8
# Winning the Peace, 1659–69

In the latter part of 1660 William Fuller, the recently appointed Dean of St Patrick's Cathedral in Dublin, penned an anthem to be sung at the consecration of two archbishops and ten bishops of the Church of Ireland in January 1661. The sentiments caught the moment:

> Now that the Lord hath readvanced the crown
> Which thirst of spoil and frantic zeal threw down,
> Now that the Lord the mitre hath restored,
> With which the crown lay in the dust abhorred . . .
> Angels look down and joy to see,
> Like that above a monarchy,
> Like that above a hierarchy.
>     Hallelujah.[1]

It was clear, in Fuller's mind at least, what that process called 'Restoration' meant. It signalled the final rejection of the sort of compromise solutions for the governance of church and state that had been in the air in 1659, particularly the possibility of some Presbyterian element in the ecclesiastical settlement, and it revelled in the return of monarchy and an episcopal church hierarchy. The penultimate line of the anthem is sufficiently vague to admit of another cause of celebration: the re-creation of social as well as ecclesiastical hierarchy. Here, then, were encapsulated the problems of those who struggled to remake Irish society in the 1660s.

## THE PROMISE OF 1659

On 3 September 1658 Oliver Cromwell, Lord Protector, died and was succeed by his eldest son, Richard. What followed in England was a gradual implosion of the Protectorate. The events are tortuous to follow, but in outline they began with the summoning of the third Protectorate parliament in January 1659. Within this structure the army and the politicians failed to reach any sort of working compromise and this was followed by the restoration in May of the Rump Parliament, the remnant of the Long Parliament that traced its origins to before the Civil War, though it had been thoroughly purged in 1648 by Colonel Pride. That parliament exerted pressure on Richard Cromwell to resign, but it, in turn, was dissolved by army radicals in October. All this reflected the uncertainty of what the future might offer in the absence of Richard Cromwell: military dictatorship or anarchy. It was clear that the Cromwellian experiment was at an end, but it was not clear what was to replace it.

Whether the Cromwellian land settlement in Ireland would survive was a pressing question for those who had benefited from that settlement. There were both diehard royalists and convinced republicans in Ireland, but whether either group would gain control or whether some other form of political solution would emerge was not clear. In June 1659 the parliament in Westminster resolved that Ireland was to be administered by commissioners nominated and authorised by parliament. Henry Cromwell, Oliver's son and Irish Lord Lieutenant, was recalled, and three commissioners, later expanded to five, were appointed to govern Ireland and the Irish army purged of, allegedly, 200 officers. All this seemed to mark a return to the army radicalism of the early 1650s, a prospect that filled many of the Old Protestants with dread. The politics of the situation were changed by a military coup on 13 December 1659, when a number of army officers captured Dublin Castle in support of the restored parliament. Elsewhere in the city soldiers seized the newly appointed parliamentary commissioners. In less than two hours a *coup d'état* had been effected. In retrospect, this was the point at which the settlement of Ireland was decided, even though it did not appear so at the time. Effective power now moved to a group of Old Protestant army officers, including Sir Charles Coote in Connacht and Lord Broghill in Munster. This was essentially a conservative coup by a group of men with differing interests and solutions for the governance of Ireland. What held them together was a concern to wrest power from extremists and to set up a mechanism by which the political nation in Ireland could make decisions on its future. The Irish Convention, which met in February 1660 to take these decisions, would be dominated by such men. Tensions within the group became clear in early 1660 when Sir Hardress Waller, a Limerick landowner and republican who supported the Rump Parliament, attempted to arrest Coote, but the attempt failed and Waller found himself behind bars. The conservative nature of the insurrectionists' agenda is apparent from the instructions drafted for their agents going to London in late December 1659 or early January 1660. The main priority was to regularise the actions of the Protectorate, especially the confirmation of land grants, and to secure an act of oblivion for those who had operated under the authority of the state in the 1650s. Whatever sort of solution was to emerge, the reputations and wealth of those involved in its making were not to be compromised.

Those who became, in essence, the new commissioners for Ireland concentrated on managing the local situation, knowing that they had little influence on decisions that would be taken elsewhere about the government of the three kingdoms. In Scotland the military commander General Monck took the initiative and, having marched from Scotland, entered London on 3 February 1660, demanding the summoning of a free parliament to prevent anarchy. In the Corporation Book of Belfast someone scribbled verses which prefigured events:

> Advance George Monck and Monck St George shall be
> England's restorer to its liberty
> Scotland's protector, Ireland's president
> Reducing all to a free parliament
> If thou dost intend the other thing
> Go on and all shall Cry God save the King.[2]

On 4 April the exiled Charles II issued his Declaration of Breda, promising amnesty, settlement of land claims and arrears of army pay for those who would support him. Again the Corporation of Belfast copied this into their minute book, suggesting that they saw this as a document of long-term importance. The Convention assembly meeting in London in April had no reservations about doing the 'other thing' and voted for a restoration of monarchy on 1 May. Four weeks later, on 29 May 1660, Charles entered London. In Ireland those who seized power in January concentrated on local matters; remodelling the military command, establishing an executive, and summoning a representative convention to legitimate their actions. While the Irish Convention could not be said to have played a significant role in the restoration of the king, it did have a vitally important one in deciding how restored monarchy would relate to Irish Protestants, many of whom held their lands by the authority of the Commonwealth. Charles was, after all, a party to the Ormond peace of 1649, which had promised concessions to Catholics. Moreover, many of those who had settled in Ireland in the 1650s were not of the same religion as the king. Although Protestant, in the language of the world before 1649, they were sectaries or dissenters. In the late 1650s, in particular, a pragmatic mainstream Presbyterianism had become both influential and acceptable in Ireland under the influence of Henry Cromwell. If there was to be a restoration of the Established Church, then the question of the degree of comprehension of other religious groups was an important one. In a real sense the Irish Convention, established as the Protectorate collapsed, had the opportunity to lay down a whole new set of social as well as political rules for the government of Ireland.

The Convention itself met in February 1660. It was elected through the normal parliamentary constituencies, but with some variations in the boroughs. It ought on that basis to have comprised 158 members, but only 138 are known to have been returned. Almost all had a personal or family connection with the area they represented. At least 98 were Old Protestants, those who had been in Ireland before and during the war, and, at most, 40 were newcomers. The majority of the latter had come to Ireland with the Cromwellian army. The Convention was not a parliament, deriving its authority from an older tradition of extra-parliamentary conventions rather than from a royal summons, but it did operate according to parliamentary rules and was certainly not a body to be dominated by religious or political radicals. Perhaps significantly for the future of a religious settlement, only two of the Ulster representatives had a Scottish background, and hence the representation of organised Presbyterianism was rather weaker than one might have expected.

Two power brokers quickly emerged: Sir Charles Coote, whose power was largely based on support from Old Protestants, and Roger Boyle, Lord Broghill (later Earl of Orrery), who drew his support from a wider mixture of Old and New Protestants, including some who had fought for the parliament in the 1640s. Orrery had been closely associated with Henry Cromwell and the Cromwellian regime in both Ireland and Scotland. Broad agreement was soon reached on the main questions, such as the nature of kingship in any restoration, and there was equal agreement concerning the need to restore Irish constitutional and political integrity after the Westminster parliament's involvement in Irish matters during the 1640s. The need for public order was also agreed on, and one of the earliest acts of the Convention was to ensure that Catholics in Connacht stayed there and that those in towns were to be removed. Given the economic difficulties which the Cromwellian regime had faced, the Convention tried to tackle financial matters, though it had little success owing to its short existence.

There was less agreement on the configuration of a religious settlement. While the restoration of religious order and the suppression of the sects seemed obvious goals, the model for the resulting national church was less clear. The fact that the Convention chose a Presbyterian minister, Samuel Coxe, to preach before it at its opening session seemed to bode well for a settlement that might include the Presbyterians at least. Within a month the Convention issued a statement that seemed to support this impression. It called for a learned and orthodox ministry, settled in parishes and funded by tithes, but made no overt mention of episcopacy. However, it declared that this would be the only form of religious organisation and there was to be no toleration of others. Some continued to believe, on good grounds, that this would be a Presbyterian system, but the episcopalian option was also organising. This was supported by political sentiment which moved ever closer towards episcopalianism the more certain it seemed that the king would be restored in England. Moreover, contact had been made with the exiled king at

Breda by Sir Charles Coote, who apparently told the king that Ireland would accept an episcopal settlement. The argument seemed all but over when Henry Jones was asked to preach at Christ Church Cathedral in Dublin on the day Charles II was proclaimed king in the city and Jones was addressed by his former title of 'Lord Bishop of Clogher'.

On 1 May 1660 the decision of the English Convention to restore the king was enthusiastically welcomed and accepted in Dublin. The republican interlude of the 1650s was now decidedly over. The details of what this meant were not fully spelled out, but it was clear that any bargaining power which Dublin may have had in shaping the settlement was now at an end. On 17 May agents for the Irish Convention travelled to London with instructions, which the Convention had been working on since early March, to represent the Irish Protestant interest there. Their instructions were to obtain what was necessary for a settlement of Ireland, in particular that bills should be laid before the Irish parliament to secure the estates of soldiers and 'adventurers' and pardons for those who had served the Commonwealth. There was no mention of the church settlement, but there were some propositions on church land and finances. It quickly became clear what was expected, and the agents speedily redrafted their proposals, taking advantage of the freedom that had been given to them by the Convention. In the redrafted proposals laid before the English Privy Council on 21 June 1660 they asked that the Church of Ireland be re-established as it had been in the time of Charles I. Within days episcopal nominations were made for Ireland. On the secular front it seemed that the Irish Convention might have more influence. While Irish Protestants agreed that they wished the king restored, they also wanted to hold on to the land and power they had recently gained. Unlike the issue of religion, they were at one on this matter. The resulting negotiations produced the king's Gracious Declaration of November 1660, which formed the basis of the later Act of Settlement and met the objectives of the Convention as far as circumstances would permit. Once a new settlement for the government of Ireland was established, Protestant unity would begin to fragment, and in the working out of the settlement each was left to fend for himself. The possibilities that the events of 1659 had seemed to offer had closed off.

## RESTORING THE KING

To restore a king was a simple matter. Charles ii was proclaimed king at a number of locations in Dublin on 14 May 1660, a fortnight before his formal entry into London. The commissioners for the government of Ireland proceeded to Christ Church Cathedral 'with all sorts of music before them'. After the religious service 'the conduit did run plentifully with wine and the ordnance several times discharged in very good order'. At a more popular level, Toby Bonnell described a mock funeral service for the Rump Parliament held on the streets of the city. As the headless effigy of the Cromwellian regime was paraded through the streets 'people with their naked swords and staves hacked and butted the rump all along', and when it came to the mayor's house 'after it had been scorned and derided of all people it was in part burnt in the bonfire before the door and part trod to dirt and mortar by the route'. The mayor, playing his part, provided cakes and ale for the 'funeral guests'.[3] All this was entertainment, albeit with a purpose.

For the Old English, at least, the sort of king they thought they might get was described in John Lynch's *Cambrensis eversus* (1662). Lynch, an Old English priest, had spend most of the 1650s in France and wrote his work, which he dedicated to Charles ii, 'to confirm your title to the kingdom of Ireland in defence of which my countrymen lately rose in arms for you and lavishly sacrificed their treasure and blood'. Beginning with early Irish kingship, Lynch, like Geoffrey Keating before him, stressed not divine-right monarchy but the alternative idea that monarchs were chosen by the people and that this implied reciprocal obligations between king and subject. Sovereignty rested with the people, who had a duty to obey a just king but were entitled to resist an unjust king by force. Lynch regarded the relationship between king and people as involving a contract whereby the king had to accept people as his subjects, and they, in turn, had to agree to become subjects. The apparent disloyalty of the Irish before 1603 was explained away by the fact that the Irish 'never fully accepted the regular rights and duties of subjects until King James ascended the throne', but that on the accession of the first Stuart king the Irish had 'renounced all thoughts of opposition', knowing his ancestry. Lynch criticised his own contemporaries who regarded Charles ii as a foreigner and argued that, since he was the legitimate King of Ireland, it was not lawful for Catholics to oppose him.[4] In the world of the early 1660s, such sentiments had powerful political possibilities.

To theorise about monarchy was important, but to make it work was a much more serious challenge. That was the responsibility of the king's representative in Ireland, the Lord Lieutenant. For a substantial part of the period between 1660 and 1690, from 1662 to 1669 and again from 1677 to 1685, that office was held by James Butler, Duke of Ormond, and by virtue of his long tenure it was he who was the main moulder of that key political post in a new political order. Ormond's world contained a number of features which would shape the viceroyalty. As a large landowner and Ireland's only duke, he possessed considerable social authority in and of himself that he brought to office. Moreover, he was rich. In 1681 he had a gross rental of £25,000 a year, together with an income from offices and fees in excess of £20,000. This was combined with very significant political power that stemmed from his period in exile with the king during the 1650s and close friendships, formed in that period, with many of the new king's most senior advisers. However, what was most important was the new Lord Lieutenant's Irish background. Ormond, although firmly Protestant, was Old English in his background and schooled in the world of Thomas Wentworth. He held firmly to the idea of an Irish kingdom, and in accordance with this some of the features of Wentworth's rule were resurrected under Ormond. He believed in the importance of a viceregal court as a centre for managing Irish affairs and in the position of the Lord Lieutenant as more than a colonial governor. As he explained to his son, 'It is of importance to keep up the splendour of the government.'[5]

Ormond spent lavishly not only to prop up the ramshackle Dublin Castle, which was not altered substantially until after a fire in 1684, but also to turn his own house at Kilkenny into a residence fit for a Lord Lieutenant. He bought tapestries, gilded leather wall coverings, mirrors, silver and brass sconces and upholstered furniture and moved possessions between the castles in Dublin and Kilkenny. Public and private functions merged in these worlds, enhancing not only the Irish state but also the duke himself as the pinnacle of the social order. The rituals of court were observed, and Wentworth's innovation of a public theatre, again under John Ogilby, who had designed the triumphal arches for Charles II's entry into London, was newly situated in Smock Alley. There was more to this than simple spectacle. One of the first works to be performed in 1661 was the Earl of Orrery's play *The general*. This was a piece of court theatre of a very specialised kind, a piece of political negotiation between Orrery, who had served Cromwell in the 1650s, and Ormond, who had gone abroad with the king. Set during a rebellion in which the legitimate king and a usurper struggle for power, the play is loaded with the language of honour and duty. Orrery himself was clearly the model for the general in the play. The allusions to the Ireland of the 1640s and 1650s are clear as Orrery tried to explain his actions during those years, but, judging by the animosity of the two men in later years, Ormond did not find the explanation convincing.

Court rituals spilled out onto the streets, and the movements of Lords Lieutenant were accompanied by public spectacles appropriate to their new status. When Ormond entered Dublin in 1662, he was accompanied by the sheriffs, a peal of ordnance and fireworks. In 1665 when he arrived in the city pageants were played along his route. When his replacement, Lord Robartes, arrived in 1669, he was met by the Privy Council and sheriffs and was escorted into Dublin for a formal entry accompanied by set speeches. All shops in the city were closed, and there was considerable revellery and drunkenness. All this echoed the entrances Wentworth had orchestrated during his progress through Ireland in 1637. Again, like Wentworth, the new Lords Lieutenant were builders. Dublin Castle, the centre of government, was refurbished in 1671 and 1684, a process hastened by fires. By the 1690s John Dunton, visiting the city, could compare it with London's Whitehall, commenting: 'and indeed the grandeur they live in here is not much inferior to what you see in London if you make allowances for the number of great men at court there'.[6] An attempt was made to move the law courts from their cramped situation at Christ Church Cathedral, but this was resisted by the corporation, mindful of the business that they brought into the city. More successful was the building of the Royal Hospital at Kilmainham for former soldiers. The classicism of the building, together with the clear parallels with Les Invalides in Paris, suggested a new set of influences at work not only in architecture but also in the shaping of Irish society as those who had spent much of the 1650s with the king in France and the Low Countries returned to power.

At least as important as his ideas about the Lord Lieutenancy was Ormond's vision about how society should work, especially at the upper social levels. The core of these ideas can be found in his comment to his son, the Earl of Arran, during the crisis of 1683, when he declared that governors should 'do their duty and then to leave the success in relation to the public and private concerns to God who governs great and little things'. Again in 1678, when rebellion seemed to threaten, he urged that men 'should pray heartily and labour in their stations'.[7] God, in Ormond's view of providence, had ordered society and appointed people to their station in the expectation that there they should behave according to their appointed duty. Thus society was held together by a set of mutual obligations which culminated in one's obligations to the king. These ideas were fused in a concept of honour demonstrated by lineage and appropriate behaviour. In this respect Ormond's ideas about the organisation of society were not very different from those espoused by the Old English in the 1620s.

This sense of hierarchy and order, underpinned by well-defined ideas about honour and duty, were mixed blessings. Many of those whom Ormond regarded as the natural rulers of Ireland, some of these being his Old English relations, were Catholic but staunch royalists. As he commented to Colonel William Legge, 'I confess it troubles me to see men of birth incapable as well by their religion as their education of those advantages and employments that would better become them than many that have them.'[8] In the context of an awareness of their duty and honour, Ormond could envision a role for Catholics in the government of Ireland. The Catholicism of men of Old English background proved a barrier for them, but also a liability to Ormond. Some among the settler community regarded him with distrust. In particular, Roger Boyle, Earl of Orrery, the powerful Munster settler who had a penchant for seeing Catholic plots everywhere, became Ormond's nemesis from the middle of the 1660s. The two had little in common. Ormond had spent the 1650s in exile with the king, Orrery in the service of the Commonwealth and Protectorate. Orrery's religion tended towards Protestant radicalism, while that of Ormond was a conventional world of a Caroline high churchman. Disputes between the two spilled over into English politics, where both had considerable influence.

The nature of the factional disputes between Ormond and Orrery highlights one further feature of the viceroyalty in the late seventeenth century: the Irish viceroy became increasingly part of the English political world. After the restoration of Charles II the position of the viceroy, particularly when held by Ormond, was a powerful one. Indeed, over time it seemed that the centralising tendencies of the Dublin administration would augment that power. In 1672 the presidencies of Connacht and Munster were abolished, as was Ormond's own Tipperary palatinate liberty in 1716. The power of local landlords, so evident in the early seventeenth century, had been shattered by war in the 1640s and economic problems in the 1650s. The towns, meanwhile, had their political power removed with the new arrangements for their working in the 'New Rules' of 1672, imposed from Dublin Castle. Yet, despite that, late seventeenth-century Ireland saw power gravitate towards London. The politics of court, and the English parliament, would become increasingly important for the stability of the Irish viceroy's position. Within two years of his appointment as viceroy in 1672 the Earl of Essex experienced the sort of campaign at court that was to become normal, involving pressure on the king, charges of mismanagement and the encouragement of complaints from Ireland. In this case the campaign against Essex was promoted by courtiers, such as the fourth-generation Irish peer and protégé of the Duke of Buckingham, Lord Ranelagh, who resented Essex's opposition to schemes for making money from Ireland, and particularly his intervention in the management of its finances. Irish affairs had become an important weapon in the struggle for political power and enrichment at the court at Whitehall, and Irish viceroys quickly learned the importance of maintaining an agent there. The gentry followed the viceroy's example, and the wealthy took to maintaining houses in London and entertaining their countrymen there. As Ormond found in the late 1670s and early 1680s, attacks would come not merely from the court but also from parliament manipulated by those, such as Orrery, who had little liking for the Irish governor. From 1665 relations were tense. Those in Ireland who expected Ormond to protect them from the actions of the English parliament, such as the imposition of the Cattle Acts, were to be disappointed. In practice, so long as the Irish viceroy could retain the confidence of the king he was safe, but the king was also the weak point in the political structure, and confidence in a viceroy could easily be undermined by those with access to the monarch. The Irish viceroyalty may have been potentially one of the most powerful offices in the British Isles, but that power was considerably limited by the political instability the post entailed.

## RESTORING THE CHURCH

In some ways restoring the church was as simple a process as restoring a king. On 27 January 1661 two new archbishops and ten bishops were consecrated in St Patrick's Cathedral, Dublin. At one stroke the Church of Ireland had a functioning episcopate. Eight bishops had survived from the pre-Cromwellian period, and the twelve new bishops filled seventeen sees created by the administrative union of small, uneconomic dioceses. Of the eight survivors, three were promoted and the remainder stayed in their old dioceses. One further appointment remained to be made. It was a remarkably cohesive bench of bishops. Their outstanding characteristic was their loyalty to the episcopal cause during the Interregnum. Most had passed those years in England, but a few had stayed in Ireland or, as in the case of John Bramhall, the new Archbishop of Armagh, gone to the royal court abroad. Of the complete bench of twenty-one bishops, nine were of English birth, two Welsh, four Scottish, and the remainder Irish. Of those with English backgrounds, most had begun their clerical careers in Ireland under Wentworth in the 1630s. Indeed, the hand of Wentworth or Ormond can be discerned in the careers of most of them. In that sense the outlook of the restored episcopate had been largely shaped in the 1630s by the theological ideas of Laud and the policies of Wentworth for the management of the Established Church. This was hardly accidental, especially given the almost undignified haste with which the bishops had been selected. Moreover, Archbishop Bramhall possessed a clear vision of what he wished to achieve in reconstructing the episcopal bench, and a sympathetic Ormond at court, and at the height of his power, was prepared to see it implemented. In time this clear vision would become cloudier. A rather different and broader vision would be taken of episcopal appointments in Ireland in which patronage rather than theology played a greater part, but the events of 1660 set the tone for what was to follow.

The second aspect of the restoration of the church was effected in June 1665 when the Act of Uniformity, prescribing the revised Book of Common Prayer, requiring episcopal ordination and prohibiting schoolmasters from teaching without a licence, was enacted. The changes in the liturgy were small, but new occasional services were introduced. Of much greater importance was the thinking behind the working of the church. In the early part of the seventeenth century the

Church of Ireland had attempted to be inclusive, building a broad Protestant consensus against Catholicism. Thus the 1615 Articles of the Church of Ireland did not require subscription to the articles either on ordination or admission to a living. Moreover, Article 36 of the Thirty-Nine Articles, which dealt with consecration of bishops, was silently dropped from the Irish Articles, again leaving room for a broadly based consensus. However, the 1665 Act of Uniformity required episcopal ordination and assent to the Book of Common Prayer and the Thirty-Nine Articles. This confirmed the existing position. Some sixty Ulster clergy were expelled from their livings in 1660 for their failure to conform to the Church of Ireland rite. The pattern of exclusion was even wider than this. The canons of 1634, which had not really taken effect before 1641, required churchwardens and sidesmen to take oaths before the bishop prior to assuming office. This effectively excluded Catholics and dissenters from participation in parochial office, although Catholics had served in at least some parishes of the Established Church in the early seventeenth century. In the parish of Crumlin in County Dublin during the 1590s, for instance, the churchwardens of the parish were important figures in local society. Hugh Harrold, proctor for 1596, had been constable of the manor two years previously, had assessed local taxes on the manor, and frequently sat on juries. Edmund Basnett, another proctor, also served regularly on the manorial jury. These men were responsible for guarding the property of the church and managing its lands and were not appointed by the parish but rather were elected by the manor court. While the confessional position of Basnett and Harrold cannot be fixed exactly, given Archbishop Bulkeley's comment in 1630 that the parishioners of Crumlin were 'for the most part recusants', there is a strong possibility that they had Catholic leanings.[9] Again in Ulster in 1615 during a dispute between Art MacTomlin O'Mullan and Brian MacShane O'Mullan, Art accused Brian that 'thou are a church warden yet do not attend thy office, according [to] thy instructions. Thou had sixteen masses said in thy house by Gillecome MacTeig, abbot . . . and then relievest the said Gillecome and then harbourest him in thy house as well as abroad'.[10] There can be little doubt about confessional allegiance here. Similarly, in the case of St John's parish, Dublin, in the early seventeenth century a number of Catholics certainly served in parochial office. By the late seventeenth century, at least in Dublin, this practice had ceased and both Catholics and dissenters assumed only lesser parochial offices such as cessers for the poor. In short, the Restoration religious settlement, drawing on the constructions of Wentworth, was intended to be exclusive rather than inclusive, as the early seventeenth-century settlement had been, in its outlook.

These signs of introversion were not all negative. The clear definition of a specifically Church of Ireland community, with its distinctive form of worship and political ideas, was an important factor in the emergence of a new religious culture within the restored church. Characteristic ways of reading the Bible, for the sense rather than scrutinising individual verses, alongside singing and listening to sermons developed among adherents of the Established Church. Also significant was the dramatic spate of church-building that took place in late seventeenth-century Dublin. This gave the church an opportunity to remodel its liturgical space to reflect a new sense of itself. Throughout the city in the 1670s communion tables were raised up and chancels railed in, reflecting a greater emphasis on sacramental worship. Some parish churches in Dublin had already done this in the 1630s in line with Wentworth's reforms, but now it seems to have been almost universal in the city, perhaps copying English practice. Outside Dublin it is more difficult to be precise about developments. In parts of Ulster it was not until the 1690s that such changes would be witnessed. Communion tables were also more frequently used. Churchwardens' accounts for Dublin in the late seventeenth century show a dramatic increase in expenditure on bread and wine for Holy Communion. In St John's expenditure grew sixfold, in St Bride's fourfold, and in St Catherine's it doubled. This reflects both the greater frequency of communion services in the city and the increased numbers of people attending them. A further indication of the increased participation of the community in liturgy is provided by the installation of organs in the Dublin churches, a feature of the 1670s onwards: St Werburgh's in 1676, St Catherine's 1678, St John's 1684, St Peter's 1686, and St Bride's c. 1686. The Church of Ireland began to think about singing as more of a communal activity. Music was introduced that could be reproduced by congregations when singing the psalter rather than psalms being said. In addition, church buildings provided the opportunity for displaying and reinforcing the social and political order of the Church of Ireland parish. In Dublin in the late seventeenth century pews in parish churches were sold or leased to those who could afford them. Inevitably this reflected the social and economic ranking of parishioners, reinforcing relationships of subordination in cultural and religious terms.

These developments had considerable ramifications for the way in which the Church of Ireland evolved in the later seventeenth century. In the course of time the church became increasingly introverted and abandoned the idea of a spiritually homogeneous state. As it saw itself, its role was not be a national church, but rather to serve those Protestants who had established themselves in Ireland. Estimates varied about how many actual, as opposed to legal, members the Church of Ireland had. Sir William Petty guessed that there were 800,000 Catholics and 300,000 Protestants in Ireland. Of the Protestants he estimated that about 100,000 were Scots, and therefore Presbyterian, and of the remaining 200,000 only half were conforming Protestants. While the contemporary estimate of one-tenth of the Irish population as members of the Church of Ireland is probably too low, it certainly does suggest that Anglican contemporaries thought themselves beleaguered. Outside Dublin little was done to improve the church. By the 1690s there had been little appreciable improvement in church fabric over what had existed in 1615. As the episcopate aged over the late seventeenth century bishops lost their enthusiasm for the unequal battle. Thus Bishop Hacket of Down and Connor, who in his youth had been the terror of Presbyterians, by the late 1680s had become a notorious absentee nicknamed the 'Bishop of Hammersmith' by his contemporaries. The new generation of reformers in the 1690s led by Bishops King, Foy and Marsh would have fruitful ground for reform.

## RESTORING SOCIAL HIERARCHY

While theologians of the restored Church of Ireland tried to justify the ways of God to man, they also tried to explain to people how their society was to be ordered. The manifesto for social change entitled *The whole duty of man* was written in the 1650s, probably by the English divine Richard Alstree. This book became so popular in Ireland that there was even an attempt to pirate it in 1663. The Lord Lieutenant, the Duke of Ormond, extracted prayers from it for his own use, and in the 1670s Robert Perceval of Cork was forced to read the book as a way of amending his life. The Rev. Samuel Ladyman of

Clonmel left his son 20s in his will to buy copies of *The whole duty of man*.[11] When it was finally published in Dublin in 1700 in an abridged form, it was attractively priced at 6d bound, presumably to sell at the lower end of the market. The social order depicted in *The whole duty of man* comprised orders and hierarchies in which one knew one's place:

> in regard that these degrees and distinctions of men are by God's wise providence disposed for the better ordering of the world, there is such a civil respect due to those, to whom God hast dispensed them, as may best preserve that order for which they were intended. Therefore all inferiors are to behave themselves to their superiors with modesty and respect and not by a rude boldness confound that order that it hath pleased God to set in the world.[12]

Individuals in this world did not so much have class positions or occupations as they had relationships, and these could be calculated with startling precision. *The whole duty of man* explained the relationship not only of people to God but of masters and servants, husbands and wives, magistrates and subjects, parents and children, rich and poor.

Precise as *The whole duty of man* was about the ties of obligation in society, it did not reckon with the fluidity of Irish politics and the social compromises that had to be made in the quest for a settlement. Charles II's Declaration of Breda, issued in April 1660, revealed the extent of that compromise by promising pardon to those who had supported the royalist cause in the 1640s, Catholic or Protestant, and offering liberty to the tender consciences of Cromwellian dissenters who had recently arrived in Ireland. Social order was to be placed under considerable strain by such compromises. One example of this is that Irish poets, most notably Dáibhí Ó Bruadair, who previously had not criticised settlers overtly, turned on the Cromwellian arrivals, accusing them of being social upstarts without the correct attributes of gentry. The Old English gentry heartily concurred with Richard Bellings, the former secretary to the Confederation of Kilkenny, when he characterised those who sought to rule Ireland in the 1660s as 'the scum of England' and 'a generation of base mechanic men, strangers to the principles of religion and loyalty', sentiments also directed against Cromwellians in England.[13] In the eyes of many, this was a dangerous situation, since, as the Duke of Ormond observed, the problems of the 1640s had been caused by 'mean and low aspirers' whose social rise had given them ideas above their station by comparison with 'peers and prelates . . . officers magistrates and judges' who were the natural advisers of the crown.[14]

Just how much social compromise had to be reached was made clear by the process of the land settlement. The land settlement rested on three key documents. The first was the Gracious Declaration of November 1660, which set out the broad principles for the settlement of the land question that were the outcome of the negotiations between the king and the Convention. This amounted, broadly speaking, to recognition of the *status quo* of 1659. Fifty-six prominent individuals or 'nominees', including twenty Catholic peers most of whom had been associated with the Confederation of Kilkenny, were singled out by name as meriting special royal favour and were to be restored to their estates. The second document was the Act of Settlement of 1662, passed by the Irish parliament to give effect to the Declaration. There were compromises here. The Catholic agents in London led by Sir Nicholas Plunkett and Richard Talbot, later Earl of Tyrconnell and Lord Deputy of Ireland under James II, also lobbied for change, although Talbot's earlier offensive lobbying during the drafting of the Act of Settlement led to his being imprisoned in the Tower of London for a period. The Earl of Orrery was equally to be seen in the corridors of Westminster, lobbying on behalf of various Irish Protestants. The final version of the act set out that 'adventurers' who had advanced money under the 1642 act, along with Cromwellian soldiers, were to be confirmed in their property. This gave them a distinct advantage over nominees and others, who had to wait until the Cromwellian settlers then in possession of their lands could be compensated elsewhere. Those Catholics found innocent of involvement in the rising of the 1640s who had nonetheless been transplanted to Connacht were to be restored, but were required to surrender their Connacht estates to the crown. Provision was also made for those known as '49 officers, Protestants who had served in the king's forces in Ireland before June 1649. A land bank of over 173,000 acres was to be created for them, comprising property in towns and in the north and west of Ireland. Perhaps inevitably with a measure of this complexity, modifications were required. In particular, it became apparent that the original conception had been based on a set of false statistics about the amount of land that would have to change hands. These figures had been provided by the Earl of Orrery in an endeavour to have his plan accepted in the early 1660s. New arrangements had to be put in place to deal with this situation as well as explaining problems and contradictions in the original act. Moreover, a good deal of lobbying at court meant that there were a number of private interests to be satisfied. These changes were given effect in the third document of the settlement, the lengthy Act of Explanation of 1665.

Nearly half the members of the Convention found themselves elected to the parliament of 1661–6. Three-quarters of the House of Commons were Protestants who had been in Ireland before 1649, and hence their interests were paramount. Although the House of Lords contained twenty-seven Catholics, they were outnumbered by Old Protestants, including bishops, who acted as staunch defenders of tradition. However, such division between Old and New Protestants did not prevent a fusion of interests between the two groups when that proved necessary to prevent too many concessions being made to Catholics. The only significant breach in this apparently solid wall of the Protestant interest was the provision in the Act of Settlement, and later in the Act of Explanation, for a court of claims to hear pleas of innocence from those who believed that they had been unfairly deprived of their lands by the Cromwellian regime. Both sides felt it would work to their advantage. Seven English commissioners were to sit, and decrees of innocence entitled the successful claimant to immediate possession of his lands without the Cromwellian owner being compensated. However, the Cromwellian owner was to be given land elsewhere. The court began to hear claimants in January 1663, and it quickly became clear that the Protestant fears that had emerged during the previous year were well founded. Through January and February alarm grew. The Irish parliament signalled its concern by throwing out the explanatory bill for the land settlement which it was then debating. Ormond gradually brought the Commons to heel, finally proroguing the parliament in April 1663. Nonetheless, tensions ran high, and after a Protestant plot led by Thomas Blood was revealed in May 1663 the court of claims had to be disbanded in August 1663. It had issued 566 decrees of innocence to Catholics, comprehending some 850,000 acres, but leaving many claims unheard. Sir William Petty claimed there were at least 8,000 Connacht transplanters' claims awaiting processing. In theory, those who lost property were all Cromwellian purchasers of land; but the nature of the land market was such that many Old Protestants had purchased Cromwellian grants, and so a number of them, such as Viscount Massereene, Sir Maurice Eustace and Ormond's secretary Sir George Lane, also lost land.

The failure of the first court of claims to make significant progress with the Restoration land settlement gave impetus to the drafting of a new act—the Act of Explanation—which was pursued fitfully from 1662 to explain the problems with the earlier act. The first attempt was rejected by the Irish Commons in 1663. Ormond himself had reservations about the workings of the Act of Settlement. Given his sense of the importance of the Old English elite in the government of the country, he felt that such deserving claimants were not being provided for, since the qualifications for innocence were so exacting. As one man expressed it to Ormond, the aim of the new act should be 'to preserve some of the ancientist families and best estates'.[15] Ormond himself had constantly worked behind the scenes to ensure that such Catholics would be restored to their estates. Since it had become clear that there was not going to be enough land to satisfy all the categories set out in the 1662 act, soldiers and 'adventurers' were to give up a third of their holdings, and the land thus freed would provide a land bank to compensate Protestants who had made way for innocent Catholics. A number of prominent Cromwellians were exempted in an effort to ensure that the bill was passed in parliament. A year's rent was also levied on all land in Catholic hands in 1641, and the proceeds were to be divided between the king, Ormond (£50,000 each) and the English Secretary of State, the Earl of Arlington (£10,000). Despite these concessions, the act passed by a majority of only nineteen votes, which suggests considerable Protestant opposition to such concessions. Again, the main means by which the Act of Explanation was to work was through a second court of claims under five commissioners, all of whom had experience in the first court of claims.

This second court met on 4 January 1666 and continued until 2 January 1669, including a number of recesses. Overall it managed to effect a settlement of sorts, although the ways by which it did so are obscure. Legal claims over individual pieces of property rumbled on for years. For some the outcome was a triumph, particularly so for the Old Protestant interest. For them, the Act of Settlement was 'Magna Charta Hibernia' or, as another put it, 'the knot and ligature of all'.[16] The act seemed to constitute a timeless, invisible trust that, as James II was to find to his cost, could not be compromised on or reformed. For others it was rather different. The '49 security set up to compensate the Protestant royalist officers in Ireland in the 1640s claimed in the 1670s that they had received less than half of their arrears. From another perspective, the Irish Lord Lieutenant from 1672 to 1677, the Earl of Essex, wrote of the land settlement: 'The truth is the lands of Ireland have been a mere scramble and the least done by way of orderly distribution of them as perhaps hath ever been known.' It was not surprising that he drew from that experience the understanding that 'Ireland is a plantation (for in reality it is little other).'[17] This point of view was to have profound implications for the history of Ireland in the latter half of the seventeenth century, since it located Ireland within a particular colonial political framework.

The land settlement had another outcome, not normally commented on. The scale of the changes in ownership in the longer term had the effect of generating a sizeable corpus of letters patent, all of which were made to a standard form. When early seventeenth-century monarchs had made land grants, particularly in Connacht, they had included in those grants residues of older claims on the land, such as 'chieferies'. This meant that land law came to incorporate a range of local customs that were sometimes difficult to understand. While Wentworth had begun the process of standardising Irish land law in the 1634–5 parliament, it was the Restoration settlement that completed it. The Restoration land grants simplified the understanding of land law by eliminating these local customs from the grants. The abolition of wardships and liveries in the 1660s aided that process. The result was that the beginnings of a standardised national structure for landownership can be discerned in the Restoration settlement in a way that was not possible before. The process created a legal coherence within the kingdom of Ireland. By the end of the century other indications of that move towards standardisation, such as the adoption of uniform weights and measures to replace local ones, can be discerned also.

Broadly speaking, the outcome of the land settlement was a significant reduction in the amount of land held by the Catholic gentry in Ireland. The proportion of profitable land held by Catholics probably fell from about two-thirds in 1641 to about 30 per cent in 1675. Protestant landowning increased proportionately. However, these bare figures mask the variety of experiences. The ability of individuals to manipulate the system for their own ends ensured that even within the Catholic community there was a diversity of experience. The experiences of three of the prominent Confederates from the 1640s demonstrate the point. Lord Mountgarrett lost out in the settlement, the Books of Survey and Distribution recording that his landholding fell from 20,356 acres in 1641 to 14,907 in the middle of the 1660s. Viscount Muskerry, by contrast, doubled his landholding over the same period from 82,037 acres to 161,629. The landholding of Richard Bellings, secretary to the Supreme Council, remained the same, and the Earl of Antrim also emerged unscathed, largely owing to his influence with the king.

There are a number of reasons for the rise of those Catholics who became known as the 'New Interest' men. Some had achieved their success through sheer persistence and force. The Catholic Viscount Mayo, for instance, in the 1640s had been one of those who had assumed that it was permissible 'to enter into possession of men's estates . . . upon no other pretence that they were known to have belonged in former times to their family'. By this means Mayo's new estate of almost 500,000 acres in the 1660s absorbed 340 older freeholds, adding over 17,000 acres.[18] Mayo was not the only landowner in Connacht to benefit from extinguishing smaller proprietors. In addition, local arrangements made between Protestants and Catholics to prevent protracted disputes in the 1660s, together with the bribery of sheriffs, allowed Catholics to continue to hold some of their land in the face of the legislation.

However, more important in holding on to land in the 1660s were political contacts at court at Whitehall by which an individual could override the Dublin administration's decisions through the mechanisms established by the Acts of Settlement and Explanation. The restoration of the Catholic Earl of Antrim, for example, was done by royal letter directly from the king. At a slightly lower level, the Talbots of Malahide quietly consolidated their position in north County Dublin through their knowledge of the finer points of law and the work of agents in the court at Whitehall, Richard Talbot and Sir Nicholas Plunkett. Richard Talbot was a particularly important figure in representing Old English gentry in this way, navigating them through the complexities of the first court of claims and brokering local deals between contesting landlords—and in the process amassing himself a personal fortune. Even if one did not move directly in this world, a patron might smooth matters along. Theobald Taaffe, Earl of Carlingford, was a major Catholic beneficiary from the land settlement, and so was one of his clients, John Bellew of Barmeath, who managed not only to have his County Louth property restored to him but also to hold on the Galway property to which he was meant to be transplanted in the 1650s; hence he ended up with two estates. The Galway property ultimately went to one of his sons, who established the Mountbellew branch of the family.

These kinds of compromise, intended ultimately to avoid alienating too many people from a king whose position was far from secure, inevitably produced tensions. At least some of these tensions were not easily resolved, and some Protestant radicals viewed with growing dismay the growth of the 'New Interest' Catholic lobby. Perhaps predictably, these frustrations manifested themselves in conspiracy, and the Presbyterian plots of the early 1660s were prompted in part by this fraught situation. The first of these was a plot conveniently discovered by Ormond while the parliamentary row about the first court of claims was in full flight in April 1663. One Captain William Hulet, a Cromwellian 'fanatic', was said to be plotting to take Dublin Castle. There may have been little to this, but there seems to have been more substance to a plot in May 1663. Led by Colonel Thomas Blood along with at least eight members of the recently prorogued parliament, together with a number of Presbyterian ministers and army officers, the conspirators planned to seize Dublin Castle and several other strategic points around the country. Their declared aim was to undo the Restoration settlement in both church and state and to return landownership to where it had been in 1659. On the eve of the attempt to take Dublin Castle they realised that the plot had been discovered, but their attempt to disperse was foiled; twenty-four conspirators were arrested, though at least ten others escaped. Three of the former members of the Dublin parliament were hanged on 15 July. One other, the Presbyterian minister William Leckey, feigned madness, but he too was finally executed. While this was not a Presbyterian plot as such, it clearly indicated that there existed considerable potential for Presbyterian support for any conspiracy based on discontent with the land settlement. Not surprisingly, in June Ormond moved against the Ulster Presbyterian ministers with mass arrests. This was not a policy that could continue. The sheer numbers of Presbyterians in Ulster made it impracticable, and Ormond had to be content with urging caution lest too severe action might provoke rebellion in Ulster. The Presbyterian problem was to be contained rather than decisively tackled.

The evolution of the land settlement resulted in an Ireland that was more diverse than previously. Whereas early seventeenth-century society had been composed of native and newcomer, the country after 1660 was populated by various sorts of newcomers who distinguished themselves from one another. Those Protestants who had been in Ireland before 1649 increasingly termed themselves 'Old Protestants', typically Church of Ireland, to differentiate them from the 'New Protestants', often religiously radical, who had arrived as part of the Cromwellian settlement. Each had minimal dealings with the other, except when a common interest forced them to co-operate. The apparent cohesion of the Convention in 1660 had rapidly disintegrated in the quest for the spoils of the land settlement.

This increasingly heterogeneous world posed questions for a religious and political establishment that was becoming exclusive to the point that the parliament of 1661–6 was the first in which only one Catholic was returned, even though there was no legal bar or oath to preclude their election. Indeed, Geoffrey Brown, the Catholic elected for Tuam, never took his seat. Several Catholic peers did take their seats in the Lords, but they were a small minority by this stage, since a number of Catholic peers had been affected by outlawry proceedings during the war of the 1640s. How could the social and political obligations of Catholic and dissenting landowners under the new settlement be legitimately expressed? The solution which the Catholic camp provided to this problem was an old one: an oath that would reconcile religious and political loyalties. This problem was certainly discussed by the Old English cleric John Lynch in his *Cambrensis eversus* published in 1662. In this analysis of kingship the historian John Lynch, unlike his predecessor Geoffrey Keating, specifically rejected the legitimacy of Henry II and the Anglo-Norman invasion of Ireland, insisting that forged papal documents had been used to deprive the Irish of their sovereignty. The Stuarts, he argued, were different. With their Milesian ancestry, the Stuart kings could be presented as legitimate successors of early Irish kings, while the issue of papal authority was kept separate from the matter of the kingship of Ireland. This allowed Lynch to argue that the Catholicism of the Old English should not be seen as evidence of disloyalty to the monarch in secular affairs. This idea underlay the Irish Loyal Remonstrance of 1661.

The primary mover in the making of the Loyal Remonstrance was Richard Bellings, the former secretary to the Confederation of Kilkenny. In December 1661 it seems that a number of Ormond supporters met to draft an oath of loyalty to the king in return for some concessions, possibly with an eye to the evolving land settlement. What may have forced their hand was that in November 1661 the Irish House of Commons asked for a bill for the suppression of the Catholic hierarchy on foot of rumours of a Catholic rising, but this was blocked by the government. However, there were also moves among English Catholics for a similar oath of loyalty to the king. The underlying assumptions of the oath were not unlike those of John Lynch's understanding of monarchy. It repudiated any power that interfered with royal authority, especially the papal deposing power, and held to a duty of obedience of subjects to legitimate monarchs. Moreover, monarchs could not be executed. Thus it emphasised the attachment of Catholics to their king, but asserted that this did not detract from their loyalty to their Catholic faith. If the oath placed strict limits on royal power, restricting it to temporal matters, it also limited papal power. In the light of the experience of Rinuccini in the 1640s, and the recriminations that followed among the Irish in exile in Europe in the 1650s, it had become clear to the Old English gentry that unchecked papal power was as dangerous as unbridled royal authority. The oath of loyalty was a delicate construction intended to balance opposing interests and advance Old English authority.

Drafted by Bellings, the oath drew on a number of sources for its inspiration, including the 1606 oath of allegiance proposed by the Westminster parliament. Indeed, some of the ideas may well have been inspired by the Treaty of Westphalia that had encapsulated the religious settlement reached in Europe at the end of the Thirty Years' War in 1648 and which Bellings and others certainly knew about. A first draft, signed by a number of the Irish clergy, was sent by Bellings to Ormond, and thence to the king, in February 1661. A second version, with a slightly altered preamble, signed by ninety-eight peers and gentry almost all of whom were of Old English background, was then submitted to the king, who signified his approval. New names continued to be added into 1662. As the land settlement took shape some Catholics clearly saw the Remonstrance as an important element in the strategy of managing the court of claims. Local versions emerged. In 1663 a Wexford variant of the document was signed by 200 gentry and merchants. The Remonstrance was exactly the sort of innovation that Ormond approved, since it would allow loyal and disloyal Catholics to be identified. The oath was championed by the Franciscan Peter Walsh, who had supported Ormond through the 1640s.

Most of those who signed the Remonstrance initially were Catholic laity with a few clergy, but attempts to broaden its support among the clergy were doomed to failure, as much due to Walsh's abrasive personality and his background as an Ormondist in the 1640s as anything else. Rome condemned the document because of its limitations on papal power, and most Irish clergy refused to sign it. Walsh persuaded Ormond to allow a national synod to be called for 1666 at which the Remonstrance could be discussed. Minds may have been focused when the normally low level of violence characteristic of banditry, or torying, erupted into a local rising, quickly suppressed, in Longford in 1666 led by the religious visionary Edmond Nangle. Even this could not overcome the opposition to the Remonstrance as a way of demonstrating loyalty, and the document was rejected. An alternative was proposed by the meeting, which agreed with the substance of Walsh's arguments but expressed them in more guarded language. The revised text was based on developments in France as set out in the first three of the Sorbonne propositions of 1663. It held that subjects could not be absolved from allegiance to their prince, rejected any attempts to kill kings, and asserted that the pope had no power over monarchs in temporal matters. This French influence was not surprising, since Walsh had powerful friends in France, including Cornelius Jansen, whose theology had influenced Bellings and other Confederates in the 1640s. Many of those involved in the drafting of the oath had also spent time in France in the 1650s. However, the parallels with France were problematical. French clergy could rely on royal support to resist Roman pressures, but Irish clergy had no such royal protector. They relied on Rome for patronage. Only Ormond's financial assistance of Peter Walsh in the 1660s allowed him to make his case so stridently. Patronage was at least as important as principle in this debate.

It seems clear that Primate O'Reilly and the Irish church wanted some sort of compromise with the state. Yet Walsh rejected this, demanding the Remonstrance or nothing. He advised Ormond not to accept the compromise. Nor did Rome look favourably on it; an envoy, the Franciscan James Taaffe, was sent to deal with the matters, but Taaffe's behaviour was such that he had to be recalled. This episode emphasised to Rome the necessity of restructuring the Catholic Church in Ireland after the depredations of the 1650s in order to maintain control. As a result, in 1669 a number of episcopal appointments were made for Ireland, and by 1671 every diocese had a bishop or a vicar general.

## THE FALL OF ORMOND AND THE SHAPE OF THE POLITICAL NATION

In 1669 the Duke of Ormond was recalled from the Irish viceroyalty. The reasons behind this are complex, but they seem to lie in the politics of the court. The state of the Irish finances was becoming increasingly perilous. While the army had been reduced in size, by 15,000 to less than 6,000, it was still consuming a substantial proportion of Irish income. External factors depressed Irish trade and hence reduced government revenue, with a resulting deficit in the Irish exchequer in 1665–7. The Earl of Orrery demanded reform and began to campaign for it at court. Ormond, no administrator and having failed to understand the complexities of the Irish finances, crossed to England to defend himself, but in the process annoyed the king. Charles II made a clean sweep of his Irish financial officials. The Earl of Anglesey, formerly the Irish Vice-Treasurer, was dismissed from the Privy Council, and Ormond himself was removed. There may have been a wider agenda at work here. Charles, emboldened by ten years on the throne, was attempting to broaden his scope for action, and this explains his dismissal of his most loyal adviser, the Earl of Clarendon. The secret Treaty of Dover with Louis XIV in 1670, by which Charles in return for subsidies from Louis, agreed to declare himself a Catholic at a suitable moment and to declare war on Holland, points to this shift in policy. The 1672 Declaration of Indulgence, removing penal measures against Catholics and dissenters, was in a similar vein. With such measures Ormond would have been profoundly unhappy, although in practice this is what developed in Ireland during the early 1670s.

The effects of Ormond's recall were significant. The implementation of the land settlement, which was already grinding to a halt under the weight of its own administrative machine, ceased, the second court of claims having done as much as it could. In the following year Richard Talbot, in the absence of Ormond, attempted to reopen the subject. Acting as an agent for fifty Irish peers and gentlemen, he petitioned the king for changes. A committee was set up to inquire into the matter, but it became a victim of the political crisis of 1672–3 and Talbot fled to France. The subject would not be reopened until Ormond's second viceroyalty in the late 1670s when a 'Commission of Grace' to remedy defective titles was established in 1683, but this proved ineffective. Secondly, whatever possibility Peter Walsh's Remonstrance had of including Catholics in political life (and it was small) died with Ormond's recall. Indeed, the 1670s were marked by a narrowing of the political boundaries. The 'New Rules' for the regulation of towns in 1672 required that the Oath of Supremacy be taken by all elected municipal officers and, in effect, gave a government veto over all nominations to senior urban posts. Rather than bringing Catholics into the political nation, it looked as though events might move in another direction.

Ormond's successors, Lord Robartes (1669–70), Lord Berkeley (1670–72) and the Earl of Essex (1672–7), proved sympathetic to Presbyterianism. In 1672, for instance, the Ulster Presbyterians received the *regium donum*, a grant of money paid to their ministers, which served as a sign of legitimacy though not toleration. However, further moves towards shifting the political boundaries were stymied by the fears of the increasing power of Presbyterianism which was becoming more organised in Ulster. The government recognised that there were two types of Presbyterians in Ulster: those who accepted the Restoration settlement, and the more radical, the Remonstrants, who did not. An indulgence was offered to the more moderate, but this had little success. Scottish-inspired Ulster Presbyterianism seemed to be expanding its influence outside the province in a desire to export the Presbyterian revolution. At least seven congregations founded outside the province of Ulster between 1660 and 1704 can be clearly identified as having accepted the authority of the Synod of

Ulster, the governing body of Ulster Presbyterians from 1690, usually at the expense of the authority of local presbyteries such as those of Dublin and Munster. Of the total number of congregations that accepted the authority of the Synod of Ulster by the end of the seventeenth century, rather over 11 per cent lay outside Ulster and some were in areas with a negligible Scottish population. These included Clonmel (1673) and Waterford (1680) in the south-east, Sligo (1676) in the north-west, and the Dublin church at Bull Alley (1667). All this inspired fear in the hearts of the bishops and the Dublin administration, who were afraid that the Covenanter influence from Scotland would result in trouble in Ireland. Moreover, as bishops and government also appreciated, the structures of Scottish-inspired Ulster Presbyterianism was becoming more effective. By the 1670s there was a 'general meeting' which had some measure of authority over the sub-presbyteries, or meetings, that had been created in the late 1650s, and within these units the church was now divided into parishes, most with their own minister. In short, this was not simply a rabble but a parallel ecclesiastical organisation for what its earliest historian, Patrick Adair, called 'the church of Ireland'. There was little possibility of a move towards greater comprehension, or even accommodation. The two organisational systems with their underlying social support reflected different patterns of belief and thought and hence acted as markers of local identity. The relations between the government and the organised Presbyterians was to produce a long and fractious story into the future.

**RESTORATION GOVERNANCE**

At best, the compromises that resulted from the process of trying to create a new structure for the government of Restoration Ireland might be described as fragile, but they were at least workable. They created a *modus vivendi* rather than a coherent social order. The governing elite became increasingly exclusivist as the Restoration church had already done. Protestant Ireland in all its varieties would become more and more fractured, with apparently little chance of rapprochement. Introversion fed fears of a Catholic or Presbyterian rebellion. Scares of risings in the 1660s and 1670s which had little foundation nevertheless contributed to already existing Protestant fears in which they saw themselves as a threatened minority. The tensions that introversion produced were most clearly seen in what was probably the most basic unit of political life, the parish. The effect of the enforcement of the canons of 1634 meant that the pool of suitably qualified candidates for parish office was reduced dramatically. Dissenters and Catholics were excluded from parish life since they were now required to take the Oaths of Supremacy and Uniformity before the diocesan bishop prior to taking up their positions. This happened at a time when the local administrative functions being assigned to the parish were growing. The burden fell heavily on those that remained. The expanding parish of St Catherine in Dublin had increasing difficultly in filling the offices of churchwarden and sidesman as more people refused to serve. In 1679 they raised the fine for those refusing to serve from £1 to £10. Despite this, they had considerable problems in finding people prepared to serve in the 1680s and had to devise ways of reducing the administrative burden on the few. Again, in the Dublin parish of St John's the sidesmen became less efficient in collecting taxes, and this resulted in the churchwardens being summoned to appear before the bishop's court. Such local experiences reveal in microcosm the problems that Restoration governance had to deal with, and its success in creating some semblance of social order in the late seventeenth century is all the more remarkable for that.

# Good King Charles's Golden Days, 1669–85

The events of the 1660s may have restored the king, and re-established the ecclesiastical hierarchy and built a social structure in Ireland, but they left uncertainty as to the limits and durability of the real power of these institutions. In the ensuing years the London administration, the Dublin government and the Irish ruling elite would try to ensure the permanence of the new order and re-establish the boundaries between the various groups. Yet the powers of each of these elements were not always complementary, and tensions were inevitable. The outworking of those tensions was often unclear. Since parliament did not meet between 1666 and the Jacobite assembly of 1689, much of the obvious political activity was conducted among a fairly small elite. However, what most contemporaries noticed about the world around them in the 1670s was not the subtle shifts in political life, but rather that prosperity finally seemed to have come to seventeenth-century Ireland. Commentators on Dublin, for instance, observed how much the city had changed in recent years. As Sir Paul Davis, the Secretary of State in Ireland, commented as early as 1664, 'It is a wonder how buildings increase in all parts of this city.'[1] In 1678 the antiquarian Robert Ware compared St Stephen's Green to Moorfields in London, the Prato in

Florence and the Prato delle Valle in Padua.[2] Another contemporary in 1686 placed Dublin in the top twelve European cities, and in 1687 Sir William Petty compared it favourably with Paris, London, Amsterdam, Venice and Rome. All this was underpinned by a rapid expansion in the city's population and trade. By 1680, according to contemporary estimates, 9 per cent of Irish people lived in Dublin, and by the 1690s the London bookseller John Dunton guessed that although Dublin was 'twelve times less than London, [it] is yet the biggest next to it in all our dominions'. Again, the proportion of national trade passing through the city was growing. In 1630 Dublin's customs revenue comprised almost a third of the national total, but this figure had grown to 47 per cent by 1662–3 and to almost 50 per cent by the beginning of the eighteenth century. Moreover, there was also an increasing concentration of national wealth in the city. Dublin accounted for 2.4 per cent of the royal subsidy of 1634, and this had grown to 4.4 per cent by 1662. As Sir William Petty pointed out in 1672, 85 per cent of the largest houses in Ireland, those with more than ten hearths, were in Dublin. That city rapidly moved from being the equivalent of a small English provincial town to being a major urban settlement. In 1600 it had a population of about 5,000, growing to 45,000 by 1685 and to 62,000 by 1706. A majority of the city's inhabitants were now Protestant thanks to the influx of settlers in the 1650s. Dublin was the fastest-growing city in the British Isles. Its importance was not confined to Ireland, for Dublin had become the most important town of the Irish Sea region, attracting settlers from north and west England, including a large number of Quakers, and fulfilling many of the functions that London did for eastern and southern England.

Evidence of prosperity was not to be found in Dublin alone. The population of Cork probably doubled between 1660 and 1685 and doubled again by 1706. In Ulster, both Belfast and Derry expanded, so that by the beginning of the eighteenth century some believed, mistakenly, that Belfast was the second largest port in Ireland. The rural world also was prospering. Admittedly, the 1660s had been difficult years. The Dutch wars, cattle disease in 1660 and 1665, and bad harvests in 1672–3 all took a serious toll. Customs revenue between 1660 and 1670 was stagnant or perhaps fell slightly. However, from 1674 matters began to improve and continued to get better until the middle of the 1680s, when an economic downturn would play a part in the worsening political crisis of the late 1680s. The growth in luxury imports, such as tobacco and fine cloth, suggests that at least some of the inhabitants of Ireland could afford a high lifestyle. Tobacco consumption, for instance, rose sharply and fairly continuously from the 1660s to the 1680s with a doubling of imports. By 1683 Irish tobacco imports were running at 2,850,193 pounds a year. By 1700 that had risen to 3,281,645 pounds a year. Wine imports rose also from 1,500 tuns in 1614–15 to 2,200 tuns between 1683 and 1686. These are, of course, official figures which make no allowance for smuggling. At the upper social levels, silver and paintings became more common in large households. The annual amount of plate assayed in Dublin between 1638 and 1644, at 1,300 ounces, was only 5 per cent of what it was to be in the 1700s. While most silversmiths had been confined to Dublin in the early seventeenth century, by the 1690s they could be found in many provincial towns. The houses this silver adorned were also changing from the tower-house type of dwelling to more modern structures, and older buildings were smartened up with new extensions in more modern styles.

This rise in the consumption of luxury goods may well indicate an increase in disposable income. The evidence is very thin, but at least in Dublin over the late seventeenth century both wages and purchasing power do seem to have increased significantly. This may well reflect, in part, the fall in agricultural prices over the late seventeenth century, which benefited urban dwellers. However, whether the wages of skilled craftsmen behaved in the same way as the incomes of the poorer sort is an impossible question to answer. For farmers, price falls were offset by growing output, thus maintaining agricultural incomes, but this was a perilous situation which meant than when a crisis did strike it was likely to be severe. Land values too were rising. In 1661 the purchase price of land was running at seven times its annual rental value, but by 1685 fifteen years' purchase was being asked for an estate. Underlying this rise in land values was an increase in rental income for landlords. Sir William Petty confidently estimated that the total rental of the country rose from £900,000 in 1672 to £1,200,000 in 1687. Not all areas were affected equally: the east benefited most, leaving the west to fall behind.

All this came about despite a number of factors that had the capacity to destabilise Irish economic expansion. One was a growth in population which threatened to reduce *per capita* growth. In 1641 the

Irish population probably stood at about 2 million. The effect of war and the plague of the early 1650s was still felt into the 1680s, when the estimates by Sir William Petty of 1.3 million might be adjusted upwards to about 1.9 million to take account of problems with Petty's data. Thereafter war probably kept population growth in check through the early 1690s. The evidence of the hearth tax suggests that this late seventeenth-century population increase exhibited strong regional variations, with the fastest growth being experienced in Ulster, while growth was more restricted in Munster. In part this reflects differential patterns of migration. Emigration from England in the late seventeenth century was discouraged, since contemporaries feared that this was a factor in the decrease in England's population. The result was that Munster relied on natural growth to boost its population. This may not have been as problematical as it appears. Studies of Irish Quakers between 1660 and 1699 have suggested that when compared with English Quakers, those in Ireland had lower marriage ages, and hence a longer child-bearing period. This may well be the result of easier access to land, making it easier to form new families. The result was that completed Irish Quaker families tended to be larger than English ones—5.4 in comparison to 4.0. In addition, Quaker infant mortality in Ireland seems to have been lower than in England, and Irish Quakers could generally expect to live up to two years longer than their English counterparts. In Ulster the faster population growth was fed by natural increase and bursts of migration from Scotland. At Lisburn, for instance, between 1660 and 1700 baptisms averaged 130 a year and burials 55, suggesting strong natural increase in the population. This was a not unmixed blessing. From the government's point of view, the continuation of Covenanter disturbances in Scotland meant that continuing migration between there and Ulster brought with it the prospect of malcontents moving to Ulster and creating trouble for the Presbyterian settlement there. Ulster's population growth in this period differed from that in the early seventeenth century in that it took place in an increasingly rigid tenurial matrix. In the first half of the century land was fairly freely available, with few existing leases, and a moving frontier of settlers ensured that Scots could be found as far south as Longford. After 1660 few new areas were opened up for settlement. In south Leinster woodland clearance as a result of ironworking opened up some regions, but in the main a well-established network of landownership existed. A growing population had to fit, not always successfully, into that grid.

A second potentially destabilising fact was the interference of government in economic expansion. This came in a number of forms. The demand for taxation by government grew dramatically in the late seventeenth century. The irregular subsidies passed when parliament met in the early seventeenth century were replaced by more regular taxation, most notably the hearth tax, that required payments to be made in cash by householders. This did not come at an opportune moment. The passage of the Cattle Acts of 1663 and 1667, which prohibited the import of live Irish cattle into England, had the potential to cause considerable problems for the Irish economy. This move was prompted by the falling prices for cattle and cereals in England, which caused discontent among cattle breeders, who felt that their trade was being undermined by the importation of Scottish and Irish livestock. The result was legislation pushed by a lobby group rather than by government. It failed completely to effect any improvement of the situation in England, however, as the recession became worse with the outbreak of the Anglo-Dutch war in 1665. As a desperate measure the English market for Irish sheep, cattle and pork was completely closed in 1667, against the wish of the Whitehall administration. The Cattle Acts are only one example of potentially destabilising legislation. The restrictions on imports contained in the Navigation Acts of 1660 and 1671 and the Staple Act of 1663 required that certain items from the colonies could not be landed directly in Ireland but had to be shipped to England and re-exported to Ireland. Thus one of the staples of the Whitehaven and Liverpool trades became the export of tobacco to Ireland. The main effect of this was to increase the cost of colonial imports into Ireland. One estimate of 1686 suggested that the restrictive terms added ½d to the price of every pound of tobacco sold in Ireland (about 8 per cent of its cost). The result was a considerable rise in smuggling, although this is impossible to quantify. While taxation and legislation were both potentially destabilising for the Irish economy, in the longer term their impact was much less than might be expected.

## ECONOMIC RESTRUCTURING

What lay behind this transformation in Dublin and the other large towns in Ireland was a sudden upsurge of economic activity in the

1670s and early 1680s, paralleling a trade boom in England. That growth was largely the result of a restructuring of the Irish economy, signs of which were already discernible before 1660. The principal shift was from the export of raw materials to processed goods, with a higher value added. Thus, while the Cattle Acts and economic trends worked against live cattle export, cattle producers turned instead to barrelled beef and dairying as a way of making profits. Late seventeenth-century international price movements favoured butter and wool over cattle and beef, and it is hardly surprising that Irish exports moved away from live cattle to processed goods. The Cattle Acts may have speeded up this process, but they did not initiate it. Barrelled beef exports in 1665 were almost twice what they had been in 1641, while live cattle exports had increased by only 26 per cent. Similarly, pork and bacon only became prominent in the Irish trade after 1665. It would be wrong to dismiss the potential of the live cattle trade altogether. During a temporary lapse in the Cattle Acts in 1679 and 1680, 8,000 and 24,000 live cattle were landed in England in the respective years. However, this was less than half the 1665 total, which suggests the shift in the structure of the economy was already well under way. While the mainstay of the Irish trade after 1665 was butter, the second most important commodity was wool. By 1685 wool and butter comprised 40 per cent of Irish exports by value. Here the underlying price trend was firm, particularly in the early 1670s, but high duties on imports into England may explain why the wool trade did not grow as rapidly as might be expected. One other reason may be that raw wool was now being worked up into cheap cloth, known as frieze, which was being exported to England. By 1695 it was claimed that some 50,000 people in Ireland were employed in the frieze trade with England.

The success of these new products was in large measure determined by the improved and expanded marketing structures that evolved in Ireland. In 1665 about 74 per cent of all Irish exports were destined for England. By 1683 that had fallen to 30 per cent, and by 1700 the English share of Irish trade had only recovered slightly to 42 per cent. One market that was exploited more intensively than before was continental Europe. In 1683, for example, France took over 20 per cent of Irish butter exports, mainly from Ulster and Munster. Belfast and Youghal between them accounted for 47 per cent of the Irish butter trade in 1683. A second highly significant market that absorbed an increasing proportion of the Irish export trade was the transatlantic trade to the West Indies and colonial North America. Between 1683 and 1685 almost 61 per cent of Irish barrelled beef and pork exports went to North America, as did more than a quarter of cheese exports. The West Indies sugar islands had their main source of beef and butter in Ireland. From the 1650s Galway was exporting significant quantities of provisions to the West Indies, and prominent Galway merchant families, such as the Kirwans, Blakes, Lynches, Frenches and Skerretts, became significant players in the Caribbean economy. In the 1660s the centre of the transatlantic trade moved to Cork, which by the 1680s was exporting almost half the Irish total of beef to the colonies. The 1680s saw further expansion of the trade as labour shortages in the American colonies drove the prices of colonially produced goods upwards, making Irish imports even more competitive. In such ways Ireland could finance the significant balance-of-payments deficit which she ran with England in the late seventeenth century.

These shifts in the nature of economic activity had important implications for marketing structures within Ireland. Specialisation within the economy meant that a much higher level of inter-regional trade than before had now become necessary. As long as live cattle dominated the market there was little need for specialisation, but with the rise of butter and provisions exports there was a need for a division between breeding and fattening areas for cattle, the latter requiring better land than the former. East Connacht and the midlands became established as fattening country, while lands of more marginal quality in Counties Roscommon, Limerick, Clare and Westmeath, together with parts of County Tipperary, were given over to sheep. Such shifts underlie the growth in livestock fairs over the late seventeenth century, with 503 fairs operating in the country by 1685. The rise of the textile trade, and the weaving of linen and woollen cloth, required local trade centres. As a result of this need for local trade to move goods within specialised regions or to ports, inland market towns became more important than they had been before. Irish trade became concentrated in a small number of large ports fed by smaller market towns. A case in point is the comparative fortunes of Drogheda and Ardee. Between 1665 and the 1680s the farm of the Drogheda customs stagnated, while those of the inland town of Ardee rose by over 300 per cent. Small towns linked to large ports flourished.

Naas, with its links to Dublin, boomed, with a threefold rise in freemen, despite having no manufactures or other visible means of support. Mullingar, Kildare and Lisburn similarly grew because of their links to Dublin and Belfast. Such physical urban expansion spoke eloquently of the economic growth that sustained it.

These infrastructural changes did not happen by accident. They were, in the main, the result of co-operation between landlords and merchants. Landlords appreciated that fairs and markets would not work without merchants. Hence Sir John Perceval commented of Kanturk, County Cork, in 1681: 'The place is capable of a woollen manufacture. But be pleased to mind the fairs first.'[3] It was the responsibility of the landlord to provide the infrastructure, such as a grant of market rights. In Munster Roger Boyle, Earl of Orrery, not only tried to attract Dutch merchants on to his estates, but also used the Munster presidency to promote economic change. He developed Charleville, County Cork, in the 1660s as a model that he hoped others would follow, and he also formed an association with a Dublin merchant, Thomas Parsons, in an attempt to create a joint-stock company, the Merchant Adventurers of Munster, in 1670. In the same way the Belfast merchant community developed in the years after 1660, trading with towns in the Lagan valley where landlords encouraged their activities. As a result, the tonnage of shipping owned by the Belfast merchants tripled from the 1660s to the 1680s. From such projects did economic growth spring.

## SOCIAL IMPLICATIONS OF GROWTH

Economic growth on this scale inevitably created difficulties within late seventeenth-century Irish society. Most fundamental was the tension between the accumulation of wealth in the hands of a few powerful merchants and the sort of consensus that the governing idea of a commonwealth of interdependent people which existed in this world created. As Thomas Phillips, surveying the state of Irish fortifications in the 1680s, argued in 1685, Irish society had been corrupted by the scramble for money, 'for there is not the true affection that subjects ought to bear to one another, besides the business of most people here is nothing but the getting of money without the least regard to their prince's service'.[4] In the early part of the seventeenth century the very rich justified their wealth on the grounds that their prosperity was good for the commonwealth as a whole. Richard Boyle, first Earl of Cork, could, without any contradiction, refer to the highly profitable business of clearing woodland and exploiting natural resources as 'commonwealth work'. Settlers who introduced new crops, established ironworks and other profitable enterprises saw themselves as contributing to long-term social development and to the religious reformation of Ireland. Profit, in this world, was a religious imperative that improved the entire commonwealth, and the experiment of the Ulster plantation was one mark of that. This idea was still alive in the late seventeenth century. Those settlers enthused by Cromwellian experiments in science became even more concerned to master and improve their landscape as a way of enhancing the moral state of its inhabitants. On the south-western edge of Ireland one landlord, Sir William Petty, established fisheries, ironworks and a timber industry. Others, operating on a much more modest scale, planted gardens to improve their diets and surroundings. In County Antrim one clergyman, Andrew Rowan, planted fruit trees and other exotica in his garden and surrounded himself with the latest fashion in cloth, glass, books, lace and tobacco. Such material improvements were taken as a sign of civility as well as of wealth. To spend was deemed a social duty, since it provided not only a mark of social status but also generated employment. However, as the complaints of the 1620s demonstrated, too radical a redistribution of wealth brought problems, since the market proved an effective social solvent. This is what at least some of those who witnessed developments in Ireland in the 1670s and 1680s feared.

In the late seventeenth century a literature of protest grew up against the sort of society that excessive personal profit might generate, encouraged by the idea of virtue beloved of old Cromwellians. Robert Ware in his unpublished 1678 history of the city of Dublin, for instance, complained of the collapse of older civic values such as hospitality, and lamented that in its stead had emerged the desire for 'vain fashions' in clothing and furniture. He complained of the 'needless expense' incurred by men's wives 'and in some particular their mis[tres]ses'.[5] To combat this trend of wasteful expenditure, there were calls for sumptuary legislation in the planned parliament of 1677. A tract of that year condemned the extravagance of the Irish in dress, coaches and French wines which depleted the resources of their estates.

A link between corruption and luxury is clear in Richard Head's pornographic novel *The miss display'd* (1675). Set in Dublin, the novel clearly links the world of the brothel with that of fine clothes, high spending, balls, coaches, rich hangings and rich furnishings. The same luxury was condemned in other language too. The Baptist Richard Lawrence in his *The interest of Ireland in its trade and wealth stated* (1682) condemned luxury and immorality equally. Prostitution cost Ireland £37,000 a year according to Lawrence, more costly than swearing, estimated at £20,000 a year, but not as expensive as gaming at £52,000 a year. Drunkenness, widely condemned, cost Ireland a massive £174,000. However, the most virulent public attack on the world of Restoration Ireland came in the plays of Richard Head, who was born in Carrickfergus but by the mid-1660s was living in London, with occasional visits to Dublin. Head objected to what he saw as the dissolution of a social order underpinned by traditional values and its replacement with a mercantile society comprising illusions generated by money. In his *The English rogue* (1665) Dublin was portrayed as a fractured world with strong amoral tendencies. It was a place of thieves, bigamists and murderers. For Head, in his play about Dublin *Hic et ubique* (1663), this was the result of the rapid expansion and commercialisation of the city, which created a society made up of immigrants with no social ties or restraints other than the need to make money. Their names suggest their backgrounds. Contriver, Bankrupt, Hopewell and Trust all fled from debt or justice in England and set themselves up in dubious occupations in Dublin. One is an astrologer, another a surgeon specialising in venereal diseases (despite a lack of training), and another dabbles in occult arts. None has any interest in religion or virtue. Again, in his *The miss display'd* the world of the brothel is portrayed in the language of commerce. Such men railed against the expanding commercial world with its atomistic society and perceived lack of social order. This may be a long way from the reality of late seventeenth-century Dublin, but it accurately reflects the fears of those that lived there as to how their society was developing.

In the notebook kept by John Yarner, the Church of Ireland minister of St Bride's in Dublin during the 1670s, he charted what he saw as a growing breakdown of moral order which was manifesting itself in the form of breaches in public order with consequent social breakdown, increased violence and disrespect for one's betters. Furthermore, moral lapses threatened punishment from God on the city, a message that godly preachers had been hammering out since the 1570s. In this world Yarner's fears reflect the sort of protests about social change that were reflected in literary sources. The rise of luxury seemed to bring decay from within. What was needed, it seemed to men such as Richard Lawrence and Richard Head, was a return to a simpler, more moral and virtuous life which would underpin the workings of the Irish polity.

The most obvious way of introducing some control over the potential dangers that commentators suggested economic growth might generate was through the corporate action of parliament. However, parliament failed to meet for most of this period, though when it did so it proved enthusiastic in its campaign for moral and social reform. In 1661 the Irish parliament had condemned the moral state of Dublin, and in particular it abhorred swearing and profanation of the Sabbath. In 1662 legislation dealing with these matters was drawn up, but it failed to become law. Two proclamations to the same effect were issued in 1661 underlining official concern about what was regarded as degeneration. It was to be the 1690s before parliament returned to the matter with a series of acts dealing with blasphemy and other moral matters. This did not prevent outbreaks of moral panic from time to time. These are most clearly seen in the activities of the Societies for the Reformation of Manners in the 1690s when vigilantes patrolled the streets of Dublin in 1698 grabbing prostitutes from both the brothels and the streets. A similar event seems to be depicted in Head's *The miss display'd*, which includes a description of the breakup of a brothel.

One way of understanding how these perceived social problems were tackled is to consider the specific problem of the poor. From the 1660s the poor came more into focus in the minds of those who lived in Ireland. Unlike England or Scotland, Ireland lacked any legal form of poor relief, and in the absence of parliament there was little prospect of resolving this difficulty. Even in 1695 when parliament agreed the heads of a bill to allow parishes to assess their residents for poor relief, this proved abortive, as did similar schemes raised in parliament in 1697 and 1698. Much therefore had to be done informally at a local level. Two agencies were primarily involved in this: the Church of Ireland parish and landlords.

The Church of Ireland parish in the late seventeenth century had a number of meanings to those who lived in it. It was a defined space which conferred rights on all its inhabitants, regardless of their background. All residents of the parish had a right to be buried in the parish graveyard; in Dublin parishes the burial fees charged were usually higher for strangers than for parish inhabitants. It was also a confessional space where members of the Church of Ireland worshipped on Sunday and days of state celebration such as 23 October, 29 May or 5 November. Finally, it was an administrative entity in which local society could be regulated and where some individuals learned the skills of management of affairs. In Dublin at least, administrative functions for the parish had grown in the course of the seventeenth century. Parliament required the parish to look after roads which ran through it, and Dublin Corporation assigned the role of road-cleaning to the parishes. Further fire-fighting duties were also assigned to Dublin parishes in 1620, and by the 1630s buckets and ladders were normal parochial property. Perhaps more significantly, in 1631 the Dublin parishes became responsible for their own poor. By 1636 St Audoen's parish was maintaining twelve poor, and in 1644 St John's marked out its own poor by issuing badges (or 'badging'). Providing for the poor meant not only raising a poor cess but also appointing a beadle to administer poor relief. It also meant contributing at parish level to the House of Correction maintained by Dublin Corporation from the 1630s.

The localising of poor relief in the parish increased during the late seventeenth century. By 1670 the practice of badging the parish poor, claiming them for the parish and hence linking them into a particular community and a hierarchy, had spread to Ulster, and by the beginning of the eighteenth century at least six parishes in Ulster were badging their own poor. By 1682 the Lord Mayor of Dublin required all the city's churchwardens to badge beggars. The unbadged were to be sent to a House of Correction. Such a structure had largely been the result of local initiative addressing a problem which government had failed to deal with. Although there had been a good deal of discussion in the early seventeenth century of the desirability of putting the poor to work, little had been done towards shaping the necessary institutions. In the 1650s the Baptist army officer Henry Barrow produced a short discourse on raising money to deal with the problem as part of a wider Cromwellian agenda of reformation of manners in Ireland driven by the need for moral reform. Few rushed in to deal with the poor in the later seventeenth century, the only significant innovation in Dublin being the foundation of King's Hospital school in 1671. Slowly in the later seventeenth century the parish's obligations to the local community and the expectations of central authority came to be outlined more clearly. In 1665 a clause was inserted in a more general statute enabling the Church of Ireland vestry of St Andrew's parish in Dublin to assess its inhabitants for, among other things, 'the relief of the poor'. In this case what had once been a charitable act was now set out as a legitimate expectation of government, although the legislation was merely enabling and restricted to a single parish. Nevertheless, the evidence of the Dublin parishes in the late seventeenth century does suggest that most of them established poor cesses. The amount spent on the poor fluctuated widely, ranging from a third to three-quarters of parochial expenditure.

The basis on which relief was offered is usually very unclear. Most parishes were interested in helping their own poor through badging schemes or maintaining poor lists. Those from outside the parish tended not to be supported, or, if they were, it was usually only on an occasional basis, with the requirement that they would move on. This control of poor relief placed considerable power in the hands of parochial officials, though precisely how they exercised it is not clear. Surviving poor lists do not state the confessional position of the recipient, and hence it is difficult to know if poor relief crossed religious divides or if it was used to achieve conversions. Again, the majority of those who appear in late seventeenth-century poor lists are women, suggesting that there was a marked reluctance to support men who might be regarded as able-bodied and who could work. The operation of poor relief by the parish was untidy and *ad hoc*, informed by discrimination, the need for discipline and often generosity. That it operated at all is a testimony to the importance of local initiative in at least some parts of late seventeenth-century Ireland. It also reflects the understanding by local communities, rather than government, that some level of social regulation was necessary, reinforcing moral boundaries within communities and differentiating the deserving and undeserving poor who were part of the parish community and those who were not. That initiative was, of course, limited by local funds and personnel, but it demonstrates the importance of local communities in the management of seventeenth-century Irish society.

Landlords and great estates dealt with poverty in a different way to that of the vestry. For such men, the problem of poverty was intimately tied to the ability to pay rent. As John Aubrey observed in his late seventeenth-century biography of the Irish polymath Sir William Petty, when the Irish Privy Council considered banning the import of coal from England so that Dublin would use turf from its hinterland, their motives were that 'they would improve their rents, set poor men on work and the city would be served with fuel cheaper'.[6] Profit and poor relief were two sides of a single coin. Most landlords therefore chose to promote poor relief by encouraging projects which drew the poor into the commercial economy to make profit. This they did by promoting projects or specific trades and occupations on their lands which would generate cash. Thus the expansion of fishing on Sir William Petty's Kerry estates was encouraged 'forasmuch as it will be an employment to the people who otherwise would be troubled to pay the rent'.[7] In Cork later in the century Sir Richard Cox offered similar reasons for implementing economic changes. The Duke of Ormond also promoted woollen weaving in his town of Clonmel because, as one correspondent pointed out to him, it would be 'an employment for many great idle poor people for they must spin most of the yarn and by degrees be taught the whole mystery'.[8] Similar ideas may well have lain behind the establishment of a linen works by Ormond at Chapelizod under the management of Richard Lawrence. From this perspective, the poor were seen as an unrealised resource rather than a liability.

One clear example of this was the promotion of linen-weaving on estates. Landlords encouraged weaving in diverse ways. On the Abercorn estate in County Tyrone in the 1690s the Earl of Abercorn promoted spinning and weaving competitions to boost the linen trade at Strabane. Perhaps more typical was the case of Arthur Brownlow at Lurgan in County Armagh. This was an area that was expanding rapidly in the later seventeenth century, mainly as a result of immigration, although by the end of the century there were twice as many baptisms in the parish church as burials, pointing to significant natural population growth. The result was pressure on land, indicated by an increase of almost 70 per cent in rents per acre over the century, and even larger increases in entry fines for land. With rising rents holdings became smaller, older holdings being divided into two or three. Agricultural activities, particularly the production of butter, provided the main support for this population, but this was clearly insufficient. Linen production was an important way of making subsistence possible on smaller holdings. At one level, linen could be used as a way of paying rent, as on the Castledillon estate in County Armagh, where, it was claimed, 'the inhabitants are all very poor. They are so far from selling corn that they can hardly get bread. They pay their rent in linen cloth having no other way.' Brownlow's contribution was to promote the development of the linen trade by creating marketing structures. As it was later claimed, 'on first establishing the linen trade here [he] bought up everything that was brought to the market of cloth and lost at first considerably but at length the thing fixing itself, he is now by the same methods a considerable gainer'. What he did with the linen cloth is not known. Some of the coarser linen may have been resold locally, hence the loss, but the finer linens probably entered the wider market through Dublin. This reflects the importance of mercantile contacts, and Brownlow may well have used the Quakers settled on his estates, especially John Hoope, a Quaker merchant and later linen draper who lived in Lurgan. Brownlow's experiment of introducing linen to supplement household income quickly caught on. By the 1690s linen-bleaching was carried on in Lurgan, and as early as the 1670s in Lisburn a very considerable linen manufacture had been established, probably containing a tenth of the looms in Ulster.[9] In such ways did landlords, often acting with merchants, promote economic growth and tackle the problem of poverty on their estates by introducing manufactures.

## POLITICAL IMPLICATIONS OF GROWTH

The problems produced by economic growth were not limited to the social sphere. In the years after 1667 a financially impecunious king sought ways of releasing himself from the controls his parliament had imposed on him. The secret Treaty of Dover of 1670, in which Charles reached a deal with Louis XIV whereby he promised to join France in war against the Dutch and to announce his own conversion to Catholicism in return for French subsidies, was one manifestation of this. As the possibility of income from an economically recovering Ireland became clear, the king and his ministers turned their attention there. After 1660 the Irish revenue, now more regular than in the early seventeenth century as a result of the hearth tax, had been farmed in return for a fixed annual payment. When the farm came up for resetting in late 1667, the Lords of the Treasury in London became interested in the profit that might come to them. When the farm was set again in 1671 to Lord Ranelagh, it was part of the undertaking that he produce a profit by 1675, a goal he achieved through ruthless administrative efficiencies in the collection system. Profit, of course, meant that the question of where that money would be spent was quickly raised. One indication of where future priorities lay was the instruction that all issues of money from the Irish exchequer were to be signed by the Treasurer in Whitehall. In the late 1670s the surplus was secretly used to pay the army in England, and £7,000 went on pensions for Whitehall courtiers, siphoned off by paying for a regiment that did not exist. By the end of the 1670s the grip of the Treasury was assured, and by 1682 it had enough confidence to abolish the farm of the Irish revenue and administer it directly from London with a specialist staff. The Irish Treasury Commissioners based in London now had direct control over Irish receipts and expenditure and operated through agents in Dublin. Ireland's control over her own finances, apparent in 1660, had now disappeared, and real power was moving to London.

This development was not merely an Irish matter. In the late 1670s imperial considerations were also in play. The London government gave serious consideration to the running of the colonies in North America and the West Indies, and the end result was the reduction of proprietary interests and an increase in royal power, culminating in the creation of the dominion of New England in 1684 and its extension in 1688. The model which was used to give effect to this was the government of Ireland. In the Westminster parliament in 1670 Sir Edward Dering, one of the commissioners in the Irish court of claims, recorded a debate on whether a salt tax imposed on England should also be applied to Ireland. The argument was whether 'Ireland was not a plantation but a distinct kingdom governed by laws and parliament of its own' or whether 'we had the same power to charge Ireland as we have of other plantations'.[10] The latter was the overwhelming consensus, based on economic considerations.

Seven years later London in effect, though not by name, tried to implement Poynings' Law in Virginia. The previous year Secretary Williamson in London had included among a set of jottings on Jamaica, wrested from the Spanish in 1655: 'Query, how was the style of king and kingdom in Ireland enacted' and asking about the relationship of Poynings' Law to this. This, in fact, was revisiting an older discussion from 1668 in which there had been an attempt to impose on Jamaica the 'law Sir Edward Poynings made in Ireland'.[11] The understanding of Poynings' Law here was thoroughly Wentworthian: its function was to constrain the workings of the legislature rather than the executive as it had been designed to do. However, what happened in 1677 was a much more thoroughgoing attempt by the Lords of Trade and Plantations to impose a system like Poynings' Law in Ireland. The debate rested on whether Jamaica, and by extension Ireland, was a conquered country or not. In fact direct rule failed, but what had been given was an answer to a question most clearly articulated by William Molyneux in 1698 as to whether Ireland was a kingdom like those of the Old World or a colony like Virginia or Maryland. In the words of one English merchants' petition of 1676, 'New England and Ireland that are but colonies purchased and settled by the blood and treasure of England'.[12] By 1685 the matter seemed so clear that Lord Keeper Guildford, advising the new Irish Lord Lieutenant, the Earl of Clarendon, told him that Ireland was 'a kingdom subordinate to England in so absolute a manner, that the king in his parliament of England may make laws that shall be binding in Ireland'. Yet he did concede that since Ireland had no representation at Westminster, it might be unreasonable for the parliament in England to 'give away their money or make laws to change property'.[13]

This might have been a *fait accompli* but for the fact that attitudes within the settler community in Ireland were changing. Some were perplexed by the practical problems these arrangements generated. Sir William Petty, for instance, found his position as a judge in the Irish Admiralty Court undermined by appeals to England which he felt challenged the authority of the crown and as a result would produce 'chaos'.[14] Those in Ireland did not accept such reduction of their status easily, although it was unclear what they could do about it. The Earl of Orrery, for instance complained at the passage of the Cattle Acts, observing: 'Our usage in England amazes me. . . . But they [the English parliament] have done what they can against us. I doubt not that His Majesty will do what he can for us. I will never so much doubt that the king's care for his own prerogative as to fancy an act in England shall be admitted to bind Ireland.'[15]

Others found themselves defending the indefensible in different places. Henry Jones, the Church of Ireland Bishop of Meath, for instance, found himself under fire in 1679 for defending the actions of the late Archbishop of Armagh, James Margetson, in spending most of his money in England rather than investing it in Ireland. From a very different confessional position, the Baptist Richard Lawrence, while railing against luxury and immorality also, in his *The interest of Ireland in its trade and wealth stated* (1682), attacked the institutional and structural deficiencies which had made his own ventures into manufacturing in Ireland such a failure. Chief among those culprits were England and the English government. Unsympathetic strangers were sent to take over Irish offices, and since the majority of those beneficiaries were absentees, they drained wealth out of the country and as a result sent interest rates soaring. He urged that the army should be equipped with Irish-made uniforms rather than imports in an endeavour to stimulate local industries. Lawrence was not alone in this sort of economic analysis. Sir William Petty in Dublin and the elder Sir Richard Cox in Cork similarly identified absenteeism by English or Scots landowners and office-holders as one of the problems of the Irish economy. These were difficulties that were experienced, and their implications partially grasped by contemporaries, but not precisely defined or resolved by all parties by the end of the century.

By the 1680s the roots of these patriotic views among the settlers were already deep. The experience of Wentworth in the 1630s had taught settlers that the assertion of their rights in shaping a form of government was more important than proving conquest. An assumption that a contract which bound the king to respect the rights of those who took risks to defend the security of his realm by settling in Ireland needed copperfastening. The events of the 1640s had inhibited the development of this insight, but the experience of a union of England, Scotland and Ireland in the 1650s proved disillusioning for some Irish M.P.s who went to Westminster. The advantages of a full union, most notably free trade, failed to emerge, and the influence of thirty Irish representatives in a parliament of 400 was minimal. On a more practical level, there seemed little they could do to ameliorate high local taxation imposed from Westminster. The failure of the bills sponsored by Old Protestants for a union between England and Ireland in 1654 and 1656, which would have dealt with these matters, was central in shaping attitudes to English interests in Ireland. English M.P.s and army interests blocked these attempts. It may be this failure to solve Irish economic grievances through a union that led the Convention of 1660 to commission a 'Disquisition' on Irish legislative independence from Sir William Domville, a second-generation settler who was later to become Attorney General. Domville, borrowing heavily from the arguments marshalled by the Old English Confederate lawyer Patrick Darcy in the early 1640s, concluded that England and Ireland remained separate kingdoms, each with its own jurisdiction under the common head of the king. Ireland, argued Domville, had never been conquered by England, but rather had willingly submitted to Henry II and in return had been given the common law of England and the right to hold parliaments. Thus drawing on Darcy's insight that the common law of England applied in Ireland, English rights were guaranteed to English settlers and could not be overridden by the metropolitan government. The text of Domville's treatise was never printed and presumably had only a restricted circulation in manuscript, and there is little evidence that it was drawn upon by anyone until his son-in-law, William Molyneux, used large sections of the text as parts of his own work, *The case of Ireland's being bound by acts of parliament in England . . . stated*, published in 1698.

Whatever about the constitutional niceties of Domville's argument, the basic principle was well established, and the Irish Convention had no reservations in telling the restructured Long Parliament at Westminster that it had no right to levy taxes on Ireland, whatever about other forms of legislation. A few months later the Convention had enough confidence to assert that Irish trade and manufactures were matters to be dealt with by an Irish parliament. However, it was wise not to push the argument too far, given the unforeseen difficulties that might rear their heads in the context of the debate about the land settlement, some of which was predicated on the Adventurers' Act of 1642 and the Act of Settlement of 1652, both pieces of legislation passed by the English parliament. Nevertheless, such ideas did provide an important foundation on which new approaches could be built. These were undoubtedly encouraged by the Duke of Ormond's style of governance, with its theatrical processions and grand buildings, all of which were intended to convince others of what Ormond already believed: that Ireland was a kingdom in its own right rather than a colony presided over by a provincial governor.

These political developments were merely signs of more fundamental changes taking place within the settler world. In the early part of the seventeenth century the registers of the University of Glasgow had noted the nationality of the sons of Irish settlers as 'Scotus' or 'Anglicus', but from the 1660s they began to record them as 'Scoto-Hibernicus' or 'Anglo-Hibernicus'. The change in terminology is significant. It reflects a growing cultural identification of settler families with Ireland. By the 1660s a second generation of settlers was growing up knowing nowhere but Ireland as their home. Many of their fathers had been forced in the 1640s to demonstrate where their loyalties lay by deciding which theatre of war they would fight in. Thus the Trevor family in south Down spent most of their time fighting in Wales in the 1640s and by 1700 had sold most of their Irish estates and left the country. By contrast, the Montgomery family, Viscounts Ards, chose to fight not in Scotland, the country from which they had come, but in Ireland, and they sold the land that they held in Scotland. This sort of process of disengagement and re-engagement was slow and uneven. The MacDonnell family, Marquises of Antrim, continued to involve themselves in a personal feud with the Campbells of Argyll into the late seventeenth century which took them into Scottish politics even though their main base was in Ireland. However, what is clear is that by the 1680s a rather unfocused sensibility was building in Protestant Ireland which proceeded hesitantly and unevenly. It was perhaps more of a sense of identification with the country than a clearly articulated political or economic programme for the development of the country. That would require a catalyst which would not appear until the 1690s.

## THE CRISIS OF THE THREE KINGDOMS

The rise of luxury and wealth in the 1670s seemed to many to presage moral decay and the decline of that essential political attribute—virtue. That much seemed apparent in the treatment of the Irish kingdom by Westminster in the 1670s and in the refusal to summon an Irish parliament, despite Ormond's lobbying for this. For some, this impending crisis was contained rather than resolved in the late seventeenth century. Its manifestation was clearly seen by some in the crises that engulfed the three kingdoms of England, Ireland and Scotland in the late 1670s. In particular, four crises which did not originate in Ireland, and which were, in the main, marginal to its political world, served to expose a range of tensions and unresolved dilemmas within Irish society. The first was the reaction to the revelations of Titus Oates to the English Privy Council of a 'Popish Plot' in 1678 which drew attention to relations between Irish Catholics and the administration. The second, the Covenanter uprising of 1679, threw the spotlight on the relations between Ulster Presbyterians and the government. The third plot, which in 1680 alleged a French-inspired Catholic plot in Ireland to massacre Protestants, and ultimately cost Archbishop Plunkett of Armagh his life, highlighted problems within Irish Catholicism. The final conspiracy, the Rye House Plot, which involved an attempt to assassinate Charles II in 1683, reveals a good deal about the state of relations between the inhabitants of Ireland and their king.

Financial difficulties may have focused England's attention on Ireland's position in the 1670s, but religious problems were not far behind. As the English parliamentarian Henry Powle declared in 1672, 'There has been a general design to set up the popish and Irish interest, to out the Protestant and English.'[16] The events of 1673–4, whereby Charles II had been forced to recall parliament in England as a result of financial demands following the second Dutch war, seemed all too familiar. Parliament opposed the Declaration of Indulgence of the previous year, forcing the king to withdraw it. A Test Act was then imposed, requiring officials to take Holy Communion in the Church of England. The English Privy Council instructed the Irish Lord Lieutenant that no Catholic could become a soldier, judge, sheriff, justice of the peace or a member of a corporation, and by the end of 1673 proclamations had been issued in Ireland for disarming Catholics, banishing bishops and regular clergy and enforcing the closure of Catholic schools. Matters seemed to worsen in 1674 when the extension of the Test Act to Ireland was contemplated. This bore some similarities to the events of 1640–41. The story was that of a king forced by the exigencies of war to summon a parliament only to be outmanouvered by a religiously unsympathetic body. Again, as in 1641, this was a period of economic downturn in both England and Ireland, occasioned by the Dutch war and a severe winter which destroyed crops. The parallel was drawn even closer by the republication of Sir John Temple's history of the Irish rebellion, originally published in 1646, sponsored by anti-Catholic figures in England. While some thought a Catholic rising might be possible, it did not materialise, but the events of 1672–4 demonstrated that the politics of England and Ireland, like their administrations, were becoming ever more closely interlinked in the later seventeenth century.

One example of that tendency was the reaction to the revelations of Titus Oates and Israel Tonge to the English Privy Council on 28 September 1678. They told a fantastical story of a Catholic plot involving Jesuits, Benedictines and several prominent English Catholics, with the support of Louis xiv and Pope Innocent xi, to assassinate Charles ii and restore Catholicism by force. A wave of anti-Catholicism swept over England, and in 1679 parliament attempted to pass an 'Exclusion Bill' which would have prevented the king's Catholic brother, James, Duke of York, from succeeding to the throne. The fallout in Ireland was speedy. Within ten days of the revelations the order was given for the arrest of Archbishop Peter Talbot of Dublin, although this did not happen for more than a year, and on 16 October 1678 proclamations were issued for the banishment of Catholic bishops and regular clergy and the closure of religious houses and schools. This was followed by an order prohibiting Catholics from carrying arms or moving into garrison towns. The militia was to be mobilised. Such orders were difficult to enforce, and they were repeated over the next two years with limited effect.

The scare exposed Ormond's weaknesses as the security issue quickly degenerated into factional politics. Although staunchly Protestant, given his Old English background Ormond had many Catholic relatives, and this led to accusations that he was soft on Catholicism. Ormond now found himself under attack in the Privy Council, in the Westminster parliament and in Ireland. The Earl of Orrery led the assault, but he was supported by others, such as the Earl of Essex, who hoped to be restored to the viceroyalty. Ormond continued to protest his loyalty, declaring 'that if I find any of them who are nearest to me acting or conspiring rebellion against the government and religion established among us I will endeavour to bring them to punishment sooner than the remotest stranger to my blood'.[17] Such declarations were part of a propaganda war which Ormond conducted in Dublin and London in 1679 in an attempt to shore up his reputation. Ormond's supporters in London, led by his son the Earl of Ossory and Sir Robert Southwell, managed his campaign there and through the manipulation of the press and factional interest were able to stave off a direct attack on the viceroy.

Protestant reaction to the rumours of the plot was swift. While Orrery's letters, which painted a picture of total anarchy in Ireland with murderous Catholics fomenting rebellion and a French invasion fleet expected daily, exaggerated the situation for political effect, there was still considerable panic. This was fuelled by further allegations in the spring of 1679 by a Catholic named Murphy, who alleged a further plot, and a sea captain, David Fitzgerald, who told Orrery about a longstanding French design to invade Ireland. Both of these allegations Ormond thought unlikely, since neither witness was credible, and investigations were carried out to no effect. However, as the allegations surrounding the Popish Plot rumbled on new intrigues arose to be dealt with.

The second set of events which had important ramifications in Ireland surrounded the murder of Archbishop Sharp of St Andrews and the Covenanter rising in Scotland which came to a head at the battle of Bothwell Brig in June 1679. The discontent that this generated in Ulster was fed by the arrival of the defeated party from Scotland. A watch was established on the ports, but since many of the Ulster justices of the peace were Presbyterian, it was widely believed that many escaped their attention. Copies of the Sanquhar Declaration by the Scottish Covenanters, basically a restatement of the now illegal Solemn League and Covenant of 1643, were found in Ireland. In the face of this, most Presbyterian ministers urged calm. In June 1679 the presbytery of Down drew up an address of loyalty to the king; in September eight Presbyterian ministers in County Londonderry promised passive obedience to the king; and in July 1680 four Presbyterian ministers in Armagh pledged their loyalty to the king. However, this did not prevent Ormond and the Dublin administration being more than usually sensitive to developments in Ulster. In February 1681 the Laggan Presbyterian meeting in County Donegal called a local public fast for the sins of the times, the judgments of God on the people, and the need to make petitions to God. This was not unusual; but given government sensitivities, the ministers involved were summoned to Dublin, since calling a fast was a function reserved to the king as governor of the Church of Ireland. One minister, William Trail, put up a particularly vigorous defence in the ensuing trial. He acknowledged the king's power and accepted most of the 1615 Articles of the Church of Ireland, which, although replaced, had not been repealed by the convocation of 1634. The ministers were imprisoned for eight months at Lifford. However, as Ormond pointed out, the legal grounds on which dissenters could be prosecuted in Ireland were uncertain, since Ireland did not have the Conventicle Acts that had been passed in England in the 1660s.

In some ways the third plot was a continuation of the earlier Popish Plot. In the spring of 1680 the Whig Earl of Shaftesbury, who had recently been removed from the Privy Council as a result of his actions during the Popish Plot, announced that he had uncovered an Irish conspiracy which was part of a French-backed plot to massacre Protestants that had been hinted at in Oates's testimony. Anti-Catholicism had been reawakened by the revelation in late 1679 of a plot by Thomas Dangerfield and others to murder Shaftesbury. A rumour was also circulating that some of the Irish Catholic bishops, including Oliver Plunkett, Archbishop of Armagh, had signed a letter to the nuncio in Brussels recommending Colonel John Fitzpatrick, Ormond's brother-in-law, as the commander of a Catholic army to invade Ireland. Once again, this threw up allegations of Ormond's partiality to Catholics in Ireland. On 6 December 1679 Archbishop Plunkett was arrested. Shaftesbury was to reveal Plunkett's role in a plot in early 1680, backed up by the statements of William Hetherington from County Louth and the Franciscan Edmund Murphy. These witnesses were joined by other Catholic clergy, James Callaghan, Anthony Daly, John McMoyer and Daniel Finan. What was being played out here was a dispute within Ulster Catholicism. Plunkett, a reforming Tridentine archbishop of Old English background, had instituted a number of reforms in his traditional, native-Irish-dominated diocese. From the perspective of social reform, he was effective in suppressing the bandits, or 'tories', of south Ulster, and, from the point of view of ecclesiastical discipline, he worked at the familiar problem of trying to bring those in religious orders under control and prevent them occupying parishes and hence collecting parochial dues which were the right of secular clergy. Plunkett had won a good deal of support from Protestants and the government for his social reforms, but he had also made enemies within the traditional clergy. Those tensions found an outlet in the accusations laid against him at his two trials, in Dundalk in July 1680 and in London in May 1681, and ultimately led to his execution for high treason on 1 July 1681.

In all these developments Ormond played a game of damage limitation, insisting, despite attempts to incriminate him, that he knew nothing of the plot and had concealed nothing. The allegations collapsed in 1681 with infighting among the witnesses and inconsistencies appearing in the evidence. These were exactly the sort of people—men perceived to be without honour or a sense of duty— that Ormond feared would gain access to the trappings of power as a result of the social mobility of the 1670s and 1680s. As he bitingly wrote of them when they returned from Plunkett's trial in England, they had gone with bad English and worse clothes and returned with all the outward signs of gentlemen in 'periwigs and broad cloth, their brogues with leather straps converted into fashionable shoes with glittering buckles'.[18] Such distinction between appearance and real worth, guaranteed by honour, mattered. As Narcissus Marsh, later Archbishop of Dublin, observed, 'the common people judge by outward appearance', which accordingly threatened to undermine the very basis of hierarchy.[19] However, opinion in England was moving away from Shaftesbury, who was arrested on a treason charge in July 1681 and, although acquitted, had to flee to Holland the following year after an unsuccessful attempt at a *coup d'état*.

The final plot that had reverberations in Ireland was the Rye House Plot of the late spring and summer of 1683. This Whig-inspired plot to manipulate the royal succession by assassinating both the king and his brother was revealed by a Baptist in June 1683. Investigations suggested that there was a connection with Ulster Presbyterians. No hard evidence was forthcoming, but Irish Presbyterians fully expected a clampdown, and this duly arrived with orders for the disarming of those said to attend dissenting meetings. By the end of July it was thought necessary to suppress unlawful dissenting meetings. In practice, most dissenting ministers conformed to government wishes; additional troops were dispatched to Ulster and those arriving from Scotland were examined. Little else could be achieved except the removal of a few suspects from the commission of the peace. Since the government did not want to be seen to single out nonconformity for particular punishment, a rather halfhearted attempt was made to close some Catholic chapels and a convent at Burrishoole in County Mayo. However, this clampdown was relatively ineffectual, and within the year there were signs of reinvigorated Catholic activity.

## WINNERS AND LOSERS

The complex whorls of plots and plotters in the 1680s had much more important consequences than seemed evident in 1682. Combined with other underlying trends, the conspiracies ensured that the political and social configurations that emerged in 1683 were rather different to those of five years earlier. The principal loser in this shakeup was the Irish viceroyalty. It had been clear from the late 1670s that control over the exercise of power in Ireland was moving to London. The changes in financial administration discussed above indicate that. But this trend extended far beyond finance. By the early 1680s the viceroy's traditional dominance over military appointments as commander-in-chief had been broken. Whitehall now made army appointments, and even before Ormond's removal from the viceroyalty the king had appointed Richard Talbot to a senior post in the army. While this undoubtedly created financial problems, more important was the reduction in patronage which resulted. The loss of patronage limited the ability of the viceroy to build a party by the disposal of posts to potential supporters. As it was explained in 1673, the Lord Lieutenant had 'some 4 or 500 places of employment' in his gift which were necessary because he 'can trust very few persons who do not depend on the favour of employment'.[20] The removal of the right of appointment to the army meant a considerable loss of viceregal control of government. The weakening of the influence of the now elderly Ormond is probably most clearly manifest in his inability to convince the king and Privy Council to summon an Irish parliament to raise funds for the reform of Ireland and to confirm the land settlement. In 1679 and again in 1680–83 bills were transmitted to the council under Poynings' Law. The first transmission probably fell victim to the Popish Plot, but even before this Ormond was losing the argument for a parliament. While Ormond's political networks had been successful in defending his position and keeping Ireland quiet throughout the plots, they were rather less successful with the king and council. For a viceroy to be successful, the ear of the king was essential, as the career of Wentworth in the 1630s had shown.

By contrast, the main beneficiary from the events of the early 1680s was the crown. The rumours of conspiracy and the desire to know how events in England might impact in Ireland evinced an enthusiasm for politics among the 'middling sort' of Protestant merchants and the professions in Ireland. One indication of this is the dramatic expansion of printed items from the Dublin press in the later 1670s and early 1680s. The number of items produced by the Dublin press between 1676 and 1680 was up 50 per cent on the previous five years, and for the period 1681–5 it was again up almost 50 per cent on the previous five years. Most of these publications were reprints of English works detailing what was happening there, but there was also an unprecedented number of local compositions. This political awareness was capitalised on in the wake of the plots. Beginning with Dublin in 1681 and followed in 1682 by counties and corporations all over Ireland, forty-four addresses were sent to Charles II pledging commitment to the king, the royal succession and the Protestant religion. Clearly these were drawn from a small segment of the population. County Antrim and the town of Belfast did not send petitions, or are not known to have done so, indicating that Presbyterians were not part of that process, and Carrickfergus and Derry were among the last towns to address the king. A further fifty-two addresses were sent to the king following the failure of the Rye House Plot in 1683. On this occasion County Antrim did send an address, though Belfast remained obdurate. There are indications of more popular enthusiasm in the celebrations of 29 May 1682, the commemoration of the Restoration, during which the Whig Earl of Shaftesbury and a local Presbyterian minister were burnt in effigy in Lifford, County Donegal. The evidence from within Irish-speaking Ireland is thin, but Dáibhí Ó Bruadair's poem *Searc na suadh* ('Love of sages'), written in May 1682 at the height of the petitioning, has flattering things to say about 'the good king of the Saxons' or 'the generous prince in the east' who 'dearly loves his people' and steers 'a kind wave of wisdom an right' over Ireland; such expressions may well be attributable to this upsurge in royalism.[21]

Clearly this demonstration of royalism in the wake of the plots, which found its counterpart in the Tory reaction in England, strengthened the king's hand considerably. From an apparent position of increased strength, Charles began to consider the possibility of making changes in the way Ireland was governed. Rumour had it that he was a secret Catholic, and, although untrue, this seemed to be confirmed by events. By 1683 Richard Talbot, later Earl of Tyrconnell, who had been in France during most of the period of plotting, was back in Ireland. It seems that he was now collecting material for a complete overhaul of the civil and military administration and had made contact with the Catholic James, Duke of York. By 1684 Ormond had been told by the king that 'very many and almost general alterations should be made in Ireland both in its civil and military parts' and that he was to leave the viceroyalty.[22] Ormond was not the only grandee leaving the political stage. The generation that had given effect to the Restoration settlement was passing. Ormond was already elderly and ill, and Lord Chancellor Boyle was in his eighties, although he continued as an archbishop. Orrery and Viscount Conway were both dead. A new generation was about to assume the reins of power. The signs of the times were the growing influence in the army of Talbot, more a courtier than a soldier, and it was rumoured that a commission was to be granted to a Catholic, Justin MacCarthy. The army itself was growing in importance. It was enlarged by 600 men and reorganised in regiments, and new fortifications were built around the coast. How far this reorganisation of the Irish polity might have proceeded had Charles lived is not known, but it was certainly a portent of what was to come.

# The King Enjoys His Own Again, 1685–91

On 6 February 1685 Charles II died suddenly. Ironically for a man with a great deal of sexual energy, he failed to produce a legitimate heir. As a result, his brother, James, succeeded to the thrones of England, Ireland and Scotland. James had converted to Catholicism in 1669 and had succeeded to the throne despite attempts in 1679, by act of the Westminster parliament, to exclude him from the succession. The outward reaction among the Protestant establishment to the sight of a Catholic on the throne was better than could reasonably be expected. Youghal Corporation celebrated the king's accession by providing beer for the local garrison, and most other corporations sent loyal addresses to the king. In County Cork Captain Henry Boyle, a nephew of the largest landowner there, Lord Burlington, wrote: 'Everyone is planting, improving and trading . . . which is a disappointment to those who do not expect to see the king proclaimed with such genuine joy and conformity.'[1] One contemporary, Lord Mountjoy, contrasted the fears before James's accession with the peacefulness of the event itself and thought that James's open Catholicism at least meant that people felt safer under a king whose religion was open rather than one who was a secret Catholic, as Charles II was alleged to have been. However, some Irish

Protestants were uneasy. The mood is caught in a letter from the Dublin Independent minister John Pinney to his daughter, Sarah, in June 1685 reporting rumours of strange happenings which seemed to presage changes, including three monsters born within the last three months and a mermaid taken near Dublin, but 'as yet we be quiet . . . but full of fears for the Irish have an health to the confusion of all P[ro]testants'.[2] Unease was certainly exacerbated by the recall of the elderly Lord Lieutenant, the Protestant Duke of Ormond, although that event had been clearly signalled up to a year previously. The succession to that office was a closely fought one in the court at Whitehall between the representative of the Irish Catholic interest, Richard Talbot, and one of James's English courtiers, Henry Hyde, second Earl of Clarendon and a Protestant.

## CLARENDON'S GOVERNMENT

In October 1685 Henry Hyde, second Earl of Clarendon, was appointed Lord Lieutenant of Ireland. Clarendon was a deeply committed royalist who, with his brother the Earl of Rochester, had played a significant part in orchestrating the royalist reaction in England after the plots of the early 1680s. There is no reason to doubt Clarendon's own account of the priorities for the government of Ireland written a year after his elevation:

> When the king first appointed me to this government . . . [he told me] that he would support the English influence which was one reason for sending me hither . . . that he would have the Irish see they had a king of their own religion and that they should enjoy all the freedom thereof yet he would have them see too that he looked upon them as a conquered people and that he would support the [land] settlements inviolably.[3]

Such views are in line with James's own sentiments. In 1692, admittedly affected by the events of the previous four years, he wrote to his son:

> As to Ireland . . . Great care must be taken to civilise the ancient families by having the sons of the chief of them bred up in England . . . by which means they will have greater dependence on the crown . . . and learn to improve their estates, by making

plantations and improving their land as the English and Scots have done wheresoever they have settled.

He added that the Irish language was to be eliminated and no natives were to hold military commands or occupy the post of viceroy.[4]

James's concerns were not merely theoretical. Irish money balanced the royal books, and to ensure that the funds continued to flow to London, the dependency of Ireland on the English crown had to be maintained and Ireland had to be kept in a governable state. This was a difficult task, as contemporaries appreciated. The social basis of taxation had changed significantly over the seventeenth century. In the early part of the century about a quarter of exchequer revenue had come from trade and another half from rents and compositions. By 1685 rents accounted for about a fifth of gross revenue and the customs for about a third. Thus most taxes now fell not on fixed capital assets but on highly mobile mercantile capital which could be easily relocated in times of crisis. In addition, about 10 per cent of James's Irish income came from the hearth tax, which fell not on the elite but on the mass of the population and as such was highly susceptible to local disturbances.[5] Royal income was therefore more volatile than it had ever been, and to maintain it political stability was imperative. Thus the Protestant interest could not be ignored. Moreover, the king had benefited personally from the Irish Restoration land settlement with the acquisition of almost 95,000 acres in Ireland, and hence he had little ambition to unwind existing arrangements, which Talbot and others had been agitating for. In this world Clarendon might hope, on the basis of his English experience of the 1680s, to build a royalist coalition of Protestants, happy with the appointment of a Protestant viceroy and an assurance that the land settlement would not be touched. Equally, Catholics might be happy that one of their own was on the throne, anticipating that this might result in some measure of toleration. To that end, Clarendon repeatedly emphasised to Protestants that the land settlement would not be tampered with, and on a number of occasions he asked for assurance from London that the king should tell men that they were safe in their possessions. On the other hand, state payments were made to Catholic bishops and archbishops from the middle of 1686, and three Catholic judges were appointed in April. At the same time Catholic officers, exempted from taking the Oath of Supremacy, were appointed to the army. All this seemed to point to a conciliation policy which had its roots in the king's unwillingness to alienate either English or Irish Protestant opinion.

Experience would prove how wrong Clarendon was in his analysis of and his strategy for the Irish kingdom. Almost as soon as he arrived in Ireland he found things not as he expected. First, the Irish were rather less enthusiastic about his understanding of the king's vision of Ireland than he had hoped. In September 1686 he commented to the Lord Treasurer: 'These gentlemen, the natives, though several of them are in the commission of the peace, yet they will not mingle with the others, nor come to any public appearance but held by themselves as if their business were to keep up a distinct interest which I am sure is not for the king's service and I hope a little time will teach them better things.'[6] He also discovered that there were diverse types of Catholic in Ireland who were concerned with different things. There were 'great differences between Irishman and Irishman; and as many feuds and animosities as between any people in the world'. There was a world of difference, he noted, between some who divorced spiritual and temporal allegiances, as the Remonstrance of the 1660s had done, and those who believed the pope could depose kings. Echoes of the debates of the 1640s still survived. Yet more worryingly, he discovered that the presence of a Catholic king on the English throne did not encourage goodwill from the Irish towards the English, but rather that the expectation of change meant they would 'hardly treat them [the English] with common civility'. Others, however, who had benefited from the land settlement he thought 'had rather live under any English governor than any of their own countrymen'.[7] To put together a royalist coalition from such material was a complex task.

Secondly, and perhaps more seriously for the management of the country, was the rumour-mongering and insurrection scares that spread across Ireland. Clarendon found Dublin, 'a very tattling town', teeming with rumours 'which are sometimes the forerunner of truth though commonly they are lies'.[8] Some rumours related to threats of an insurrection. This was a sensitive issue, for, as he reported, people 'say they have still in their memories the cruelties they suffered in the late rebellion [of the 1640s] from the natives . . . and some say can we help being frighted when we see that some of those very men who were most active in the rebellion now in command'.[9] Other stories and allegations referred to political or administrative changes about to be made, but the most alarming were those about imminent alterations to the land settlement or to the army. Such tales Clarendon sought to defuse. He observed in July 1686: 'The future prosperity of this country and the settling of His Majesty's interest here depends upon the speedy composing of men's minds and the freeing them of the apprehension that they are now under that they shall lose their estates which they are possessed by law and upon which they have laid out so much expense and labour.'[10] In November 1686 Clarendon instructed the justices of the peace to present at the assizes all such stories spread with 'malicious intent'. The judges on circuit in July 1686 tried to calm matters by declaring from the bench the king's resolution that the land settlement would not be tampered with and urged people not to leave the country. The degree of success is not known.

In this volatile situation, Clarendon became increasingly aware that his authority in Dublin was being undermined. As Irish viceroys had discovered in the past, their principal handicap was the simple fact of being in Ireland. James was more influenced by the immediate arguments of courtiers around him in London than by dispatches from remote Dublin, many of which might be several days old. Indeed, Clarendon complained in October 1686 that his letters were not even being shown to the king. Those the king turned to were the Irish courtiers in London, of whom the most forceful was Richard Talbot, later Earl of Tyrconnell, who was in London for most of the early part of 1686 and returned there again after August that year. His appointment as commander of the Irish army in June 1686 was obviously part of a move to undermine Clarendon, since Catholic appointments to the judicial bench in April had been made without consulting the Lord Lieutenant, the king having been convinced by Tyrconnell that they were necessary. Clarendon complained in October that he was being dictated to by Tyrconnell who gave him a list of those to be appointed sheriffs for the entire country rather than leaving this to the judges as was customary. He wrote to the Lord Treasurer that, while it appeared that the king's policy towards Ireland was unchanged, events indicated otherwise, with power being transferred to the Irish. Manouvering in the English court saw the collapse of the faction controlled by Clarendon's brother, the Earl of Rochester, and his replacement with the Earl of Sunderland. The inevitable consequence had been clear since September: the recall of

Clarendon. This happened at the beginning of 1687. Finding a replacement was not easy, and there was a reluctance in London to appoint Tyrconnell in his place. However, his lobbying was too strong, although, significantly, he was only appointed as Lord Deputy rather than to the more exalted office of Lord Lieutenant which was the normal title for viceroys in the late seventeenth century. Again, he was not allowed his choice for the office of Chief Secretary. James appointed a Meath man, Thomas Sheridan, to that post despite the fact that Sheridan's relationship with Tyrconnell was fraught at best. However, Sheridan was there to report Tyrconnell's actions to the king and to attempt to ensure that the Lord Deputy did not stray far from royal policy.

## REIMAGINING IRELAND
The recall of Clarendon and the appointment of the Catholic Old Englishman Richard Talbot, recently created Earl of Tyrconnell, in January 1687 opened a number of new possibilities for how the kingdom of Ireland was to be organised. There was a range of possibilities available. The first one was a reinvigoration of a world based on the values of Gaelic Ireland. That this seemed likely is indicated by the publication in 1685 of *Ogygia* by Roderick O'Flaherty, the last member of a learned Connacht family. Like Keating's *Foras feasa ar Éirinn* fifty years earlier, O'Flaherty's book grappled with the fragments of the mythic Irish past in an attempt to create a usable narrative explaining the origins of the peoples of the country. O'Flaherty treated the Irish origin myths as fictions, but fiction with a core of truth which in his interpretation showed the *Gaeil* as originating in Phoenician civilisation, and in particular Egypt. As such, Ireland's ancient culture on the evidence of texts, language and monuments predated that of Britain and, indeed, Rome. As O'Flaherty concluded, it was through this line of the ancient kings of Ireland that Charles, and latterly James—to whom the volume was dedicated—was King of England and Ireland.

The impact this volume had in convincing anyone of its arguments in support of the supremacy of Irish culture is uncertain. That it was written in Latin probably ensured that, unlike Keating's vernacular work, it circulated only among the learned. However, the fact that it was written at all was significant, since for the first time in almost a century a version of the Irish past was available to the European world of scholarship. In the early part of the seventeenth century, and again in the early eighteenth century, poets in the Irish language regularly had recourse to history to support or illustrate arguments. From the 1660s to the 1680s almost no one in Gaelic Ireland looked to the past. Indeed, almost all the writers born in years of the 1640s and 1650s fell silent, with the exception of the poems of Dáibhí Ó Bruadair and a handful of works by Séafraidh Ó Donnchadha an Ghleanna and Diarmaid mac Seáin Bhuidhe Mhic Chárthaigh. It is as if the generation who lived through the traumas of the 1640s and 1650s did not want to look back to the past, preferring to forget what had happened in those decades. O'Flaherty's *Ogygia* marks a new beginning of literary activity from a native Irish perspective. This interest in reinventing the Irish past spread more widely. In 1685 the Dublin almanac writer Patrick Bourke included in his almanac for that year a work on early Irish kings. A few years later, when Sir Neil O'Neill of Killileagh in County Antrim had his portrait painted, he was depicted in the traditional costume of an Irish chief. The family also arranged for the compilation of a traditional family *duanaire*, the *Leabhar Chloinne Aodha Buidhe*, and in Munster about the same time the Cotters likewise compiled a traditional *duanaire*. In Kells, County Meath, one of the early Christian high crosses was used to make a market cross. Most dramatically, in County Limerick the poetry of Dáibhí Ó Bruadair praised James II, in whose veins ran, according to Ó Bruadair, the blood of Corc, son of Lughaidh, the first king of the race of Éibhear. History and language became visible markers of belonging, and it was language that Ó Bruadair used to appropriate a number of those of Old English background to his cause in the 1680s by imputing support for the language to their political outlook. In the early 1680s Ó Bruadair deemed it appropriate to salute the Protestant judge John Keating in Irish because of his Old English background. Thus was a Gaelic Ireland reimagined.

Given the attitude of both the king and the viceroy to Gaelic Ireland, this option does not seem to have been a viable one. Much more significant were the sort of ideas set out in the writings of the Old Englishman Nicholas Plunkett, second son of the second Earl of Fingal. Plunkett was a moderniser, urging in one tract that 'What is past cannot be recalled: therefore 'tis for the future our solicitude must be.' His library contained books on agricultural improvement, as well as a number of tracts on trade and money which reflect contemporary mercantilist concerns with the balance of trade and optimism in the power of legislation to solve economic problems. He had also read the historical works of Geoffrey Keating, to which he refers. While all these concerns are reflected in Plunkett's economic writings, his interests engage more closely with issues of estate management and the moral improvement of the inhabitants of Ireland. In this he revealed his social conservatism, condemning social mobility since 'wealth is no lasting companion to nobility' and urging the importance of honour in one's dealings.[11] His political writings exhibit similar traits, arguing a classic Old English view of the Irish polity as a distinct kingdom, although the succession to the kingship was by blood, rather than by election. His primary loyalties were to Ireland rather than James II whom he regarded as having been 'infected with this rotten principle—provoke not your Protestant subjects'.[12] The sort of building blocks that Plunkett used for his argument seem to have been commonly available in parts of Ireland. Lists of books seized from Jacobites after 1690 and given to the library of Trinity College Dublin contain up-to-date works on a wide range of subjects from a variety of European countries which could have promoted the sort of modernising trends evident in Plunkett's work. In terms of religion also, the library of Luke Wadding, Catholic Bishop of Ferns, reflected a modern French-influenced spirituality as well as the more solid theological standbys of the Counter-Reformation. More importantly, Wadding purchased recently published small pious books in large quantities which he gave away to those in his diocese. Again the French influence is clear from these works. Similar books were on sale in the Dublin shop of William Weston in 1688. All this suggests a vibrant Old English culture, influenced strongly by the ideas of France in religion as well as in other areas.

The presence of two political traditions is also clear in contemporary writings. In his political fable *Macariae excidium*, written after the Williamite wars, the native Irishman Charles O'Kelly wrote of 'both races of the Irish, or those of aboriginal and colonial descent', but equally he argued that they had 'blended together and became a united nation' cemented by 'community of blood and interest'.[13] It would be wrong to stress this harmony of interest too strongly, especially in light of later divisions, but it does suggest that, in the two generations since Keating had given historical sanction to the emergence of the idea of the 'Irish person' (*Éireannach*) and the first coherent attempts to apply it in the 1640s, the idea had become commonplace. Manuscript copies of Keating's work had proliferated, and it had spawned imitators, most prominently Peter Walsh's *Prospect of the state of Ireland* (1682), which brought the message to new readers of printed works in English. By the 1680s what held the various Jacobite groups in Ireland together was their common religious ideas, which in contemporary minds, created a new community, albeit one that was rather unstable and with many potential and real fault-lines. The poet Dáibhí Ó Bruadair caught the spirit of this development by describing the Irish as 'Clann Phádraig', or the family of Patrick, a saint who had traditional elements to his cult, for instance in the form of holy wells, but who also had received a thoroughly Tridentine makeover in the course of the century.[14]

## RESHAPING IRELAND

Significant as such ideas were for the reform of Ireland they required political and administrative action to turn them into realities. That was the task of the Lord Deputy from 1687, Richard Talbot, Earl of Tyrconnell. Tyrconnell had extensive experience of Irish affairs through the court in Whitehall, where he had lived intermittently since the early 1660s, having acted as agent for Catholics attempting to obtain land under the Restoration land settlement. His approach was that of an Old English aristocrat of the Pale who disliked, and distrusted, those from native Irish backgrounds. Significantly, he gave very few commissions in the army to those of native Irish backgrounds. The feelings were reciprocated. Charles O'Kelly, in his account of the war from the perspective of the native Irish, alleged that Tyrconnell passed himself off as an Englishman, and that he took advice from the Old English 'New Interest' men. He described him as proud and of 'an unbounded ambition', 'inconstant' in friendships and happy to dispose of individuals once he had achieved his own ends.[15] O'Kelly was not alone in offering an unflattering picture. Thomas Sheridan, his secretary, painted similarly unflattering portraits of Tyrconnell's ambition and 'cunning'. Notwithstanding the shared Catholicism of the groups in Ireland, Tyrconnell's main concern was to re-establish the Old English interest where he felt it should belong, in government and landownership. These were sentiments shared by the king, anxious to strengthen the monarchy, who saw the Old English as 'reliable' Catholics who could act as a royalist bulwark against Cromwellian settlers, whom the king suspected as having republican leanings, and the native Irish who required anglicisation. The difference between the two men was one of degree. While James argued for balance, Tyrconnell pushed for more thoroughgoing reform. Tyrconnell won the argument, mainly through sheer force of personality and the exploitation of James's religious sensibilities. To this end there were three main interconnected strands in his approach to Ireland. The first was to remove arms from the Protestant community, a process begun with the disarming of the militia in 1685, and to allow Catholics to carry arms, which they were previously forbidden to do. Secondly, he wished to Catholicise the army and civil and municipal administration. In the case of the army, Tyrconnell had been pressing for reform on exactly this line since 1685. Thus far these ideas fitted with James's English policy of creating a world in which Catholics could be part of the political nation, albeit that Tyrconnell would take this to extremes. What was different about the Irish experience was the final part of the strategy. Tyrconnell demanded the unwinding of the Restoration land settlement, as a way of underpinning Catholic power through the control of landownership. In short, he hoped to use the opportunity provided by the accession of a Catholic king to strengthen the Catholic interest dramatically. What would happen after the king's death if there was no heir was another matter. There were certainly political options in the event of this happening, such as trying to join the crown of Ireland to that of France or Spain, but circumstances dictated that these remained only possibilities that would not be fulfilled.

Tyrconnell's first move for the control of Ireland was essentially opportunistic. The Rye House Plot in 1683, followed in May 1685 by a rising against James by the Earl of Argyll in Scotland, had created fears of unrest among the Scots in Ulster. Orders were given to disarm the militia and inspect the number of firearms in private hands, as in England. These orders continued to be enforced by Tyrconnell after the immediate danger of the plot had passed. How rigorously they could be enforced, given the limited resources of the administration, is another question. While the disbanding of the militia certainly removed a structure of the organisation of local defence, the events of

1689 in Ulster suggest that there were still substantial quantities of arms in Protestant hands. Apart from their practical functions, firearms were expensive and hence a mark of status that was not to be easily surrendered.

The introduction of Catholics into military and civil offices had already begun before Tyrconnell's appointment to the Irish Lord Deputyship. His period as commander of the army from June 1686 had seen significant progress in this area, although there had been movements in this direction even before this. By the end of September 1686, out of a sanctioned strength of 7,485 men, there were 5,043 Catholic privates (67 per cent) but only 166 Catholic officers out of 406 (40 per cent). By 1688, however, the great majority of officers were Catholic. Again, before Tyrconnell assumed office, changes were already under way in the judiciary, with three Catholic judges appointed on instructions from London. Eleven Catholics had also been admitted to the Privy Council. In terms of corporations, Clarendon had already sent a circular to towns instructing them to admit Catholics as freemen without taking the Oath of Supremacy. Under Tyrconnell this process speeded up rapidly with the appointment of new judges and Privy Councillors, so that by 1687 Catholics had the majority on both the judicial bench and the Privy Council. The new Attorney General, Sir Richard Nangle, was also a Catholic, as were the sheriffs appointed for 1687 and 1688, with one exception. Protestant contemporaries complained that the new appointees lacked both experience and social standing to carry out their offices. Only the revenue administration, where considerable experience was necessary and hence few short-term changes could be made, was left untouched. Almost as important was the fact that Church of Ireland bishoprics becoming vacant were left unfilled.

This reshaping of the political and administrative structure was unlikely to endure unless the ground on which it was built—the land settlement—could be restructured in order to provide an economic and social basis for the new elite. Before his appointment as Lord Deputy Tyrconnell had prevented attempts by some to get the king to confirm existing land titles. To achieve this, a parliament was needed to alter the Acts of Settlement and Explanation. By June 1687 James II had agreed, at least in principle, to the summoning of a parliament. New charters were to be issued to corporate towns as part of the electoral strategy. Corporations were remodelled in the way that their counterparts in England were also altered by removing the Oath of Supremacy as a requirement for office. In Dublin ten of the twenty-four aldermen named in the city's new charter were Protestant, as were fifteen of the forty-eight burgesses, although eleven of these did not take their seats in the corporation. This opened the corporations not only to Catholics but to nonconformists also as two Quakers were named in the Dublin charter and one Presbyterian in the case of Belfast, but in both cases Catholics dominated. Two months later the king agreed that draft legislation concerning the land settlement could be drawn up by Tyrconnell for consideration by the new parliament. The evidence of what was agreed at this meeting at Chester is very confusing and contradictory, but the Acts of Settlement and Explanation were certainly discussed. James still refused to commit himself to a date of meeting for the Irish parliament, claiming that he wanted the English parliament to meet first to repeal the penal legislation against Catholics there, a natural reaction given the potential storm that would erupt in the English parliament over changes in Ireland. Despite Tyrconnell's assurances, James was still concerned about Protestant reaction in Ireland. Two alternative bills modifying the land settlement were sent from Dublin to London in March 1688. The formula preferred by Tyrconnell proposed to reverse all Cromwellian confiscations that had not already been undone by the Restoration land settlement. The property so affected was to be divided between the old inhabitants and those now in occupation. The scheme was obviously biased in favour of the Old English, since the older plantation settlements were left intact. This would have left settlers with some 60 per cent of Irish land, and the king was prepared to accept such a compromise deal. Both sets of proposals were opposed by the English Privy Council, which was required to consent under Poynings' Law, and thus the legislation became bogged down until the Irish parliament actually met under very different circumstances a year later.

### REACTIONS

Understandably there were widely varying reactions to Tyrconnell's changes in the government of Ireland. Among those who considered that they would benefit from the changes there was exultation. This manifested itself in a number of ways, not least in raids on Protestant houses in parts of rural Ireland in search of arms. The dissolution of the militia meant that the forces that might have kept law and order in the countryside could not do so. This law-and-order problem was made worse by deteriorating economic conditions. The expansion in the late seventeenth-century economy had been characterised by significant growth in volumes of agricultural output in an age when European agricultural prices were falling. Thus a reversal in output growth, for example as a result of harvest failure or cattle disease, had a greater effect on rural society than might appear at first glance. Two exceptionally good harvests, in 1686 and 1687, although increasing exports, drove prices down to unrealistic levels. The harvest of 1688, by contrast, was poor. The 1688 customs yield fell dramatically, and by 1689 it was less than half what it had been in 1687. This reflected the downturn in economic conditions, which in the ensuing war became even worse. Supporting an army, which Tyrconnell had increased in size in 1688, in this context was an impossible task. The tensions this engendered were exacerbated by the fact that that army was now largely Catholic with little empathy for the Protestant population on which it was quartered. Sectarian tensions would both feed and be fed by the sort of difficulties created by harvest failure. Increasing local violence gave rise to rumours that a general massacre, like that of 1641, was to occur again. Such rumours, Clarendon declared, were usually 'idle plots and shams raised by the natives against the English'. In Waterford there were rumours of plots and counterplots: 'Sometimes it was pretended that the English would cut the throats of the Irish and sometimes the Irish would do the same to the English which caused great fears among the poor people insomuch as many of them left their houses and lay in the fields.'[16] Such rumours only grew in the telling.

It might well be expected that Protestant reactions to these developments would be vociferous, if not violent. Yet what is striking about the Protestant response is how muted it in fact was. In south-west England some Protestants under the command of the Duke of Monmouth had risen against James II in the middle of 1685. Given the well-established connections between this region and Ireland, it might be expected that at least some would have joined Monmouth's force; yet very few did so. Indeed, Monmouth's defeat was celebrated by Irish Protestants with bonfires and a loyal address to the king. There were, of course, allegations that some were involved, including a group of Irish Baptists in Munster. Similarly, in the case of the Earl of Argyll's insurrection in Scotland, Irish Protestants, despite the closeness of Ulster, stubbornly refused to take part. Perhaps the best evidence for any overt resistance to a Catholic king in Ireland in the late 1680s was at Downpatrick, where one man was arrested for speaking 'traitorous words' at the proclamation of the king's accession. However, he was later discovered to be drunk and was released. Similar allegations were made in Tyrone, where one man was supposed to have called the new king a 'popish knave', but such examples are rare. Even the Ulster Presbyterians seem to have been generally prepared to wait and see what a Catholic king might do. Thus they silenced one minister, David Houston, who preached to the effect that the accession of a Catholic king removed the bonds of loyalty and invited rebellion. The much-vaunted rumours of a massive exodus from Ireland by Protestants between 1685 and 1687 were mainly that: rumours. In 1687 Irish customs revenue was higher than the average yield of the previous four years, which does not suggest a significant disruption of trade caused by the flight of Protestant merchants. Reconstructing the movements of the Dublin Independent minister John Pinney from his correspondence suggests that, although concerned about developments, he remained in Dublin through 1685. In August 1686 he was in England, but by October was back in Dublin again. He remained in Dublin during 1687, and by January 1688 he had fled to north Wales. In August he was back in Dublin, and by the end of 1689 he was in Somerset. The Protestant flight from Jacobite Ireland may have been more complex and irregular than might appear on the basis of reported rumour alone. Rather than suggesting that there was a mass renunciation of loyalty to the king by Protestants on his accession or as a result of the Catholicisation policy, it is better to think of a process of progressive disengagement which extended over a long period of time. However, those who did leave carried with them stories, real and imagined, which grew in the telling. The Scottish Convention, for example, collected such stories, but there was not enough for them to interfere in events in Ulster as they had done in the 1640s.

More positively, Protestants took to the printing-press to defend themselves. In March 1687 the Dublin Jacobite bookseller Christopher Jans produced a work of religious controversy penned by Peter Manby, the Dean of Derry and convert from the Church of Ireland. Though written up to six months earlier, this was now put into print as part of the Catholicisation policy pursued after Tyrconnell's arrival in Ireland in February 1687. The issuing of Manby's work may also be a response to the failure of the Catholic authorities to organise a formal religious disputation, and even had they done so, the Church of Ireland Archbishop of Dublin forbade his clergy to take part in such debates. William King, then rector of St Werburgh's in Dublin, replied to Manby in a pamphlet which was issued under the *imprimatur* of the Archbishop of Dublin as a direct challenge to the Jacobite licensing system. In the latter half of the year the Dublin Presbyterian minister Joseph Boyse also entered the fray with a work against Manby and King, published by the Dublin Presbyterian bookseller Patrick Campbell. Printed propaganda became an integral element of the response to Catholicisation. Both sides issued pamphlets in the latter half of 1688 describing Charles II's conversion to Catholicism and the iniquities of the Catholic Church. One of these by Neal Carolan, a former Catholic priest who converted to the Church of Ireland, was probably written much earlier and held in reserve for an occasion such as this.

## THE KING ENJOYS HIS OWN AGAIN

The situation in Ireland was transformed in March 1689 when James II, the first King of Ireland to visit the country since the creation of the Irish crown in 1541 and the first English king since Richard II to do so, arrived in Kinsale. In the latter half of 1688 William of Orange from Holland, James II's son-in-law, had been invited to accept the crown of England and arrived at Torbay in Devon in November. James's position in England quickly collapsed, not because of outright resistance but because his supporters did nothing. After one failed attempt James fled to France in December 1688, leaving the English to ponder whether he had abdicated or whether William had conquered England—a point of considerable constitutional import, the ramifications of which were to be debated for some time.

James II, however, remained as king of Ireland and Scotland (as James VII), and with the support of William III's continental enemy Louis XIV he sailed for Ireland, arriving in Kinsale, where the local Protestant landlord paid for beer to be drunk at the bonfires that were lit in celebration and entertained the king himself with large quantities of wine. The king marched straight to Dublin. James arrived in the city in some splendour, to be met by an army regiment, the Privy Council, most of the Jacobite nobility and the corporation of the city in full regalia. At Christ Church Cathedral a Scotsman in the crowd named Beaton cried 'Long live the king', and the pipers who preceded the procession struck up a royalist song from the English Civil War: 'The king enjoys his own again'. These resounding words proclaimed: 'But all to no end for the times they will mend / When the king comes home in peace again.' As they passed from Christ Church to Dublin Castle the king was preceded by virgins who scattered rose petals on the road. Unfortunately virgins appear to have been rather scarce in Dublin, and one observer was sure he saw a number of prostitutes from the brothel he had frequented the previous evening in their midst. The streets were decked with flags, and, for want of bunting, many of the householders along the route hung curtains and chair covers from their window.

One of James's first priorities after a journey north to Derry was the calling of a parliament. The day after his arrival in Dublin he issued a proclamation summoning parliament on 7 May. The reorganisation of the corporations and the sheriffs, who acted as returning officers, which Tyrconnell had carried out the previous year, provided the basic tools for selecting a manageable body. Some 230 members were returned out of a possible 300 (most of the missing M.P.s being from Ulster). Most members were from Old English backgrounds. Forty-one peers sat in the House of Lords, including at least five Protestant peers and four Church of Ireland bishops (three others were excused on grounds of age or illness); these constituted about a quarter of the house, suggesting that the king had not yet alienated himself from all Protestants. How many Protestants actually attended the full sessions is not clear.

Summoning of the parliament was hardly unexpected. The king needed money, and to get that concessions would have to be made. However, much of what the parliament did was conservative. It did not repeal Poynings' Law or the acts restricting trade. The position of the Church of Ireland, and its endowments, remained unchanged, and the royal supremacy over the church continued. The Catholic Church was not established, although its clergy were to be supported from the proceeds of vacant Church of Ireland livings. While the king agreed to the effects of the Acts of Supremacy and Uniformity being suspended, they remained as active pieces of legislation. The king also agreed, reluctantly, to an act declaring that the English parliament had no right to pass legislation for Ireland—an argument to be heard most vociferously from Irish Protestants within ten years. However, the two most radical pieces of legislation were those relating to the land settlement and the Act of Attainder. The proposals relating to land proved more controversial than might seem to be the case. A substantial number in the Commons urged the complete appropriation of all lands granted under the Restoration land settlement, but some Catholics who had benefited from the land settlement as 'New Interest' men opposed the changes, as did James's English advisers. James was inclined to seek a compromise, but this slowed up the passage of the subsidy. Finally the king agreed to an act which repealed the Acts of Settlement and Explanation. Those who had been landowners in 1641, or their heirs, were allowed to take steps to recover their property. A court of claims was to be established to deal with the rights of individuals, although this does not seem to have been set up. Nothing was done about those families who had lost land before 1641.

There was also provision for the forfeiture of lands belonging to those who had rebelled against James or had dealings with rebels. The identity of these rebels was defined by the second radical piece of legislation, the Act of Attainder, which named 1,340 individuals who were regarded as traitors for their failure to acknowledge James as king. To these were added an indeterminate number of persons who had left the kingdom. The lands of these groups were to be vested in the king. There was much in this programme to disillusion James's supporters. The king's political stock was fast becoming depleted, and by July 1690 Irish verse was depicting him as more of a liability than a saviour. James's focus was still the recovery of England rather than the reform of Ireland, and concern with English responses to his actions proved to be effective in placing limits on what was possible. This certainly explains the horror with which James's English supporters regarded the disunity and division among his Irish supporters.

Protestant reaction to James II's arrival in Ireland was mixed. It is certainly the case that tensions were heightened as settlers became increasingly nervous about what was to happen. The strange events, which may have been seen as portents, reported by one Protestant diarist, reflect the tensions abroad. In January 1688 a meteor was seen over Dublin, on 7 April a cross was seen on the moon in Wexford and Wicklow, and on 30 October two armies were seen engaged in a supernatural battle in the clouds near Dublin. Ghosts were also walking, and Tyrconnell had to move out of his house in Chapelizod because the house was so disturbed by evil spirits. However, all was not straightforward. In the case of Fermanagh, for example, a number of prominent Protestant gentry, including the former Belfast merchant John Corry, refused to declare for William III before fleeing Ireland in April 1689. It is also worth noting that the attitude of the citizens of Derry was not initially favourable to William. After the first closing of the gates of Derry on 7 December 1688, in response to the fears generated by a rumour of massacre, the inhabitants swore an oath to be loyal to their sovereign lord the king—James II. Again, the Protestant reaction to the seizing of their churches by Catholics from early 1689 was to appeal for restitution to the Catholic King James rather than William III. The case of Thomas Bligh, a Protestant landowner from near Athboy, County Meath, suggests how Protestant reaction evolved. In September 1688 Bligh was in London and wrote to his brother-in-law in Dublin that there were strange reports circulating at court that the Dutch intended to land an army in England, but it was clear that 'His Majesty [James II] and his loyal people here will be soon able to beat them out to their eternal ruin'. By the summer of 1689 Bligh had undergone a change of heart and was welcoming the dispatch of Schomberg and the Williamite force to Ireland.

There were two fundamental reasons for this change in attitude. The first was that the proposed land settlement threatened to wrest power not simply from Protestants but from an elite that now regarded itself as the rightful rulers of Ireland. The second reason was that James had been unable to protect his people in the face of mounting disorder in Ireland. The sort of violence involved was usually low level. At Old Leighlin, for example, Narcissus Marsh, Church of Ireland Bishop of Ferns, complained that the newly appointed Catholic burgesses, 'very mean men', destroyed the bishop's enclosures and seized his land on the pretext that it was originally common land. On another occasion Marsh and others witnessed the arrival of the burgesses in 'a great rabble' with a piper in front of them to destroy more of the enclosures, claiming that they were riding the franchises of the corporation. Attempts to get redress in law resulted in Marsh and his followers being charged with riot.[17] The king in a proclamation of 3 September 1689 pleaded for restraint in violent actions towards his loyal subjects, but he could not control rapparee pillage which, by this stage, had become part of the Jacobite war effort.

The failure of the Dublin government to maintain law and order and to relieve fears of an insurrection led many Ulster Protestants to band together for their own defence. As it was explained by William Montgomery of the Ards, bands were formed because of 'these distracted times wherein no lawful government is established in the kingdom of Ireland'. As one Monaghan man wrote in March 1689, 'we have no civil government among us'.[18] By April 1689 many of the Protestant landlords of Antrim and Down, including William Waring of Waringstown, Arthur Brownlow of Lurgan, and Robert Colville of County Antrim, had fled Ireland. However, they had not gone to support William in England. Rather, they had fled to the Isle of Man, which remained neutral in the dispute between James and William. Others did go to England. One list of 1688 records that 1,055 adult males had fled to England, while another the following year records almost 1,300 Irish Protestants in Chester. Most of these had come from the area around Dublin and Cork, though other parts of the country were less affected by this emigration. In all, perhaps no more than 5 per cent of Protestants left Ireland in 1688–9. In the case of Whitehaven in Cumberland, settlers from Ireland began arriving there in December 1688, but by September 1689 they were returning to Ireland. Others stayed at home and simply kept their heads down, unwilling to be forced to choose between the two candidates for the crown. Perhaps the best example of a trimmer in the 1680s was William King, later Bishop of Derry, who after the war wrote the most important defence of the Protestant position in late 1680s Ireland, *The state of the Protestants in Ireland*, which was frequently reprinted in the eighteenth century. King was imprisoned in Dublin in 1689 by the Jacobite force. In a search of his study they had found what they regarded as Williamite propaganda. This took the form of a document setting out the shape of the Church of Ireland under a Williamite regime. Had they looked harder, as the historian can now do by examining King's papers a little more carefully, they would have found a second document setting out the shape of a Church of Ireland settlement under a Jacobite regime.

## THE WAR OF THE TWO KINGS

By 1689 James's relationship with his Protestant subjects was disintegrating rapidly. By late January there were a growing number of declarations for William from Ulster. On 4 January the Sligo Association declared for him, on 19 January the gentry of Antrim and Down joined them, and on 29 January the Ulster Presbyterians sent William a congratulatory address. In March Enniskillen declared for William. The most dramatic example of this accelerating breakdown of relations was the second closing of the gates of Derry against James, this time in person, on 18 April 1689, which tied down Jacobite forces in north-west Ulster for five months. The Jacobite parliament with its Act of Attainder and restructuring of the land settlement speeded up the disengagement between James and what Protestant support he had left. The English Jacobite diarist James Stevens noted: 'The Protestants that before might have perhaps stood neuter or hoped for some reconciliation, their estates being taken away, were in a manner necessitated to espouse the rebellion which alone could restore them to their . . . fortunes.'[19]

William himself, unlike James, remained reluctant to intervene in Ireland. By February 1689 a group of Irish Protestants in England had given up waiting for William to act and were prepared to return to Ireland if James would give them terms. William's reluctance to become involved in Ireland can best be explained by his European background. The Dutch wars of the 1670s were a defining moment in the life of William of Orange, for they gave him a profound hatred of King Louis xiv and of France. That hatred was sharpened after 1682 when French troops occupied William's principality of Orange in south-east France. The battle-lines of European politics hardened as England joined the War of the League of Augsburg against France on 12 May 1689. This war was to be William's priority for the remainder of his military life, and Ireland may be seen as a small part of it. William found himself in league with a wide range of anti-French powers, including the papacy, which viewed Louis xiv's ambitions as dangerous for European stability. Such alliances explain why many Catholic European powers, not least the papacy, welcomed the defeat of Louis's ally, King James, at the battle of the Boyne.

William's intervention in Ireland should be seen in this European context rather than as a championing of Protestantism. His Irish involvement was not central to his plans; rather, it was forced on him by Louis xiv's support of James ii in Ireland. That support proved to be a liability to James, as the French soldiers who accompanied him were detested by the Irish. Louis could not be left with Ireland as a jumping-off point for a possible invasion of England. William, however, was anxious to leave Ireland as soon as he could and head for the main theatre of European war. His presence in mainland Europe was made all the more urgent by the fact that Louis xiv declared war on William's United Provinces in November 1688.

It was within this context that William arrived at Carrickfergus, County Antrim, on 14 June 1690 with 15,000 men, a train of artillery, a printer and a war-chest of £200,000. A Williamite force had already landed at Bangor the previous August under Marshal Schomberg and had consolidated a bridgehead in Ulster stretching as far south as Dundalk, but he had refused to engage James's forces as his army had been ravaged by disease. William marched south, but it was James who had time on his side and was able to choose the site of engagement at the River Boyne on 1 July 1690. William had some 40,000 men in total, including mercenaries from a number of European countries. These faced a Jacobite force of probably no more than 25,000, including some French soldiers. The fighting was not particularly heavy or prolonged, a fact reflected in the modest casualties—about 1,000 on the Jacobite side and 500 Williamites. The result was a long-remembered victory for the Williamite forces. In purely Irish military terms, the Boyne was probably less important than the later battle of Aughrim in undermining Jacobite morale and military strength. However, the psychological importance of William's victory was considerable in European terms. A failure by William to win in a direct conflict would have placed considerable pressures on the loose European coalition, of which William was a key player, known as the Grand Alliance. As the contemporary winners were to represent events, the Boyne was as much a piece of political theatre as it was a battle.

### PEACE TACTICS

James's flight to Waterford and then to France on 4 July 1690, after the battle of the Boyne, may well have proved to be more decisive than the battle itself. In a diary kept by a Kilkenny Protestant, references to 'the king' before the Boyne had always been to James ii, but after that date they were always to William iii. Indeed, after the battle at least some settlers began destroying papers that might incriminate them, while declaring their undying support for William. By November reaction had set in and there were demands for those Protestants who had collaborated with James to be tried for high treason. William King, Dean of St Patrick's and later Bishop of Derry, produced a defence of this species proving, at least to his own satisfaction, that those who had served James in 1689 had done so because of their loyalty to William.[20] After the Boyne Jacobite Ireland, with no king, had to rely on its own resources.

The first problem that the Williamite victory brought was a dissolution within the Protestant interest. While various Protestant groups in Ireland might come together to face immediate danger, once that danger passed they rapidly fragmented into a range of divergent interests. Even before the war was over, Ulster Protestants would begin to accuse each other of betraying the Williamite cause. In County Down, for example, various members of the association formed to resist the Jacobite advance in 1688 began accusing each other of using the war to advance their private interests and political fortunes at the expense of others. James Hamilton of Tollymore, for instance, was accused by other members of the association of preserving his private fortune at the expense of the public interest. It was claimed that he was only prepared to admit to the association those who would readily assent to his orders. Even more seriously, the splits between Presbyterians and members of the established Church of Ireland, briefly buried during the siege of Derry, exploded again as soon as the siege was over. One Presbyterian minister, Alexander Osborne, was accused of being a traitor, and the role of others in the Williamite campaign was denigrated. The king had first-hand experience of this factionalism almost as soon as he arrived at Belfast. A number of Presbyterians presented a petition to him when he arrived in the town, asking for his protection in return for the services they had rendered during the siege of Derry. As they were doing so the hero of the siege, George Walker, took on the mantle not of Protestant champion but of defender of the Established Church. He contradicted the Presbyterian petitioners at every point with what the Secretary at War, George Clarke, described as 'a good deal of warmth'. As a Derry soldier, Joseph Aicken, who had served during the siege put it in *Londerias*, a poem published in 1699,

The Church and kirk do thither jointly go
In opposition to the common foe
Though in times of peace they disagree
Yet they sympathise in adversity.

Once the siege was over, sympathy had been firmly placed in the background. Such factionalism the king saw as minor provincial quarrels which detracted from the main issues of the war. William himself was quite prepared to support Presbyterianism in Ireland, and indeed had established it in Scotland. He certainly continued and increased Charles II's grant of the *regium donum* to support the Presbyterians, but at the same time the Church of Ireland gentry who controlled parliament ensured that the king would not be allowed to undermine their position.

Secondly, the prospect of victory after the Boyne and the flight of James II reshaped the priorities in the Irish war. As the Duke of Würtemberg, commander of the Danish mercenaries in William's force, noted in September 1690, 'The state of Ireland is such that if an amnesty could be given to the leading people the war would soon come to an end . . . as the English are very eager for the confiscation of the Catholics' estates. For the Irish say openly "we are fighting not for King James, nor for the Popish religion but for our estates".[21] The desires of both parties could not be met. King William's priority for the Irish war was to reach a rapid settlement which would free both himself and his men for action in what he regarded as the main theatre of war, continental Europe. To that end he was prepared to reach a rapid compromise settlement with the Jacobites. As early as February 1689 the king issued a proclamation allowing Irish Jacobites to surrender, keep their estates and practise their religion in private to the extent that the law allowed. Such tolerance in the face of religious diversity may stem from the Netherlands, where William had grown up. By the standards of the seventeenth century, the Netherlands was a remarkably tolerant society, and the resulting absence of religiously motivated violence played a significant part in its economic rise to become one of the richest countries in seventeenth-century Europe. While William was a convinced Calvinist and member of the Dutch Reformed Church, this was not an established church in the Netherlands in the way the Church of Ireland was in Ireland. In the United Provinces Catholics, Calvinists and other forms of Protestants had managed to reach an accommodation, and William believed that some similar arrangement could be reached in Ireland.

Until William's victory the issue of how far pardons would be extended was an academic one, but after the Boyne it became a live one. William's principal Secretary of State for Ireland, the Cork landowner Sir Robert Southwell, struggled manfully to produce recommendations. The solution was the royal declaration at Finglas within days of the Boyne victory in which William promised pardon to the Jacobite followers who surrendered, saying nothing about religion, but that gentry were to be pursued unless they could show they repented their actions. The failure of the declaration to elicit any response saw a shift in policy towards a negotiated settlement with the Jacobites, a policy which seemed the only way forward after William failed to take Limerick following the first siege in August 1690. Negotiations were conducted with a Jacobite lawyer, John Grady of Clare, through the winter of 1690, and there seems to have been some progress. By February 1691 a declaration was issued that the king had no wish to persecute Jacobites for their religion or ruin their estates and urged submission, but this was too vague to produce any real effect. It was July 1691 before a proclamation was issued offering pardon and security of property to any Jacobite officers who surrendered their garrisons, and to citizens in Galway or Limerick, who were still holding out, to procure the surrender of those towns. Adverse Protestant reaction in Ireland and England was swift, although Ginkel, William's Dutch adviser and military commander in the field, thought the terms not lenient enough. The matter crystallised at the end of July when Galway proposed to surrender to Ginkel on terms. But what would those terms be? Given the fast approach of winter, the war needed to be concluded quickly. The articles Ginkel negotiated were generous, guaranteeing the estates of both the garrison and the inhabitants of the town; the Catholics of the town were to be allowed to practise their religion privately, and clergy were to be protected. Not surprisingly, Ginkel's actions were the subject of much Protestant criticism.

Military events now moved quickly, as the commanders wanted the war concluded before the end of the campaigning season. By late August Ginkel was besieging Limerick, held by a demoralised force, disheartened after their loss of the battle of Aughrim in July. In this context, they were more than willing to agree terms, although

Tyrconnell, already fatally ill, attempted to prevent individual officers capitulating by forcing them to swear an oath that this would only be done by unanimous decision. Tyrconnell's death, combined with repeated offers of the terms of the July proclamation, eventually persuaded the besieged to begin negotiations.

On 3 October 1691 the Treaty of Limerick was signed, comprising military articles which allowed the Irish army to serve with James in France, and civil articles which promised Catholics the religious privileges they held according to the laws of Ireland or in the reign of Charles II (Article 1); guaranteeing pardon and restoration of property (Article 2); and making the oath of allegiance the only one required of those who submitted to the crown (Article 9). The Treaty of Limerick was not therefore a decision taken by Ginkel in the field, but the result of a policy which had developed over the previous two years. The articles were a compromise, giving neither side what they demanded, and, not surprisingly, both Jacobites and Irish Williamites were unhappy. Even the eccentric Archbishop Marsh of Cashel, who had fled Jacobite Ireland, confided his prayer on hearing about the treaty to his diary: 'Spare us O Lord and bring not thy heritage in this kingdom to confusion, we beseech thee, though our sins have deserved it and the times threaten it and 'tis to be feared that 'twill be the effect of the unhappy condition that (I know not how or why) have been granted to a rebellious people that were not able to defend themselves, but will in a very little time again offend and go near to destroy us.'[22] Another Protestant poet put it like this:

> Hard fate that still attends our Irish war,
> The conquerors lose, the conquered gainers are,
> The pen's the symbol of our sword's defeat,
> We fight like heroes, but like fools we treat.[23]

However, the promise that the civil articles were to be confirmed by parliament quickly ran into political problems, and it was only in 1697 that the Irish parliament confirmed them. Even then, what was actually confirmed was somewhat short of what had been agreed. The bill made no reference to the crucial first or ninth articles. In terms of landholding, the Jacobites fared rather better, with 491 claims under the treaty being heard before the Irish Privy Council by 1694, of which 483 were allowed. A further spate of 781 claims under the articles of

Galway and Limerick were heard after 1697, of which all but eight were allowed.

If the Jacobite world after Limerick was to be dealt with by the Irish parliament, it was also a reasonable expectation that the Irish parliament would be left to share the spoils. It quickly became clear that this was not going to be the case. William intended to use a large part of the confiscated property to reward his friends. Most dramatically, the Irish estate of James II, comprising just over 95,500 acres, went to the king's mistress, Elizabeth Villiers, who had originally come from The Hague as a maid of honour to Queen Mary. Some 60 per cent of the forfeited lands were granted to foreign favourites of the king, including the Frenchman de Ruvigny, who became Earl of Galway, and Ginkel, who became Earl of Athlone. Two other grantees, Thomas Prendergast and Francis de la Rue, were to be involved in a Jacobite plot to assassinate William in 1696. They turned king's evidence at the last moment.

There were, of course, Irish Protestants who benefited from the Williamite settlement, but the sight of such royal largesse annoyed many others who felt they should have benefited from their efforts during the war. Nor was the Westminster parliament happy with such signs of royal munificence. The result was the establishment of a commission of inquiry into the settlement in 1699. Seven commissioners were appointed. Five were members of the Protestant Irish House of Commons. One of these was James Hamilton of Tollymore, who had set up the pro-Williamite County Down association in 1688. They attacked the king and his prerogative violently, and even his most staunch supporters frankly admitted that the grants were indefensible. The result was the Resumption Act of 1700, which appointed trustees to administer the confiscated property. By 1702 the trustees had sold off the property, the vast majority of the purchasers being people whose families had been well established in Ireland before 1688. Those who had fought in the war of the 1690s had at last got what they regarded as their due reward, but with no thanks to William, whose cause they had supported. They, it might be said, were the fortunate ones. All the unfortunate defender of Derry, Colonel John Mitchelbourne, received for the £10,000 due to him by the time of his death was two periods of imprisonment in the Fleet in London. Something of the disillusionment which the defenders of Derry felt at their treatment is caught in a pamphlet published in 1721 by their agent William Hamill, who had also been imprisoned for debt, entitled *A view of the danger and folly of being public spirited and sincerely loving one's country*.

By the time of William III's death on 8 March 1702, six months after that of James II—who had spent his years in French exile in pious contemplation of his life in an attempt to gain a heavenly kingdom to replace the earthly ones he had lost—there was little love lost between William and his Irish supporters. That was revealed in the parliament of 1692, which had proved to be unusually fractious as the Dublin Castle government tried to impose its will on Protestant Ireland. Nor for that matter did William have much regard for his Irish supporters. What the Irish Williamites loved was not the reality of a hunchbacked, asthmatic king, but his sophisticated image, carefully cultivated in print, porcelain, glass and medallions after the Boyne. Much of this was initially directed to the Dutch and English market, but it quickly made its way to Ireland. William became a symbol of the political arrangements which had evolved in the 1690s, and his birthday on 4 November became a day for the celebration of the political *status quo*: an established church, Protestant parliament and limited monarchy. It is no accident that when Dublin Protestants wished to erect a statue of William III in College Green in the heart of the city they chose to depict him not as the victor of the Boyne but as a Roman emperor, a symbol of classical, republican government and an embodiment of virtue. The realities of William were being fast forgotten, and his image had become public property to be remade and reshaped in every generation to meet the needs of eighteenth-century politics and culture.

# Epilogue: Post-War Reconstruction, 1691–5

The end of one war in 1691, perhaps, invites comparison with the end of others: the Nine Years' War and the war of the 1640s. Yet the immediate consequences of the Williamite war were nowhere near as traumatic as those of previous conflicts. The most recent war had been a shorter, more focused campaign, and, unlike the 1650s, the country had not experienced the problems of epidemic disease in its aftermath. Nor was a significant military campaign being waged in England or Scotland, the main market for Ireland's exports. The effects of the war were heavily regional, and recovery was patchy. By 1700, however, rent levels had returned to those seen in the boom years of the early 1680s, unlike the 1640s when rents slumped and took almost forty years to recover their pre-war level. Part of the explanation for this dramatic recovery lies in the rapid resettlement of Ireland after the Williamite war. After 1690 there was considerable immigration into the country, prompted in part by bad harvests from 1695 to 1699 in Scotland and to a lesser extent in England, though not in Ireland, which made the country an attractive settlement option. The Jacobite author of the early eighteenth-century tract *A light to the blind* noted of the Ulster landlords that 'their tenants for the most part were Roman Catholics until after the Battle of the Boyne . . . when Scottish men came over into the north with their families and effects and settled there so that they are at this present the greatest proportion of the inhabitants of Ulster'.[1] In Ulster this gave rise to the longer-term problem of the treatment of a substantial and organised body of dissenting Protestants, but in the more immediate circumstances of the 1690s it represented a considerable inflow of capital in the aftermath of war, evidenced by the ability to finance an adverse balance of trade. The economic recovery is particularly clear in the case of the woollen trade, and by 1698 the export of new draperies was twice what it had been in 1687. Such recovery gave rise to concerns among English merchants, and in this can be discerned the origins of the Woollen Act of 1699, which restricted the import of Irish woollens into England.

If the economic changes of the 1690s were benign, the political and social ones were less so. The Treaty of Limerick which brought the Williamite wars to a conclusion provides a convenient end point from which to view the changes which Irish society underwent in the seventeenth century. For some, such as the Irish poet Dáibhí Ó Bruadair, it was the end of an era. His 1692 poem 'The shipwreck of the men of Ireland' shows no optimism for the future, but rather it is characterised by social breakdown and internal dissension among Irish Catholics on a scale that had not been known before. From such dissension there could be no recovery, and Ó Bruadair ended his poem with the comment 'Finis be unto my writing for the men of Fódla's shores'. In fact he did write more poems, but these were increasingly stylised works composed to raise money from individual patrons. In the 1690s he lamented the dramatic decline in the poetic art—a new theme in his poetry. Such writing seems to point to the development of a cultural amnesia about the Irish past and its literary forms. A new generation of poets, born after 1660, were in the process of devising a different set of strategies for dealing with the trauma of the 1690s on its own terms, and most especially the projection of redemption into the future in the *aisling* form which became popular in the eighteenth century.

From the perspective of settler society, a rather different world presented itself. Writing at the beginning of the eighteenth century, William Montgomery of Rosemount in County Down described the early years of the settlement of north Down:

> Now everybody minded their trades and the plough and the spade, building and setting fruit trees etc. in orchards and gardens and by ditching in their grounds. The old women spun, and the young girls plyed their nimble fingers at knitting, and everybody was innocently busy. Now the golden peaceable age renewed, no strife, contention, querulous lawyers or Scottish or Irish feuds between clans and families and surnames disturbing the tranquillity of those times, and the towns and temples were erected with other great works done.[2]

This hopelessly over-romanticised picture says nothing about the early settlement of Ulster, but it reveals a great deal about the aspirations of William Montgomery and at least some of the Scots in Ulster at the close of the seventeenth century. The image of society portrayed here is of a co-operative venture in which the various groupings, both native and newcomer, have well-defined social roles to act out. It is a picture of a set of complex social networks. These roles are not colonial arrangements, but rather the world of hierarchy and social negotiation that the Old English had been advocating in the first half of the century. Those social roles occurred within a specific political context. William Montgomery was at great pains to stress the distinctiveness of the Irish family. He pointed out that the motto of the Viscounts Ards in Ireland was the same as the Earls of Eglinton in Scotland 'because our Montgomeries were from that family'. At the same time he pointed out that the arms of the two families were different, 'but now Sir Hugh's posterity (and none else) may pretend to carry the arms and use the motto of the Lord Viscount Ards'. The creation of the third viscount as Earl of Mountalexander in 1661 meant that they were now at least the Irish equivalent of the Earls of Eglinton, and the fourth viscount could claim the title 'the chief of that nation or tribe in Ireland'. In short, the sort of social authority on which the creation of a harmonious Irish society had to rely now rested with the settlers.

By the 1690s the settlers of the early part of the century had thus adopted a political outlook not unlike that of the Old English political elite whom they displaced. Their view of Ireland comprised a complex set of obligations which bound those in the country back to their king. However, the events of the late 1680s ensured that the king was not in the same relation to elites as had been the case earlier. Concurrently the parliament in London showed an interest in Irish affairs of a sort that would not have been tolerated by the monarchy a century earlier. The Irish Lord Lieutenant in the early 1690s, Henry Viscount Sidney, was seen by many in Ireland as a minor provincial figure. He was regarded by some not as part of the process of guaranteeing the rights of the parliament of Ireland, and its Protestant elite, on an equality with that of England, but rather as part of the problem that the demands for those rights presented. As a result, post-war developments saw not a reconstruction of Irish society as it had appeared in the 1680s, but rather a crystallisation of ideas, some of which had been implicit in that earlier period. The débâcle of the 1692 parliament, with its demands from the country gentry for parliamentary rights, and the publication in Dublin in 1698 of William Molyneux's *The case of Ireland's being bound by acts of parliament in England . . . stated*, which provided a configuration of ideas to give meaning and shape to events, both indicate this process at work. The Protestant-controlled Irish parliament became not merely the symbol of the pre-eminence of the new landed class, as it had been in 1660, but also a mechanism by which they could influence, or at times control, the government of Ireland. Moreover, the appearance on the Dublin stage of William Philips's *St Stephen's Green* in 1699 marked the beginning of a dramatic tradition of political discourse set in contemporary Dublin rather than under the cover of the classical allegory, as with Henry Burnell's *Landgartha* in 1640.

All of this demonstrated the extent to which Ireland had been reshaped in the seventeenth century to become a recognisably modern society. The economy had reaped the benefits of a spreading market economy with urban growth and a commercial land market. All this was reflected in improving material circumstances, at least for the wealthy, over the century. The power of the settler elite had been confirmed by the Williamite victory and was now underpinned by a range of cultural achievements. Not least of these was their interest in new late seventeenth-century developments in science which led to the establishment of the Dublin Philosophical Society at a time when Edinburgh, the capital of the Scottish kingdom, failed to support such a body of inquiring minds. This cadre of Protestant gentry, tied together by intermarriage and commercial connections and the possessors of titles of honour from the crown, were firmly in command. By the 1690s something of the outlines of the 'Protestant interest', which would become clearer in the eighteenth century, can already be discerned. The framework of political discourse and the participants in the political world had changed and expanded since 1600, but the essential question of how Ireland was to be managed remained the same and similar solutions were being canvassed. The only real resolution to the problem of governance of Ireland was a clarification of the ambiguities that had been necessary to allow society in the seventeenth century to exist, in particular the tension between the two conflicting understandings of Ireland as kingdom or colony. A clarification for Scotland appeared with the Act of Union of 1707. Such an idea was canvassed in an Irish context from the 1670s by Sir William Petty. Apart from any other consideration, relocating Ireland with its Catholic majority in a British Isles context would immediately shift the demographic balance. Thus, as well as advocating a union, Petty argued for transplanting Irish Catholics to England and English Protestants to Ireland.[3] In the 1690s some believed a union might become a reality as a way of guaranteeing equality with England. But as William Molyneux admitted in 1698, this was 'an happiness we can hardly hope for', since the London parliament would not be prepared to admit Irish M.P.s on an equality with themselves.[4] The failure to grasp that nettle would dominate the eighteenth century.

# Abbreviations

| | |
|---|---|
| *Anal. Hib.* | *Analecta Hibernica* |
| B.L. | British Library, London |
| Bodl. | Bodleian Library, Oxford |
| *Cal. Carew MSS* | *Calendar of the Carew manuscripts preserved in the archiepiscopal library at Lambeth* (6 vols, London, 1867–73) |
| *Cal. S.P. col.* | *Calendar of state papers, colonial series* (London, 1860– ) |
| *Cal. S.P. dom.* | *Calendar of state papers, domestic series* (London, 1856– ) |
| *Cal. S.P. Ire.* | *Calendar of the state papers relating to Ireland* (24 vols, London, 1860–1911) |
| H.M.C. | Historical Manuscripts Commission |
| *I.H.S.* | *Irish Historical Studies* |
| T.C.D. | Trinity College Library, Dublin |

# References

**Chapter 1: Introduction: Seventeenth-Century Ireland and its Questions (pp 1–30)**

1. *Journals of the House of Commons* [*of England*] (London, 1742), i, 461.
2. John Morrill, 'The British problem, c. 1534–1707' in Brendan Bradshaw and John Morrill (eds), *The British problem, c. 1534–1707* (Basingstoke, 1996), p. 14.
3. John Hanly (ed.), *The letters of Saint Oliver Plunkett, 1625–1681* (Dublin, 1979), p. 74.
4. T.C.D., MS 829, f. 310v.
5. Bonaventure Ó hEodhasa (ed.), *An teagasg Críosdaidhe*, ed. Fearghal Mac Raghnaill (Dublin, 1976), p. 67.
6. H.M.C., *Report on the manuscripts of the Earl of Egmont* (2 vols, London, 1905–9), i, 49, 59.
7. H.M.C., *Report on the Franciscan manuscripts* (London, 1906), p. 61.
8. Ibid., p. 63.
9. John Davies, *A discovery of the true causes why Ireland was never entirely subdued* . . . (London, 1612), p. 119.
10. J. T. Gilbert (ed.), *History of the Irish Confederation and the war in Ireland* (7 vols, Dublin, 1882–91), i, 1.
11. B.L., Harley MS 3298, f. 30.
12. Philip Sidney, *The Countess of Pembroke's Arcadia*, ed. Ernest Baker (London, 1907), p. 677.
13. Gilbert (ed.), *Irish Confederation*, i, 28.
14. Geoffrey Keating, *Foras feasa ar Éirinn: The history of Ireland*, ed. David Comyn and P. S. Dinneen (4 vols, London, 1902–14), i, 5–7.
15. Joseph McLaughlin (ed.), 'Richard Hadsor's "Discourse" on the Irish state' in *I.H.S.*, xxx, no. 119 (1997), p. 346.
16. *Journals of the House of Commons of the kingdom of Ireland* (19 vols, Dublin, 1796–1800), i, 437.
17. T.C.D., MS 826, f. 299.
18. *Cal. S.P. Ire., 1625–32*, pp 499, 509, 513.
19. T.C.D., MS 817, f. 185; MS 834, f. 64v.
20. Steven Jerome, *The soul's centinell ringing an alarm against impiety and impenitence* (Dublin, 1631), sig. A3.

21. Bodl., Carte MS 39, f. 561.

22. John Davies, *Le primer report des cases & matters en ley resolves et adjudges en les courts del roy en Ireland* (Dublin, 1615), preface.

23. *Journal of the House of Lords [of Ireland]* (8 vols, Dublin, 1779–1800), i, 443.

24. Based on Waring's travel diaries in Public Record Office of Northern Ireland, D/695.

25. Raymond Gillespie, *Devoted people: belief and religion in early modern Ireland* (Manchester, 1997), pp 76–8, 94.

26. J. T. Harwood (ed.), *The early essays and ethics of Robert Boyle* (Carbondale, 1991), pp 60, 146; Michael Hunter, *Robert Boyle: scrupulosity and science* (Woodbridge, 2000), esp. pp 72–92.

27. Michael Hunter *et al.* (eds), *The correspondence of Robert Boyle* (6 vols, London, 2001), i, 169–70.

28· William Congreve, *Incognita and The way of the world*, ed. A. N. Jeffares (London, 1966), p. 33.

## Chapter 2: Distributing Power, 1603–20 (pp 33–63)

1. Compare P. A. Breatnach (ed.), 'Metamorphosis 1603: dán le hEochaidh Ó hEodhasa' in *Éigse*, xvii (1977), pp 169–80 and Osborn Bergin (ed.), *Irish bardic poetry* (Dublin, 1970), no. 30.

2. John Harrington *Nugae antiquae*, ed. Henry Harrington (3 vols, London, 1779), ii, 149–53.

3. *Cal. S.P. Ire., 1603–6*, p. 26.

4. Hanly (ed.), *Plunkett letters*, p. 318.

5. *Commons' journals, Ireland* i, 56.

6. Bodl., Carte MS 38, ff 655–6.

7. *Acts of the Privy Council of England, 1618–19*, pp 157, 181, 490.

8. R. M. Young (ed.), *Historical notices of old Belfast* (Belfast, 1896), p. 39.

9. R. D. Edwards (ed.), 'Letter-book of Sir Arthur Chichester, 1612–14' in *Anal. Hib.*, no. 8 (1938), p. 56.

10. Davies, *A discovery of the true causes why Ireland was never entirely subdued . . .*, pp 6–7.

11. *Cal. S.P. Ire., 1606–8*, pp 275–7.

12. T. W. Moody (ed.), 'Ulster plantation papers' in *Anal. Hib.*, no. 8 (1938), pp 281–6.

13. Davies, *Discovery*, pp 280–82.

14. *Cal. S.P. Ire., 1611–14*, pp 538–40.

15. *Cal. S.P. Ire., 1608–10*, pp 116, 356.

16. Ibid., p. 406.

17. The National Archives: Public Record Office, London, SP 63/229/135, 150.

18. B.L., Add. MS 4756, ff 104v, 118rv.

19. *Cal. Carew MSS, 1603–25*, p. 168.

20. H.M.C., *Franciscan MSS*, p. 67.

21. Based on Bríd McGrath, 'The membership of the Irish House of Commons, 1613–15' (M.Litt. thesis, Trinity College Dublin, 1985).

22  *Cal. S.P. Ire., 1615–25*, p. 167; H.M.C., *Franciscan MSS*, p. 66.

## Chapter 3: Money, Land and Status, 1620–32 (pp 64–91)

1. Bodl., Carte MS 30, f. 161.

2. Thomas Ryves, *The poor vicars plea for tithes* (London, 1620), pp 1–2.

3. B.L., Add. MS 4756, ff 52, 97, 124, 127, 129.

4. Ibid., Harley MS 3292, ff 40–45.

5. Ibid., Harley MS 3292, f. 28.

6. Ibid., Harley MS 4297, f. 168v

7. Henry E. Huntingdon Library, San Marino, California, Elsmere MS 1746, f. 21.

8. *Cal. Carew MSS, 1603–25*, pp 305–10.

9. Paul Walsh (ed.), *The life of Aodh Ruadh Ó Domhnaill transcribed from the book of Lughaidh Ó Clérigh* (2 vols, London, 1948–57), i, 347.

10. Paul Harris, *The excommunication published by the L. Archbishop of Dublin, Thomas Fleming alias Barnwell* (Dublin, 1633), pp 41–2.

11. David Rothe, *Analecta sacra*, ed. P. F. Moran (Dublin, 1884), pp 100, 309.

12. George O'Brien (ed.), *Advertisements for Ireland* (Dublin, 1923), pp 4–5.

13. Charles McNeill, 'Rawlinson Class C' in *Anal. Hib.*, no. 2 (1931), pp 14–15.

14. Ibid., p. 17.

15. *Cal. Carew MSS, 1603–25*, p. 205.

16. B.L., Add. MS 4756, f. 31.

17. Breandán Ó Bric, 'Galway townsmen as the owners of land in Connacht, 1585–1641' (M.A. thesis, University College Galway, 1974), pp 712–14.

18. Keating, *Foras feasa*, iii, pp 182–3.

19. Ibid., pp 10–11.

20. Ibid., ii, 132–3.

21. C. R. Elrington and J. H. Todd (eds), *The whole works of . . . James Ussher* (17 vols, Dublin, 1847–64), xv, 336.

22. Keating, *Foras feasa*, i, 33; John O'Donovan (ed.), *Annála ríoghachta Éireann: Annals of the kingdom of Ireland by the Four Masters* (7 vols, Dublin, 1851), i, p. lvi.

## Chapter 4: The Challenge to the Old World, 1632–9 (pp 92–120)

1. 'A survey of the government of Ireland' (Sheffield Archives, Wentworth Wodehouse papers, Strafford letter-books, 39).

2. Ibid., Strafford letter-books, 8 no. 11.

3. Thomas Carte, *A history of the life of James, first Duke of Ormond* (6 vols, Oxford, 1851), v, 201.

4. Sheffield Archives, Wentworth Wodehouse papers, Strafford letter-books, 8 no. 11.

5. William Knowler (ed.), *The Earl of Strafford's letters and despatches* (2 vols, London, 1739), i, 200.

6. Edmund Spenser, *A view of the state of Ireland*, ed. Andrew Hadfield and Willy Maley (Oxford, 1997), pp 20, 29–30.

7. Ibid., pp 159–60.

8. Ibid., p. 67, 144.

9. Royal Irish Academy, MS 24 G 16, ff 32v, 33v, 34rv.

10. Henry Leslie, *A treatise tending to unity* (Dublin, 1622), p. 50.

11. T.C.D., MS 6404, f. 116v.

12. *Cal. S.P. Ire., 1633–47*, pp 47, 156.

13. *Winthrop papers* (5 vols, Boston, 1929–47), iii, 193.

14. W. Scott and J. Bliss (eds), *The works of Archbishop Laud* (7 vols, Oxford, 1847–60), vi, 543–4.

15. James Howell, *Epistolae Ho-Elianae* (London, 1655), p. 281.

16. Knowler (ed.), *Strafford letters*, i, 200–1; B.L., Add. MS 29587, ff 24v–25r.

## Chapter 5: Destabilising Ireland, 1639–42 (pp 123–151)

1. J. T. Gilbert (ed.), *A contemporary history of affairs in Ireland* (3 vols, Dublin, 1879), i, 364–5.

2. John Lynch, *Cambrensis eversus*, ed. Matthew Kelly (3 vols, Dublin, 1848–52), i, 28.

3. The text of the queries with Darcy's replies are in C. E. J. Caldicott (ed.), 'Patrick Darcy, *An argument*' in *Camden Miscellany XXXI* (London, 1992), pp 191–320.

4. Davies, *Le primer report des cases & matters en ley*, preface.

5. This passage is not in Caldicott's edition but in the original text, Patrick Darcy, *An argument . . .* (Waterford, 1643), pp 133–4.

6. *Cal. S.P. Ire., 1633–47*, p. 302.

7. B.L., Egerton MS 2541, f. 245.

8. Gilbert (ed.), *Irish Confederation*, i, 255–6.

9. Ibid., p. 11.

10. H.M.C., *Egmont MSS*, i, 146.

11. B.L., Egerton MS 80, f. 6.

12. Bodl., Carte MS 2, f. 203.

13. Eoin Mac Cárthaigh, 'Dia libh, a uaisle Éireann, 1641' in *Ériu*, lii (2002), pp 89–121.

14. T.C.D., MS 839, ff 32, 45v.

15. H.M.C., *Egmont MSS*, i, 144.

16. Gilbert (ed.), *Irish Confederation*, i, 18–19, 22, 54–5, 69, 70.

17. For examples, T.C.D., MS 836, f. 165; MS 832, f. 143v, 166; MS 839, f. 118.

## Chapter 6: The Quest for a Settlement, 1642–51 (pp 152–181)

1. Gilbert (ed.), *Irish Confederation*, i, 2; John Temple, *The Irish rebellion* (London, 1646), pt 1, p. 14.

2. B.L., Add. MS 25277, f. 58.

3. Gilbert (ed.), *Contemporary history*, i, 365.

4. B.L., Add. MS 4781, ff 151–6, 276–300 for Plunkett's views.

5. Gilbert (ed.), *Contemporary history*, i, 382–3.

6. Gilbert (ed.), *Irish Confederation*, ii, 70–80.

7. T.C.D., MS 817, f. 185; MS 834, f. 64v.

8. Gilbert (ed.), *Irish Confederation*, ii, 35.

9. H.M.C., *Franciscan MSS*, pp 113, 134.

10. W. T. Latimer (ed.), 'The old session book of Templepatrick' in *Journal of the Royal Society of Antiquaries of Ireland*, xxxi (1901), p. 271.

11. W. K. Tweedie (ed.), *Select biographies edited for the Woodrow Society* (2 vols, [Edinburgh], 1845–7), i, 166.

12. Patrick Adair, *A true narrative of the rise and progress of the Presbyterian Church in Ireland*, ed. W. D. Killen (Belfast, 1866), p. 115.

13. Quoted in Michael Perceval-Maxwell, 'Ireland and Scotland 1638 to 1648' in John Morrill (ed.), *The Scottish National Covenant in its British context, 1638–51* (Edinburgh, 1990), pp 205–6.

14. *Cal. S.P. Ire., 1599–1600*, pp 279–81.

15. Annie M. Hutton (ed.), *The embassy in Ireland of Monsignor G. B. Rinuccini, Archbishop of Fermo* (Dublin, 1873), pp 144, 254.

16. Gilbert (ed.), *Contemporary history*, i, 66.

17. Hutton (ed.), *Embassy*, pp 142, 143–4.

18. Gilbert (ed.), *Irish Confederation*, v, 286–308.

19. Michael Perceval-Maxwell, 'The Anglesey–Ormond–Castlehaven dispute, 1680–1682' in Vincent Carey and Ute Lotz-Heumann (eds), *Taking sides? Colonial and confessional mentalités in early modern Ireland* (Dublin, 2003), pp 213–30.

20. St John D. Seymour (ed.), *Adventures and experiences of a seventeenth-century clergyman* (Dublin, 1909), p. 24.

21. Aidan Clarke (ed.), 'A discourse between two councillors of state, the one of England and the other of Ireland (1642)' in *Anal. Hib.*, no. 26 (1970), pp 159–75.

## Chapter 7: Cromwellian Reconstruction, 1651–9 (pp 182–211)

1. This data is from Royal Irish Academy, MS 4 A 42/2c; Raymond Gillespie, 'The Irish economy at war, 1640–50' in Jane Ohlmeyer (ed.), *Ireland from independence to occupation, 1641–1660* (Cambridge, 1995), pp 161–80.

2. Calculations in Raymond Gillespie, 'War and the Irish town: the early modern experience' in Pádraig Lenihan (ed.), *Conquest and resistance: war in seventeenth-century Ireland* (Brill, 2001), pp 305–7.

3. The poems are printed in Cecile O'Rahilly (ed.), *Five seventeenth-century political poems* (Dublin, 1977).

4. Pádraig de Brún *et al.* (eds), *Nua-dhuannaire*, i (Dublin, 1975), p. 38, line 24.

## Chapter 8: Winning the Peace, 1659–69 (pp 215–243)

1. Andrew Carpenter (ed.), *Verse in English from Tudor and Stuart Ireland* (Cork, 2003), pp 354–5.

2. R. M Young (ed.), *The Town Book of the Corporation of Belfast* (Belfast, 1892), p. 79.

3. T.C.D., MS 2929, ff 11–12.

4. Lynch, *Cambrensis eversus*, i, 3; iii, 53.

5. H.M.C., *Report on the manuscripts of the Marquess of Ormond* (new series, 8 vols, London, 1902–20), vii, 189.

6. John Dunton, *Teague land: or A merry ramble to the wild Irish*, ed. Andrew Carpenter (Dublin, 2003), p. 139.

7. Bodl., Carte MS 219, ff 478–9; B.L., Add. MS 21484, ff 42v.

8. H.M.C., *Report on the manuscripts of the Earl of Dartmouth* (3 vols, London, 1887–96), i, 15.

9. Myles Ronan (ed.), 'Archbishop Bulkeley's visitation of Dublin, 1630' in *Archivium Hibernicum*, viii (1941), p. 74.

10. *Cal. S.P. Ire., 1615–25*, pp 54–5. For futher examples see B.L., Add. MS 4756, f. 62v.

11. Mary Pollard, *Dublin's trade in books, 1550–1800* (Oxford, 1989), p. 68; H.M.C., *Egmont MSS*, ii, 74; W. P. Burke, *History of Clonmel* (Waterford, 1907), p. 333.

12. [Richard Alstree], *The whole duty of man* (Dublin, 1756), p. 225.

13. Bodl., Carte MS 214, ff 292v, 293.

14. Carte, *Ormond*, v, 33–4.

15. Bodl., Carte MS 32, f. 732.

16. H.M.C., *Egmont MSS*, ii, 115; Thomas Morrice (ed.), *A collection of the state letters of the . . . first Earl of Orrery* (2 vols, Dublin, 1743), ii, 41.

17. Osmond Airey (ed.), *Essex papers*, i (London, 1940), p. 201.

18. Gilbert (ed.), *Irish Confederation*, iii, 8–9.

## Chapter 9: Good King Charles's Golden Days, 1669–85 (pp 244–271)

1. Bodl., Carte MS 33, f. 626.

2. Robert Ware, MS 'History and antiquities of Dublin', p. 19 (Armagh Public Library).

3. H.M.C., *Egmont MSS*, ii, 85.

4. H.M.C., *Dartmouth*, i, 132.

5. Ware, 'History and antiquities of Dublin', pp 148–51 (Armagh Public Library).

6. O. L. Dick (ed.), *Aubrey's brief lives* (Harmondsworth, 1972), p. 402.

7. Quoted in T. C. Barnard, 'Fishing in seventeenth-century Kerry: the experience of Sir William Petty' in *Journal of the Kerry Archaeological and Historical Society*, xiv (1981), p. 24.

8. H.M.C, *6th report* (London, 1872), p. 742.

9. For this and sources of quotations see Raymond Gillespie (ed.), *Settlement and survival on an Ulster estate* (Belfast, 1988), pp xxxiii–xxxix.

10. B. D. Henning (ed.), *The parliamentary diary of Sir Edward Dering, 1670–1673* (New Haven, 1940), pp 14–16.

11. *Cal. S.P. col., 1661–8*, p. 558.

12. *Cal. S.P. dom., 1676*, p. 587.

13. W. Singer (ed.), *The correspondence of Henry Hyde, Earl of Clarendon* (2 vols, London, 1828), i, 183–5.

14. Marquis of Landsdowne (ed.), *The Petty–Southwell correspondence* (London, 1928), pp 50–51, 66–7.

15. Morrice (ed.), *Orrery letters*, ii, 93–4, 145–6, 150.

16. Anchitel Grey (ed.), *Debates in the House of Commons from the year 1667 to the year 1694* (10 vols, London, 1763), iii, 119–20.

17. H.M.C., *Report on the manuscripts of the Marquess of Ormond* (old series, 2 vols, London, 1895–1909), ii, 280.

18. Bodl., Carte MS 219, f. 312.

19. Lambeth Palace Library, MS 1942/133.

20. National Library of Ireland, MS 17845.

21. J. C MacErlean (ed.), *Duanaire Dháibhidh Uí Bhruadair* (3 vols, London, 1910–17), ii, 274–5, 282–3.

22. Carte, *Ormond*, v, 166.

## Chapter 10: The King Enjoys His Own Again, 1685–91 (pp 272–298)

1. Edward MacLysaght (ed.), *Calendar of the Orrery papers* (Dublin, 1941), p. 307.

2. Geoffrey Nuttall (ed.), *Letters of John Pinney, 1679–1699* (Oxford, 1939), p. 19.

3. *The state letters of Henry, Earl of Clarendon, Lord Lieutenant of Ireland* (2 vols, Oxford, 1765), ii, 38.

4. Printed in Charles Petrie, *The Jacobite movement: the first phase, 1688–1716* (London, 1948), pp 226–7.

5. Figures from Seán Egan, 'Finance and the government of Ireland' (Ph.D. thesis, Trinity College Dublin, 1983), appx 1.

6. *Clarendon state letters*, ii, 8.

7. Ibid., i, 115, 407; ii, 140, 166.

8. Ibid., i, 69, 237.

9. Ibid., p. 303.

10. Ibid., p. 301.

11. Patrick Kelly (ed.), 'The improvement of Ireland' in *Anal. Hib.*, no. 35 (1992), pp 47–84.

12. J. T. Gilbert (ed.), *A Jacobite narrative of the war in Ireland, 1688–91* (Dublin, 1892), pp 63, 182–4.

13. Charles O'Kelly, *Macariae excidium or The destruction of Cyprus*, ed. J. C. O'Callaghan (Dublin, 1850), pp 8, 28, 173.

14. MacErlean (ed.), *Duanaire Dháibhidh Uí Bhruadair*, iii, 76–7.

15. O'Kelly, *Macariae excidium*, pp 79, 146–7.

16. *Clarendon state letters*, ii, 89–90, 160.

17. Raymond Gillespie (ed.), *Scholar bishop: the recollections and diary of Narcissus Marsh, 1638–1696* (Cork, 2003), pp 67–71.

18. George Hill (ed.), *The Montgomery manuscripts* (Belfast, 1869), p. 273; Public Record Office of Northern Ireland, T/2529/6/108.

19. R. H. Murray (ed.), *The journal of John Stevens* (Oxford, 1912), p. 70.

20. For this fascinating document see J. I. McGuire (ed.), 'A *remora* to King James's affairs: William King's defence of Protestant office-holders, 1689–90' in Christopher Fauske (ed.), *Archbishop William King and the Anglican Irish context* (Dublin, 2004), pp 36–46.

21. Quoted in Kevin Danaher (ed.), *The Danish force in Ireland* (Dublin, 1962), p. 76.

22. Gillespie (ed.), *Scholar bishop*, p. 38.

23. *The British muse: including a smart poem on the generous articles of Limerick and Galway* (London, 1691).

**Epilogue: Post-War Reconstruction, 1691–5 (pp 299–303)**

1. Gilbert (ed.), *Jacobite narrative*, p. 556.
2. Hill (ed.), *Montgomery manuscripts*, p. 66.
3. Marquis of Lansdowne (ed.), *The Petty papers* (2 vols, London, 1927), i, 13–16, 57–63.
4. William Molyneux, *The case of Ireland stated*, ed. J. G. Simms (Dublin, 1977), p. 84.

# Bibliographical Guide

## GENERAL

There is no modern single-volume history of seventeenth-century Ireland. The best narrative history of the period is to be found in the relevant chapters of T. W. Moody, F. X. Martin and F. J. Byrne (eds), *A new history of Ireland*, iii: *Early modern Ireland* (Oxford, 1976; reprinted with bibliographical supplement, 1991), which also contains specialist thematic chapters. This is particularly useful for its bibliography, which provides a guide to older works. However, the most important bibliographical resource is www.irishhistoryonline.ie, which is a user-friendly way of constructing a bibliography of post-1939 writings on the seventeenth century, especially crucial local studies. On religion, an important overview is P. J. Corish, *The Catholic community in the seventeenth and eighteenth centuries* (Dublin, 1981), and for a wider perspective the early modern chapters of Brendan Bradshaw and Dáire Keogh (eds), *Christianity in Ireland: revisiting the story* (Dublin, 2002) provide a convenient narrative. On war, Pádraig Lenihan (ed.), *Conquest and resistance: war in seventeenth-century Ireland* (Leiden, 2001) offers a series of essays on the conduct and impact of warfare.

There are a number of specialist studies covering the whole period. The main developments in religion and print are charted in Raymond Gillespie, *Devoted people: belief and religion in early modern Ireland* (Manchester, 1997) and Raymond Gillespie, *Reading Ireland: print, reading and social change in early modern Ireland* (Manchester, 2005). For the curious position of Catholic settlers see David Edwards, 'A haven of popery: English Catholic migration to Ireland in the age of plantations' in Alan Ford and John McCafferty (eds), *The origins of sectarianism in early modern Ireland* (Cambridge, 2005). On economics, an overview is provided by Raymond Gillespie, *The transformation of the Irish economy, 1550–1700*, Studies in Irish Economic and Social History 6 (Dundalk, 1991), and for settlement there are good chapters in B. J. Graham and L. J. Proudfoot, *An historical geography of Ireland* (London, 1993) and in T. B. Barry (ed.), *A history of settlement in Ireland* (London, 2000). On theatre, the first chapter of Christopher Morash, *A history of Irish theatre, 1601–2000* (Cambridge, 2002) provides an introduction, but for the early seventeenth century this should be supplemented by Alan J. Fletcher, *Drama, performance and polity in pre-Cromwellian Ireland* (Cork, 2000). On literature, see Deana Rankin, *Between Spenser and Swift: English writing in seventeenth-century Ireland* (Cambridge, 2005). There is, as yet, no book-length survey of Gaelic literature in this period, but Parts I and II of Breandán Ó Buachalla, *Aisling ghéar* (Dublin, 1996) is an incisive analysis of political thought using Gaelic literary sources. Little has been written on Dublin, but for an introduction see Raymond Gillespie, 'Dublin 1600–1700: a city and its hinterlands' in Peter Clark and Bernard Lepetit (eds), *Capital cities and their hinterlands in early modern Europe* (Aldershot, 1996), which provides an analysis of the changes in the city. Cultural and social history have been the poor relations in historical writing on this period. On women, there is a selection of essays in Margaret MacCurtain and Mary O'Dowd (eds), *Women in early modern Ireland* (Dublin, 1991), and there is an overview of the subject in Mary O'Dowd, *A history of women in Ireland, 1500–1800* (London, 2005), although this is more concerned with the eighteenth century. There are two important works on cultural history which can be read with profit: Joep Leerssen, *Mere Irish and fíor-Ghael* (Cork, 1996) and Clodagh Tait, *Death, burial and commemoration in Ireland, 1550–1650* (Basingstoke, 2002). On art and architecture, the best introductions are the relevant chapters in Anne Crookshank and the Knight of Glin, *Ireland's painters, 1600–1940* (New Haven & London, 2002) and Maurice Craig, *The architecture of Ireland from the earliest times to 1880* (London, 1982).

## PRIMARY SOURCES

The best overall guide to early seventeenth-century sources is R. W. Dudley Edwards and Mary O'Dowd (eds), *Sources for early modern Irish history, 1534–1641* (Cambridge, 1985). The late seventeenth century awaits similar treatment. A good selection of primary source material is accessible in Séamus Deane (ed.), *The Field Day anthology of Irish writing* (5 vols, Derry & Cork, 1991–2002); vols i and iv contain the early modern material. Andrew Carpenter (ed.), *Verse in English from Tudor and Stuart Ireland* (Cork, 2003) contains evidence of a particular sort that is entertaining and informative. References to older editions of texts discussed in this book can be found in the bibliography of Moody, Martin and Byrne (eds), *New history of Ireland*, iii.

## SECONDARY SOURCES

### 1600–1640

There are some overview essays in Ciaran Brady and Raymond Gillespie (eds), *Natives and newcomers: essays on the making of Irish colonial society, 1534–1641* (Dublin, 1986). Undoubtedly the most important work on this period in recent years has been Nicholas Canny, *Making Ireland British, 1580–1650* (Oxford, 2001), which approaches early seventeenth-century Ireland using plantation and colonisation as the main explanatory forces for social change.

In the main, three themes have dominated historical writing in this period: plantation, politics and religion. Plantation has been described in a number of regional studies. Munster is well served by Michael MacCarthy-Morrogh, *The Munster plantation* (Oxford, 1986); Terence Ranger, 'Richard Boyle and the making of an Irish fortune' in *Irish Historical Studies*, x, no. 40 (1957) and Nicholas Canny, *The upstart earl: a study of the social and mental world of Richard Boyle, first Earl of Cork, 1566–1643* (Cambridge, 1982). The later history of the settlement is dealt with in David Dickson, *Old World colony: Cork and south Munster, 1630–1830* (Cork, 2005). The Ulster scheme is covered generally in Philip Robinson, *The Ulster plantation* (Dublin, 1984), with specialist studies of the Scots in Michael Perceval-Maxwell, *The Scottish migration to Ulster in the reign of James I* (London, 1975) and of the English by R. J. Hunter, 'The English undertakers in the plantation of Ulster' in *Breifne*, iv (1973–5). For the area outside the escheated counties see Raymond Gillespie, *Colonial Ulster* (Cork, 1985). There is little on the midland plantation schemes, but Brian Mac Cuarta, 'A planter's interaction with Gaelic culture: Sir Matthew De Renzy' in *Irish Economic and Social History*, xx (1993) is of particular interest. However, historians must continually remind themselves that not all of Ireland was planted. Three monographs on unplanted areas are Mary O'Dowd, *Power, politics and land: early modern Sligo, 1568–1688* (Belfast, 1991), the final chapter of David Edwards, *The Ormond lordship in County Kilkenny, 1515–1642* (Dublin, 2003) and the brilliant evocation of north Dublin in Maighréad Ní Mhurchadha, *Fingal, 1603–60: contending neighbours in north Dublin* (Dublin, 2005). Suggestions on how new societies were created are contained in Patrick Little, 'The Geraldine ambitions of the first Earl of Cork' in *Irish Historical Studies*, xxxiii, no. 130 (2002) and Raymond Gillespie, 'Negotiating order in early seventeenth-century Ireland' in Michael Braddick and John Walter (eds), *Negotiating power in early modern society: order, hierarchy and subordination in Britain and Ireland* (Cambridge, 2001). The second theme which has preoccupied historians is politics, dominated by the anomalous position of the Old English magisterially described in Aidan Clarke, *The Old English in Ireland* (London, 1966) and his *The Graces* (Dundalk, 1968). The views of one influential Old English historian are well set out in Bernadette Cunningham, *The world of Geoffrey Keating: history, myth and religion in seventeenth-century Ireland* (Dublin, 2000). Less attention has been given to what might be seen as 'bread-and-butter' politics of faction and conflict. John McCavitt's *Sir Arthur Chichester: Lord Deputy of Ireland* (Belfast, 1998) and his *The flight of the earls* (Dublin, 2002) have gone some way to redressing this imbalance for the period before 1615, and V. C. Rutledge, 'Court-castle faction and the Irish viceroyalty' in *Irish Historical Studies*, xxvi, no. 103 (1989) deals with the period immediately after Chichester. For the 1620s Victor Treadwell, *Buckingham and Ireland, 1616–1628* (Dublin, 1998) is a sure, and detailed, guide. There is almost no writing on political thought, though some key figures, including Ussher and Rothe, are dealt with in Hiram Morgan (ed.), *Political ideology in Ireland, 1541–1641* (Dublin, 1999), and some of the political ideas of Sir John Davies are atomised in Hans Pawlisch, *Sir John Davies and the conquest of Ireland* (Cambridge, 1985). Alan Ford, 'James Ussher and the creation of an Irish Protestant identity' in Brendan Bradshaw and Peter Roberts (eds), *British consciousness and identity: the making of Britain, 1533–1707* (Cambridge, 1998) casts a good deal of light on the ideas of a key Protestant thinker.

The third theme is that of religious change. On the Reformation, Alan Ford, *The Protestant Reformation in Ireland* (2nd ed., Dublin, 1997) remains the best study, while Phil Kilroy, 'Sermon and pamphlet literature in the Irish reformed church' in *Archivium Hibernicum*, xxx (1975) provides an important analysis of Protestant thought. From the perspective of the Counter-Reformation, there are two seminal articles: John Bossy, 'The Counter-Reformation and the people of Catholic Ireland' in T. D. Williams (ed.), *Historical Studies VIII* (Dublin, 1971) and Donal Cregan, 'The social and cultural background of a Counter-Reformation episcopate, 1618–1660 ' in Art Cosgrove (ed.), *Studies in Irish history* (Dublin, 1979). The Franciscan mission has always been recognised as centrally important to reform, and there is a good introduction to this in Cathaldus Giblin, 'The contribution of Irish Franciscans on the continent in the early seventeenth century' in Michael Maher (ed.), *Irish spirituality* (Dublin, 1981). A cultural perspective on religion is provided by Aidan Clarke, 'Colonial identity in seventeenth-century Ireland' in T. W. Moody (ed.), *Nationality and the pursuit of national independence: Historical Studies XI* (Belfast, 1978). Two important articles encapsulate the political ideas of Irish Catholics in Europe: Thomas O'Connor, 'A justification for foreign intervention in early modern Ireland: Peter Lombard's *Commentarius*' in Thomas O'Connor and Mary Ann Lyons (eds), *Irish migrants in Europe after Kinsale* (Dublin, 2003) and his 'Towards the invention of the Irish Catholic *natio*: Thomas Messingham's *Florilegium* (1624)' in *Irish Theological Quarterly*, lxiv (1999).

On Wentworth, the standard work remains Hugh Kearney, *Strafford in Ireland* (Manchester, 1959; reprinted with a new introduction, Cambridge, 1989). Some of the problems which the 1630s generated have been examined in detail in Michael Perceval-Maxwell, 'Strafford, the Ulster Scots and the Covenanters' in *Irish Historical Studies*, xviii, no. 72 (1973), Aidan Clarke, 'Sir Piers Cosby: Wentworth's tawny ribbon' in *Irish Historical Studies*, xxvi, no. 102 (1988), and more generally in Michael Perceval-Maxwell, 'Ireland and the monarchy in the early Stuart multiple kingdoms' in *Historical Journal*, xxxiv (1991).

### 1640–1660

There has been a significant shift in recent years in our understanding of what happened in the 1640s. On the origins of the rising, Aidan Clarke, 'The genesis of the Ulster rising' in Peter Roebuck (ed.), *Plantation to partition* (Belfast, 1983) and Michael Perceval-Maxwell, *The outbreak of the Irish rebellion of 1641* (Dublin, 1994) have shifted thinking on the matter. Equally important is Chapter 10 of Conrad Russell, *The fall of British monarchies* (Oxford, 1991), which provides a vital British perspective on Irish events.

Three collections of essays are of central importance in understanding the dynamics of the 1640s in Ireland: Brian Mac Cuarta, *Ulster 1641* (Belfast, 1993); Jane Ohlmeyer (ed.), *Ireland from independence to occupation* (Cambridge, 1995); and Micheál Ó Siochrú (ed.), *Kingdoms in crisis: Ireland in the 1640s* (Dublin, 2001). These multifaceted explorations effectively complement a more specialist literature. Most effort has gone into untangling the Confederate position. Micheál Ó Siochrú, *Confederate Ireland, 1642–1649: a constitutional and political analysis* (Dublin, 1999) complements Donal Cregan, 'The Confederate Catholics of Ireland' in *Irish Historical Studies*, xxix, no. 116 (1995). Pádraig Lenihan, *Confederate Catholics at war, 1641–9* (Cork, 2001) is a masterly analysis of the mechanics of warfare. From a diplomatic and religious point of view, Tadhg Ó hAnnracháin, *Catholic reformation in Ireland: the mission of Rinuccini, 1645–1649* (Oxford, 2002) provides a clear introduction to a complex period. The exploration of the complexities of Protestant responses to the war were first explored in J. A. Murphy, 'The politics of the Munster Protestants, 1641–9' in *Journal of the Cork Historical and Archaeological Society*, lxxvi (1971) and David Stevenson, *Scottish Covenanters and Irish Confederates* (Belfast, 1981) and have now been elucidated with great care by Robert Armstrong, *Protestant war: the British of Ireland and the Wars of the Three Kingdoms* (Manchester, 2005).

On Cromwell's military campaign, James Scott Wheeler, *Cromwell in Ireland* (Dublin, 1999) provides the definitive account. Fundamental to understanding Cromwellian Ireland is T. C. Barnard, *Cromwellian Ireland* (Oxford, 1975) and his 'Planters and policies in Cromwellian Ireland' in *Past and Present*, no. 61 (1973). The 'adventurers' as a group have been anatomised in Karl Bottigheimer, *English money and Irish land* (Oxford, 1971). Much new light has been thrown on the high politics of this difficult period in Patrick Little, *Lord Broghill and the Cromwellian union with Ireland and Scotland* (Woodbridge, 2004). On overall political ideas, Aidan Clarke, 'Colonial constitutional attitudes in Ireland, 1640–60' in *Proceedings of the Royal Irish Academy*, xc, sect. C (1990) is important. The destruction of the Cromwellian archive in the 1922 Public Record Office fire means that older works have a particular importance for this period, particularly St John D. Seymour, *The Puritans in Ireland* (Oxford, 1921), which utilised much archival material now destroyed.

### 1660–1690

There is no overall survey for this period, but the early chapters in T. C. Barnard, *The kingdom of Ireland, 1641–1760* (Basingstoke, 2004), Sean Connolly, *Religion, law, and power: the making of Protestant Ireland, 1660–1760* (Oxford, 1992) and, especially, David Dickson, *New foundations, 1660–1800* (2nd ed. Dublin, 2000) provide reliable and insightful introductions. There is much of relevance to the late seventeenth century in the writings of Toby Barnard, particularly his *A new anatomy of Ireland: the Irish Protestants, 1649–1770* (New Haven & London, 2003) on society, and his *Making the grand figure: lives and possessions in Ireland, 1641–1770* (New Haven & London, 2004) on material life. His selected essays, *Irish Protestant ascents and descents, 1641–1770* (Dublin, 2004), also contain much to inform and entertain on the later seventeenth century. Edward McParland's study of public buildings, *Public architecture in Ireland, 1680–1760* (New Haven & London, 2001) is fundamental in understanding not only taste but how various groups in Ireland wished to present themselves to a wider world.

On the Restoration process itself, Aidan Clarke's *Prelude to restoration in Ireland: the end of the Commonwealth, 1659–60* (Cambridge, 1999) is surely the definitive account of these years. On the mechanics of what followed, L. J. Arnold, *The Restoration land settlement in County Dublin* (Dublin, 1993), his 'The Irish court of claims of 1663' in *Irish Historical Studies*, xxiv, no. 96 (1985) and Karl Bottigheimer, 'The Restoration land settlement: a structural view' in *Irish Historical Studies*, xviii, no. 69 (1972) provide a guide through the complexities of the land settlement. Some of the anomalies of the settlement can be traced in two excellent case studies: Harold O'Sullivan, *John Bellew: a seventeenth-century man of many parts* (Dublin, 2000) and Joseph Byrne, *War and peace: the survival of the Talbots of Malahide, 1641–1671* (Dublin, 1997).

On the man who dominated Restoration Ireland, the Duke of Ormond, there is a meagre literature. The standard biography remains that by Thomas Carte published in 1735–6. This had been supplemented by the slight but readable J. C. Beckett, *The Cavalier duke* (Belfast, 1990) and the more rigorous essays in Toby

Barnard and Jane Fenlon (eds), *The Dukes of Ormond, 1610–1745* (Woodbridge, 2000). One important issue in Ormond's career is examined in J. I. McGuire, 'Why was Ormond dismissed in 1669?' in *Irish Historical Studies*, xvii, no. 71 (1973). An insight into the mind of Ormond's nemesis is provided by John Kerrigan, 'Orrery's Ireland and the British problem, 1641–1679' in David Baker and Willy Maley (eds), *British identities and English Renaissance literature* (Cambridge, 2003). On wider issues of governance, T. C. Barnard, 'Scotland and Ireland in the later Stuart monarchy' in S. G. Ellis and Sarah Barber (eds), *Conquest and union* (London, 1995) and J. C. Beckett, 'The Irish viceroyalty in the Restoration period' in *Transactions of the Royal Historical Society*, 5th ser., xx (1970), reprinted in J. C. Beckett, *Confrontations: essays in Irish history* (London, 1972), provide important insights; for a wider context see Ronald Hutton, *Charles the Second, King of England, Scotland and Ireland* (Oxford, 1989).

Restoration political ideas have hardly begun to be explored, but a variety of offerings are in Jane Ohlmeyer (ed.), *Political thought in seventeenth-century Ireland* (Cambridge, 2000). T. C. Barnard, 'Crisis of identity among Irish Protestants, 1641–80' in *Past and Present*, no. 127 (1990) provides an incisive look into Protestant minds. The crises of the latter part of Charles ii's reign are well charted in a 'three kingdoms' context in Tim Harris, *Restoration: Charles II and his kingdoms, 1660–1685* (London, 2005).

Religion in the late seventeenth century has attracted more attention than has politics. Phil Kilroy, *Protestant dissent and controversy in Ireland* (Cork, 1994) provides a fine overview of the problem of dissent; and this can be amplified by Raymond Gillespie, 'The Presbyterian revolution in Ulster, 1660–90' in W. J. Sheils and Diana Wood (eds), *The churches, Ireland and the Irish*, Studies in Church History xxv (Oxford, 1989), Raymond Gillespie, 'Dissenters and nonconformists' in Kevin Herlihy, *The religion of Irish dissent* (Dublin, 1996) and J. I. McGuire, 'Government attitudes to religious nonconformity in Ireland, 1660–1719' in C. E. J. Caldicott *et al.* (eds), *The Huguenots in Ireland* (Dublin, 1987). Catholicism has attracted less attention, but Celestine Murphy, 'The Wexford Catholic community in the late seventeenth century' in R. V. Comerford *et al.* (eds), *Religion, conflict and coexistence in Ireland* (Dublin, 1990) provides an important window into parish life in Ireland in this period. On the Remonstrance of 1661, see Anne Creighton, 'The Remonstrance of December 1661 and Catholic politics in Restoration Ireland' in *Irish Historical Studies*, xxxiv, no. 133 (2004).

For the Jacobite period J. G. Simms, *Jacobite Ireland* (London, 1969) remains indispensable. Simms's interpretation has been fleshed out in John Miller, 'The Earl of Tyrconnell and James ii's Irish policy' in *Historical Journal*, xx (1977). A 'three kingdoms' perspective on the period is provided in Tim Harris, *Revolution: the great crisis of the British monarchy, 1685–1720* (London, 2006). The position of the Irish Protestants is more fully explored in Andrew Carpenter, 'William King and the threats to the Church of Ireland in the reign of James II' in *Irish Historical Studies*, xviii, no. 69 (1972) and Raymond Gillespie, 'The Irish Protestants and James II' in *Irish Historical Studies*, xxviii, no. 110 (1992). The first chapter of Eamonn Ó Ciardha, *Ireland and the Jacobite cause* (Dublin, 2002) provides a Gaelic Irish perspective using the evidence of the political poetry. From the military perspective, Pádraig Lenihan, *1690: the battle of the Boyne* (Stroud, 2003) is an incisive account of one battle. More generally, W. A. Maguire (ed.), *Kings in conflict* (Belfast, 1990) provides a good collection of well-illustrated essays that deal with the course and consequences of the war. On the outcome, three essays shed much light on William III and Ireland: Karl Bottigheimer, 'The Glorious Revolution and Ireland' in L. G. Schwoerer (ed.), *The Revolution of 1688–1689* (Cambridge, 1992); David Hayton, 'The Williamite Revolution in Ireland, 1688–1691' in J. I. Israel (ed.), *The Anglo-Dutch moment: essays on the Glorious Revolution and its world impact* (Cambridge, 1991); and P. H. Kelly, 'Ireland and the Glorious Revolution: from kingdom to colony' in Robert Beddard (ed.), *The revolutions of 1688* (Oxford, 1991). Despite this wealth of recent writing, much remains to be done in analysing and understanding this intriguing and seminally important age.

# Index